# THE ILLUSTRATED PROJECT BOOK OF
# MAKING GIFT CARDS AND SCRAPBOOKING

360 EASY-TO-FOLLOW PROJECTS AND TECHNIQUES WITH
2300 LAVISH PHOTOGRAPHS

CHERYL OWEN AND ALISON LINDSAY

southwater

# CONTENTS

THE ILLUSTRATED PROJECT BOOK OF

# MAKING GIFT CARDS
# AND SCRAPBOOKING

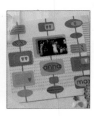

# INTRODUCTION

In recent years two craft subjects have enjoyed massive popular appeal on an unprecedented scale. The crafts of scrapbooking and making greetings cards have much in common and both appeal to a creative craft audience.

The pleasure of these crafts is in the opportunity to create a small-scale piece of art that has a meaningful message, taps into our creative skills and will be valued by the recipient as well as the maker. For many of us the chance to make something for family and friends adds to the pleasure. Greetings cards, like scrapbook pages, can be perfectly tailored to suit the event that they celebrate. Highly personalized motifs can be designed to celebrate life's special events, as well as for the people that matter most.

Scrapbooking as a pastime has grown and developed from a visual way of recording events to creating collections of objects that may be important, cherished or whimsical. Once we may have used scrapbooks as a means of bringing together objects and ephemera with a common theme, or collecting together precious mementoes of

▲ *This attractive dragonfly card uses a simple papercutting technique and decorative photo corners. A similar motif could be made to decorate a scrapbook album page with a summer theme, or photographs from a trip to the insect house at the zoo.*

special days and holidays. Memories invested in the items, such as theatre and travel tickets, and receipts for special purchases, for example, could be safely stored and recorded to create a lasting record to be cherished. Scrapbooking now still retains the sentiment of such collections, but today's scrapbookers have brought the craft up to date by combining it with the content of the traditional photograph album, and adding a whole host of decorative crafts to the pages.

All of the crafts used to embellish greetings cards can be used on a larger scale to decorate scrapbook pages, and vice versa. There is limitless opportunity to add any number of creative decorations to the face of a greetings card or album page. Paper collage,

◀ *Vintage-style charms made of colour-coordinated beads, ribbon and old-fashioned pretty fabrics are easy to make and perfect for adding to gift cards for a female friend or relative. A similar decoration could be made for an album page.*

paint techniques (most of which do not require an artistic ability), simple sewing, beadwork and hand embroidery, modelled clay shapes and embossed metal designs are just some of the crafts that can be used in a decorative way.

Each craft is fully explained in detail. All the equipment needed for each is listed, and step-by-step photographs and clear instructions show you how to master each skill so that a professional finish can be achieved quickly, even by an absolute beginner. As well as making the focal point of a greetings card design, many of these craft skills can be used to create tinted, textured and layered scrapbook backgrounds that will be embellished further with motifs, words, ephemera and photographs. Crafts can also be used to enhance the theme of the photographs included in albums, pulling the design together in a subtle way.

Each stage of construction of the greetings card or album page is set out. Consider first the event to be celebrated and choose motifs and colourways that are appropriate – confetti, rings, doves, and even a cake for a wedding celebration, for example. Next look at the people involved in the event, or the person who will receive the card. Take account of their interests and how the piece can be tailored to take them into account. Then choose a design style that fits. If you are making a scrapbook page, it may be the content or colours of the photograph that is

▲ *Old black and white photographs of family have an enduring charm. Today's scrapbookers have the technology to duplicate these precious images quickly and easily. The images are often used in heritage-style album pages.*

the focal point and which suggests a design style. A child playing in a flower garden might suggest a bold and colourful treatment, whereas an old sepia photograph of your ancestors might require a more romantic and sentimental design to reflect the old-fashioned charm of a bygone age.

Whatever your choice, you will find a suitable project in this compendium of 350 inspirational ideas. More than 2200 photographs will inspire you and show you how to master each technique.

▼ *Traditional scrapbooks contained themed collections that may have included postcards, magazine cuttings and fabric swatches.*

▼ *A contemporary scrapbook page has been carefully manufactured using digital technology.*

# GREETINGS CARDS AND STATIONERY

# HAND-CRAFTED GREETINGS

Greetings cards have a wide appeal across many cultures. We send them to mark special occasions such as birthdays or Christmas, to keep in touch, and to express goodwill. In sending these tokens to family and friends we are subscribing to a long tradition. Greetings have been sent in written form for hundreds of years, though originally cards were the preserve of the rich, who commissioned them as elaborate gifts that were expensively produced. It was not until the modernization of printing methods and the ability of printers to reproduce colours accurately and at low cost that the market proliferated with cards for Christmas and Valentine's Day. In recent years cards have been produced for every occasion imaginable, as well as plain pictorial

▲ *For a greetings card with a romantic feel, paint two gold hearts in the centre of a mottled paper card. The symbol is universally recognized and an easy shape to form. Add a lavish organza ribbon for a final flourish.*

▼ *Simple stylized motifs, such as those found in childrens' colouring books or on old-fashioned wallpaper, can be made to look fresh and appealing when cut from strongly contrasting coloured papers and applied to a plain card background.*

cards, providing an easy way to communicate with friends. A small and inexpensive gesture, a greetings card can be kept and treasured, and for this reason the tradition is unlikely to be surpassed by contemporary text messaging or email.

The craft of making greetings cards has increased in popularity, alongside the wider availability of specially designed craft materials, beautiful handmade papers, and the use of the internet for exchanging ideas. As handcrafted cards form a larger part of stationery ranges in gift shops, and are perceived to be of a high value, so the fashion for designing and making them has grown.

Choosing to make and send a greetings card that is handcrafted to suit the style, interests and specific occasion to be celebrated by the recipient makes the gift more personal. It shows how much you care, and the receiver will appreciate the thought and effort that has gone into making the card. Greetings cards can be quickly made with minimal materials and

A wide range of design styles are presented too, to cater for every taste. There are retro ideas, such as a card for passing a driving test featuring an old black and white photograph, with photo corners and styled like an old-fashioned album. Traditional Christmas cards with a red and green theme sit alongside a contemporary card for Diwali, cute and colourful cards for children's birthdays, feminine, lacy and embroidered creations for female relatives, as well as sport-themed cards for men.

A comprehensive techniques chapter at the start of the chapter shows all the basic skills that are required for the projects, from stencilling images and painting backgrounds, to adding modelled clay motifs and making envelopes. In addition, templates are provided for every card where needed, so that you can ensure a professional finish is achieved. Once you have mastered different crafts for card making, you can be inventive and create your own innovative designs.

▼ *A pretty card decorated with beads, buttons, sequins and ribbon, arranged to resemble a bouquet of flowers, could be appropriate for plenty of occasions as well as to keep in touch with female relations and friends.*

▲ *Card-toppers are available from many supermarkets as well as craft stores. Choose your motifs carefully and arrange them artfully on a contrasting coloured card for maximum impact.*

financial outlay. Because they are quick to make they are an ideal craft for people with busy lives, who will enjoy the pleasure and satisfaction of making a professional-looking card that will be appreciated.

Within these pages are 140 unique greetings card, gift tag and notelet ideas for every landmark occasion, such as Christmas, Easter, wedding anniversaries, engagements and the arrival of a new baby, as well as cards to send just to keep in touch. There are projects for beginners as well as for accomplished card makers. All the projects featured are described with concise step-by-step instructions and easy-to-follow photographs. Many are simple enough to make quickly, and in multiples, so are suitable for invitations or for Christmas cards, for example. Or you could lavish time and care to create a one-of-a-kind card for a special person.

# Card-making techniques

However original and inspired your designs, they need to be perfectly crafted to make really beautiful, effective greetings cards. This section covers the basic techniques used in the book, from simple card-making to achieving different paint effects, and includes lots of clever tips to give your creations a professional finish. Always read all the instructions for a project before embarking upon it and, if it includes skills that are new to you, experiment on scrap materials first. Follow either the metric or imperial measurements but not a combination of the two.

# EQUIPMENT

For safety and comfort, work on a clean, flat, well-lit surface. Keep all sharp tools and adhesives beyond the reach of children and pets. Clean tools thoroughly after usage.

## Cutting tools

*Always use sharp tools for cutting, and change your knife blades frequently, as blunt blades are liable to tear paper.*

### Knives
Craft knives cut materials neatly and are better than scissors for cutting straight lines, especially on card (stock). Always use a craft knife on a cutting mat, preferably one with a self-healing surface. Cut straight edges with a craft knife against a metal ruler. Retract the knife blade when it is not in use.

Card can be scored with the back of a craft knife blade, but for the best results use a bone folder. This traditional bookbinder's tool will impress the surface of the card but will not cut or weaken it. After making the fold you can also use the bone folder to sharpen the crease by running it flat along the fold.

▼ *Careful measuring and cutting is important: a cutting mat with a printed grid keeps right angles accurate; a clear ruler is useful for positioning lines but you will also need a metal ruler to guide your craft knife.*

### Scissors
Choose scissors that are comfortable to handle. You may find it easier to cut intricate shapes with small, sharp-pointed scissors rather than a craft knife. Cut fabric, ribbon and threads with fabric or embroidery scissors and do not use these on paper or card as they will blunt quickly. Use pinking shears and other decorative-edged scissors to give interesting, shapely edges to your creations.

### Guillotines and die cutters
If you intend to make lots of cards, consider purchasing a guillotine. It should have a measured grid for accurate cutting, and some models will cut decorative edges and rounded corners. Plastic templates and low-level cutters are also available for use with

Synthetic sponge

Cutter

Natural sponge

Cookie cutter

Fancy-edge scissors

▲ *As well as special punches and cutters, standard household equipment such as cookie cutters and pinking shears can be useful in card-making. Small sponges are handy for applying paint.*

die-cutting equipment. Paper punches are available in many different designs and are mainly used to cut out decorative shapes, but the larger sizes can be used to punch out the windows of window cards.

### Punching holes
Use a standard desk double-hole punch to make pairs of holes to thread with ribbon or cord for fastening, or a single hole punch for single holes. A hole punch, which has heads in a number of different sizes arranged on a wheel, is a useful tool for making single holes. To pierce small holes you can use a bradawl, resting on a cutting mat.

### Cutting wire and sheet metal
Use wire snippers to cut wire and round-nosed pliers to manipulate it. Cut sheet metal with metal cutters or an old pair of scissors, bearing in mind that the metal will blunt the blades.

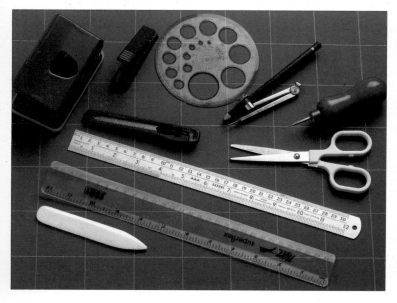

# Drawing, painting and sticking

*As with all crafts, you will get the best results if you always buy the best quality materials you can afford. It is sensible to start with a few basic items and build up your collection gradually.*

## Drawing

Use an HB pencil for drawing. Keep pencils sharpened to a point or use propelling pencils. Draw squares and rectangles using a ruler and set square so that all the lines are straight and the angles accurate. Draw circles with compasses or use a circular stencil for small sizes. Plastic or metal stencils in various shapes are available for drawing around and cutting out. Consider cookie cutters for simple shapes too – they can be good for children's motifs.

▼ *Spray adhesive, glue sticks and PVA (white) glue all stick paper, and glue dots hold small ornaments securely. Double-sided tape is neat and clean, and masking tape is helpful when positioning components.*

**Paint palette**

▼ *Buy a few good water-colour brushes in a range of sizes, plus a flat-tipped stencil brush. You can buy palettes for mixing paint, but an old white plate is just as good.*

**Flat artist's brush**

**Stencil brush**

**Fine artist's brush**

## Applying paint

Paint with good quality artist's paintbrushes and clean the brushes immediately after use. A flat brush, a medium round brush and a fine brush are the most versatile. Stencil with a flat-ended stencil brush. Paint can also be applied with natural or synthetic sponges to create particular effects.

## Adhesives

Read the manufacturers' instructions for all adhesives and test them on scrap materials before use. Work in a well-ventilated room and protect the work surface with scrap paper or newspaper.

Use spray adhesive to stick layers of paper and card together. PVA (white) glue is cheap and very versatile. It will stick paper, card, fabric and wood. All-purpose household glue is strong and will stick many materials, but is best for

**PVA (white) glue**

**Spray adhesive**

**Glue stick**

**Glue spreader**

**Glue dots**

**Clear glue**

**Round-nosed pliers**

**Pliers**

**Double-sided tape**

gluing small pieces as it does not spread evenly over a large surface. Leave items stuck with PVA and all-purpose household glue flat while the glue dries. Paper glue will stick lightweight paper, and is clean and easy to use.

Double-sided tape is a neat way to join paper and card. It is available in a few widths, with 15mm/$^5$/$_8$in being the most versatile. Motifs can be cut from double-sided adhesive sheets and sprinkled with glitter or accent beads (minute beads without holes).

Glue dots, supplied on a backing tape or sheet, stick small items quickly as no drying time is needed. Use adhesive foam pads to raise motifs above a surface, layering them for extra height. They are available in very small sizes but larger pads can be cut to fit. Attach photographs and other pictures with photo mounts at the corners.

Use low-tack masking tape to stick items temporarily, or to mask areas to be painted (but check first that it will not tear the surface when you remove it).

## Using adhesives

Spread glue with a plastic glue spreader or improvise and use a scrap of card. Use a cocktail stick (toothpick) to apply tiny spots of glue. Spray adhesive must be used in a well-ventilated room. Spraying into a large cardboard box stops it drifting on to other surfaces.

# MATERIALS

**Apart from the papers that form the foundation of your gift cards, plus suitable adhesives, all the materials you will need are decorative.**

# Paper and paint

*A fabulous range of paper and card (stock) is widely available nowadays, and a single sheet of beautiful paper can be enough to make or decorate many cards. Envelopes can be bought ready-made in standard sizes, and you can design your cards to fit these. Alternatively, you can make your own envelopes from matching or co-ordinating paper in any size you choose.*

**Card blanks**

Ready-made card blanks are available in a wide range of shapes and styles. They will fit standard-size envelopes and often come with their own envelopes. Window cards and gift tags are also available. Cutting card to make your own greetings cards offers more variety, however, as you can use the material you like and cut it to the exact size required.

**Paper and card**

Art shops and specialist paper suppliers stock papers from all over the world. Mass-produced paper and card is available in a vast array of colours, weights and textures and lots of different prices depending on quality, texture and

finish. Some are coated to give pearlescent, metallic, glittery and even futuristic holographic effects. Tactile embossed and textured papers add interest to a greetings card. Realistic papers resembling fabric, animal skin and wood are lightweight and not as bulky as the real thing. Look for papers incorporating petals, metallic fragments or textural fibres. Mulberry paper is lightweight, but very strong. It is very fibrous and should be torn rather than cut to look most effective.

Papers printed with beautiful patterns or even embroidered need little other embellishment to make stunning greetings cards. These are often sold as gift wrap, so you could make a card that

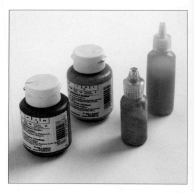

▲ *Water-based paints such as acrylics are ideal for use on paper and card. They are easy and clean to use, fast-drying and available in a vast range of colours. Water-based fabric paints and other special media come in containers with thin nozzles for direct application.*

co-ordinates with the gift wrap. Packs of origami papers and books or packs of patterned papers can be used together to create a theme for your cards, but you can also use scraps of wallpaper to introduce pattern. Many papers are specially packaged in small quantites with co-ordinating colourways or themes for scrapbooking. They are useful for providing small quantities of lots of different types of paper. Copyright-free books offer printed motifs suitable for every occasion. Layer them with translucent and vellum papers to create designs full of depth and interesting colour effects. This technique is especially good for creating nostalgic and "aged" pieces of work.

◀ *Ready-made window cards, with their accompanying envelopes, can be used to frame a photograph or drawing for an instant personalized greeting.*

## Paints

These are used to decorate and transform a plain piece of paper or card with colour and texture. Paint is a versatile medium and can be used to create lots of different effects for background coverage, or to add tiny details as a finishing touch.

Before using any paint, test it on a spare piece of paper or card, as some paints may cause plain paper to warp or soak through to the other side of the sheet. In general, water-based paints are most suitable for use on paper. Acrylic paints, which are water-based, are very versatile: they come in many colours, mix well, dilute, and dry quickly. You can apply thicker paints to the surface of a card and make an impression in the paint with stamps.

Use silk paints to create beautiful effects on silk panels. These water-based paints are applied in areas outlined with outliner (gutta) on silk stretched in an embroidery frame. Large areas need to be coloured quickly before the paint starts to dry, otherwise watermarks will result. Different effects can also be achieved by adding salt crystals to the drying paint.

Relief paints and glitter paints are fun to use. They come in plastic tubes and are applied straight to the surface through a thin nozzle. Try these first on spare paper to ensure that you can achieve a smooth, continuous line of paint with a professional finish. Masking fluid has a similar consistency to paint. Use it to mask areas that should remain unpainted. Allow the fluid to dry before applying paint to the surface. Once the design has been painted over, and the paint has dried, the dried mask is rubbed away.

Frosting spray gives an etched glass effect. Use it on acetate, masking off a design with sticky-backed plastic.

## Rubber stamping

Ready-made rubber stamps are made to suit every imaginable theme, and enable cards to be produced quickly and with a highly professional finish. They are available as "mounted" designs, meaning they are attached to a block of wood, or "unmounted" so that you can apply them to clear plastic, which helps accurate positioning of the motif. You can also make your own simple stamps from Neoprene foam. Stamp designs on to the greetings card using an ink pad and enhance the image with embossing powder, before the paint dries, if you wish. Watercolour stamp paints give the appearance of hand-painted images. Rubber stamps can also be used to impress polymer clay before hardening.

▲ *Plain, printed and textured papers of every description are available from art, craft and stationery suppliers. While some handmade and decorative papers can be expensive, a single sheet can be used to make a number of original cards, and offcuts can be saved for future use.*

▼ *Rubber stamps are easy to use and can be used with inks or paint. You can also apply embossing powder to produce a raised motif.*

Paint

Rubber stamps

Embossing powder

Ink pad

# Embellishments

*Greetings cards can be decorated with all kinds of unexpected materials. The main limitation is that they should not be too heavy, or they will tip the card over. Many companies now manufacture "card toppers", which are pre-formed decorations that need only glue dots to hold them in place. However, making your own is far more satisfying.*

### Fabric and haberdashery

If you are a keen needleworker, you will undoubtedly already have a stash of fabric and ribbon offcuts, ornamental buttons, embroidery threads (floss), beads and sequins. These are all ideal for decorating greetings cards and can be stuck in position using PVA (white) glue. A tiny panel of embroidery or appliqué is quick and easy to sew but can have a lot of impact as a feature of a greetings card. Small panels of silk or other fabrics can also be decorated with fabric paints.

Backing fabric with medium-weight iron-on interfacing stops it fraying and makes it easier to handle and cut out.

### Natural materials

Look to the natural world for materials to decorate your cards. Small pieces of driftwood and balsa wood may be light enough to use. Feathers have a natural resilience that will allow them to be folded into a card without being crushed, and they will add a delicate look to your creations.

Collect fallen leaves and twigs or pick flowers to press in a flower press or between the pages of a heavy book. Specialist shops sell seashells to underline a nautical theme.

### Moulded decorations

Polymer clay is available in lots of colours, as well as metallic and other special finishes. The colours can also be blended to create new shades or partly blended for a marbled effect. Bake the clay in an oven to harden it, following the manufacturer's instructions. Neoprene foam is also very useful for three-dimensional decorations. It is soft and pliable and should be glued in position with all-purpose household glue.

Relief paint

Buttons and toggles

Embroidered motifs

▲ *Relief paints can be applied straight from the container to make simple raised designs. All kinds of buttons and embroidered motifs also add three-dimensional interest, but need to be very securely attached.*

▼ *Tiny ornaments, glitter, sprinkles and wire add lustre to card designs. Embellish them further with decorative fastenings and finish by tying the layers together with pretty ribbon or cord.*

Polymer clay

Lurex cord

Embroidery thread (floss)

Wire

Ribbon

Glitter

Eyelets

Snap fasteners

Brads

Sequins

Metal plaques

Photo corners

## Metallics

Apply fine metallic leaf over a coat of gold size to create luxurious gilded greetings cards. For the finest effects you can use tiny amounts of real gold and silver leaf, but a cheaper option is Dutch metal leaf, which is available in gold, silver, copper and other colours. Alternatively, you can rub metallic wax on embossed paper and clay surfaces to highlight the raised areas.

You can also enhance your designs using fine metal sheet, embossed with simple images. Aluminium, brass and copper foils of suitable thickness for embossing are available from craft suppliers. Wire is another option for adding the gleam of metal to cards, and is easy to shape into coils, frames and motifs. Fine wire is available in different thicknesses and colours from craft stores and jewellery-making suppliers.

## Stickers and glitter

Create a greetings card instantly by sticking on a row of ready-made stickers. There are stickers for every occasion, made of card, plastic, fabric or even diamanté jewellery stones. All have an adhesive backing so they are ready for use. There are also ready-made three-dimensional motifs to attach to make an instant greetings card, but you can give any sticker or cut-out an extra dimension by attaching it to a foam pad. Consider, too, charms, embroidered patches and woven or printed labels. Save broken or unwanted costume jewellery, such as odd earrings, and

dismantle it so that you can use the individual elements as hanging ornaments on the front of cards.

Card decorations can be further embellished with tiny elements such as glitter, accent beads and sequin dust (the tiny holes punched from sequins). "Sprinkles" are tiny plastic shapes like miniature sequins but without holes. Use them in the same way as sequin dust, pouring them over a coat of glue then shaking off the excess.

▲ *Haberdashery stores provide rich pickings for greetings card decoration, from scraps of pretty fabrics to novelty buttons, ribbons, sequins and embroidery threads, which are all light in weight and easy to attach to card.*

## Fastenings

As an alternative to gluing layers together invisibly, you can turn mounts and fastenings into decorative features by using items such as brads, snap fasteners, and eyelets. Snap fasteners, available from craft suppliers, resemble those used for dressmaking but have attractive tops. Brads, similar to regular stationery paper fasteners, are available in many styles and finishes. Eyelets give a utilitarian look to a greetings card: they are applied with eyelet pliers or an eyelet tool and a tack hammer.

You can also lace or tie layers together using lengths of ribbon, thonging, cord, paper, hemp string or raffia. Ribbon is available in numerous widths and textures. Wire-edged ribbon will hold its shape when tied in a bow.

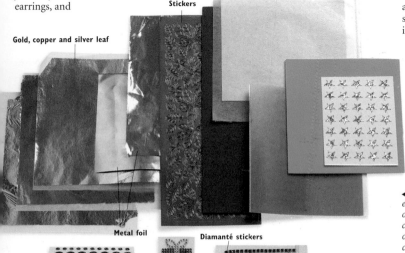

◄ *Sparkling touches of metallic leaf or embossed foil can be used to enhance your own designs, but you can also create effective cards using ready-made motifs in foil, glitter or tiny gems. For more subtle effects, add contrasts of texture in the form of vellum, tissue or interesting handmade papers.*

# WORKING WITH PAPER

**Paper and card (stock) come in many different weights and qualities, so it is wise to experiment with the basic techniques to check that your chosen material will produce the effect you want.**

## Papercraft techniques

*Most paper is easy to fold and cut, especially if it is lightweight, but you need to aim for accuracy in all these basic tasks to achieve satisfying, professional-looking results.*

### CUTTING

For best results, cut straight lines using a craft knife against a metal ruler rather than a pair of scissors. Always take care when handling blades.

**1** Rest the sheet on a cutting mat and cut straight lines using a craft knife, guiding the blade along a metal ruler. When cutting card (card stock), do not press very hard or attempt to cut right through with the first pass, but gradually cut deeper and deeper.

**2** You may find it easier to cut intricately shaped motifs or small circles with a small pair of sharp-pointed scissors. Hold the scissors in one position and turn the paper in the other hand, rather than trying to move the scissors round the shape.

### SCORING

Although paper can be folded simply by aligning the edges and flattening the fold, scoring the surface of card first gives a neater, sharper finish.

**1** A bone folder is recommended for scoring as it will indent a line to fold along without breaking the surface of the card. The right or wrong side of the card can be scored. Lay it on a firm surface and score along the fold line with the pointed end of the folder resting against a ruler.

**2** Alternatively, lightly score the card with the back of a craft knife blade, taking care to break the top surface only and not to cut right through the card.

### FOLDING

Make sure the edges are perfectly aligned before creasing the fold.

When folding card, score it first, then fold along the scored line. Press the flat of a bone folder on the fold and run it smoothly along its length. If you do not have a bone folder, run your thumb along the fold to flatten it.

### USING SPRAY ADHESIVE

The room must be well ventilated when you are using spray adhesive.

Protect the surrounding area with scrap paper or newspaper, or place the card inside a large cardboard box. If sticking large sheets, smooth them outwards from the centre to avoid creases and air bubbles.

# STICKING MOTIFS

Motifs cut from card and other materials can be made to stand proud of the card front by mounting them on adhesive foam pads or glue dots.

 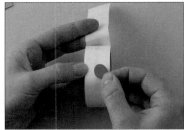

**1** Select a foam pad that is smaller than the motif, or cut an appropriate shape from a large pad. Stick it to the back of the motif, positioning it centrally. Peel off the backing paper then press the motif in position.

**2** Press a glue dot on its backing paper to the back of a motif, positioning it centrally. Peel away the backing paper leaving the glue dot in place, then press the motif in position on the card.

# STRENGTHENING PAPER

Mounting paper on a sheet of card makes it sturdy enough to use for the main body of a greetings card.

**1** Cut the paper 1cm/⅜in larger all round than the required size. Apply spray adhesive to the back of the paper then stick it to a sheet of card.

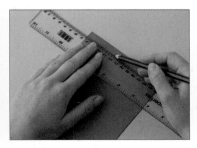

**2** Turn the card over and draw the size required for the greetings card. Resting on a cutting mat, cut out the card and paper together using a craft knife and metal ruler.

## USING VELLUM

Translucent vellum paper can be used to overlay patterns or pictures to create subtle colour effects.

Change the colour of vellum by applying it to card of a contrasting or deeper colour. Here, light blue is applied to pink card to create lilac. Attach vellum with spray adhesive or "invisible" glue dots.

▲ Here, a glittery striped paper has been applied to pink card. A wooden decoration is tied to the front with cord.

# Tearing paper

*Softly torn paper edges can add extra interest to a greetings card, especially if you are using a fibrous material such as mulberry paper. Torn edges usually look best when contrasted with the sharp, neatly cut edges of other elements in the design. The overall effect of torn edges is quite feminine.*

## CREATING A TORN EDGE AGAINST A RULER

Tearing paper against a ruler controls the tear, so that the edge is attractively torn but straight. This is particularly useful if you are using a handmade paper that has a deckle edge but needs two sides of the paper to be torn to make the overall size smaller. Tearing the third and fourth edges to size will match the deckle edges. For stronger paper dampen the tear line first to weaken the fibres.

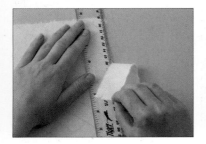

**1** Hold a ruler firmly on the paper where you wish to tear it. Tear the paper against the ruler. If you are using a printed paper with a white core, this will appear uppermost along the edge: to avoid it tear with the printed side down.

**2** If the paper is too thick or strong to tear easily, run a moistened artist's brush along the intended tear line first to soften and weaken the fibres. Allow the paper to absorb the water for a few moments then tear it against a ruler as before.

**3** For a freer effect you can simply tear the paper between your fingers. If you follow the grain of the paper the torn edge will still be relatively straight.

## CREATING A TORN-EDGE MOTIF

Simple collages and other applied paper designs in a naive style can be enhanced by tearing rather than cutting out the motifs. This method suits pictures of natural, curved forms such as leaves and flowers.

**1** Draw the motif on the back of the paper, leaving a margin of at least 5mm/¼in around the motif. Tear along the drawn line by holding the motif between the thumb and fingers of one hand close to the drawn line and pulling the paper around the image toward you with the other hand. Tear slowly and carefully and, for accuracy, gradually move the fingers holding the paper along the line.

▲ *The torn flower motif on this colourful card has the naive quality of folk art.*

# Working with templates

*All the templates you will need in order to make the greetings cards in this book can be found together in a section at the end. You will need to trace or photocopy them and scale them up or down as necessary before use.*

## TRANSFERRING TEMPLATES

If you need to use the template only once it may be sufficient simply to transfer your tracing. If a template is to be used repeatedly, it is worth cutting it out of stiff card (card stock), which you can then draw round.

1 Trace the template on to tracing paper. Redraw it on the wrong side using a soft pencil. Tape the tracing right side up on paper or card with masking tape. Redraw the design with a sharp pencil to transfer it.

2 Transfer the template to a piece of card if you intend to use it more than a few times. Cut out the card template, which can then be drawn around many times.

## ENLARGING AND REDUCING TEMPLATES ON A GRID

If you don't have access to a photocopier you can rescale a template by redrawing it on a smaller or larger grid.

1 To enlarge or reduce a motif on a grid, tape a piece of tracing paper over the original design with masking tape. Draw a square or rectangle on top, enclosing the image, and divide it up with rows of vertical and horizontal lines, making equal-sized squares or rectangles. Draw a square or rectangle of the required finished size to the same proportions as the shape on the tracing paper. Divide it with the same number of vertical and horizontal lines.

2 Redraw the image, working on one square or rectangle at a time.

3 Look at the new design as a whole and redraw any areas that do not seem to match up or to "flow" well.

## ENLARGING AND REDUCING ON A PHOTOCOPIER

It is sometimes necessary to enlarge or reduce a motif. For accuracy and speed, use a photocopier to do this.

1 Decide what width you want the final motif to be. Next, measure the width of the original motif you intend to photocopy in millimetres. Divide the first measurement by the second and multiply the result by 100 to find the percentage by which to enlarge the motif. For example, a motif needs to be enlarged to 50mm and the original width is 40mm (50 divided by 40 = 1.25, and 1.25 × 100 = 125). Therefore, the motif must be photocopied at 125 per cent. Remember that an enlargement will be more than 100 per cent and a reduction less than 100 per cent.

## USING READY-MADE TEMPLATES

Lots of ready-made plastic or metal templates of useful motifs are available to draw round. Clear plastic makes it easy to position the template correctly.

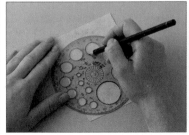

1 A number of motifs of different shapes or sizes are often available on a single sheet. A circle template is particularly useful.

# Window cards

*It is easy to make window cards to your exact requirements. They can be cut to any shape. If you plan to make a series of cards, use a large paper punch to punch matching windows. If you have embroidered a card front, or attached motifs with brads, or sewn a motif in place with wire, the underside of the card front can be covered with a facing, which will hide any fixings.*

▼ *These ready-made window cards have metallic paper behind the windows and display a decorative leaf and a fabulous metal elephant.*

## MAKING A TRIPLE-SECTION WINDOW CARD

For neatness, a window card is usually constructed in three sections: two of the three sections form the card front and back, and the last section is a facing that is next to the front but 5mm/¹⁄₄in narrower than it. The facing is stuck to the underside of the front to hide the raw edges of whatever is shown in the window and the backs of any fixings. The piece of card is folded into three sections with the left-hand section being the facing that is slightly narrower than the card front and back.

**1** Draw the dimensions of the card on the wrong side of a piece of card (stock). For example, if you want your folded card to measure 18cm/7in high × 10cm/4in wide, you need to draw a rectangle measuring 29.5 × 18cm/11¾ × 7in. Cut out the rectangle using a craft knife and metal ruler and working on a cutting mat.

**2** Still working on the wrong side of the card, score and fold it 9.5cm/3¾in from the left-hand short edge and 10cm/4in from the right-hand short edge, keeping the folds parallel with the short edges. Open the card out flat again.

**3** Draw the window on the wrong side of the middle section, positioning it centrally between the folds. Cut out the window with a craft knife, resting on a cutting mat.

▶ *This pretty card has strings of sequins behind the window. Three additional sequins are stuck to the card front using glue dots.*

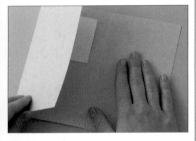

**4** Cut the motif, or the background paper or card that will go behind the motif in the window, making it approximately 1cm/⅜in larger all round than the window. Apply 5mm/¼in-wide double-sided tape all round the window on the wrong side.

**5** Peel off the backing strips and stick the motif behind the window. Apply 5mm/¼in-wide double-sided tape to the cut edges of the facing section. Peel off the backing strips and stick the facing section to the underside of the front.

# Working with inserts

*A greetings card with an insert, or inner sheet, always looks very classy. The insert is also practical as it hides any fixings inside the card front, and a pale insert inside a dark-coloured or heavily textured card provides a good surface on which to write your greeting legibly.*

## MAKING AN UNFOLDED INSERT

If you are making a card with a separate front and back bound together, the insert can also be made from one or two loose sheets of paper.

**1** Cut one or two sheets of lightweight paper 5mm/¼in smaller on all sides than the front and back of the card.

**2** Arrange the insert on the card back, matching the left edges of the sheets. Place the front on top.

**3** Join the layers along the left edge in your chosen style, using brads or eyelets.

**4** Alternatively, punch a pair of holes in the left edge and tie with ribbon.

## MAKING A FOLDED INSERT

In a standard folded card, a paper insert is simply folded to match and glued near the fold so that it opens with the card.

**1** Cut the insert 5mm/¼in smaller on all sides than the card. Fold the insert in half and run a line of paper glue along the fold.

**2** Stick the insert inside the card, matching the fold lines and making sure the border is even at the top and bottom.

# Punching holes

*It's often necessary to punch holes when making cards and gift tags, either for decoration, such as when you want a contrasting colour to show through the holes, or for practical purposes, such as to sew or thread ribbon through. Make sure the holes you make will be large enough for practical applications before you begin, and for a more professional finish, ensure that they are lined up correctly by marking their position with a pencil and ruler.*

**I** Punch holes for inserting ribbon or cord fastenings with a single or double hole punch. The holes made by a standard desk hole punch will be 5mm/¼in in diameter.

**2** A single hole punch usually has heads of different sizes that screw into the handle. Resting on a cutting mat, hold the hole punch upright on the card and hit the end with a tack hammer to punch the hole.

**3** Alternatively, rest the card on a cutting mat and twist the hole punch to cut the hole. This works well with new punches and on paper rather than card (stock), but will be less effective as the punch blunts.

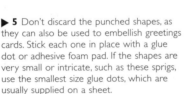

◀**4** Use a shaped paper punch to create decoratively shaped holes.

▶ **5** Don't discard the punched shapes, as they can also be used to embellish greetings cards. Stick each one in place with a glue dot or adhesive foam pad. If the shapes are very small or intricate, such as these sprigs, use the smallest size glue dots, which are usually supplied on a sheet.

◀ *This bright card uses decorative punched holes to great effect. Leaf sprigs are punched in a band of turquoise paper and the punched shapes are then applied with glue dots. A strip of turquoise paper cut using decorative-edged scissors and punched with a 2mm/¹⁄₁₆in hole punch is used as a border on the contrasting lime green card. The remaining punched shapes can be slipped inside the card as confetti.*

# USING BRADS

Attach motifs or fasten the front and back of cards together with brads. Numerous decorative styles are available, and they are simple to use and very versatile as they can be opened to remove or add items.

1 Resting the card on a cutting mat, pierce small holes through the pieces to be joined using a bradawl.

2 Insert the brads through the holes.

3 Splay open the prongs on the underside of the card.

# USING SNAP FASTENINGS

Join layers together with craft snap fasteners. They are the same as dressmaking fasteners but have decorative tops.

1 Press the pointed end of the top section of the snap fastener through the card layers. If the layers are too thick to do this make a hole with a bradawl before inserting the snap fastener.

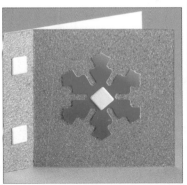

▲ This frosty Christmas card has a punched snowflake attached with a snap fastener. The front of the card is joined to the back with snap fasteners too.

# APPLYING EYELETS

Eyelets can be used for the same purposes as brads, except that once they are fixed, they cannot be removed. They can, however, have ribbons or hanging charms threaded through them.

1 Make a hole for the eyelet with a bradawl or a hole punch. Insert the eyelet into the hole.

2 Position the eyelet into the recess of a pair of eyelet pliers. Squeeze the handles of the pliers to flatten the eyelet.

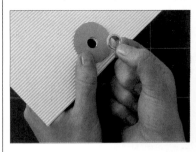

3 Alternatively, use an eyelet tool kit, following the manufacturer's instructions.

# Making envelopes

*Many of the cards you make will fit ready-made standard envelopes, and plastic templates are available to draw around and cut out to make envelopes in your own choice of paper. However, it is easy to make your own envelopes when you need them for cards in unusual sizes. It is also worth making your own template if you find a size that suits your purposes.*

## BASIC ENVELOPE

You can adapt this basic design to make square or long envelopes.

▶ *A plain envelope is easy to make in any size or shape, and can be tailored to match and co-ordinate with your cards.*

**1** Draw the size of the card front on scrap paper, adding 5mm/¼in to each edge. Draw the flap at the upper edge half the depth of the front. Draw the back at the lower edge, reducing the depth by 2cm/¾in.

**2** Draw a tab 2.5cm/1in wide at each side of the front. Draw a curve at each corner, using a circle stencil or drawing around the side of a coin so that all the curves are the same shape. Cut out the template.

**3** Draw round the template on your chosen paper and cut out the envelope. Fold in the side tabs, back and flap along the edges of the front. Open the back and flap out flat again.

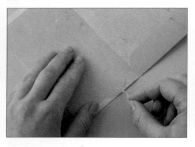

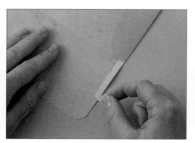

**4** Apply 5mm/¼in-wide double-sided tape along the side edges of the back, starting below the curves.

**5** Peel off the backing strips and stick the back over the tabs.

**6** To fasten, tuck the flap inside the back or seal with double-sided tape. Alternatively, seal the flap with a sticker.

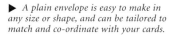

◀ *If you prefer, trim the flap of the envelope with decorative-edged scissors, or cut it to a point, trimming the tip in a curve.*

# CUTWORK DESIGN

Stamp your personal style on the envelope as well as its contents by adding a punched or cutwork decoration before making it up.

▼ *A cascade of punched holes appears to flow across the front of this envelope.*

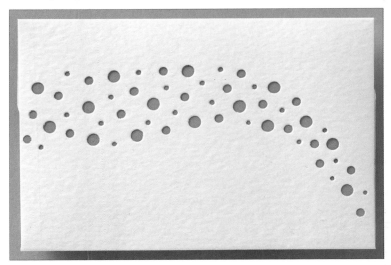

**1** Open out the envelope and rest it on a cutting mat. Cut a design or punch decorative holes across the front, working from the right side. For the best result, the card that goes inside should be of a contrasting or different shade.

# MAKING A CLASSIC WALLET

This simple envelope has no flap and can be fastened in various ways. Its plain design is ideal when you want to use a beautiful printed paper.

▼ *This classic wallet has holes punched at the top and is tied with ribbon. In sumptuous gold and cream paper it makes a lovely container for a wedding card or gift.*

**1** To make a template, measure the card front and draw it on scrap paper, adding 2cm/¾in to the side edges and 5mm/¼in to the top and bottom edges. Draw the back at the lower edge the same size as the front. Draw a tab at each side of the front 1.5cm/⅝in wide. Draw a curve at each end of the tab. Cut out the wallet template.

**2** Cut the envelope out of paper. Fold in the tabs and back along the front edges, then open the back out flat. Apply 5mm/¼in-wide double-sided tape to the side edges of the back, stopping 5mm/¼in from the top and bottom. Peel off the backing strips and stick over the tabs.

# MAKING A PADDED ENVELOPE

Present a delicate greetings card in a padded envelope for protection.

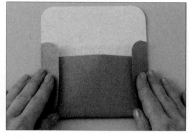

**1** Draw the dimensions of the card front on scrap paper, adding 1cm/⅜in to each edge, and make a template as for the Basic Envelope. Cut bubble wrap to fit the front and back sections and glue inside the envelope, with the smooth side uppermost.

**2** Fold in the back then fold the side tabs over. Open the tabs out flat again.

**3** Apply 5mm/¼in-wide double-sided tape along the outer edges of the tabs, starting 2cm/¼in from the upper edges. Peel off the backing strips and stick the tabs over the back. Seal the envelope by sticking the flap over the back with double-sided tape.

# MAKING A CARD-BACKED ENVELOPE

To prevent a greetings card being bent or folded in the mail, send it in a stiffened envelope.

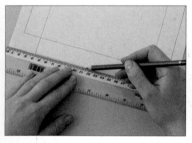

**1** Measure the card front and draw it on scrap paper, adding 5mm/¼in to each edge. Draw the flap at the upper edge half the depth of the front. Draw 2.5cm/1in-wide tabs on the other three sides of the front.

**2** Draw a curve at each corner using a template or coin. Cut out the template and use it to cut the envelope from paper. Fold the envelope along the edges of the front then open all the sides out flat again.

**3** Apply 5mm/¼in-wide double-sided tape along the outer edges of the tabs, between the curves.

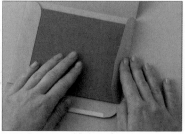

**4** Cut the back from stiff card (stock) the same size as the front, then trim 1cm/⅜in from the top and 3mm/⅛in from one side. Place the card back on the front.

**5** With the lower edges matching, peel off the backing strips and stick the side tabs, then the lower tab, over the back.

**6** To fasten, seal the flap to the back with double-sided tape. Alternatively, seal the flap with a sticker.

# MAKING A LINED ENVELOPE

A lining in a matching or contrasting colour gives a touch of luxury to an envelope. Choose lightweight paper so it is not too bulky.

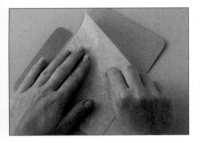

**1** Cut out the basic envelope. Cut the front and flap from the lining paper, trimming 3mm/⅛in from the outer edges. Stick the lining to the inside of the envelope using spray adhesive.

**2** Continue making up the envelope. For best results, seal the envelope by tucking the flap into the back.

▲ *An elegant tissue lining enhances the appearance of the envelope as well as giving greater protection to the contents.*

# NOVELTY ENVELOPE

Create an amusing envelope for a child in a special shape. Your design must have an opening large enough to slip the card into. Alternatively make an attractive envelope to hold a small gift.

**1** Cut a pair of elephants from paper. Resting on scrap paper, apply paper glue along the edges on the back of one elephant, leaving the straightest edge open.

**2** Stick the elephants together. Stick on card ears and joggle eyes. Punch matching holes at the top to fasten with ribbon.

▲ *The elephant template at the back of the book is used to make this funny envelope to contain a tiny card. Enlarge the template as necessary for a larger card. A joggle eye and a scythe-shaped sequin for a tusk are stuck in place using glue dots. Curling gift-wrap ribbon is tied through punched holes to fasten the envelope.*

## MAKING A BOX ENVELOPE

For a three-dimensional greetings card you may need to custom-make a box especially to fit it. These are quick and easy to make. For added protection for the card, you can line the box and lid with bubble wrap, fill the box with shredded tissue, or wrap the card in tissue paper.

**1** To make a template, measure the card front and draw it on scrap paper, adding 5mm/¼in to each edge. This will be the base. Lay the card flat on its back and measure its depth. Draw a side to the box along each edge that is the depth of the card plus 3mm/⅛in.

**2** Add a tab 1.5cm/⅝in wide to each end of two opposite box sides, drawing a slanted side to each tab from the corner of the box base. Cut out the template and use it to cut the box from card (stock), using a craft knife and metal ruler and working on a cutting mat.

**3** Score along the lines using a bone folder and fold up the sides of the box. Stick the tabs inside the ends of the adjacent sides using double-sided tape. Make a lid in the same way as the box, adding 2mm/¹⁄₁₆in to each edge of the lid top so that it fits over the sides of the box.

## QUICK WALLETS

The sides of a simple wallet can be fastened decoratively with brads or eyelets. Cut the wallet wide enough to allow for the side fastenings as well as taking the greetings card.

**1** Fold a sheet of paper in half and punch a row of holes along the sides.

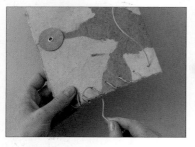

**2** Starting at the lower edge, oversew each side with paper string. Work back to the lower edge and tie the ends together.

▲ *The top of this handmade paper wallet fastens with paper string tied around circles of paper attached to the front and back using eyelets – this should be done with the paper opened out flat, before the side edges are stitched together. The holes along the side edges are punched 2cm/¾in apart and threaded with paper string.*

## NOW TRY THIS

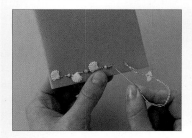

▲ The sides of a quick wallet can be joined using various stitches. In this back-stitch version using a double length of silver embroidery thread (floss), a shell-shaped sequin and a small bead are threaded on to each stitch on the wallet

front. The wallet is made of Neoprene foam, which is very quick and easy to cut and sew, and it is sealed with a length of ribbon wrapped around the centre and tied with another length of silver thread trimmed with more sequins and a larger bead.

▲ This handmade paper wallet has bands of beaded trim glued along the side edges. It is fastened with ribbons glued in the centre of the top edges. Flower sequins conceal the join and trim the ends of the ribbon.

# MAKING QUICK ENVELOPES

The simplest envelopes can be made with a few folds and no side flaps.

▼ *Toile de jouy wallpaper is used for this quick envelope. The flap is edged with glitter paint to emphasize its curvaceous shape.*

I Make an instant envelope with a flap by folding a rectangle of paper into thirds. The sheet should be 2cm/¾in wider than the height of the front of the greetings card and three times the width of the front plus 3cm/1¼in. Open it out flat again and stick the front to the back with 5mm/¼in-wide double-sided tape at each side. Cut the flap edge in a decorative shape if you wish.

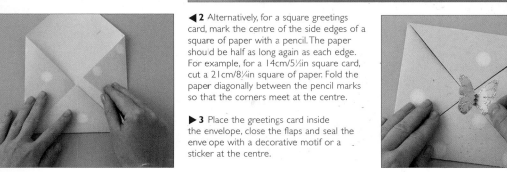

◄ 2 Alternatively, for a square greetings card, mark the centre of the side edges of a square of paper with a pencil. The paper should be half as long again as each edge. For example, for a 14cm/5½in square card, cut a 21cm/8¼in square of paper. Fold the paper diagonally between the pencil marks so that the corners meet at the centre.

▶ 3 Place the greetings card inside the envelope, close the flaps and seal the envelope with a decorative motif or a sticker at the centre.

# DESIGN THEMES FOR CARDS

Your original designs for cards will be unique to you: if you wish you can tailor each one to suit the recipient, but your own taste is likely to influence the style of most of your creations. Clarifying the themes you wish to follow can be helpful as you build up stocks of paper and decorative materials.

## Contemporary style

*Greetings cards immediately look up-to-date when made with modern materials. Acetate and plain translucent papers have a contemporary look, and superbly realistic papers resembling distressed metals are also appealing. Experiment with shiny materials on a matt background of the same colour for an understated look. Make envelopes and wallets of Neoprene foam or acetate fastened with plastic thonging for a funky way to present cards or gifts.*

Natural motifs with distinctive outlines are very popular now and are best when used boldly. Even antique-style motifs can be given a modern twist, maybe by enlarging just a section of the design. Update traditional designs by working them in unexpected materials – such as stencilling with metallic paint on paper incorporating metallic fragments. Spray acetate with frosting spray for an etched glass effect. Clever laser-cut designs occur throughout contemporary interior design, and the style also suits greetings cards, using cutwork motifs in stylish papers.

Glamour plays an unashamed part in modern style. Wrap a gift in pearlized paper and bind it with a length of diamanté trim. Add gemstone stickers or sprinkle loose glitter or accent beads on shapes such as a candelabra or high heeled shoes cut from a double-sided adhesive sheet.

Alternatively, use sugar paper in subdued colourways, graph paper or lined writing paper for a utilitarian look. Type a message in a simple font then cut the wording into strips and use as tape to bind a present. Punch out a name on a metal tag to tie on a gift or attach it to a greetings card using a chrome brad or eyelet.

### Going digital

The computer, an essential tool in modern life, can be used to create entire cards or just background papers on which to apply decorations. Digital photography offers many creative possibilities, and if you are a keen photographer you will have a wealth of images to choose from. Changing the background colour of an image is a useful manipulation technique, and distracting background details can also be removed. Image-editing software is sophisticated and can produce extraordinary effects.

◀ *For an understated modern Easter card (below left), a repeat design of egg shapes cut from plain and lined translucent paper is arranged on lime green pearlized paper. A traditional flock wallpaper design is given a modern twist (above right) by enlarging it and cutting it from double-sided adhesive sheet, which is then applied to copper-effect card (stock) and sprinkled with copper glitter.*

# Vintage style

*There are many occasions when a vintage-style greetings card fits the bill. These unashamedly romantic creations make perfect Valentine cards and are also ideal for weddings and engagements. To make this style work well you need to develop a magpie's talent for hoarding a multitude of small treasures for possible future use: printed scraps and engraved images, tickets, tags and other ephemera, old letters, fragments of lace or frail patterned silks, ribbons, buttons and bows. All these disparate elements are held in harmony by their soft textures and faded colours, allowing them to be combined in beautiful designs of tremendous richness and depth.*

Traditional materials such as handmade paper and natural fabrics have soft textures and colours to match with vintage embellishments. Marbled papers also suit cards with a vintage theme. And not everything you use needs to be old: there are clever ways to create the look. You can scan or photocopy old letters, or samples of copperplate handwriting, and age your photocopies by painting them with a weak solution of tea. Sprinkle a few instant coffee granules sparingly on the surface before the tea dries. You can buy books of papers printed with vintage handwriting or music scripts to use as backgrounds and borders, and reproductions of 19th-century colour-printed paper scraps. Cotton lace will also age realistically if dyed in a cup of strong, cold tea for a few hours. Rinse in water and spread out to dry naturally.

Sort through old family photographs for useful images. Don't use the originals but photocopy or scan them then age them digitally with a sepia tone, or add a little delicate hand tinting. Frame them with borders of lace or ribbon.

## Vintage embellishments
There are lots of antique-style accessories available to create heritage greetings cards, but you may already have suitable items. Old sewing accessories are ideal: mother-of-pearl buttons are particularly pretty. Small fragments of lace and pieces of embroidery can be framed in a window card. Hang tiny charms and lockets on a luggage label.

Pressed flowers are perfect embellishments for vintage cards, with their soft, faded colours and timeless charm.

▶ *Scraps of old textiles, manuscripts and printed ephemera are staple ingredients of vintage style. An exquisite scrap of a beaded and embroidered panel is mounted on a background of dark marbled paper (left), while the border of fine lace has a piece of broken jewellery sewn to it. Another eclectic assembly (right) features a pair of distressed luggage labels decorated with a lace fragment and postage stamp and bound with silk ribbon. They are stuck to a section of an old map, tinted with tea and mounted on handmade paper. The strings of the labels are cleverly used to fasten the pages together.*

Apply a mass of dainty pressed forget-me-nots in a heart shape or linked rings for an engagement card.

Paper doilies are cheap and easily available, but pieces used sparingly as backgrounds can lend vintage designs the look of old cut-paper greetings cards. Books of copyright-free images are another useful resource: photocopies of old engravings stuck to cards make instant greetings cards or sets of invitations or notelets.

Make vintage-style envelopes and wrappings too. Tie up your parcels with string, seal them with sealing wax and decorate them with old stamps or tickets and labels from foreign holidays.

# Retro style

*The bold designs of the not-so-distant past are now being rediscovered and reinterpreted by modern designers, and the best of them retain their freshness while also evoking fond memories of the 1950s, '60s and '70s. Be inspired by these graphic patterns and images and create witty, retro cards that chime perfectly with today's style.*

Stereotypical images from 1950s advertising, books and periodicals, portraying manly men, domesticated women, perfect children and streamlined homes, are perfect for funny, ironic cards, especially when you want to send an irreverent greeting to a friend: just add your own pithy caption or personalized speech bubbles. Hunt through your older relatives' bookshelves and attics for suitable images, or try second-hand book stores, postcard dealers and charity shops.

Stylized organic motifs dominated 1950s graphic design, and relief paints are ideal for work in this style. The kidney shape was a popular outline and was used for all kinds of items, from the tops of coffee tables to textile motifs. Try stamping the shape with a handmade Neoprene foam stamp on plain paper for retro-style gift wrap. A grey, red and black colour scheme would work well.

Images of basic everyday utensils such as kitchenware were also popular in wallpaper and printed textile designs of the time.

Many of the printed papers available from craft stores for scrapbooking feature retro images of this kind, and they can be used as background designs or cut up as sources of decorative motifs.

### The 1960s

The confident wild designs of the 1960s are easy to reproduce. After the previous decade's insistence on modernism, 1960s designers revived Victorian and Edwardian styles, but with a contemporary twist. This was also the age of op art and psychedelia. Keep the colours bold and vibrant: orange was particularly popular, often combined with sizzling pink or purple. Cut bulbous shapes such as stylized flowers from brightly coloured towelling and cotton fabrics. Chunky plastic buttons and coloured synthetic lace flowers are great for appliqué effects. Cut out curvaceous letters and numbers from suitably patterned papers to add to cards and tags.

### The 1970s

For true 1970s glam-rock style, create a glittery frame for a photograph on the front of a greetings card. Using spray adhesive stick gift wrap or wallpaper with a loud repeat pattern to a card as a background, then top with a slinky silhouette of a dancer cut from glossy sticky-backed plastic. Photocopy or scan a computer image from comics of the time.

Cut stylish Scandinavian furniture shapes from realistic wood veneer paper and apply to a greetings card covered with a scrap of suitable wallpaper to make a quirky card for friends with an interest in interior design. If you can crochet, work a square medallion to adorn the top of a square gift box for a touch of 1970s folksiness.

To complete the retro effect, type your messages and captions in decorative fonts that evoke the period that inspires you.

◀ *This gift box (right) is decorated with simple retro motifs reminiscent of 1950s designs inspired by the dawning space age. Circles are cut freehand from red paper and stuck at random to the box lid, then decorated with smoky blue and black relief paints. On the card (left) a vibrant pop art flower has petals applied in layers cut from orange and grey card and applied to a circle of grey. The background is orange polka-dot gift wrap applied to grey card.*

# Natural style

*Nature provides lots of beautiful materials for card making. Gather feathers, seed pods and twigs when you are out for walks in the countryside, or pick flowers and leaves from the garden to press for future greetings card projects. Pressed ivy and bay leaves are sturdy enough to be painted or rubbed with metallic wax.*

When you visit the sea, go beachcombing for small pieces of driftwood and fragments of sea-washed glass. Do not collect seashells but buy them from a reputable supplier. Some have holes already drilled for threading on to twine or raffia, but if you wish to drill holes yourself, use a small drill bit and support the shell on a lump of plastic clay. Shells can be attached to cards using glue dots. Make a tiny boat for the front of a card, using driftwood for the hull and adding a twig mast and a fabric sail.

Collect flowers and leaves and press them for future use. Many flowers also dry well. Dried roses, hydrangeas, heather and cornflowers make lovely trimmings for gift-wrapped wedding and birthday presents. Tie a sachet of dried lavender to the front of a greetings card for a delightful fragrant gift. You could even re-create a 17th-century knot garden by arranging seeds and dried lentils on areas spread with PVA (white) glue in symmetrical patterns.

These natural materials look most effective on backgrounds of handmade paper. There are some fabulous papers available incorporating petals, leaves or onion skins. If you make your own paper, making it into greetings cards is a great way to show it off. You can match the natural deckle edge of handmade paper on the other edges of a sheet by tearing it to size against a ruler. If necessary, moisten the paper first with a wet paintbrush to make it easier to tear.

## Natural materials

Use rustic fabrics such as hessian (burlap) and linen in natural, warm tones and fray the edges. Cottons woven in plaids and stripes can be cut and stuck to the front of a card in a simple patchwork design. Apply iron-on interfacing to the back of the fabrics before cutting if you wish to cut out shapes from them. Decorate the fabrics with simple embroidery stitches, keeping the colours simple or matching them to your natural decorations.

Cards and wallets can be fastened with neutral-coloured twine or string, or a few strands of undyed raffia. Make up a bouquet garni with cinnamon sticks and bay leaves and tie it on to the front of a card. Sweet-smelling sheets of beeswax are available from candle-making suppliers, and can be cut with scissors and stuck to the front of a

card with glue dots – a beehive shape accompanied by a tiny drawn bee would make a lovely design.

Recycled materials go well with natural decorations. Brown parcel paper can be stamped or painted, and wallets made from corrugated card (stock). Cut motifs from printed waxed paper cartons and attach them to cards with coloured eyelets.

Hand-deliver cards decorated with natural materials in padded envelopes for protection or put them in a box envelope.

▼ *This quick wallet of handmade paper incorporating marigold petals (right) has its side edges oversewn with dyed raffia. A pressed grass seedhead and leaf sprig decorate the front. The wallet is fastened with a raffia tie. A pretty scallop shell is the focal point of the greetings card (below left), edged on two sides with colourful handmade papers. A row of pressed forget-me-not flowerheads is applied with PVA (white) glue and a small sea-worn limpet shell is sewn to the card front with string.*

# Ethnic style

*Many nations have distinctive identities that inspire themes and styles for card making. Studying the folk art of another country is a great way to explore new craft techniques. For example, paper cuts have been a popular pastime in China, Mexico, North America, Germany and Poland for hundreds of years, and often have spiritual associations. They all have their own style and look stunning on greetings cards or adapted to make stencils.*

▲ *Characterful printed and patterned papers from all over the world can be used to make unusual and beautiful cards. This Mexican-style card (below right) has a stylized South American bird embossed on fine metal and glued to a paper coaster doiley on a bright pink card. For the Indian-inspired card (above right), scraps of printed and embroidered papers are applied in bands to the front and decorated with narrow strips of self-adhesive holographic floral designs and stickers using a paisley motif, which is a popular Indian design.*

Paper was invented by the Chinese and many of their folk crafts use it ingeniously. Traditionally, Chinese paper cuts are displayed at windows, so that the light shows through the delicate patterns. The carp, signifying wealth, is a favourite motif. Colourful Chinese paper cuts can be bought ready-made and mounted on a greetings card using spray adhesive. Chinese supermarkets sell imitation money, which can be used in découpage decorations. The Japanese also have a strong affiliation with papercrafts, with origami being the best

known. Many of the more unusual and delicate papers available today are manufactured in Japan. Thin squares of plain coloured and patterned papers for origami are widely available: use them to make origami gift boxes or assemble a collage of different patterns, which co-ordinate beautifully, to decorate a greetings card. *Washi chigiri-e* is the ancient Japanese craft of arranging torn pieces of coloured paper to make a picture, with results that can resemble watercolour or pastel. The soft washi paper can be manipulated to produce very subtle colour effects.

## National traditions

Papercrafts are very popular in Mexico, and many are incorporated in traditional festive occasions. The Aztecs made a primitive paper from bark called *amate*, and simple paper cuts of amate were thought to have magical qualities. Today, vibrantly coloured paper cuts called *papel picado* are strung up outside churches for weddings and saints' days. Try recreating traditional Mexican motifs on fine embossing metal and mounting them on brightly coloured card. Pink, lime green, orange and acid yellow are the characteristic colours of Mexican folk art. The Day of the Dead is commemorated on 31 October, when the dead are believed to return to see their loved ones. Images such as skeletons and skulls are typical features of this important festivity.

Create Indonesian batik-style designs or freehand African patterns on watercolour paper using masking fluid. Paint the paper, leave it to dry, then rub away the dried masking fluid to reveal the design and mount the picture on the front of a greetings card. Paint an Australian aboriginal design with relief paints on the top of a set of stationery.

Beautiful hand-printed and embroidered papers from India are available from specialist paper suppliers. Use them with shisha glass and bindi-style decorations on greetings cards.

Many ready-made decorations from all over the world are readily available to us nowadays. Ethnic designs are popular subjects on rubber stamps. Wood block stamps used for printing on fabric in the Far East are also available for authentic effects.

# Cards for children

*It is great fun to make cards to send to children and this is an occasion to let your imagination run wild. Go for bright colours and simple motifs. Children will especially appreciate personalized greetings, so including their name on the front of the card will make them feel special. Use a computer to write the name in a suitable font and cut it out to use as a label. Alternatively, use letter stickers or write the name using a letter stencil.*

If you are making a birthday card, add the age number, as age is very important to children and they feel very grown-up when they reach a new year. If the child has a special enthusiasm — for trains or dinosaurs, for example — create a card with that in mind. Cookie cutters are often available in the appropriate shapes, or you can find a suitable picture to use as a reference for your own template.

There are lots of novel and tactile embellishments that you can buy from craft suppliers to add to children's cards. Joggle eyes will give a comical look to a character, whether you add them to a figure you have drawn or cut out, or to a photograph. Squishy pompoms are available in different sizes and colours, and can be stuck in place with glue dots. An animal cut from felt or fleece could enclose a flat, plastic toy-making growler or squeaker, which will sound when the animal is pressed. Make sure that the felt or fleece is stuck down firmly, so prying fingers can't open it.

Small gifts can be incorporated with a child's card to make it extra interesting: you could pin a birthday badge to the front for example, or glue a few foil-wrapped chocolate coins to a Christmas tree shape to resemble baubles.

On a cautionary note, there are safety considerations to think about when making childrens' cards, and you should always bear in mind the age of the recipient. Do not decorate cards for young children with any sharp embellishments, and make sure that all decorations are stuck down securely. Use glitter paint rather than loose glitter, which could moult. If you are using brads in your design, make sure that the prongs are enclosed under a facing of card or paper, or apply stickers or tape over them, firmly stuck down.

### Child's play
Children will love to help make cards for their friends and family, and to create their own party invitations. PVA (white) glue is non-toxic, as are many water-based paints. Poster paints are an inexpensive choice for children to use, and come in bright colours that they can use straight from the pots. Cover the work surface with old plastic carrier bags cut open and laid flat to catch any spillages.

Glow-in-the-dark relief paints will make super decorations for a set of Halloween invitations. Pre-cut Neoprene shapes are available for children to stick on their cards and decorate with glitter paints, and older children love using glue and plenty of glitter to make sparkling designs. Plastic pony beads are inexpensive and are available in round, heart and star shapes. They have a large hole and are easy for little fingers to thread on to cord or thonging to make fastenings for boxes and envelopes.

▼ *This robot made of silver card (right) is trimmed with feet, hair and ears made from red sticky-backed plastic. A "door" cut in his front opens to reveal the age of the recipient. The mouth is cut out and a pair of amusing joggle eyes complete the effect. A little pair of summer sandals cut from Neoprene foam decorate a simple square card (left), which would be lovely to send to a little girl going on a trip to the seaside. The sandals are decorated with flower stickers and dots of light green glitter paint.*

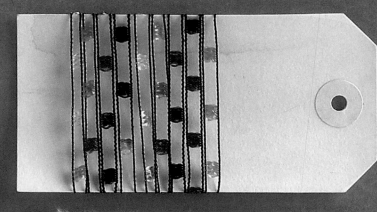

# Decorating
# paper and cards

This section presents masses of innovative ideas for decorating paper to use as gift wrap and to make cards and stationery. It covers background colours and ways of treating the surface of the paper, such as gilding and embossing, as well as showing the best ways to apply many different embellishments, from glitter to polymer clay motifs and pressed flowers. All the techniques described are suitable for beginners, so you can have fun mastering new crafts as well as rediscovering old ones.

# Using stencils

*Stencilling is very popular, and many ready-made stencils are suitable for adding decoration to greetings cards. Choose small-scale stencils with lots of detail, or if you like, it's quite easy to create your own stencils too.*

**1** Tape tracing paper over the design and redraw it, drawing along each side of any inner outlines to thicken them.

**2** You will need to add "bridges" between the sections to be cut out, such as on the circles on the wings of this butterfly.

**3** Transfer the stencil design on to oiled stencil board. Resting on a cutting mat, cut out the design using a craft knife.

## STENCILLING WITH A SPONGE

For a softer, textured look, paint can also be applied through a stencil using a small natural or synthetic sponge. Don't overload the sponge with paint. Dab lightly to control the sponged effect.

**4** Tape the stencil to the card with masking tape. Pick up a small amount of acrylic paint with a stencil brush and dab off the excess on kitchen paper. Dab the paint through the stencil, holding the brush upright and moving it in a circular motion.

**5** Leave the first colour to dry before shading the design. Pick up a small amount of paint in a slightly different colour and apply it lightly in your chosen areas, aiming for a soft, stippled effect. Leave to dry then remove the stencil.

◀ *This vibrant stencilled butterfly card is quick to produce once the stencil has been cut, so you could easily create a whole set of the same design, to send as party invitations for example.*

▶ *A golden cocktail glass is stencilled using a sponge and embellished with sequin dust and star-shaped sprinkles.*

# REVERSE STENCILLING

In this alternative stencilling technique, the area surrounding the design is painted, leaving the motif the same colour as the card background. Distinctive, solid shapes work most effectively.

Draw the design on stencil card and cut out. Resting on scrap paper and working in a well-ventilated room, spray the back of the stencil with stencil mount and stick it in place. Stencil the surrounding area with a stencil brush or spray paint. Leave to dry then peel off the stencil.

▶ *An elegant dragonfly is reverse stencilled with pink spray paint on a bright yellow background, then mounted on a wavy-edged card of the same colour.*

# STENCILLING ACETATE

Stencilling paint and frosting spray on acetate gives a contemporary look to your creations. Cut stencils from sticky-backed plastic, which adheres well to the smooth surface.

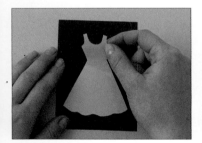

I Cut a stencil from sticky-backed plastic and stick the stencil to the acetate.

2 Place the acetate on scrap paper or old newspaper. Working in a well-ventilated area, spray with paint or frosting spray.

◀ 3 Leave the paint to dry before carefully peeling off the stencil.

▲ *A stunning dress is reverse stencilled with turquoise spray paint on acetate, then embellished with stickers and silver plastic discs. The acetate is mounted on a white card trimmed with matching turquoise brads.*

# Making polymer clay motifs

*Playing with polymer clay is a great way to try out ideas for three-dimensional motifs to decorate greetings cards. After modelling, bake the clay in a domestic oven to harden it.*

**1** Roll a piece of polymer clay to about 3mm/⅛in thick on baking parchment.

**2** Stamp the clay with a cookie cutter. Press the cutter firmly into the clay.

**3** Pull away the excess clay around the cutter. Remove the cutter.

**4** If you need a threading hole, pierce a hole in the clay with a cocktail stick (toothpick), wiggling it to enlarge the hole to take a ribbon or cord. Decorate the motif if you wish, then bake following the manufacturer's instructions. Leave to cool.

**5** Varnish the hardened motif using a specially formulated polymer clay varnish for protection if you wish. Leave to dry.

**6** Suspend the motif from the card on thread or cord or attach it with double-sided tape, adhesive foam pads or glue dots.

◀ *Two polymer clay elephants, joined with a bow of fine ribbon threaded through holes pierced in their trunks, are attached to the front of this card using double-sided tape.*

## USING A RUBBER STAMP ON CLAY

Rubber stamping on polymer clay produces subtle motifs that can be highlighted with metallic wax.

## MAKING A POLYMER CLAY FLOWER

Pretty clay flowers are deceptively easy to model from small balls of clay with a little simple shaping, and they have lots of decorative uses. The size of the flowers can be varied, but you need to make sure that very large motifs will not be too heavy for the front of a card.

**I** Roll clay out flat on a sheet of baking parchment to about 3mm/⅛in thick and stamp firmly with a rubber stamp. Do not rock the stamp. Trim the clay around the stamped motif and bake to harden it.

**I** Roll a 5mm/¼in ball of polymer clay for the flower centre and press it on to baking parchment. Roll six 5mm/¼in balls of contrasting coloured clay for the petals and press them around the flower centre.

**2** Indent the flower centre at random with the head of a dressmaking pin.

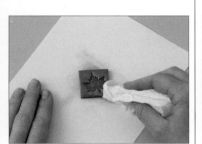

**2** Resting the hardened motif on scrap paper, use kitchen paper to rub metallic wax sparingly on to the surface to distinguish the raised areas.

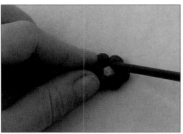

**3** To shape the petals, indent each one close to the flower centre with the handle of a fine artist's paintbrush.

**4** Bake the flowers following the manufacturer's instructions. Leave to cool then stick each flower in position on a greetings card using a glue dot.

▲ A row of delightful clay flowers are applied to a torn strip of pale green card (stock) on the front of this charming greetings card.

# Gilding

*The glimmer of fine gold, silver or copper leaf will add a touch of glamour to your handcrafted cards. Dutch metal leaf is supplied on backing paper, making it much easier to handle than real gold leaf. The effect adds a luxury element, so use this technique for cards that mark a significant occasion.*

**1** Lightly draw the outline of your design in pencil on the card. Apply gold size to the shapes. Set aside for 15 minutes until the size has become clear and tacky.

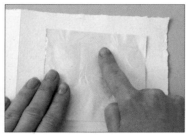

**2** Cut a piece of transfer metal leaf slightly larger than the sized area. Lay the metal leaf face down on the size and gently press in place. Peel off the backing paper.

**3** Sweep away the excess metal leaf using a soft brush.

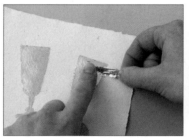

**4** If the metal leaf has not adhered in places, simply press a little of the left-over metal leaf into the gaps.

## USING METALLIC WAX

Fabulous gilded effects can be achieved very easily by rubbing on metallic wax, which is available in a range of colours. This is a good way to add lustre to embossed papers and other raised designs: when applied sparingly, the wax will adhere just to the raised areas and highlight the embossing. Rest a small stamped motif on scrap paper, or mask a sheet of embossed paper with scrap paper or a stencil, then rub the metallic wax lightly over the motif using a piece of kitchen paper.

◄ *This sumptuous card decorated with a pair of gilded champagne flutes would be ideal for a special wedding greeting. The design is finished with jewellery stone bubbles and the insert is attached with a length of fine gold cord.*

# GILDING A GIFT BOX

Transform a plain cardboard box into a beautiful gilded presentation container for an important gift. Fill with shredded coloured tissue paper and tie with ribbon and beads.

**1** Resting on scrap paper, use a flat paintbrush to paint the box and lid with acrylic paint. Set aside to dry.

**2** Using a flat paintbrush, apply a coat of gold size to the painted box and lid. Set aside for 15 minutes until the size has become clear and feels tacky.

**3** Cut a sheet of metal transfer leaf into manageable pieces. Place a piece of leaf face down on the size and gently press in place. Peel off the backing paper. Apply further sheets of metal leaf, overlapping the edges, until the box and lid are covered.

**4** Sweep away the excess leaf with a soft brush. Allow the paint to show through at any gaps or at the corners of the box.

▲ *This gilded box would be lovely to use to present a gift of jewellery. For a traditional look, use light blue paint under aluminium gilding, red paint under gold gilding and aquamarine paint under copper gilding to create a verdigris effect.*

# GILDING ON POLYMER CLAY

Apply this fabulous technique to polymer clay plaques to create solid decorations. The gilding is applied before the clay is baked.

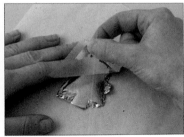

**1** On a sheet of baking parchment, roll a piece of polymer clay out flat to a thickness of about 3mm/⅛in. Cut out a motif using a cutter or knife. Carefully place a piece of metal leaf face down on top of the clay.

**2** Roll over the backing paper with a rolling pin. Lift off the backing paper and gently pull away any large excess pieces of the metal leaf, saving them to use again. If the gilding has not adhered in places, press a piece of the left-over metal leaf in the gaps, replace the paper and roll over it again to adhere it to the surface.

**3** To create crackles in the gilding, place a piece of baking parchment on top of the motif and roll over the surface again with a rolling pin. Remove the baking parchment and bake the clay following the manufacturer's instructions.

▲ *This dramatic Christmas card has a festive tree cut from white polymer clay gilded with copper metallic leaf. The motif is applied to a midnight blue card with double-sided tape. A white paper insert allows the card to be written in clearly.*

# Creating backgrounds

*While there is a huge selection of appealing printed and patterned papers to choose from in greetings card shops, you can also make unique backgrounds using these easy printing and painting techniques.*

## PAINTING WITH A NATURAL SPONGE

Applying paint using a sponge creates a subtle, organic-looking random pattern. Use colours that harmonize well for the best effects.

1 Using a broad, flat paintbrush, apply acrylic paint to an old plate or ceramic tile.

2 Moisten a natural sponge. Squeeze it in kitchen paper to remove the excess water. Dab at the paint with the sponge then dab the paint at random all over the paper. Repeat with a second colour if you wish.

▲ *This orange paper has been sponged with red paint then more sparingly with off-white. The paper can be used as gift wrap or as a background for a greetings card.*

## PAINTING WITH A SYNTHETIC SPONGE

Using a synthetic sponge to apply paint gives a denser coverage of colour.

1 Paint the top surface of a synthetic sponge with acrylic paint using a flat paintbrush.

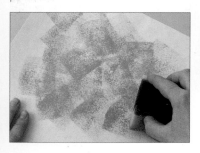

◄ 2 Dab the sponge all over the paper. Press down on the sponge to release more paint and change the direction of the sponging to create a random effect.

▲ *Applying light pink paint at random all over cream paper using a synthetic sponge gives a simple textured effect.*

# USING MASKING FLUID

Masking fluid is used to protect areas that are to remain unpainted. After painting, the dried fluid can be rubbed away to reveal a pattern.

  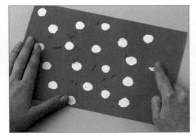

**1** Paint a simple motif or pattern with masking fluid using an artist's paintbrush on watercolour paper. Set aside to dry.

**2** Paint the paper all over with a strong colour. Leave to dry.

**3** Rub away the masking fluid patches with your finger to reveal the unpainted areas of paper underneath.

# BLEACHING

Paint freehand designs on strongly coloured papers using bleach to remove the colour from the paper. This is a super way to decorate tissue paper.

◀ Use a fine or medium artist's paintbrush to paint a simple design with household bleach. The colour should come out quickly.

▶ *Flamboyant freestyle swirls decorate this sheet of tissue paper.*

# USING CHALKS

Coloured chalks are good for creating a large patterned sheet of paper quickly. Keep the designs simple: stripes and checks work particularly well.

  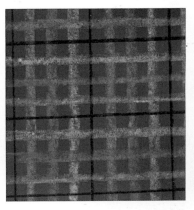

**1** Hold the chalk upright to draw a stripe the width of the chalk. Hold the chalk on its edge for finer lines. Draw rows of multi-coloured stripes, then add stripes in the other direction to create a check pattern.

**2** Working in a well-ventilated room and protecting the surrounding area with scrap paper, spray the chalked paper with fixative to prevent the chalk from smudging.

▲ *This checkered chalked paper could be used to cover a box to make a great presentation box for a baby shower present.*

# Using rubber stamps

*Applying designs with rubber stamps is a popular craft. The technique is particularly suitable for making cards, and a wide variety of styles can be created with it. Ready-made stamps are available to suit almost any theme.*

**1** Press the rubber stamp on the ink pad. If the stamp is larger than the pad, restamp it a few times to get an even coverage. Press the rubber stamp firmly on the paper or card. Do not rock the stamp. Lift off the stamp and leave the image to dry.

**2** If you wish, add a little colour to the image using felt-tipped pens.

▲ *This stamped image is mounted on a square of orange card and applied with foam adhesive pads to the card front over torn strips of green paper and floral gift wrap.*

## EMBOSSING STAMPED MOTIFS

Embossed stamped motifs have a very professional finish, which is achieved by applying embossing powder and then melting it.

**1** Resting on scrap paper, sprinkle embossing powder on the stamped image before the ink dries.

**2** Shake off the excess powder on the scrap paper. Tap the back of the image a few times to release all the excess powder. Pour the excess embossing powder back into the container.

◀ **3** Hold the stamped image over a heat source such as an electric toaster or hotplate. Alternatively, warm the image with a heat gun until the powder melts and amalgamates into a shiny, raised motif.

▲ *This regal gift tag has a feather stamped with gold ink on red card. The feather is embossed with gold embossing powder.*

# STAMPING WITH WATERCOLOUR STAMP PAINTS

Create delicate effects with watercolour paints specially formulated for rubber stamps. The paints can be blended together to produce the appearance of a hand-painted image.

**1** Paint the rubber stamp with watercolour stamp paints using a medium artist's paintbrush and blending the colours together on the stamp.

**2** Stamp the image on absorbent paper such as handmade paper or rough watercolour paper. Leave to dry.

### CLEANING RUBBER STAMPS

Remember to clean your stamps after use, otherwise the fine detail of the design will become clogged with ink. You also need to clean a stamp if you want to print the motif in a different colour.

Clean the stamp with alcohol-free baby wipes or a designated stamp cleaner. An old toothbrush is good for cleaning stubborn areas. Finish by blotting the stamp with kitchen paper.

## MAKING A FOAM STAMP

If you want a simple shape for a repeating stamped pattern it's easy to cut your own. Neoprene foam is ideal for this purpose, as you can cut it with a craft knife and it takes both ink and paint well.

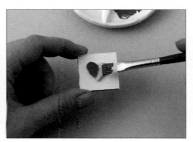

**1** Resting on a cutting mat, cut out a simple shape from Neoprene foam using a craft knife. To mount it, cut a square or rectangle of corrugated cardboard slightly larger than the foam shape. Stick the foam shape to the corrugated cardboard using all-purpose household glue.

**2** Use a flat paintbrush to paint the foam shape with acrylic paint.

**3** Stamp the image firmly on to paper or card. Repaint the foam stamp before stamping each motif.

# Adding embellishments

*All kinds of decoration can be glued on to your cards and tags to provide accents of colour and sparkle, as well as to establish a theme. The only proviso is that they should not be too heavy.*

## LOOSE GLITTER

Use loose glitter for a dense, sparkling effect on small or large areas. Pour on a generous amount to get a good even coverage: the excess can be collected and returned to the container. Glitter is widely available in a range of colours to match your designs, and can be applied to detailed shapes quite accurately if you apply the glue using a fine brush.

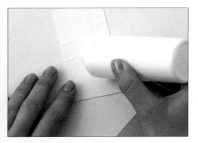

1 Resting on scrap paper, spread PVA (white) glue on the area where glitter is to be applied. Depending on the size of the area, use the nozzle of the container, a glue spreader or an old paintbrush.

2 Sprinkle glitter over the glued area and set aside to dry. Shake the excess glitter on to the scrap paper, tapping the card to remove the loose grains, and pour it back into the glitter container.

▲ *The decorated panel on this card is simple enough to work freehand with silver glitter and accent beads.*

## USING ACCENT BEADS

Use these tiny, shiny ballbearing-like beads without holes in the same way as glitter to create sparkling shapes with a crunchy texture.

1 Resting on scrap paper, spread glue on the area to be decorated. Sprinkle the accent beads on the glue.

2 Tap the card on the scrap paper to release the excess accent beads and carefully pour them back into the container.

## GLITTER AND BEAD SPOTS

Glitter and accent beads adhere well to glue dots, so this is a useful way to make sparkly spots of a regular size and shape.

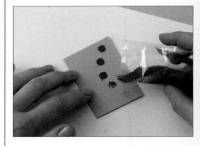

Press the glue dots on to the card surface. Resting on scrap paper, sprinkle glitter or accent beads on to the glue dots. Shake off the excess.

# USING DOUBLE-SIDED ADHESIVE SHEET

A double-sided adhesive sheet can be cut to shape and stuck to card or paper, providing a sticky surface on which to pour glitter and accent beads.

**1** Draw a motif on the paper backing of an adhesive sheet and cut it out. Peel off the backing paper and stick it in place. Peel off the protective plastic top sheet.

**2** Resting the card on scrap paper, sprinkle glitter or accent beads thickly on to the motif. Pour off the excess.

▲ *The fine particles on this demure flamingo motif catch the light beautifully. A jewellery stone eye is the only other decoration needed.*

# USING A READY-MADE ADHESIVE MOTIF

Ready-made adhesive motifs are an easy way to get a professional finish.

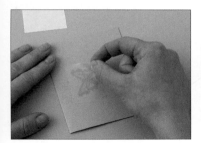

**1** Roughly cut out the motif. Peel off the backing paper and stick the motif firmly to the card. Peel off the plastic top sheet.

**2** Resting the card on scrap paper, sprinkle glitter on the motif. Pour off the excess.

▲ *The pretty butterfly on this card is a ready-made adhesive motif that has been sprinkled with copper glitter.*

# RELIEF PAINT AND GLITTER PAINT

Both these special-effect paints can be applied straight from the container.

**1** Gently squeeze the tube to apply the paint. Leave to dry.

**2** For a glamorous effect, sprinkle sequin dust, tiny sequins or sprinkles on the paint before it dries. Gently shake off the excess.

▲ *This gift tag has wavy lines of relief and glitter paint. For extra sparkle, one line has been sprinkled with sequin dust.*

# APPLYING STICKERS

Ready-made stickers come in a huge choice of designs that are suitable for adults as well as children. The easy-to-use adhesive backing makes them easy to apply to the background.

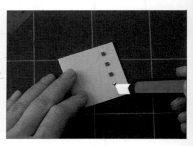

**1** Stickers are usually supplied on a backing sheet. Peel them off the sheet and stick in place. Some come loose with a backing tape protecting the adhesive backing. Peel off the backing tape to apply the sticker.

**2** Tiny diamanté stickers are often supplied on an adhesive strip. To release the stickers singly, cut between them with a craft knife, resting on a cutting mat.

**3** Position tiny stickers by picking up the sticker on the blade of a craft knife. Lightly press the sticker in place and slide the blade out. Press the sticker firmly in place.

# MAKING STICKERS WITH A PUNCH

It is easy and quick to make your own stickers using double-sided tape and a paper punch.

**1** Apply double-sided tape to the wrong side of paper or card (stock).

**2** Punch out the shape with a paper punch. Peel off the backing paper and press the stickers in place.

# USING STICKY-BACKED PLASTIC TO MAKE STICKERS

Cut or punch shapes from sticky-backed plastic to make stickers. This is particularly useful for large-scale designs, which can be drawn on the paper backing. Choose bright colours to give cards a contemporary look.

Draw the motif on the paper backing of a piece of sticky-backed plastic. Remember that the motif will be a mirror image of what you draw. Cut out the motif using a craft knife, resting on a cutting mat, or with a pair of scissors. Peel off the backing paper and press the sticker in position.

▲ *This vibrant card using shiny lime green sticky-backed plastic shows just how effective this material can be when used to make decorative motifs.*

# USING NEOPRENE FOAM

This pliable material is light in weight, easy to cut and available in bright colours. It's great for light-hearted images.

◀ Resting on a cutting mat, cut the foam with a craft knife held upright. It is easier to cut small pieces with a pair of scissors. Stick Neoprene foam to cards using all-purpose household glue.

▶ *Colourful Neoprene foam is used for the various elements of this underwater scene. Jewellery stones and metallic plastic circles add sparkle and a change of texture.*

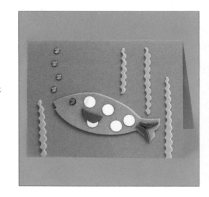

# PRESSING FLOWERS

Flower pressing is a traditional pastime that also has stunning contemporary applications. For best results, pick the flowers on a dry day. Delicate blooms with thin petals, such as pansies and poppies, are usually the most successful. As they take time to press, it's a good idea to pick flowers at every opportunity and build up a collection for future use.

**1** Gently arrange the flowers or leaves on blotting paper. Cover them with another piece of blotting paper and press flat in a flower press or between the pages of a heavy book for about 10 days.

**2** Carefully lift off the top piece of blotting paper to reveal the pressed flowers.

**3** Use a cocktail stick (toothpick) to spread PVA (white) glue sparingly on the underside of the flower.

**4** Lift the flower with a pair of tweezers. Turn it over and stick in place.

## PIN PRICKING

This delicate technique suits simple designs best, and involves pricking a row of tiny holes with a bradawl around the outline of the motif. To begin, draw the motif on tracing paper and tape it with masking tape to the paper or card. Pierce holes at regular intervals along the outline using a bradawl. When the shape is complete remove the tracing. If you wish, carefully enlarge the holes with the bradawl.

▲ *Here, an elegant pin-pricked motif is applied to the front of a greetings card of smartly striped gift wrap.*

# Fabric and sewing skills

*Embroidery stitches and other sewing techniques allow you to add luxurious textures to your greetings cards and give them an unmistakably handmade look. Making too many holes in paper will weaken it, so keep your stitches large and bold, using chunky thread, string or narrow ribbon, and go for simple designs.*

## APPLYING FABRIC MOTIFS

Backing fabric with interfacing makes a flimsy fabric stiffer, and therefore makes it easier to handle when used in conjunction with paper and card (stock). It also stabilizes frail fabrics and helps prevent them from fraying excessively. The outline of the motif can be drawn on the interfacing, but bear in mind that the fabric motif will be a mirror image of the template.

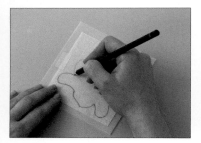

I Trace the outline of the motif using a black pen. Tape a piece of iron-on interfacing, shiny (adhesive) side down, on the wrong side of the tracing. Resting on a sheet of white paper so that you can see the black outline clearly, trace the motif on to the interfacing using a pencil.

2 Roughly cut out the motif, leaving a margin all around. Position the interfacing on the wrong side of the fabric, shiny side down, and iron it on.

3 Cut out the motif with fabric scissors and attach it to a card using spray adhesive.

▲ *A simple fabric rabbit motif has been applied to a card covered in fibrous paper. Buttons provide its bobtail and eye.*

## RUNNING STITCH

Embroidery stitches work well on paper. Holes for each end of the stitch should be pierced first so that you do not crease the surface when sewing. Do not use lightweight paper unless it has been applied to card (stock) first, as it is likely to tear. Choose threads that complement the texture and colour of the paper.

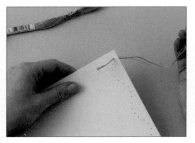

I Mark an even number of dots on the card for the stitches. If you prefer, mark the dots on tracing paper to use as a template. Tape the template to the card with masking tape. Resting the card on a cutting mat, pierce a hole at each dot using a bradawl.

2 Thread a crewel embroidery needle with stranded embroidery thread (floss) and knot the end. Start the stitches on the front or back of the card: if you start stitching on the front, the end knots will be visible.

3 Sew a running stitch in and out of the holes. Finish with a knot over the last hole and cut off the excess thread.

# LAZY DAISY STITCH

Flowers are traditional embroidery motifs, and the "lazy daisy", worked in single chain stitches, is the most familiar. It looks very pretty on a card.

**1** To make a template, draw a circle for the flower on tracing paper. Divide the circle into six even segments. Place a button or jewellery stone at the centre and mark a dot on each segment around the centre piece. Mark another dot at the end of each spoke to mark the tips of the petals.

**2** Tape the template in position on the greetings card. Resting the card on a cutting mat, pierce a hole at each dot using a bradawl. Remove the template and glue the button or jewellery stone in position at the centre of the flower.

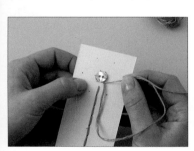

**3** Thread a crewel needle with stranded embroidery thread (floss) and knot the end. Bring the needle to the right side of the card through a hole close to the centre. Return the needle through the same hole but do not pull the thread right through.

**4** Bring the needle to the right side through the outer hole of the petal, passing it through the loop of thread. Pull the thread gently until the loop forms a rounded petal shape flat on the card.

**5** Push the needle back through the same outer hole to secure the petal. Repeat to form the other five petals, keeping the tension even throughout, and tie off the thread at the back.

▶ *An embroidered long-stemmed flower makes a lovely panel on the front of this greetings card. The button centre is applied with a glue dot. A wavy line of running stitch borders the inside of the card.*

## BACK STITCH

This classic embroidery stitch is used to create a solid single line of stitching. Before working it on paper, pierce a row of evenly spaced holes.

Bring the needle through to the right side through the second hole, then make a backward stitch through the first hole. Bring the needle out again through the third hole and insert it in the second. Continue, taking the needle two holes forward and one back, to the end of the line.

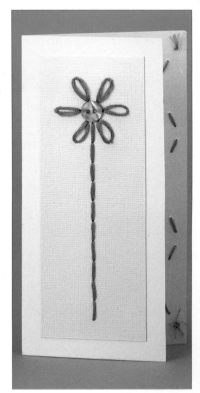

# USING RIBBON

Short scraps of ribbon can be used to embellish cards and envelopes. Ribbon looks very effective applied in bands across the front of a card, either singly or in multiples as stripes.

**DECORATING WITH BUTTONS**

A beautiful button combined with a scrap of lace or ribbon can be enough to create an instant greetings card.

**1** Cut the ribbon 2cm/¾in longer than the card front. Stick double-sided tape to the back of the ribbon. If the ribbon is narrower than the tape, stick the tape to a cutting mat and cut a strip of the right width using a craft knife and metal ruler.

**2** Peel the backing strip off the double-sided tape. Stick the ribbon across the card front, lining it up against a ruler to ensure that it is straight.

**1** To attach a small button to a card, press it on to a glue dot then lift the dot off the backing tape. Press the button in position.

**3** Turn the card over and cut the ribbon ends level with the card edges using a pair of scissors.

**4** For a looser look, cut a short piece of double-sided tape and stick it to the centre of the ribbon only. Peel off the backing tape and stick the ribbon in place.

**2** If you wish to sew the button to the card, pierce holes for the stitches first. Open the card out flat and rest it on a cutting mat. Holding the button in place, pierce the holes with a bradawl, using the holes in the button as guides.

▼ *These ribbons are attached only at the centre so that the ends hang free. The heart motif is sewn to the card with running stitch.*

▼ *This understated card is trimmed with a vintage button tied to a band of gingham ribbon using stranded thread.*

▼ *The simple decoration on this small card focuses attention on the beautiful handmade paper with its attractive deckle edges.*

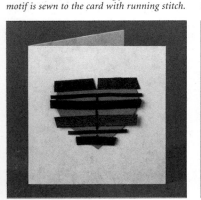

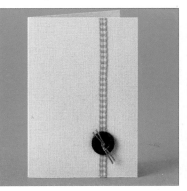

# USING BEAD EDGING

Bead edging comes in lots of designs, from simple fringing to elaborate crystal creations. Avoid heavy edging as it could make the card fall over.

**1** The edging is usually supplied with the beads suspended from a length of ribbon. Pull off the last few beads to the beginning of a complete sequence of beads or a single piece of fringe. Stick the ribbon end to the underside using PVA (white) glue. Repeat at the other end of the ribbon, making sure that the edging fits the card.

**2** Stick a length of double-sided tape to the back of the ribbon. Peel off the backing strip and stick the ribbon in place on the card with the beads hanging down. Draw a pencil guideline or use a ruler to make sure that the ribbon is straight.

## THREADING BEADS

A vast selection of beads is available, and small individual beads of any kind can be attached to cards using thread, wire or fine ribbon or cord.

Resting the card on a cutting mat, pierce a hole at each end of each intended stitch using a bradawl. If necessary, tape a template drawn on tracing paper to the card as a guide and pierce holes through the template into the card. Sew on the beads using a running stitch or back stitch.

# USING SEQUINS

Sequins are available in a host of shapes and sizes, either loose or stitched in strips and motifs. They all make ideal card decorations.

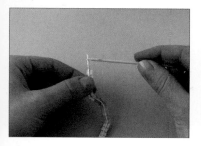

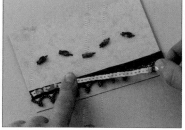

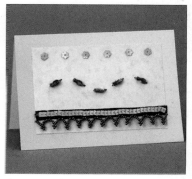

**1** To stop a sequin string unravelling, cut the string approximately 4cm/1½in longer than the length you need. Pull a few sequins off each end. Stick the string behind the last few sequins with PVA (white) glue, applying the glue with a cocktail stick (toothpick).

**2** Stick the sequin string in place with PVA glue or all-purpose household glue, spreading the glue along the string with a cocktail stick. If necessary, line the sequins up against a ruler to get a straight line.

◀ **3** Stick loose sequins with glue dots. Press the sequin to the glue dot then lift it off the backing tape. Press the sequin on to the card. To make it easier to position a small sequin, lodge it on the tip of a craft knife blade to move it to the right place, then press down to secure.

▲ *A range of techniques are used to make this pretty card decorated with beads, bead edging and sequins. The completed panel is mounted on a larger card so that the ribbon ends at the back are neatly concealed.*

# Holiday celebrations

Fabulous festive occasions are annual highlights in the lives of people all over the world. For some celebrations, such as Valentine's Day, Mother's Day and Father's Day, you will have a particular loved one in mind and can handcraft a personal card just for them. You may want to mark other times of religious, spiritual or patriotic significance with large numbers of cards, which need to be more general and simpler to create. This chapter has all the options covered, with many ideas for elaborate one-off creations as well as cards that can be made quickly and simply.

# New Year calendar

*This clever design emphasizes the meaning of New Year's Day as the first day of a new calendar, as you peer through the giant date to see the rest of the year cascading behind it. A shiny gold card strikes the right celebratory note.*

**1** Cut off a 10cm/4in strip from one side of the gold card and reserve. Score lightly along the centre of the remaining card on the metallic side. Fold along the score line and smooth the crease using a bone folder.

**2** Trace the template of the numeral 1 at the back of the book. Cut it out carefully, and centre it on the front of the card. Draw around the outline using a sharp pencil.

## materials and equipment

- craft knife
- metal ruler
- cutting mat
- 30 x 25cm/12 x 10in gold card (stock)
- bone folder
- tracing paper
- pencil
- small calendar pages
- glue stick

**3** Cut out the numeral carefully using a craft knife. Use a metal ruler to get straight edges and cut the curves freehand.

**4** Trim 5mm/¼in from one long and one short edge of the reserved piece of metallic card. Use the template to draw the numeral centrally on the card. Cut out the separate months from the calendar and arrange them inside the outline. When you are happy with the arrangement glue the pieces in position using a glue stick. Finally, glue the calendar card to the inside of the card front so that the calendar pages appear in the window.

# New Year celebration

*Capture the exuberant tone of New Year festivities with a mass of colourful balloons. As well as the balloon motifs stuck on the front of the card, balloon-shaped windows reveal shiny acetate in a design of depth and varied textures.*

## materials and equipment

- tracing paper and pencil
- scissors
- coloured paper in several shades and weights
- craft knife
- cutting mat
- white card blank
- coloured acetate
- glue stick
- star stickers

**1** Trace the balloon templates at the back of the book and cut out the shapes. Draw around these with a sharpened pencil on to the various coloured papers so that you have seven different coloured balloons.

**2** Cut out the shapes with scissors and then cut out the highlight shapes on each balloon using a craft knife and working on a cutting mat.

**3** Using the templates, draw three balloon shapes on the front of the card blank and cut them out with the craft knife. Cut a rectangular piece of acetate, slightly smaller than the card, and attach it to the inside of the card front using a glue stick. Cut out the three highlight shapes from the offcuts of white card and glue them in position on the acetate balloons.

**4** Arrange the coloured paper balloons across the card and, when you are pleased with the design, glue them in place. Finish off by adding a few twinkling star stickers.

# Gift tag to mark the year

*Welcome the New Year with a clay plaque gift tag. Polymer clay is stamped with the appropriate Roman numerals and spattered with metallic paint.*

**1** Draw the relevant number in Roman numerals, measuring and spacing them accurately, on a 5.5 × 3.5cm/2¼ × 1½in rectangle of tracing paper. Cut a strip of mounting board 3cm/1¼in wide. Cut the strip into sections the lengths of the various lines of the numerals.

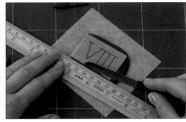

**2** On a sheet of baking parchment, roll out some dark green metallic polymer clay to a thickness of 3mm/⅛in. Place the tracing on top and cut round it with a small kitchen knife, cutting against a metal ruler.

**3** Mark the ends of all the lines of the numerals by pricking through the tracing into the clay with a dressmaking pin. Remove the tracing.

**4** Using the pricked marks as guides and holding the pieces of mounting board upright, press the relevant strips firmly into the clay to indent it.

**5** Bake the clay plaque following the manufacturer's instructions and leave to cool. Put the hardened plaque on a large sheet of scrap paper. Dip an old toothbrush into silver acrylic paint. Dab off the excess paint on kitchen paper, then flick the bristles with your finger to spatter the paint on to the clay plaque. Leave to dry.

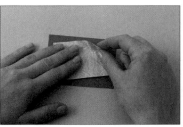

**6** Cut out a 9 × 7cm/3½ × 2¾in rectangle of metallic grey card using a craft knife and metal ruler and working on a cutting mat. Cut a 7.5 × 5.5cm/3 × 2¼in rectangle of silver marbled paper, cutting the paper freehand with a craft knife. Use spray adhesive to attach the paper to the card, positioning it at an angle.

**7** Punch a hole with a single hole punch in the top left corner of the card.

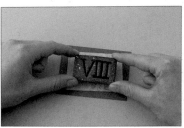

**8** Stick the clay motif to the front of the tag using double-sided tape. Thread a length of organza ribbon through the hole and knot the ends together.

# Chinese New Year

*In China red is believed to be lucky, so it is a good choice of colour to use for this pretty fan-shaped card to wish friends a happy Chinese New Year.*

## materials and equipment

- red card (stock)
- craft knife and metal ruler
- cutting mat
- bone folder
- tracing paper
- pencil
- stencil board
- masking tape
- gold acrylic paint
- stencil brush
- kitchen paper
- single hole punch
- 30cm/12in gold cord
- embroidery scissors

**1** Cut a 16 × 12cm/6¼ × 4¾in rectangle of red card using a craft knife and metal ruler. Use a bone folder to score and fold it across the centre parallel with the short edges. Trace the fan template at the back of the book and transfer the outline to the card, aligning one straight side with the fold. Cut out the fan shape using a craft knife.

**2** Open the fan out flat, right side up. Using a bone folder and a ruler, score and fold across the front of the card 5mm/¼in from the central fold to form a hinge. Refold the fan in half.

**3** Use the template to draw the Chinese character on stencil board. Cut out the stencil with a craft knife, resting on a cutting mat. Tape the stencil to the card front with masking tape. Pick up a small amount of gold paint with a stencil brush and dab off the excess paint on kitchen paper. Dab the paint through the stencil, holding the brush upright and moving it in a circular motion. Leave to dry, then remove the stencil.

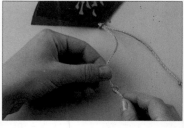

**4** Resting the card on a cutting mat, make a hole at the dot marked on the template using a single hole punch. Thread with gold cord and tie in a loop. Tie a knot 2cm/¾in from each end of the cord and fray the cord ends beyond the knots.

# Scandinavian Valentine

*This charming woven heart is a traditional Scandinavian motif. It has been given a modern twist with bold pink papers and contemporary gift wrap.*

**materials and equipment**

- brown and silver gift wrap
- pale pink card (stock)
- spray adhesive
- craft knife
- metal ruler
- cutting mat
- bone folder
- tracing paper
- pencil
- bright pink, light pink and silver paper
- glue stick
- scallop-edged scissors
- adhesive foam pads

**1** Apply brown and silver gift wrap to pale pink card using spray adhesive. Cut a 20 x 13cm/8 x 5¼in rectangle from the card using a craft knife and metal ruler and working on a cutting mat. Use a bone folder to score and fold the card across the centre, parallel with the short edges.

**2** Trace the template at the back of the book and use it to cut one heart section from bright pink paper and one from light pink paper. Cut the slits. Weave the straight ends of the heart sections together.

**3** Fold the ends of the sections to the underside of the heart and stick in place using a glue stick.

**4** Cut a 4.5cm/1¾in square of silver paper. Next cut a 5.5cm/2¼in square of bright pink paper using scallop-edged scissors. Stick the silver square on the bright pink square using spray adhesive. Stick the bright pink square to the card front with adhesive foam pads. Stick the heart to the silver square with an adhesive foam pad.

# Valentine shoe

*This fabulous shoe is decorated with a spray of colourful hearts. The shoe and card are made of beautiful printed papers that have the look of silk fabrics.*

## materials and equipment

- deep pink printed paper
- card (stock) in white, purple, deep pink, mauve, light green and pale pink
- purple printed paper
- spray adhesive
- craft knife
- metal ruler
- cutting mat
- bone folder
- white fibrous paper
- tracing paper
- pencil
- 0.4mm purple wire
- wire snippers
- glue dots

**3** Cut a total of five small hearts from deep pink, mauve, light green and pale pink card and a large heart from deep pink card. (The hearts can be punched using heart-shaped paper punches.) Snip six 4cm/1½in lengths of purple wire. Stick each wire to the back of a small heart with a glue dot.

**1** Apply deep pink printed paper to white card and purple printed paper to purple card using spray adhesive. Cut a 25 × 18cm/10 × 7in rectangle of white covered card using a craft knife and metal ruler. Score and fold it across the centre, parallel with the short edges, using a bone folder.

**2** Cut a 13 × 7.5cm/5 × 3in rectangle of white fibrous paper. Stick the paper centrally to the front of the greetings card using spray adhesive. Use the template at the back of the book to cut out a shoe from the purple card and stick it centrally on the card front using spray adhesive.

**4** Stick the other ends of the wires to the back of the large heart with glue dots, trimming some wires so that the small hearts are at different levels. Stick the large heart to the shoe using glue dots.

# Winged heart Valentine

*The message is clear as a winged heart leaps out of this Valentine card on a wire spring. The spring is easily made by wrapping fine wire around a pencil.*

## materials and equipment

- card (stock) in turquoise, red holographic hearts and gold
- craft knife
- metal ruler
- cutting mat
- bone folder
- tracing paper
- pencil
- 5mm/¼in wide double-sided tape
- 30cm/12in length of 0.4mm gold wire
- clear adhesive tape
- white paper

**1** Cut a 41.5 x 14cm/16¼ x 5½in rectangle of turquoise card. On the wrong side, score and fold the card parallel with the short edges, 13.5cm/5¼in from the left edge and 14cm/5½in from the right edge. Open out. Draw a 6.5cm/2½in square on the central section, 2.5cm/1in from the top edge and right foldline. Cut out.

**2** Use the template at the back of the book to cut a heart from red holographic hearts card and the wings from gold card. Stick the wings to the back of the heart using double-sided tape

**3** Wind the wire around a pencil. Slip the coil off the pencil and pull it slightly open. Stick one end of the wire to the back of the heart using clear adhesive tape.

**4** Apply double-sided tape around the window on the wrong side. Stick the end of the wire coil behind the window with adhesive tape. Cut an 8.5cm/3½in square of white paper. Peel the backing strip off the double-sided tape and stick the square behind the window. Stick the facing behind the front using double-sided tape.

# Envelope Valentine

*This smart card features a tiny envelope into which you can insert a romantic message for your beloved's eyes only. The idea of mailing a love letter inspired the decorative use of lovely old stamps, franked with cherub "postmarks".*

**materials and equipment**

- tracing paper and pencil
- 10 x 12cm/4 x 5in rectangle of white handmade paper
- scissors
- ruler
- bone folder
- glue stick
- 12.5 x 25cm/5 x 10in rectangle of grey Ingres paper
- old postage stamps
- cherub rubber stamp
- black ink pad
- red heart sticker

**3** Fold the Ingres paper in half to make a square card. Press the crease with a bone folder. Glue the envelope to the card, face down, then add a few vintage stamps.

**4** Finish off by printing a few cherub images across the stamps, using a black ink pad. Place your secret message in the envelope and seal the flap with a red heart sticker.

**1** Trace the envelope template from the back of the book and transfer the outline on to white handmade paper. Cut out carefully around the outside edge.

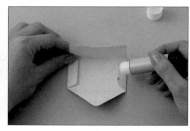

**2** Carefully score along the four marked lines. Fold in the side flaps and use a glue stick to secure them to the back flap. Fold down the triangular flap.

# Victorian Valentine

*Valentine cards were among the first commercially produced greetings cards in the mid-19th century, and many early examples were lavishly trimmed with coloured scraps and paper lace. This gorgeous confection echoes that style.*

**materials and equipment**

- 2 paper doilies
- scissors
- gold tissue paper
- spray adhesive
- pink paper
- 30 x 25cm/12 x 10in rectangle of marbled lilac card (stock)
- selection of reproduction scraps, including cherubs, hearts and flowers
- 1 gold doily
- glue stick
- paper insert

**1** Choose a round motif, about 12.5cm/5in in diameter, from the centre of one of the doilies. Cut it out roughly, then cut a piece of gold tissue slightly larger all round. Stick the tissue to the back of the doily using spray adhesive, then cut out the motif neatly around the edge.

**2** Select a pair of motifs, each about 5 x 12.5cm/2 x 5in, from the other doily. Back these motifs with pink paper as before.

**3** Fold the card in half widthways and sharpen the crease with a bone folder to give a crisp finish. Glue the round motif centrally to the front of the card, then stick one of the narrow motifs on each side. Glue a large scrap to the centre of the round motif then add the flowers, heart and cherubs.

**4** Carefully snip a few flower shapes from the gold doily and add them to the arrangement. Glue in a paper insert inscribed with your own special message and decorated with another cherub.

# St Patrick's Day wallet

*This pretty wallet decorated with cutwork shamrocks is ideal to contain a card or small gift for St Patrick's Day.*

## materials and equipment

- green paper
- craft knife
- metal ruler
- cutting mat
- pencil
- tracing paper
- 50cm/20in of 2.5cm/1in-wide aquamarine ribbon
- 5mm/¼in wide double-sided tape
- embroidery scissors

**1** Cut out a 22 × 16.5cm/8⅝x 6½in rectangle of green paper using a craft knife and metal ruler and working on a cutting mat. Fold the paper in half parallel with the short edges.

**2** Draw four lines 3cm/1¼in long across the centre of the wallet, parallel with the fold and 2.5cm/1in, 4.5cm/1¾in, 7cm/2¾in and 9cm/3½in above it. Resting the folded paper on a cutting mat, cut along the lines through both layers using a craft knife and a metal ruler, to make four slits.

**3** Open the card out flat. Use the template at the back of the book to draw a shamrock on the front of the wallet, 2cm/¾in from one side edge. Turn the template over and repeat on the opposite side. Resting on a cutting mat, cut out the designs with a craft knife.

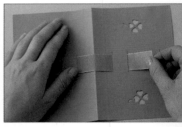

**4** Thread ribbon in and out of the slits. Apply 5mm/¼in-wide double-sided tape to the side edges on the wrong side of the front and stick the front to the back. Slip the card or gift inside and fasten the ribbon. Trim the ends of the ribbon diagonally.

**Tip**
Punch motifs along the side edges of the wallet using a paper punch if you prefer.

# Easter card with velvet chicks

*This pretty collage uses interesting materials of contrasting texture – stiff, crunchy crepe paper for the spiky grasses and soft velvet for the fluffy yellow chicks. The sky-patterned background gives the card a springlike feel.*

## materials and equipment

- double-sided olive green crepe paper
- scissors
- 10 x 15cm/4 x 6in rectangle of sky-patterned card (stock)
- glue stick
- tracing paper and pencil
- fusible bonding web
- iron and pressing cloth
- 5 x 15cm/2 x 6in strip of pale yellow velvet
- 3 black rocaille beads
- fine needle and black thread
- tiny fabric flowers

**1** Cut a 5 x 20cm/2 x 8in strip of crepe paper and snip into one edge so that it resembles blades of grass. Cut two "tufts" from one end, then attach the "grass" to the lower half of the card using a glue stick.

**2** Copy the chick template at the back of the book three times on to fusible bonding web. Iron the adhesive side to the back of the velvet and cut out the shapes.

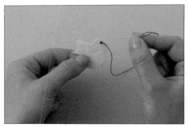

**3** Sew a black bead on to each chick to represent an eye. Iron the chicks on to the card in the spaces between the grass tufts, using a pressing cloth to protect the card.

**4** Stick a few tiny fabric flowers to the grass to complete the design.

# Millefiori Easter cards

*The clay egg motifs on these stylish Easter cards are decorated using the millefiori technique: different coloured clays are stretched and rolled together into multicoloured "canes", then sliced and embedded in the clay surface.*

## materials and equipment

- polymer clay in white, apricot, lilac and violet
- rolling pin
- chopping board
- egg-shaped cookie cutter
- craft knife
- 8mm/³/₈in-wide ribbons in toning shades
- scissors
- all-purpose household glue
- textured card blanks
- adhesive foam pads

**3** Gently roll the cane with the tips of your fingers until it is about 8mm/⅛in in diameter. Use a craft knife to cut off 2mm/¹/₁₂in slices. Arrange these over the surface of the clay oval, then roll it gently until the slices sink into the surface of the clay and no joins are visible.

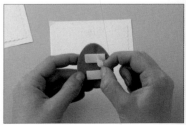

**4** Cut out an egg shape with the cookie cutter. Experiment with the remaining clay to make more millefiori patterns for other cards. Bake the egg motifs to harden them following the clay manufacturer's instructions and leave to cool. To complete each card, tie a 15cm/6in length of ribbon into a small bow, trim the ends and stick to the egg using all-purpose household glue. Attach the egg to the card front using adhesive foam pads.

**1** Cut off a quarter of one clay block and knead it until malleable. Roll it out on a chopping board to a depth of 4mm/⅙in, forming an oval shape slightly larger than the egg-shaped cookie cutter.

**2** Cut and knead 2cm/¾in squares of the remaining three clay blocks. Roll each one out into a 4mm/⅙in sausage. Cut one length of one colour and three each of the other two. Arrange these lengths alternately around the single colour and press gently together to make a cane.

# Easter egg card

*Choose papers in subtle colours to make this unusual Easter card. The eggs are made from scraps of co-ordinating gift wrap and tied with fine string. Keep the colours neutral for a sophisticated look.*

## materials and equipment

- grey mulberry paper
- grey card (stock)
- spray adhesive
- craft knife
- metal ruler
- cutting mat
- bone folder
- crinkled copper paper
- pinking shears
- white writing paper with embedded fibres
- scraps of 3 different but co-ordinating gift wraps
- tracing paper
- pencil
- fine hemp string or embroidery thread (floss)
- scissors
- adhesive foam pads

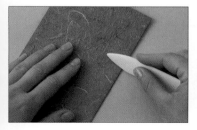

**1** Apply grey mulberry paper to grey card using spray adhesive. Cut a 22 × 20.5cm/ 8½ × 8in rectangle of the covered card using a craft knife and metal ruler and working on a cutting mat. Score and fold the card across the centre, parallel with the short edges, using a bone folder.

**2** Cut a 16.5 × 7cm/6½ × 2¾in rectangle of crinkled copper paper, using pinking shears to create a decorative edge. Cut a 15 × 5.5cm/6 × 2¼in rectangle of white writing paper with embedded fibres. Stick the copper paper centrally to the card front using spray adhesive, then attach the white paper in the centre of the copper panel in the same way.

**3** Apply scraps of three gift wrap papers to offcuts of the grey card using spray adhesive. Use the egg template at the back of the book to draw matching egg shapes on each design and cut them out using a craft knife.

**4** Tie a length of hemp string around each egg in a double knot and trim the ends. Alternatively, tie the eggs with embroidery thread (floss). Stick the eggs in a row to the card using adhesive foam pads.

# Easter basket

*Nestle tiny Easter eggs in this charming woven basket to make a small Easter gift that will delight children and adults alike. The basket is lined with silver tissue paper and trimmed with a mesh ribbon bow on the handle.*

## materials and equipment

- light ochre and cream card (stock)
- craft knife
- metal ruler
- cutting mat
- masking tape
- bone folder
- double-sided tape
- scissors
- silver tissue paper
- 40cm/16in of 2.5cm/1in-wide wire-edged silver mesh ribbon

**1** Cut eight strips of light ochre card, each 18 × 1.5cm/7 × ⅝in, using a craft knife and metal ruler and working on a cutting mat. Arrange four strips side by side then weave the remaining four strips in and out. Adjust the strips to centre the weaving.

**2** Stick masking tape over the weaving to hold the strips in place. Score the strips along the edges of the woven section using a bone folder. Fold the extending ends of the strips upwards along the scored lines to form the basket sides.

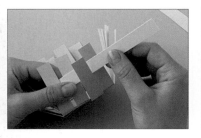

**3** Cut three strips of cream card and one of light ochre, each 29 × 1.5cm/11½ × ⅝in. Weave one cream strip in and out of the sides of the basket, folding the strip neatly at the corners.

**4** Push the strip down to the base and stick in place with masking tape. Overlap the ends inside the basket and cut off the excess strip. Join the ends using double-sided tape.

**5** Weave the second cream strip then the light ochre strip in the same way, sticking the overlapped ends inside the basket with double-sided tape. Push the strips down the basket and secure with a few pieces of masking tape. Trim the extending ends level with the top of the basket using scissors.

**6** Score and fold the remaining cream strip along the centre with a bone folder. Open the strip out flat again. Stick double-sided tape to the wrong side of the strip. Stick the strip around the top of the basket on the outside, gradually peeling off the backing and matching the foldline to the top of the basket. Overlap the ends. Cut off the excess.

**7** With a pair of scissors, snip the top half of the cream strip down to the foldline at the corners of the basket. Fold the top half of the strip down inside the basket, enclosing the ends of the vertical strips. Carefully peel off the masking tape.

**8** Cut a strip of card 20 × 1.5cm/8 × ⅝in to make the handle. Stick the ends inside opposite sides of the basket using double-sided tape. Using scissors, cut two 18cm/7in squares from silver tissue paper and cut the edges in a deep zigzag. Place the tissue paper in the basket, folding under the fullness at the corners. To finish, tie wire-edged silver mesh ribbon in a bow around the handle.

# Mother's Day gift

*Here is a thoughtful gift for Mother's Day of a pretty book covered with a vintage scarf. Old silk scarves eventually fray at the edges, but their beautiful patterns and textures can be enjoyed again when recycled in such a way. The book has pages of handmade paper and a traditional pamphlet binding.*

## materials and equipment

- white card (stock)
- craft knife
- metal ruler
- cutting mat
- bone folder
- fabric scissors
- vintage scarf
- PVA (white) glue
- speckled cream paper
- spray adhesive
- 4 sheets of cream handmade A4 paper
- bradawl
- large-eyed needle
- 60cm/24in of 3mm/⅛in-wide satin ribbon

**1** Cut a 31 × 22cm/12¼ × 8⅝in rectangle of white card for the cover of the book, using a craft knife and metal ruler and working on a cutting mat. Score and fold the card across the centre, parallel with the short edges, using a bone folder. Open the card out flat.

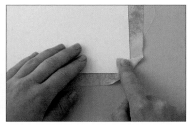

**2** Using fabric scissors, cut a 34 × 25cm/13½ × 10in rectangle from a vintage scarf, positioning the best part of the design on the right-hand side. Place the fabric wrong side up then centre the card cover on top. Stick the fabric corners on one short edge to the card cover with PVA glue, then stick the short edge to the cover.

**3** Fold the cover in half. Adjust the fabric so that it lies smoothly. Lift the front cover and stick the remaining corners of the fabric inside the back cover using PVA glue. Stick the short edge inside the back cover.

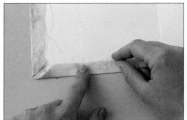

**4** Open the cover. Turn in the long fabric edges and stick them to the cover using PVA glue. Leave to dry.

**5** Cut a 30.5 × 21.5cm/12 × 8⅜in rectangle of speckled cream paper. Centre the paper on the inside of the cover and stick in place using spray adhesive to conceal the raw edges of the fabric.

**6** Stack the sheets of A4 handmade paper on a cutting mat. Place the cover centrally on top of the sheets.

**7** Pierce a hole through all the layers at the centre of the central fold, using a bradawl. Pierce two more holes, 5cm/2in to each side of the centre.

**8** Thread a large-eyed needle with ribbon. Starting on the outside of the cover, insert the needle through the centre hole then bring it out through the hole to one side of the centre. Take the ribbon through the hole on the other side of the centre and then out through the centre. Adjust the ribbon ends so that they are level and tie in a bow around the threaded ribbon. Fold the book in half.

# Mother's Day gift card

*This is more than just a greetings card. It's a great way to present your mum with a bracelet as a Mother's Day gift.*

**1** Cut a 21 × 14cm/8⅛ × 5½in rectangle of pale green card using a craft knife and metal ruler and working on a cutting mat. Score and fold the card across the centre, parallel with the short edges, using a bone folder.

**2** Open the card out flat on the cutting mat. Arrange the bracelet on the front of the card. Using a bradawl, pierce pairs of holes on each side of the bracelet at the top and bottom.

**3** Remove the bracelet. With a pencil, draw a small motif such as a leaf halfway between the pairs of pierced holes. Paint the motif with acrylic paint using a fine artist's paintbrush. Leave to dry.

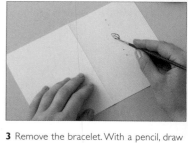

**4** Cut two 30cm/12in lengths of ribbon and thread one length through each pair of holes. Tie each ribbon around the bracelet in a bow and trim the ends.

# Mother's Day appliqué

*Here is an elegant flamingo of textured silk. Its eye and long legs are drawn with pink relief paint and its plumage is delicately highlighted with sequins.*

## materials and equipment

- white on cream printed paper
- cream card (stock)
- spray adhesive
- craft knife
- metal ruler
- cutting mat
- bone folder
- tracing paper and pencil
- 11cm/4¹/₂in square of iron-on interfacing
- 11cm/4¹/₂in square of pink silk dupion
- iron
- fabric scissors
- pink relief paint
- pink sequins
- glue dots
- tweezers

3 Stick the flamingo to the card front using spray adhesive. Draw the bird's legs on the card lightly with a pencil. Use pink relief paint to draw an eye and redraw the legs. Set aside to dry.

1 Stick white on cream printed paper to cream card. Cut a 20cm/8in square of the covered card using a craft knife and metal ruler and working on a cutting mat. Score and fold it across the centre.

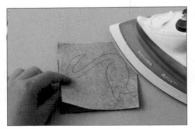

2 Trace the flamingo template at the back of the book on to the rough side of iron-on interfacing. Place the interfacing, adhesive side down, on a piece of pink silk dupion and iron it on. Cut out the flamingo.

4 Stick a few pink sequins to the flamingo with glue dots, positioning them on the wing tips and tail with tweezers.

# Father's Day card

*This greetings card decorated with a handsome feather will appeal to a nature lover. The feather is protected with a piece of acetate held in place with a smart set of pewter brads, which match the elegant grey card.*

### materials and equipment

- pewter-grey card (stock)
- craft knife
- metal ruler
- cutting mat
- bone folder
- white textured writing paper
- spray adhesive
- feather
- clear acetate
- bradawl
- 4 x 12mm/¹/₂in pewter-coloured brads

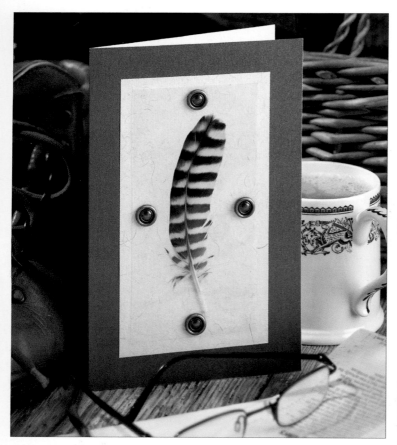

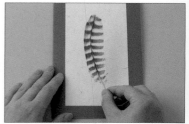

**3** Select a feather of a size that fits well on the paper panel, leaving room for the decorative brads. Spray the back of the feather with spray adhesive and stick it centrally to the paper.

**4** Cut a 15 x 7.5cm/5⅞ x 3in rectangle of clear acetate. Open the card out flat on a cutting mat. Centre the acetate rectangle on the paper panel. Pierce a hole with a bradawl through all the layers at the centre of each edge of the acetate, 8mm/⁵⁄₁₆in in from the edges. Insert a brad through each hole. Splay open the prongs inside the card.

**1** Cut a 26 x 20cm/10¼ x 8in rectangle of pewter-grey card using a craft knife and metal ruler and working on a cutting mat. Score and fold the card across the centre, parallel with the short edges, using a bone folder.

**2** Cut a 16.5 x 9cm/6½ x 3 ⅝in rectangle of white textured writing paper. Stick the paper centrally to the front of the card using spray adhesive.

**Tip**
If you wish to conceal the prongs inside the card, add a white paper insert.

# Golfing Father's Day card

*If your dad is a keen golfer this is the card to make for him. Coloured bands are painted across the card and wooden golf tees are slotted through velvet ribbon – they can be slipped out later to use on the golf course.*

## materials and equipment

- white card (stock)
- craft knife
- metal ruler
- cutting mat
- bone folder
- scrap paper
- 2.5cm/1in-wide masking tape
- acrylic paint in gold, green and smoky blue
- flat paintbrush
- 20cm/8in of 1cm/³/₈in-wide ridged smoky blue velvet ribbon
- 4 wooden golf tees
- double-sided tape
- embroidery scissors

**1** Cut a 23 × 19cm/9 × 7½in rectangle of white card. Score and fold the card across the centre, parallel with the short edges, using a bone folder. Resting on scrap paper, apply two lengths of masking tape across the card front, to mask off a band 7cm/2¾in wide, 4.5cm/1¾in below the upper edge. (Test the tape on a scrap of the card first to check it doesn't damage the surface.)

**2** Stick two lengths of masking tape lightly to a cutting mat and cut two 5mm/¼in-wide and two 1cm/⅜in-wide strips. Apply each to the card front above and below the masked band. Paint the card between the tapes, leaving the wide band clear. Peel off the masking tape before the paint dries.

**3** When the paint is dry, open the card out and cut four pairs of 1.2cm/½in vertical slits, 1cm/⅜in apart, across the wide band. They should be 1.5cm/⅝in in from the sides, with 1.5cm/⅝in gaps between the pairs of slits.

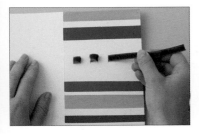

**4** Thread velvet ribbon in and out of the slits. Slip a golf tee behind each ribbon loop. Stick the ends of the ribbon to the underside of the card front with double-sided tape. Snip off the excess ribbon.

# Greetings for Diwali

*Wish family and friends peace and happiness with this celebratory Diwali card depicting a lit diya.*

## materials and equipment

- red and yellow card (stock)
- craft knife
- metal ruler
- cutting mat
- bone folder
- tracing paper and pencil
- lilac pearlized card (stock)
- gold paper
- spray adhesive
- double-sided tape
- 7 x 6mm/¹/₄in red round glitter stickers
- 4 x 8mm/⁵/₁₆in purple teardrop glitter stickers

**1** Cut an 11cm/4⅜in square of red card using a craft knife and metal ruler and working on a cutting mat. Score and fold the card across the centre using a bone folder.

**2** Use the template at the back of the book to draw the diya on the card front, with the fold along the top. Resting on a cutting mat, cut out the diya.

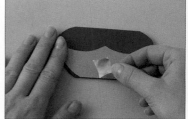

**3** Use the template to cut the diya front from lilac pearlized card, the outer flame from yellow card and the diamond and inner flame from gold paper. Stick the diya front to the card front, the diamond to the diya front and the inner flame to the outer flame using spray adhesive.

**4** Stick the outer flame to the card front using double-sided tape. Stick red round stickers along the upper edge of the diya front and decorate the diamond with purple teardrop stickers, positioning them with the blade of the craft knife.

# Halloween party invitation

*Invite guests to a Halloween party with this scary invitation. Visit a joke or party shop to find a selection of frightful accessories, such as this wiggly worm, to adorn the ghostly character.*

### materials and equipment

- tracing paper
- pencil
- white card (stock)
- broad black felt-tipped pen
- cutting mat
- craft knife
- plastic worm
- soft plastics glue

**I** Trace the ghost template at the back of the book and transfer it to a sheet of white card using a pencil.

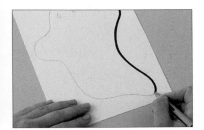

**2** Redraw the ghost outline using a broad black felt-tipped pen. Draw the eyes too.

**3** Resting on a cutting mat, cut out the ghost with a craft knife, cutting along the outer edge of the black outline.

**4** Write your message on the back of the invitation. Stick a plastic worm across the front of the card with soft plastics glue, following the manufacturer's instructions.

# Halloween card

*Here is a fun idea for a Halloween card. A scary foam spider bounces on a length of elastic, staring eerily from a pair of joggle eyes.*

**materials and equipment**

- bright green mottled card (stock)
- craft knife
- metal ruler
- cutting mat
- bone folder
- tracing paper
- pencil
- black Neoprene foam
- metallic pen
- two 6mm/¹/₄in joggle eyes
- glue dots
- bradawl
- 15cm/6in fine black round elastic

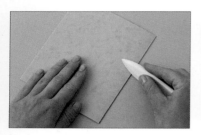

**1** Cut a 26 × 16cm/10¼ × 6¼in rectangle of bright green mottled card using a craft knife and metal ruler and working on a cutting mat. Score and fold the card across the centre, parallel with the short edges, using a bone folder.

**2** Use the template at the back of the book to draw a spider on black Neoprene foam using a metallic pen. Cut out the spider using a craft knife on a cutting mat. Stick a pair of joggle eyes on the spider using glue dots.

**3** Pierce a hole in the centre of the spider with a bradawl, resting on a cutting mat. Thread elastic through the hole. Knot the end of the elastic under the spider.

**4** Open the card out flat. Resting it on a cutting mat, pierce a hole in the card front using a bradawl, 1.5cm/⅝in below the centre of the upper edge. Insert the end of the elastic in the hole and knot the elastic inside the card.

**Tip**
When you are cutting shapes from dark-coloured Neoprene foam, a metallic pen is best for drawing lines as it shows up clearly.

# Thanksgiving garland card

*This pretty circlet in the rich colours of the American fall is made using coloured paper leaves, but if you have planned ahead and have a store of colourful pressed real autumn leaves you could use them instead in a similar design.*

## materials and equipment

- tracing paper or three small leaves
- pencil
- scissors
- paper in shades of brown, green and orange
- fine knitting needle, crochet hook or large tapestry needle
- 18 x 30cm/7 x 12in duck-egg blue card (stock)
- bone folder
- glue stick

**1** Trace the three leaf templates at the back of the book and cut them out. Alternatively find a few small leaves and use them as templates. Use the templates to draw 11 outlines on to the different coloured papers.

**2** Cut out the leaf shapes with sharp scissors, carefully following the outlines.

**3** Use the point of a knitting needle, crochet hook or tapestry needle to score a pattern of veins across the front of each leaf. Gently fold along the curves to give a three-dimensional look to the leaves.

**4** Fold the card in half lengthwise and rub over the crease with a bone folder. Arrange the leaves in a circle on the card front, overlapping them to create a garland. Use a glue stick to fix them in place.

# Sampler for Thanksgiving

*Recreate the look of an old sampler with this appliqué Thanksgiving card. The design features a stylized tree on a fringed square of checked fabric.*

## materials and equipment

- pale green card (stock)
- craft knife
- metal ruler and cutting mat
- bone folder
- 10cm/4in square of multi-coloured checked fabric
- fabric scissors
- tracing paper and pen
- iron-on interfacing
- masking tape
- sheet of white paper
- pencil
- pale green and yellow fabric
- spray adhesive
- iron
- handmade cream paper

**3** Roughly cut out the pieces, leaving a margin all round. Apply the leaves to patterned pale green fabric and the trunk to patterned yellow fabric by ironing the interfacing on to the fabric. Cut out the pieces. Stick the leaves, then the trunk, to the fabric square using spray adhesive.

**1** Cut a 26 x 13cm/10¼ x 5⅛in rectangle of pale green card using a craft knife and a metal ruler and working on a cutting mat. Score and fold the card across the centre, parallel with the short edges, using a bone folder. Cut a 10cm/4in square of checked fabric. Fray the edges for 5mm/¼in.

**2** Use the template at the back of the book to draw the tree and trunk on tracing paper with a black pen. Use masking tape to attach a piece of iron-on interfacing, shiny side down, to the wrong side of the tracing. Resting on a sheet of white paper so that you can see the image clearly, trace the trunk on to the interfacing. Tape a second piece of interfacing to the tracing and trace the leaves of the tree.

**4** Tear an 11.5cm/4⅝in square of handmade cream paper, tearing the paper against a ruler. Stick the paper square to the card front then stick the fringed fabric square on top using spray adhesive.

# Thanksgiving pumpkins

*Pumpkin pie is a traditional part of a Thanksgiving dinner, so these warmly coloured autumnal fruits make a lovely theme for a seasonal greetings card.*

## materials and equipment

- tracing paper
- pencil
- orange paper
- scissors
- textured rust brown paper
- ruler
- decorative-edged scissors
- A4 sheet of peat brown card (stock)
- bone folder
- glue stick
- 6 small skeleton leaves

**1** Trace and cut out the pumpkin template at the back of the book. Draw round it six times on the orange paper and cut out carefully around the outlines.

**2** Cut six 5cm/2in squares from the rust brown paper. Use a pair of scissors with decorative-edged blades to trim the edges of the squares.

**3** Fold the A4 card widthwise to make a long rectangle. Rub along the fold with a bone folder. Stick the rust brown squares in a checked pattern with a glue stick. Glue a pumpkin to each square.

**4** Glue a skeleton leaf in each of the spaces between the squares, making sure they all point in the same direction.

# Thanksgiving notebook

*Get all your loved ones to write their thoughts in this rustic notebook when you gather to celebrate Thanksgiving. The cover and pages are made from handmade papers and hinged with a twig and raffia. A pressed autumn leaf is a lovely simple motif to apply to the front cover.*

**materials and equipment**

- autumn leaf
- blotting paper
- flower press or heavy book
- bone folder
- ruler
- 2 x A5 sheets of dark green handmade paper
- cutting mat
- 8 x A5 sheets of light green handmade paper
- twig, approximately 12.5cm/5in long
- bradawl
- large-eyed needle
- undyed raffia
- scissors
- A5 sheet of sage green handmade paper
- PVA (white) glue

**1** Press a leaf between sheets of blotting paper in a flower press or a heavy book for about 10 days. Using a bone folder and ruler, score and fold an A5 sheet of dark green handmade paper 3cm/1¼in from one short edge. Open the sheet out flat again. This will be the front cover; the remaining sheet will be the back cover.

**2** Resting on a cutting mat, stack eight A5 sheets of light green handmade paper on top of the back cover. Place the front cover on top with the scored fold to the left to form the hinge.

**3** Lay the twig on the hinge. Using a bradawl, pierce two pairs of holes on each side of the twig at the top and bottom to make cross stitches.

**4** Thread a large-eyed needle with undyed raffia. Leaving a trailing end of raffia at the back, sew through the holes using cross stitches to anchor the twig to the hinge at the top and bottom.

**5** Tie the ends of the raffia together securely on the back cover. Cut off the excess raffia with a pair of scissors.

**6** Tear a 9cm/3½in square of sage green handmade paper by tearing the paper against a ruler. Stick the square to the front cover of the book using PVA glue. Finally, stick the leaf on the square with PVA glue.

# Hannukah greeting

*The seven-branched candelabrum is associated with Hannukah. Create this distinctive symbol using relief paint and beads to send good wishes.*

## materials and equipment

- maroon and white card (stock)
- craft knife and metal ruler
- cutting mat
- tracing paper
- pencil
- bradawl
- gold relief paint
- 7 x 3mm/$^1$/$_8$in square diamanté stickers
- embroidery needle
- silver thread
- 7 x 10mm/$^3$/$_8$in silver bugle beads
- gold glitter paint
- bone folder
- spray adhesive

**1** Cut a 9.5 x 7cm/3¾ x 2¾in rectangle of maroon card using a craft knife and metal ruler and working on a cutting mat. Use the template at the back of the book to draw the menorah in the centre of the rectangle. Resting on a cutting mat, pierce a hole at each dot using a bradawl.

**2** Dot gold relief paint along the drawn lines and set aside to dry. Stick a 3mm/⅛in square diamanté sticker at the top of each branch of the menorah.

**3** Thread an embroidery needle with a double length of silver thread. Knot the ends together and sew a silver bugle bead between each pair of holes to resemble candles. Apply gold glitter paint above each bead to look like flames. Set aside to dry.

**4** Cut a 22 x 14.5cm/8⅝ x 5¾in rectangle of white card. Score and fold the card across the centre, parallel with the short edges, using a bone folder. Glue the maroon rectangle to the centre of the card front using spray adhesive.

# Christmas landscape

*This icy winter scene is created by masking purple acetate with sticky-backed plastic then spraying it with glass-frosting spray.*

## materials and equipment

- purple acetate
- cutting mat
- craft knife and metal ruler
- tracing paper and pencil
- sticky-backed plastic
- scrap paper or old newspaper
- glass frosting spray
- pinking shears
- grey card (stock)
- bone folder
- masking tape
- bradawl
- 4 x 4mm/$^5$/$_{32}$in gold brads
- white paper
- paper glue

**1** Cut an 8.5cm/3⅜in square of purple acetate. Use the template at the back of the book to cut the landscape and moon from sticky-backed plastic, working on a cutting mat. Stick the stencil to the acetate.

**2** Place the acetate on scrap paper or old newspaper and spray with frosting spray. Leave to dry then carefully peel off the stencil. Trim the acetate to 7.5cm/3in square using pinking shears.

**3** Cut a 21 × 19cm/8¼ × 7½in rectangle of grey card. Score and fold the card across the centre, parallel with the short edges. Open the card out flat. Cut a 5.5cm/2¼in square window on the card front, 2.5cm/1in from the top and side edges and the fold.

**4** With the open card right side up on a cutting mat, tape the acetate centrally over the window. Pierce a hole 5mm/¼in inside each corner with a bradawl. Insert a brad in each hole and remove the tape. Cut a 20 × 18cm/7¾ × 7in white paper insert. Fold the paper in half parallel with the short edges. Glue the insert inside the card, matching the folds.

# Dove of peace Christmas card

*This three-dimensional paper dove would look lovely perched among the branches of a festive tree, but it will also stand on a flat surface, balanced by its tail, so it can be displayed on a shelf with other Christmas cards. Write your festive message on the back of the body and fold the bird flat for mailing.*

**1** Stick speckled cream paper to cream card using spray adhesive. Use the template at the back of the book to cut the bird's body from the covered card.

**2** Cut out two 8cm/3¼in squares of speckled cream paper and fold them in half. Use the template at the back of the book to draw a wing and tail on each piece, matching the folds. Draw the feathers. Cut out the pieces using a craft knife, resting on a cutting mat.

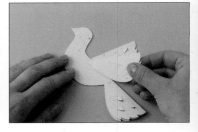

## materials and equipment

- speckled cream paper
- cream card (stock)
- spray adhesive
- tracing paper
- pencil
- craft knife
- cutting mat
- all-purpose household glue
- crystal jewellery stone sticker

**3** Cut the notches representing the feathers with a craft knife, resting on a cutting mat. Open the wings and tail out flat. Cut the wing section in half to make a pair. Lift the feather tips outwards.

**4** Dot all-purpose household glue on the underside of the tail near the point. Stick the tail over the end of the bird.

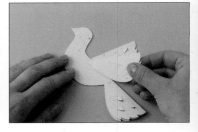

**5** Dot all-purpose household glue on the undersides of the wings at the points. Stick the wings to each side of the bird.

**6** Stick a jewellery stone sticker to the bird's head to represent an eye. To apply it, lift the sticker from its backing sheet with the tip of a craft knife blade. Place in position, remove the craft knife then press the sticker down firmly.

# Christmas baubles gift wrap

*Give an original treatment to an easy-to-wrap present such as a CD or book by creating a boldly coloured gift wrap on the theme of festive baubles. The bright tissue paper underneath shows the cutwork motifs to great effect. The design is easy to achieve but great accuracy is needed for a professional finish.*

**1** Wrap the present in deep yellow tissue paper. Cut a piece of bright pink paper, large enough to wrap the present in one direction and 3cm/1¼in narrower than the top of the present in the other. Trace the template at the back of the book and transfer it twice to the part of the pink paper that will lie on top of the gift.

**2** Resting the paper on a cutting mat, cut along the solid outlines of the first motif using a craft knife.

## materials and equipment

- deep yellow tissue paper
- bright pink paper
- tracing paper and pencil
- masking tape
- cutting mat and craft knife
- double-sided tape
- 2mm/¹⁄₁₆in hold punch
- tack hammer

**3** Cut away a narrow sliver of paper along the edge of the wavy string and the bauble. Cut out the other bauble in the same way.

**4** Resting the paper on a cutting mat, punch holes at random on the baubles with a 2mm/¹⁄₁₆in hole punch and tack hammer. Wrap the present, sticking the edges of the paper with double-sided tape underneath. Gently lift the cut edges of the baubles and bauble hangers so that the yellow tissue can be seen beneath them.

# Stamped gift wrap

*It is simple and economical to make your own gift wrap. This baroque repeat design is stamped in silver on coloured tissue paper. For this kind of repeating design, choose a rubber stamp with a regular shape such as a square or rectangle, so that it is easy to align the motifs accurately to produce an even all-over pattern.*

### materials and equipment

- mauve tissue paper
- scissors
- scrap paper
- 6cm/2¹/₂in square block design rubber stamp
- silver ink pad

**1** If necessary, cut a straight line across the tissue paper with a pair of scissors to make a straight edge. Place the tissue paper on a sheet of scrap paper to protect the work surface from any ink that seeps through the paper. Press the rubber stamp firmly on to the ink pad. Press it a few times to get an even coverage if the stamp is larger than the ink pad.

**2** Stamp the paper, matching the upper edge of the stamp to the cut edge. Remove the stamp by lifting it straight up.

**3** Press the stamp on to the ink pad again. Stamp the paper, matching the upper edge as before and lining up the left-hard edge with the first stamped image. Continue stamping a row of images.

**4** Stamp more rows in the same way to cover the paper completely, lining up the upper edge of the stamp with the lower edge of the motif in the previous row.

# Beaded snowflake Christmas card

*This luxurious greetings card with its beautiful snowflake is easier to create than it looks. The spokes of the snowflake are made from sparkling beads threaded on to fine wire and held in place on the back of the card opening.*

**1** Apply cream paper with metal fragments to cream card using spray adhesive. Cut a 32.5 x 11cm/12½ x 4⅓in rectangle of the covered card using a craft knife and metal ruler and working on a cutting mat. On the wrong side, score the card parallel with the short edges, 11cm/4¼in from the right edge and 10.5cm/4in from the left edge. Fold along the score lines.

**2** Trace the snowflake template at the back of the book on to tracing paper using a black pen. Open the card out flat on a cutting mat, right side up. Place the template on the middle section, which will be the card front. Pierce a hole through the card at the end of the lines using a bradawl.

## materials and equipment

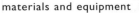

- cream paper with embedded metal fragments
- cream card (stock)
- spray adhesive
- craft knife
- metal ruler
- cutting mat
- bone folder
- tracing paper
- pen
- bradawl
- 70cm/28in of 0.4mm silver wire
- clear sticky tape
- 12mm/½in diameter red jewellery stone
- 72 x 3mm/⅛in red plastic beads
- wire snippers
- 5mm/¼in double-sided tape
- 6 x 6mm/¼in red square sequins
- glue dots

**3** Insert the wire in one outer hole, bend the last 2cm/¾in flat against the back of the card and tape in place. Glue the 12mm/½in diameter red stone to the centre front.

**4** Thread eight 3mm/⅛in red plastic beads on to the wire. Insert it in the hole next to the red stone and out through the hole at the opposite side of the stone.

**5** Thread on eight more beads and insert the wire into the outer hole. Bring the wire to the front again through another outer hole. Repeat steps 4 and 5 to make all the spokes of the snowflake.

**6** Insert the wire through one of the remaining holes. Thread on four beads and insert the wire into the hole on the other side of the spoke. Bring the wire out through one hole beside the next spoke and repeat to make the cross pieces on all the spokes.

**7** On the back, snip the wire 2cm/¾in from the card with wire snippers. Bend the end flat against the back of the card and tape down. Fold in the card facing and stick it behind the front using double-sided tape along the edges. Stick square sequins between the spokes using glue dots.

# Metal plaque Christmas card

*Here is a design that is ideal if you want to produce a set of Christmas cards, as it is very quick to make. Packs of metal plaques with Christmas motifs and an adhesive backing are available from craft suppliers.*

**1** Cut a 21 x 12cm/8¼ x 4¾in rectangle of pale yellow card using a craft knife and metal ruler and working on a cutting mat. Score and fold the card across the centre, parallel with the short edges, using a bone folder.

**2** Peel the backing strip off the plaque and stick it to the centre of the card front.

## materials and equipment

- pale yellow card (stock)
- craft knife
- metal ruler
- cutting mat
- bone folder
- 3.5 x 2.5cm/1³/8 x 1in metal Christmas plaque
- pencil
- silver relief paint

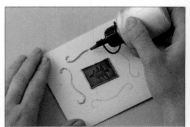

**3** In pencil, draw a simple swirling border on the card around each side of the plaque. Draw along the pencil lines with silver relief paint and leave to dry.

**4** As a finishing touch, draw another swirl inside the card with a pencil. Draw along the pencil line with silver relief paint then leave the card open to dry.

### Tip
Relief paints are sold in small bottles with thin nozzles, allowing them to be applied straight from the container. The technique takes a little practice, so try some swirls on scraps of card first so that your lines are confident and smooth.

# Silver charms Christmas card

*This vibrant Christmas card is easy to assemble using a few ready-made trimmings bought from craft stores. The metal charms are highlighted with dainty jewellery stones and attached to the card with metallic brads.*

## materials and equipment

- bright pink card (stock)
- craft knife
- metal ruler
- cutting mat
- bone folder
- star, snowflake and spiral metal charms
- tiny pink star and circular jewellery stone stickers
- bradawl
- 3 x 4mm/$^5$/$_{32}$in pink brads
- light pink paper
- paper glue

**1** Cut an 18 x 15cm/7 x 6in rectangle of bright pink card. Score and fold the card across the centre, parallel with the short edges, using a bone folder.

**2** Decorate the charms with a few jewellery stone stickers. To apply, lift the stickers one at a time from their backing sheet with the tip of a craft knife blade. Place them on the charms, remove the craft knife then press the stickers in position.

**3** Open the card out flat on a cutting mat. Arrange the charms on the card front. Use a bradawl to pierce holes in the card through the holes in the charms.

**4** Insert a brad through each charm into the card and open the prongs inside. Cut a 17 x 14cm/6⅝ x 5½in rectangle of light pink paper for the insert. Fold it in half parallel with the short edges. Apply paper glue to the fold and insert, matching the folds.

# Christmas stocking

*This colourful felt stocking holds a present for a sweet-toothed recipient.*
*The card front is attached to the back with co-ordinating checked ribbon.*

**materials and equipment**

- yellow card (stock)
- craft knife
- metal ruler
- cutting mat
- bone folder
- tracing paper
- pen
- red and green felt
- fabric scissors
- PVA (white) glue
- double hole punch
- 60cm/24in of 2.5cm/1in-wide green checked ribbon
- candy cane

**1** Cut two rectangles of yellow card, each measuring 19 x 15cm/7½ x 6in, using a craft knife and metal ruler and working on a cutting mat. Use a bone folder to score and fold one rectangle, which will be the front of the card, 2.5cm/1in from the long left-hand edge to make a hinge. The other rectangle will be the card back.

**2** Use the template at the back of the book to cut a Christmas stocking from red felt and four spots from green felt. Stick the spots on the stocking using PVA glue.

**3** Run a line of glue along the edges of the stocking on the wrong side, leaving the upper edge free of glue. Stick the stocking on the card front, pushing the side edges slightly inwards so that the upper edge bows open. Leave to dry.

**4** Arrange the card front on the back. Punch a pair of holes centrally in the hinge using a double hole punch. Thread the ribbon through the holes and tie in a bow. Cut the ribbon ends diagonally. Slip the candy cane into the stocking. To protect the front the card will need to be hand-delivered in a padded envelope.

# Christmas reindeer

*This elegant black reindeer is created very simply, using humble flock-effect sticky-backed plastic. A diamanté collar and jewelled eye give it a touch of glamour that suits its rather haughty demeanour.*

## materials and equipment

- tracing paper
- pencil
- black flock-effect sticky-backed plastic
- craft knife
- cutting mat
- pearlized lilac card (stock)
- metal ruler
- bone folder
- 1.5cm/⁵⁄₈in length of lilac and crystal diamanté trim
- glue dots
- 3mm/¹⁄₈in crystal stone sticker

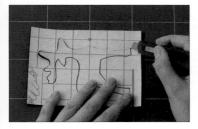

**1** Trace the reindeer template at the back of the book and transfer it to the paper backing of a piece of black flock-effect sticky-backed plastic. Cut out the reindeer using a craft knife, resting on a cutting mat.

**2** Cut a 22 × 16cm/8½ × 6¼in rectangle of pearlized lilac card. Score and fold the card across the centre using a bone folder. Peel the backing paper off the reindeer.

**3** Stick the reindeer centrally on the card front. Stick a 1.5cm/⅝in length of diamanté trim to the reindeer as a collar with a glue dot at each end.

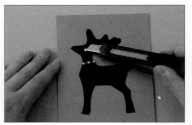

**4** To apply the crystal sticker for the eye, lift it from its backing sheet with a craft knife blade. Place in position, remove the knife then press the sticker to the reindeer.

# Pressed ivy leaf gift tags

*Press a number of ivy leaves to make a set of these natural gift tags, which look particularly good tied on parcels wrapped in brown paper.*

## materials and equipment

- ivy leaves
- blotting paper
- flower press or heavy book
- scrap paper
- copper metallic wax
- kitchen paper
- dark green and light green handmade paper
- ruler
- spray adhesive
- PVA (white) glue
- single hole punch
- yellow ochre hemp string
- scissors

**1** Select unblemished ivy leaves and press them between sheets of blotting paper in a flower press or within the pages of a heavy book. Set aside for about 10 days.

**2** Resting each leaf on a piece of scrap paper, rub copper metallic wax sparingly over the surface using kitchen paper.

**3** Tear a 7.5cm/3in square of dark green handmade paper and a 6.5cm/2½in square of light green handmade paper, tearing the paper against a ruler. Stick the light green square centrally on the dark green square using spray adhesive.

**4** Punch a hole in the top left corner of the gift tag using a 3mm/⅛in hole punch. Tie a length of hemp string through the hole for hanging. Stick the leaf to the front of the tag using PVA glue. Cut four 30cm/12in lengths of hemp string. Hold the lengths together and tie in a bow around the hanging string at the corner of the tag.

# Organza tree gift tag

*This charming festive gift tag is simple to make using offcuts of organza and a single bird-shaped sequin, so you can make enough for all your presents.*

**materials and equipment**

- cream card (stock)
- craft knife
- metal ruler
- cutting mat
- bone folder
- fabric scissors
- scraps of gold and pink organza
- spray adhesive
- tracing paper
- pen
- bird-shaped sequin
- glue dot
- single hole punch
- 30cm/12in of 12mm/¹/₂in-wide gold organza ribbon

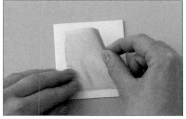

**1** Cut a 14 x 8.5cm/5½ x 3⅜in rectangle of cream card using a craft knife and metal ruler and working on a cutting mat. Score the card across the centre, parallel with the short edges, using a bone folder, then fold in half and sharpen the crease with the side of the folder.

**2** Using fabric scissors, cut a 6.5 x 5cm/2⅝ x 2in rectangle of gold organza. Stick the rectangle centrally to the front of the gift tag using spray adhesive.

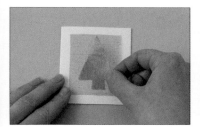

**3** Using the template at the back of the book, cut a tree from pink organza. Stick to the front of the tag using spray adhesive.

**4** Stick a bird-shaped sequin to the tree using a glue dot. Punch a hole in the top left corner of the gift tag and tie a length of organza ribbon through the hole.

# Birthdays

All age ranges are catered for in this chapter of birthday cards, from a first to a magnificent 100th. It is always fun to make cards for children, so there are all sorts of ideas here using fantastic innovative materials. Many include numbers for specific ages, but you can of course substitute any number you want.

Adults love to receive birthday cards too, and there are plenty of themed cards for special interests such as surfing, rugby or music, plus lots of gift-wrapping suggestions to make your presents extra special.

# Baby's first birthday card

*Most one-year-olds will hardly notice the card you send them, but their proud parents definitely will, and any older brothers and sisters will certainly be enchanted by this fluffy bunny. And as children love to look at their collections of cards from previous birthdays, the recipient too will eventually come to treasure this one.*

**1** Cut a 24 × 15cm/9 × 6in rectangle of turquoise card using a craft knife and a metal ruler and working on a cutting mat. Score and fold the card across the centre, parallel with the short edges, using a bone folder.

**2** Use the template at the back of the book to cut the rabbit from pale pink fleece and the number 1 from yellow felt. Stick the rabbit to the front of the card using spray adhesive, positioning it 1.5cm/⅝in above the lower edge. Stick the numeral in the top left corner.

## materials and equipment

- turquoise card (stock)
- craft knife
- metal ruler
- cutting mat
- bone folder
- tracing paper
- pencil
- pale pink fleece
- yellow felt
- spray adhesive
- deep pink coloured pencil
- black relief paint
- 2cm/¾in bright pink pom-pom
- glue dot

**3** Shade the inner ears with a deep pink coloured pencil and colour the cheek to blush it. Draw the eye and nose with black relief paint. Set aside to dry.

**4** Add a bright pink pom-pom to make the rabbit's tail, attaching it with a glue dot.

# Second birthday party invitation

*These realistic gingerbread character cards make great party invitations. Use a cookie cutter as a template and imitate the traditional white icing with relief paint. A jaunty gingham ribbon around the neck completes the effect. The invitations are quick to make so you can easily produce a whole batch to send to the birthday person's friends.*

## materials and equipment

- gingerbread man cookie cutter
- pen
- terracotta-brown card (stock)
- white relief paint
- cutting mat
- craft knife
- 20cm/8in of 5mm/¹/₄in-wide gingham ribbon
- fabric scissors

**1** Draw around a gingerbread man cookie cutter on terracotta-brown card.

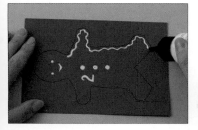

**2** Decorate the character with white relief paint. Working out from the centre so that you do not smudge the paint, apply a row of buttons, a number 2, two eyes and a mouth, then outline the character with a wiggly line. Set aside to dry.

**3** Resting on a cutting mat, cut out the character using a craft knife.

**4** Tie a length of narrow gingham ribbon around the neck and trim the ends.

# Concertina caterpillar

*Masking fluid is applied to areas that you do not want to be painted. After paint has been applied, the dried fluid is rubbed away to reveal the unpainted paper beneath. It is ideal for the patterns on this friendly caterpillar.*

**1** Cut a 33 × 6cm/13⅛ × 2⅜in strip of watercolour paper. Score it at 5.5cm/2³⁄₁₆in intervals, parallel with the short edges, using a bone folder. Fold the strip in accordion folds. Open the paper out flat again.

### materials and equipment

- watercolour paper
- cutting mat
- craft knife
- metal ruler
- bone folder
- masking fluid
- medium artist's paintbrush
- watercolour paints in light green, lemon yellow and cerulean blue
- scrap paper
- tracing paper and pencil
- red relief paint

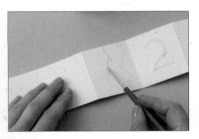

**2** With masking fluid, paint a 2 on the second section from the right. Paint wavy lines and dots on the rest of the strip, leaving the right-hand section free.

**3** Leave the masking fluid to dry then rest the strip on scrap paper and paint it with vertical stripes of light green, lemon yellow and cerulean blue watercolour paints, blending the colours together on the paper. Leave to dry.

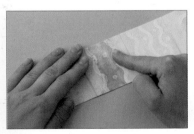

**4** Rub away the masking fluid with your finger to reveal the number and the patterns on the paper. Refold the strip.

**5** Use the template at the back of the book to draw the shape of the caterpillar on the top section, matching the foldlines.

**6** Cut through the layers using a craft knife. Draw the face on the front and outline the number using red relief paint. Leave to dry.

# Stencilled birthday car

*This card is bound to appeal to a young child who is keen on cars. The smart red vehicle has wheels that really turn and there are also three silver star stickers inside the card to mark a third birthday.*

**materials and equipment**

- pale blue, dark blue and silver card (stock)
- craft knife
- metal ruler
- cutting mat
- bone folder
- tracing paper
- pen
- stencil board
- masking tape
- red and yellow acrylic paint
- stencil brush
- kitchen paper
- double-sided tape
- bradawl
- 2 x 12mm/½in diameter green star brads
- 3 x 2.5cm/1in diameter silver star stickers

**1** Cut a 22 × 16cm/8¾ × 6½in rectangle of pale blue card using a craft knife and metal ruler and working on a cutting mat. Score and fold the card across the centre, parallel with the short edges, using a bone folder.

**2** Trace the template at the back of the book and transfer the outlines of the car and the number 3 to stencil board. Cut out the two stencils using a craft knife, resting on a cutting mat.

**3** Tape the car stencil to the card front with masking tape. To stencil the car, pick up a small amount of red paint with a stencil brush and dab off the excess on kitchen paper. Dab the paint through the stencil, holding the brush upright and moving it in a circular motion. Leave to dry, then remove the stencil.

**4** To judge the position of the number 3 stencil, hold the traced template over the card. Slip the number 3 stencil underneath, matching its position. Tape the stencil in place. Stencil the number with yellow paint. Remove the stencil.

**5** Refer to the template to cut two wheels from dark blue card and two hub caps from silver card. Stick the hub caps to the wheels with small pieces of double-sided tape.

**6** Open the card out flat on a cutting mat. Arrange the wheels on the car. Pierce a hole through the centre of each hub cap into the card using a bradawl.

**7** Insert star-shaped brads in the holes in the hub caps and through the card. Splay open the prongs inside the card.

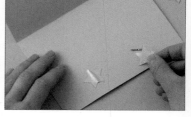

**8** To protect small hands from the prongs, stick a star sticker on top of each brad inside the card. Stick on a third star at random inside the card.

# Cute birthday dog

*Delight a child with this comical dog. He has a real removable balloon for a tongue, so don't give this card to a child younger than four.*

## materials and equipment

- white and black card (stock)
- craft knife
- metal ruler
- cutting mat
- bone folder
- tracing paper
- pencil
- grey writing paper
- spray adhesive
- black medium felt-tipped pen
- double-sided tape
- red balloon

**1** Cut a 23 × 12cm/9 × 4¾in rectangle of white card using a craft knife and metal ruler and working on a cutting mat. Score and fold the card across the centre, parallel with the short edges, using a bone folder.

**2** Use the template at the back of the book to draw the dog's face on the folded card, leaving the fold to form the left-hand edge. Cut round the outline using a craft knife.

**3** Roughly tear a patch of grey paper between your fingers. Stick the patch to the face using spray adhesive.

**4** Lightly draw the facial features on the face with a pencil. Redraw the features with a black medium felt-tipped pen.

**5** Resting on a cutting mat, use a craft knife to cut along the mouth just below the drawn line.

**6** Use the template to cut a pair of ears from black card. Score and fold along the broken lines with a bone folder.

**7** Glue the ears to the back of the card using double-sided tape and fold so that they drape over the front.

**8** Carefully slip the balloon through the slit under the mouth and pull it inside the card until it resembles a dog's tongue.

# Birthday cake gift tag

*This professional-looking birthday cake is stamped with a rubber stamp, then coloured with felt-tipped pens and highlighted with glitter paint.*

## materials and equipment

- pale yellow and mid-blue card (stock)
- decorative-edged scissors
- birthday cake rubber stamp about 4cm/1½in square
- black ink pad
- felt-tipped pens in pale blue, pale pink and deep pink
- glitter paint in blue and gold
- craft knife
- metal ruler
- cutting mat
- bone folder
- spray adhesive
- single hole punch
- 25cm/10in of 10mm/³⁄₈in-wide yellow ribbon

**1** Cut a 6.5 x 6cm/2⅝ x 2¼in rectangle of pale yellow card using a pair of decorative-edged scissors. Stamp a birthday cake rubber stamp on to a black ink pad. Stamp the image on to the centre of the yellow card. Leave the ink to dry.

**2** Colour the stamped image using felt-tipped pens, colouring the plate pale blue, the cake pale pink and the cake band and candles deep pink.

**3** Dot the cake with blue glitter paint and the candle flames with gold glitter paint. Set aside to dry.

**4** Cut a 15 x 8cm/6 x 3¼in rectangle of mid-blue card using a craft knife and metal ruler and working on a cutting mat. Score and fold the card across the centre, parallel with the short edges, using a bone folder. Stick the pale yellow card to the front of the tag using spray adhesive. Punch a hole in the top left corner and fasten a length of ribbon through the hole.

# Spotty gift wrap

*Get the children to help you make this colourful gift wrap. The spots are stamped at random over the paper using simple stamps cut from thin foam. Use a range of bright paints or just one colour for a more subtle effect.*

## materials and equipment

- circle stencil
- pencil
- Neoprene foam
- cutting mat
- craft knife
- scrap of corrugated cardboard
- metal ruler
- all-purpose household glue
- flat paintbrush
- acrylic paint in red, orange and pink
- yellow paper

**1** Use a circle stencil and a pencil to draw circles measuring 3cm/1¼in, 2.5cm/1in and 2cm/¾in diameter on Neoprene foam. Resting on a cutting mat, cut out the circles using a craft knife. Cut three 3.5cm/1½in squares of corrugated cardboard. Stick each circle to a cardboard square using all-purpose household glue.

**2** With a flat paintbrush, paint one of the foam circles with red acrylic paint.

**3** Stamp the circle firmly on to yellow paper. Repeat to stamp spots at random all over the paper, repainting the foam circle each time before stamping.

**4** Clean the brush. Paint another foam circle with orange acrylic paint and stamp orange spots at random between the red ones. Clean the brush. Paint the remaining foam circle with pink acrylic paint and stamp pink spots in the gaps on the paper. Leave to dry.

# Cowboy card

*Nimble-fingered older children will enjoy making this dapper cowboy for their younger siblings. The various elements of the figure, his clothes and the age number are torn from a selection of plain and patterned papers.*

### materials and equipment

- fawn textured card (stock)
- craft knife
- metal ruler
- cutting mat
- bone folder
- tracing paper
- pencil
- masking tape
- salmon pink, black, blue, light brown and bright green plain paper
- green checked paper
- pale blue spotted paper
- black felt-tipped pen
- glue dots
- 12mm/½in silver holographic star sequin
- 2 silver star confetti
- paper glue

**1** Cut a 26 × 19cm/10¼ × 7½in rectangle of fawn textured card using a craft knife and metal ruler and working on a cutting mat. Score and fold the card across the centre, parallel with the short edges, using a bone folder. Set aside.

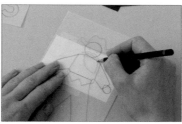

**2** Trace the cowboy templates at the back of the book and transfer the different pieces, right side down, to the wrong side of coloured and patterned papers as follows: head and hands on salmon pink paper, shirt on green checked paper, hat, moustache and boots on black paper, trousers and number 5 on blue paper, waistcoat on light brown paper and neckerchief on pale blue spotted paper. Leave a margin of at least 5mm/¼in around each image to make them easier to tear.

**3** Tear all the pieces along the drawn lines by holding the image between the thumb and fingers of one hand close to the drawn line and pulling the paper around the image toward you with the other hand. Gradually move your fingers along the line.

**4** Arrange all the pieces on the card front, being careful to place the shoes and hands below the trousers and shirt. Add the head after the shirt. Stick the pieces in place using spray adhesive.

**5** Dot the eyes on the head with a black felt-tipped pen. Using glue dots, stick a silver holographic star sequin to the waistcoat and a confetti star to each boot as spurs.

**◀6** Cut a 25 × 18cm/9¾ × 7in rectangle of bright green paper for the insert. Fold the paper across the centre, parallel with the short edges. Run a line of paper glue along the fold and stick inside the card.

# Birthday medallion card

*Award a medal to your champion with this glittery card. The polymer clay medal is hung on ribbon and can easily be removed for the recipient to wear on their birthday, proclaiming their new age.*

## materials and equipment

- polymer clay in red, gold glitter and green glitter
- baking parchment
- drinking straw
- small kitchen knife
- 75cm/30in of 1cm/³/₈in-wide red ribbon
- fabric scissors
- blue glitter card (stock)
- craft knife
- metal ruler
- cutting mat
- bone folder

**1** Roll a 2.5cm/1in ball of red polymer clay. On a sheet of baking parchment, flatten the clay to a 4.5cm/1¾in diameter circle for the medal. Stamp a hole at the top of the circle using a drinking straw.

**2** Roll 1.5cm/⅝in balls of gold glitter and green glitter polymer clay. Roll the balls into two logs 11.5cm/4½in long on baking parchment. Twist the logs together.

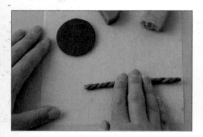

**3** Roll the twisted log until it is about 5mm/¼in thick, then bend the log into a number 6.

**4** Carefully place the numeral on the red disc of clay and press it gently in place. Cut off the excess clay. Bake the medal to harden it following the clay manufacturer's instructions. Leave to cool.

**5** Thread a length of red ribbon through the hole in the medal. Knot the ribbon ends together and trim diagonally.

**6** Cut a 24 x 16cm/9½ x 6¼in rectangle of blue glitter card using a craft knife and metal ruler and working on a cutting mat. Score and fold the card across the centre, parallel with the short edges, using a bone folder.

**7** Open the card out flat. Cut two 2cm/¾in slits in the upper edge of the card front, 5cm/2in apart.

**8** Slot the ribbon through the slits so the medal hangs on the front of the card.

**Tip**
If the blue glitter card sheds glitter, spray it with fixative spray before cutting it.

# Russian dolls

*This pretty design is based on traditional Russian matryoshka or nesting dolls, and if you wish you can make a trio of cards: reduce the size of the card to make a smaller one for another friend to send, and make an even smaller card for a gift tag, so the birthday person receives a complete set of dolls.*

## materials and equipment

- cream and red card (stock)
- craft knife
- metal ruler
- cutting mat
- bone folder
- tracing paper
- pencil
- spray adhesive
- double-sided tape
- salmon pink, black, turquoise and pink paper
- black, pale pink and red felt-tipped pens
- 12mm/½in tulip paper punch

**1** Cut a 20 × 16.5cm/8 × 6½in rectangle of cream card using a craft knife and metal ruler and working on a cutting mat. Score and fold the card across the centre, parallel with the long edges, using a bone folder.

**2** Trace the template at the back of the book and use it to draw the Russian doll on the folded card, aligning the lower left side of the doll with the fold. Use the template to cut a scarf, knot and feet from red card. Stick the scarf, then the knot, to the doll using spray adhesive. Stick the feet to the doll using double-sided tape.

**3** Resting the card on a cutting mat, use a craft knife to cut out the doll, cutting through both layers and cutting around the right-hand curved edge of the feet.

**4** Use the template to draw the face lightly on salmon-pink card with a pencil. Dot the eyes with a black felt-tipped pen and the nose with a pale pink felt-tipped pen. Draw the mouth with a red felt-tipped pen.

**5** Cut the hair from black paper and stick it to the face using spray adhesive. Cut out the face and stick it in the centre of the scarf using spray adhesive.

**6** Cut the number 7 from turquoise paper. Use spray adhesive to stick the number to the card front.

**7** Apply double-sided tape to a strip of pink paper to make stickers to decorate the doll. Punch six tulips with a 12mm/½in tulip-shaped paper punch.

**8** Peel off the backing papers and stick a row of three tulips down each side of the doll's dress, positioning them with a craft knife blade.

# Butterfly birthday card

*Transfer paint is a special non-toxic water-based paint that dries to form a soft, pliable film which can then be heat-transferred to many surfaces such as card and clothes. It can also be peeled off and reused. This transfer-painted butterfly has been applied to a turquoise card laced with ribbon and heart-shaped beads.*

**1** Trace the butterfly and the number 8 template at the back of the book on to tracing paper with a black pen. Tape a sheet of plastic on top of the tracing. Draw the butterfly using purple transfer paint.

**2** Fill in the outline of the butterfly with transfer paints. Draw the numeral with red transfer paint. Set aside for 24 hours for the paint to dry.

**materials and equipment**

- tracing paper
- black pen
- sheet of plastic
- masking tape
- transfer paints in purple, silver, red, pink and yellow
- turquoise card (stock)
- craft knife
- metal ruler
- cutting mat
- bone folder
- transfer paper
- iron
- 3mm/¹/₈in hole punch
- tack hammer
- 30cm/12in of 3mm/¹/₈in-wide red ribbon
- 4 heart-shaped pony beads in assorted colours
- fabric scissors

**3** Cut a 16.5 x 14.5cm/6½ x 5¾in rectangle of turquoise card, using a craft knife and metal ruler and working on a cutting mat, for the card front. Score and fold 2cm/¾in from one short side, using a bone folder, to form the hinge. Cut another rectangle of turquoise card measuring 19.5 x 14.5cm/7¾ x 5¾in for the back.

**4** Place the card front on an ironing board, right side up with the hinge to the left. Carefully peel the designs off the plastic sheet. Position the butterfly on the card front. Place transfer paper on top. With the iron set to a silk setting, iron over the transfer paper. Do not use steam. Leave the motif to cool.

**5** Place the card back on the ironing board, and place the front on top, matching the left-hand edges. Position the numeral on the right-hand edge of the back. Remove the front. Place transfer paper on the numeral and iron it on. Leave to cool.

**6** Tape the front to the back, matching the left-hand edges. With a pen, draw a row of ten holes 1.5cm/⅝in apart along the centre of the hinge. Resting on a cutting mat, punch a hole at each dot using a 3mm/¹/₈in punch and a tack hammer.

**7** Make a double knot at the end of the ribbon and thread it in and out of the punched holes, threading on a pony bead on each stitch at the front of the card. Make a double knot over the last hole and cut off the excess ribbon. Remove the tape. Enclose a piece of transfer paper with the card, with instructions telling an adult how to peel the motifs off the card and iron them on to the child's clothing by ironing over the transfer paper on a silk setting.

# Funky foam monster birthday card

*This friendly monster will bring a smile to the recipient's face. He is made from foam and proudly holds a number showing the child's age. The face and glitter spots are applied with relief paint.*

materials and equipment

- yellow card (stock)
- craft knife
- metal ruler
- cutting mat
- bone folder
- tracing paper
- pencil
- pen
- Neoprene foam in red and aquamarine
- relief paint in lime green and silver
- all-purpose household glue
- glue dots

**1** Cut a 26 × 17cm/10¼ × 6¾in rectangle of yellow card using a craft knife and metal ruler and working on a cutting mat. Score and fold the card across the centre, parallel with the short edges, using a bone folder.

**2** Using the template at the back of the book cut out a monster from red Neoprene foam and a number 9 from aquamarine foam, using a craft knife and resting on a cutting mat.

**3** Draw a face on the monster using a pen. Redraw the lines with lime green relief paint. Set aside to dry.

**4** Stick the numeral to the centre of the monster using all-purpose household glue.

**5** Apply a few glue dots to the fingers of the monster. Bend the fingers over and stick them to the numeral. Press firmly in place.

**6** Stick the monster to the front of the card using all-purpose household glue.

**7** Dot the monster with silver glitter relief paint. Leave to dry.

# Flying fairy birthday card

*Delight a child on their birthday with this pretty fairy bringing good wishes. She is made of scraps of pink silk fabrics and highlighted with lots of glitter paint and tiny star sprinkles.*

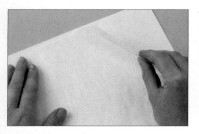

**1** Apply white mulberry paper to white card using spray adhesive. Cut a 29 × 17.5cm/11½ × 7in rectangle of the covered card using a craft knife and metal ruler and working on a cutting mat. Score and fold the card across the centre, parallel with the short edges, using a bone folder.

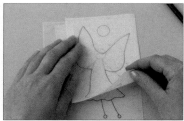

**2** Trace the fairy template at the back of the book using a black pen. Tape a piece of iron-on interfacing, shiny side down, to the wrong side of the tracing using masking tape. Trace the dress and wings on to the interfacing with a pencil. Trace the head on another part of the interfacing.

### materials and equipment

- white mulberry paper
- white card (stock)
- spray adhesive
- craft knife
- metal ruler
- cutting mat
- bone folder
- tracing paper
- black pen
- pencil
- 12.5 × 10cm/5 × 4in piece of iron-on interfacing
- masking tape
- scraps of bright pink and salmon pink silk dupion fabric
- fabric scissors
- glitter paint in gold and pink
- tiny star sprinkles
- tweezers
- glue dots

**3** Roughly cut out the pieces, leaving a margin all round. Apply the dress and wings to bright pink silk dupion and the head to salmon pink silk dupion by ironing the interfacing, shiny side down, on to the fabric. Cut out the pieces.

**4** Centre the dress and wings on the card front, then move it slightly left. Stick to the card front using spray adhesive. Stick the head on top in the same way.

**5** Draw the arms, legs, feet, numeral, eyes, mouth and wand on the card lightly in pencil. Create the hair by applying blobs of gold glitter paint around the sides and top of the head. Before the paint dries, carefully place a few tiny star sprinkles on the hair using tweezers. Set aside to dry.

**6** Use pink glitter paint to outline the dress, wings and head, then draw the arms, feet and numeral and dot the eyes and mouth. Before the paint dries, carefully place a star sprinkle on each "ankle" using tweezers. Draw the wand with gold glitter paint. Set aside to dry.

**7** Stick a few star sprinkles around the numeral, on the dress and on the tips of the wings, using glue dots. Dot gold glitter paint around the number and the stars. Set aside to dry.

# Fluttering kite card

*This breezy card is designed with a grown-up brother in mind, but no one can fail to be charmed by the little fabric kite with its flyaway tail.*

## materials and equipment

- scraps of shirting fabrics
- fabric scissors
- needle and thread
- fusible bonding web
- iron
- pencil and tracing paper
- A4 sheet of handmade paper
- bone folder
- 45cm/20in thin string
- bradawl
- glue dots
- adhesive tape
- 5 mother-of-pearl buttons
- red thread

**1** Cut out four pieces of fabric, each roughly 7.5cm/3in square, then sew them together to make a square. Trace the kite motif from the back of the book on to fusible bonding web and iron it to the back of the fabric with the crossed lines matching the seams. Cut out the kite. Fold the paper in half lengthwise and smooth the crease with a bone folder. Peel off the backing paper and iron the kite to the top right corner of the card. Draw two pencil lines for the string and the tail.

**2** From the remaining fabric cut eight 3 x 1cm/1¼ x ½in strips to make the bows on the tail. Starting 4cm/1½in from one end, knot the string over the centre of the first strip and pull the ends tightly. Do the same with the other strips, leaving regular intervals between them.

**3** Pierce holes in the card with the bradawl at both ends of the pencil tail line. Thread the string through both holes, then stick the bows down with glue dots so that the string lies along the curvy line. Cut a strip of blue fabric to go along the bottom of the card. Cut a wavy line along the top edge and fray it slightly, then attach it to the bottom edge with bonding web.

**4** Add another length of string to make the kite's string, trim the loose ends and secure on the wrong side with adhesive tape. Stitch a scattering of small buttons across the sea using red thread.

# Happy birthday cake

*For a sister who is no longer announcing her age on her birthday, make this sweet card bearing a little cake with just one candle.*

## materials and equipment

- 12 x 15cm/5 x 6in rectangle of foam board
- craft knife
- metal ruler
- cutting mat
- 14 x 17cm/6 x 7in rectangle of striped paper
- double-sided tape
- silver paper lace
- glue stick
- 10cm/4in square of patterned wrapping paper
- tracing paper and pencil
- scraps of beige and lilac card (stock)
- white ridged paper
- pinking shears
- birthday cake candle

**1** Mark an 8cm/3in square on the foam board and cut it out using a craft knife and metal ruler and working on a cutting mat. Cover the back of the striped paper with double-sided tape and remove the backing strips. Place the foam board centrally on the sticky tape and press it down firmly. Trim the surplus paper to 5mm/¼in all round and fold the edges down.

**2** Cut four narrow strips of paper lace to make a frame around the opening. Stick them in place using a glue stick. Attach the wrapping paper to the back of the opening using double-sided tape, ensuring the pattern is straight and the paper lies flat.

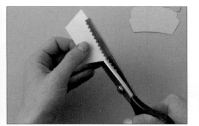

**3** Trace the cake, icing and cake paper templates at the back of the book. Cut the cake from beige card, the icing from lilac card and the cake paper from white paper. Trim the cake paper using pinking shears.

**4** Assemble the three parts to make a fairy cake. Fold back the tabs and bend the cake slightly to give a three-dimensional appearance, then stick the tabs to the wrapping paper with glue dots. Glue the birthday candle behind the cake.

# Music lover's birthday card

*The CDs on this music-inspired card are made from hologram card, attached with shiny coloured brads. An insert in a contrasting colour protects the prongs of the brads and provides a light-coloured surface to write on.*

## materials and equipment

- purple and silver hologram card (stock)
- craft knife
- metal ruler
- cutting mat
- bone folder
- circle stencil and pencil or circular paper punch
- bradawl
- 8 x 4mm/$^5$/$_{32}$in metallic brads in assorted colours
- light green paper
- paper glue

**1** Cut a 19 x 15cm/7½ x 6in rectangle of purple card using a craft knife and metal ruler and working on a cutting mat. Score and fold the card across the centre, parallel with the short edges, using a bone folder.

**2** Draw and cut out or punch eight 2.5cm/1in diameter circles of hologram card. Resting on a cutting mat, pierce a hole in the centre of each circle using a bradawl.

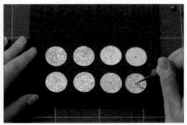

**3** Open the card out flat on the cutting mat. Arrange the circles on the front and pierce the card using the holes in the circles as guides. Insert the brads and splay open the prongs on the inside of the card.

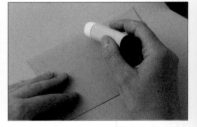

**4** Cut an 18 x 14cm/7 x 5½in rectangle of light green paper. Fold the paper in half parallel with the short edges. Run a line of paper glue along the fold and stick the insert inside the card, matching the folds.

# Surfboard card

*Make a stand-up surfboard birthday card for a keen surfer, using a glossy graphic gift wrap that captures surfing style. The card folds flat for posting.*

## materials and equipment

- white patterned gift wrap
- turquoise and red card (stock)
- spray adhesive
- cutting mat
- craft knife
- metal ruler
- bone folder
- tracing paper
- pencil
- 5mm/¼in-wide double-sided tape
- purple paper

**1** Apply white patterned gift wrap to turquoise card using spray adhesive. Cut a 20 x 12cm/8 x 4¾in rectangle of the covered card. Score and fold the card across the centre, parallel with the long edges, using a bone folder.

**2** Use the template at the back of the book to cut the surfboard from the folded card, matching the folds. Open the card and cut a slit in the front as marked on the template.

**3** Use the template to cut a fin from red card. Score and fold the fin along the broken lines. Apply 5mm/¼in-wide double-sided tape to the tab. With the fin pointing down, insert the tab through the slit on the front of the card. Peel off the backing strip and stick the tab to the underside of the card front.

**4** Cut the number 18 from purple paper. Use spray adhesive to stick the numerals across the front of the card, allowing them to extend beyond the edges of the surfboard. Turn the card over and trim off the extending edges of the numerals.

# Clothes closet birthday card

*Make this delightful card for a female friend who loves clothes. The panelled doors, with a little tag swinging from one handle, open to reveal a pretty print dress hanging on a little wire coat hanger.*

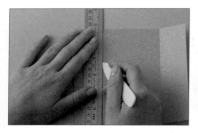

**1** Cut a 16 × 14.5cm/6½ × 5¾in rectangle of light pink card using a craft knife and metal ruler and working on a cutting mat. For the doors, score and fold the card 4cm/1⅝in in from, and parallel with, each short edge, using a bone folder.

**2** Open the card out flat and draw "door panels" on the doors with bright pink relief paint. Use the template at the back of the book to cut a label from white card. Draw the number 21 on the label with the pink relief paint. Set aside to dry.

## materials and equipment

- light pink and white card (stock)
- craft knife
- metal ruler
- cutting mat
- bone folder
- bright pink relief paint
- tracing paper
- pencil
- gift wrap with small-scale floral pattern
- spray adhesive
- 20cm/8in of 8mm/⁵/₁₆in-wide deep pink ribbon
- fabric scissors
- turquoise flower sticker
- 15cm/6in of 0.8mm blue wire
- round-nosed pliers
- wire snippers
- glue dots
- 2 × 4mm/⁵/₃₂in blue square diamanté stickers
- tiny pink flower diamanté sticker
- bradawl
- 4mm/⁵/₃₂in turquoise brad

**3** Apply patterned gift wrap to a piece of white card using spray adhesive. Use the template to cut a dress from the covered card. Tie ribbon around the waist of the dress, knotting it at the front. Trim the ribbon ends diagonally. Stick a turquoise flower sticker at the neck of the dress.

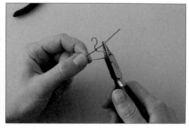

**4** Referring to the template, bend a length of thin blue wire into a coat hanger shape using round-nosed pliers. Start at the hook and finish the hanger by twisting the wire tightly around the hook. Snip off the excess wire with wire snippers.

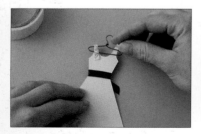

**5** Lay the dress face down and position the hanger on top of the shoulder straps. Fold the dress tabs over the hanger and stick to the wrong side of the dress with glue dots.

**6** Stick a blue diamanté sticker to the label at the dot and a pink flower diamanté sticker at the other end. Stick the label to the left door as if the diamanté sticker was a door knob. Stick another diamanté sticker in a matching position on the other door.

**7** Open the doors. Resting on a cutting mat, pierce a hole centrally in the card back 1.5cm/⅝in below the upper edge using a bradawl. Insert a brad through the hole. Hang the hanger on the brad. Splay open the prongs on the back of the card.

# For a rugby fan

*On this sporty card the ball stands proud of the surface, raised on adhesive foam pads, and the distinctive black lines are applied with relief paint.*

## materials and equipment

- dark brown, light green and terracotta card (stock)
- craft knife
- metal ruler
- cutting mat
- bone folder
- tracing paper
- pencil
- black relief paint
- cream paper
- glue dots
- adhesive foam pads
- paper glue

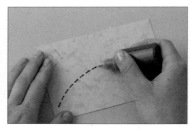

**1** Cut a 22 × 15.5cm/8½ × 6¼in rectangle of dark brown card using a craft knife and metal ruler and working on a cutting mat. Score and fold the card across the centre, parallel with the short edges, using a bone folder.

**2** Cut a 14.5 × 10cm/5¾ × 4in rectangle of light green mottled card. Use the template at the back of the book to draw the broken line and age number lightly in pencil. Redraw the broken line and number with black relief paint. Leave to dry.

**3** Draw the rugby ball on terracotta card. Draw the seam with black relief paint. Draw the lacing panel on cream paper, with the lacing in black relief paint. Leave to dry then cut out the pieces. Stick the lacing panel to the ball using glue dots.

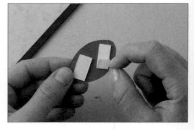

**4** Stick the light green rectangle to the card front using spray adhesive. Stick the ball to the light green rectangle using adhesive foam pads. Cut a 21 × 14.5cm/8⅛ × 5¾in rectangle of cream paper for the insert and fold it in half. Run a line of paper glue along the fold and stick the insert inside the card, matching the folds.

# Sponged foliage gift wrap

*Shapely real leaves, such as the leaves of a Japanese acer tree, are held temporarily in place on a sheet of coloured paper using stencil mount, then the paper is sponged all over with acrylic paint.*

## materials and equipment

- leaves
- blotting paper
- flower press or heavy book
- stencil mount
- orange paper
- red acrylic paint
- old plate or ceramic tile
- flat paintbrush
- natural sponge
- craft knife

**1** Press the leaves between sheets of blotting paper in a flower press or between the pages of a heavy book for a few days. When they are flat, spray the leaves with stencil mount, arrange them on a sheet of orange paper and press in place.

**2** Apply some red acrylic paint to an old plate or ceramic tile and spread it out using a flat paintbrush.

**Tip**
Test your colour choices and choice of stencil on spare paper first.

**3** Dab at the paint with a natural sponge.

**4** Sponge the paint all over the paper. Leave to dry then peel off the leaves, lifting the edges with the tip of a craft knife blade.

# Paisley birthday card

*Here, an elegant paisley design is stencilled on an easel-style greetings card, highlighted with silver paint. A panel with a matching stencilled border holds the card upright. The card folds flat to fit a standard envelope.*

**1** Cut a 53 x 9cm/20¾ x 3½in strip of lilac card using a craft knife and metal ruler and working on a cutting mat. Score the card using a bone folder, parallel with the short edges, 4cm/1½in, 11cm/4¼in and 32cm/12½in from one end.

**2** Fold the card along the scored lines to form the easel shape. Crease the folds with a bone folder. Open the card out flat again.

**3** Trace the templates of the paisley shape and the border at the back of the book and transfer them to stencil board. Cut out the stencils using a craft knife, working on a cutting mat.

**4** Tape the paisley stencil to the front section using masking tape. Pick up a small amount of jade green paint with a stencil brush, dabbing off the excess paint on kitchen paper. Dab the paint through the stencil, holding the brush upright and moving it in a circular motion. Leave to dry.

**5** Tape the border stencil to the 4cm/1½in end section and stencil the border with jade green paint. Leave to dry.

**6** Stencil the centre and outer edges of the paisley, and the upper edge of the border, with silver acrylic paint. Leave to dry then remove the stencils.

# Shell and pearl-trimmed card

*This charmingly feminine card in shades of pink combines pearlized paper with a little string of pearls and a delicate shell. It's multilayered for an extra touch of luxury, and would make a perfect birthday greeting for your mother.*

## materials and equipment

- 3 x A5 sheets pearlized paper, white, pale pink and pink
- 7cm/2³/₄in square of silver paper
- glue stick
- scallop shell
- adhesive pads
- scissors
- clear bead elastic
- pearl and pink rocaille beads
- craft knife
- metal ruler and cutting mat
- adhesive tape

**3** Cut a 50cm/20in length of bead elastic and make a double knot close to the centre. Thread on a few pearl beads, alternating them with tiny pink rocailles. Make another knot to secure the beads.

**1** Fold the three sheets of paper in half. Using a craft knife and metal ruler and working on a cutting mat, trim 6mm/¼in from the open side of the pale pink sheet and 1.2cm/½in from the white sheet.

**2** Glue the silver paper to the centre front of the white sheet. Stick adhesive pads to the back of the shell, trim any protruding edges, then attach the shell to the centre of the silver paper.

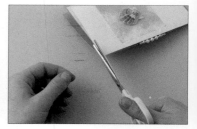

**4** Slip the pink papers inside the white paper and make a tiny notch at each end of the fold through all the layers. Tie the elastic so that it lines up the spine of the card and secure with tiny pieces of adhesive tape.

# Exotic flowers and lace

*The smallest scraps of fabric can be turned into gorgeous cards: combine an exuberant print like these tropical flowers with fragments of old lace.*

## materials and equipment

- white card (stock)
- craft knife
- metal ruler
- cutting mat
- white card blank
- cream tissue
- glue stick
- double-sided tape
- white lace
- green and white printed paper
- flowery fabric
- fabric scissors
- fusible bonding web
- iron
- scrap paper

**1** Cut a piece of white card the same size as the card blank. Cut a piece of tissue 2cm/¾in larger all round and stick the card in the centre using a glue stick. Fold the edges to the back and stick with double-sided tape. Glue a strip of lace to each side and stick the raw edges down at the back.

**2** Use double-sided tape to stick a strip of patterned paper to the centre of the card, overlapping the edges of the lace panels.

**3** Roughly cut out three flower motifs from the patterned fabric. Iron them on to fusible bonding web, following the manufacturer's instructions, then cut out carefully.

**4** Peel off the backing, arrange them attractively on the card and iron in place with a cool iron. Use a sheet of paper to protect the surface of the card when pressing. With double-sided tape, stick the card to the front of the card blank.

# Punched gift tag

*Experiment with decorative-edged scissors and paper punches in a range of designs to make dramatic gift tags from contrasting card and paper.*

**materials and equipment**

- red card (stock)
- wavy-edged scissors
- ruler
- bone folder
- olive green textured paper
- spiral paper punch about
  10 × 8mm/³/₈ × ⁵/₁₆in
- cutting mat
- 4mm/⁵/₃₂in hole punch
- tack hammer
- 3mm/¹/₈in hole punch
- 2mm/¹/₁₆in hole punch
- pale blue paper
- spray adhesive
- double-sided tape

**1** Cut a 12 × 7cm/4¾ × 2¾in rectangle of red card with wavy-edged scissors. Score the card parallel with the short edges, 5cm/2in from one side, using a bone folder.

**2** Cut a 6 × 4cm/2¼ × 1½in rectangle of olive green textured paper using wavy-edged scissors. Punch a row of four spirals along each long edge using a paper punch.

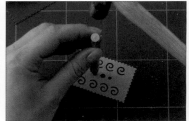

**3** Resting on a cutting mat, punch a 4mm/⁵/₃₂in hole in the centre of the olive green rectangle using a hole punch and a tack hammer. Punch 3mm/¹/₈in and 2mm/¹/₁₆in holes above and below the centre. Stick the rectangle to the front of the tag using spray adhesive.

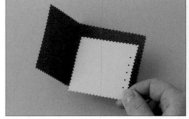

**4** Cut a 6cm/2½in square of pale blue paper using wavy-edged scissors. Resting on a cutting mat, punch a row of five 2mm/¹/₁₆in holes, 5mm/¼in from one edge. Stick the square inside the tag using spray adhesive. Stick a piece of double-sided tape to the back of the tag ready to stick to the gift.

# Greek urn card

*Make this classically inspired birthday card for a friend who is keen on antiques or travelling. The Greek urn is made of beautifully textured paper.*

**materials and equipment**

- beige paper with embedded fibres and metallic fragments
- cream card (stock)
- spray adhesive
- craft knife
- metal ruler
- cutting mat
- bone folder
- tracing paper
- pencil
- fine black pen
- black paper
- double-sided tape
- 15mm/⅝in leaf sprig paper punch

**1** Apply beige paper with embedded fibres and metallic fragments to cream card using spray adhesive. Cut a 19 x 14.5cm/7½ x 5¾in rectangle of the covered card using a craft knife and metal ruler and working on a cutting mat. Score and fold the card across the centre, parallel with the short edges, using a bone folder.

**2** Use the template from the back of the book to cut the urn from the folded card, aligning the left side with the folded edge. Refer to the template to draw the harp strings on the card using a black pen.

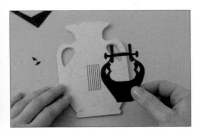

**3** Use the template to cut the harp from black paper. Stick the harp to the front of the card using spray adhesive.

**4** Stick double-sided tape to the back of a piece of black paper. Use a 15mm/⅝in leaf sprig paper punch to punch three sprigs. Peel off the backing paper and stick the sprigs in a row around the neck of the urn.

# Toolkit card

*You could send this card to a practical father (or mother, or partner) whose DIY skills you admire: it might persuade them to start on the next job.*

### materials and equipment

- 25cm/10in square of parchment-effect card (stock)
- bone folder
- 10 x 12cm/4 x 5in rectangle of parquet-effect paper
- 8 x 12cm/3 x 5in rectangle of brick-effect paper
- spray adhesive
- images of old tools from copyright-free book
- scissors
- glue stick

**1** Fold the square of parchment effect card in half and smooth along the crease with a bone folder.

**2** Stick the two pieces of decorative paper to the card front using spray adhesive and smooth down carefully.

**3** Cut out the images of the tools using scissors, following the outside edges carefully to eliminate the white background.

**4** Arrange the tool cutouts across the card and stick them down using a glue stick.

# Card for a keen traveller

*The design of this card was inspired by the plane motif on the envelope, and the border is copied from a standard airmail envelope.*

## materials and equipment

- airmail envelope
- colour photocopier
- scissors
- A4 sheet of dark grey Ingres paper
- bone folder
- 10 x 16cm/4 x 6¹/₂in rectangle of parchment paper
- glue stick
- luggage label
- adhesive foam pads
- airmail sticker
- adhesive tape

**1** Colour photocopy the envelope, enlarging it to 200 per cent of the original size. Cut out the red and blue border strips and the plane image.

**2** Fold the Ingres paper in half and rub over the crease with a bone folder. Glue the parchment to the centre front of the card using a glue stick, setting it at a slight angle.

**3** Glue the red and blue border strips around the edge of the parchment.

**4** Stick the plane across the luggage label using a glue stick, then attach the label to the parchment using adhesive foam pads. Add an airmail sticker to one corner of the card and secure the loose ends of the string on the label on the back of the card with a small piece of adhesive tape.

**Tip**
Photocopy any collection of interesting stamps, postmarks and travel souvenirs to make similar collage cards.

# Origami gift box

*This handsome box with its well-fitting lid is constructed using a traditional Oriental paper folding technique, though the modern papers used here give it an up-to-the-minute look. The box needs no adhesive to hold its shape and can be used to present a lightweight birthday gift such as a silk scarf, or be filled with shredded tissue to enclose a piece of jewellery.*

### materials and equipment
- 30cm/12in square sheet of green handmade paper
- 30cm/12in square sheet of pale blue flock gift wrap

**1** Refer to the diagrams at the back of the book to fold the squares along the solid and broken lines with the wrong sides of the papers facing. Open the squares out flat again. (The box can be made in any size. The finished container will be a third of the size of the paper. For example, a 30cm/12in square of paper will make this 10cm/4in square box.)

**2** Refold the green paper for the box diagonally in half. Fold the corners at the end of the diagonal fold inwards along the broken lines.

**3** Stand the corners upright along the broken lines then squash them flat, matching the diagonal fold line to the broken lines. Crease along the new folds. Open the paper out flat and repeat steps 2–3 on the other diagonal fold.

**4** With the wrong side facing upwards, fold the green paper along two adjacent base lines to form two sides of the box. Bring the broken lines together, folding the excess paper at the corner inside.

**5** Fold the triangle at the top of the corner over the corner to hold it in place. Recrease the corner fold to define it. Repeat to form the remaining corners of the box.

**6** To make the lid, with the wrong side of the pale blue flock gift wrap facing upwards, fold two opposite corners to meet at the centre. Fold again so that the broken lines meet at the centre.

**7** Lift the edges along the last pair of folds to form two opposite sides of the lid. Lift and fold the third side of the lid by bringing the third broken line level with the upright sides, folding the excess paper inwards at the corners.

**8** Repeat with the fourth broken line on the fourth side. Fold down along the broken lines so that the points meet at the centre on the underside of the lid.

# Exotic insect birthday card

*Silk painting is a very popular pastime. If you are new to the craft, making a panel for a greetings card is a great way to start as it is a fairly small-scale project. Practise on some spare fabric to see how the paints and the outliner work. This fabulous creature is set in a card of marbled paper trimmed with metallic cord and beads.*

**1** Trace the template at the back of the book using a black pen. Tape the silk centrally on top with masking tape. Trace the design lightly on the silk with a pencil. Stretch the silk in an embroidery hoop.

**2** Draw the design on the silk with silver silk outliner, starting at the centre of the design and working outwards so that you do not smudge the outliner. Leave to dry. If any lines are very thin or do not join up, go over them again so that the paint colour will not be able to seep through.

**3** Dip the paintbrush into the green silk paint and press the brush into the centre of one area. The paint will flow within the outline. Add more paint if necessary until the area is filled. Paint all the areas green or blue. Leave to dry then press the silk between two layers of white tissue paper.

**4** Stick the silk to a piece of white paper with spray adhesive, smoothing the silk outwards from the centre. Use a pencil to draw a 10.5 × 8cm/4⅛ × 3⅛in rectangle on the silk with the insect centred inside it. Cut out the rectangle with scissors.

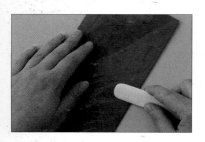

**5** Apply marbled paper to blue card with spray adhesive. Cut a 22 × 20cm/8¾ × 8in rectangle of the covered card using a craft knife and metal ruler and working on a cutting mat. Score and fold the card across the centre, parallel with the long edges, using a bone folder. Open the card out flat.

## materials and equipment

- tracing paper and pen
- 20cm/8in square of white habotai silk
- masking tape
- pencil
- 15cm/6in embroidery hoop (frame)
- silver silk outliner (gutta)
- green and blue silk paints
- medium artist's paintbrush
- white tissue paper
- white paper
- spray adhesive
- scissors
- iron
- blue and green marbled paper
- blue card
- craft knife
- metal ruler and cutting mat
- bone folder
- 5mm/¼in-wide double-sided tape
- light green paper
- paper glue
- 1.4m/55in silver cord
- 2 blue beads with large holes

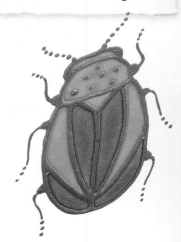

**6** For the window, draw an 8.5 × 6cm/3⅜ × 8⅜in rectangle centrally on the card front, 2cm/¾in down from the upper edge. Cut out the rectangle using a craft knife and metal ruler on a cutting mat. Apply double-sided tape around the window on the wrong side. Peel off the backing strips and stick the silk behind the window.

**7** Cut a 21 × 18cm/8¼ × 7in rectangle of light green paper for the insert. Fold the paper in half parallel with the short edges. Run a line of glue down the fold using a glue stick and insert the paper in the card, matching the folds.

**8** Double the silver cord and lay it inside the card with the loop at the top of the spine. Bring the loose ends up the outside of the card and thread them through the loop, pulling the cord tight. Thread a blue bead on to each end of the cord and tie knots to hold the beads in place.

# Cupcake gift box

*You could make a set of these delightful gift boxes to give your guests at a special birthday tea party. The cake is "iced" with white relief paint.*

## materials and equipment

- light brown and white card (stock)
- craft knife
- metal ruler
- cutting mat
- bone folder
- double-sided tape
- pair of compasses and pencil
- bright pink corrugated card (stock)
- all-purpose household glue
- tracing paper
- pencil
- masking tape
- white relief paint
- tiny pink star-shaped sprinkles
- bradawl
- 10cm/4in fine green thonging
- 12mm/¹/₂in diameter red bead

**1** Cut a 20 × 5cm/8 × 2in strip of light brown card for the side of the box. Score and fold the box side 1.5cm/⅝in from, and parallel with, one long edge for the tabs. Open the strip out flat again. On the wrong side, stick double-sided tape along the tab section and to one end of the strip. Cut a line of V-shaped tabs along the taped edge.

**2** With compasses, draw a 5.5cm/2⅛in diameter circle on light brown card for the base and cut it out. Starting at the untaped end, wrap the box side around the base, sticking the tabs under the box. Overlap the ends of the box side and stick together.

**3** Cut a 21 × 2.5cm/8¼ × 1in strip of bright pink corrugated card, cutting the short edges parallel with the corrugations. Glue the corrugated strip around the side of the box using all-purpose household glue, matching the lower edges and overlapping the ends of the strip.

**4** Cut a 21 × 1.5cm/8¼ × ⅝in strip of light brown card for the lid rim. Apply double-sided tape to one end of the rim on the wrong side. Starting at the untaped end, wrap the lid rim around the box side, resting it on the corrugated card. Do not pull the strip tight, as it needs to slip on and off the box easily. Overlap the ends of the lid rim and stick together.

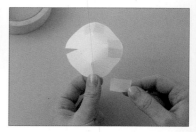

**5** Use the template at the back of the book to cut a lid from white card. Bring the straight edges together and join them with strips of masking tape.

**6** Run all-purpose household glue along the top of the lid rim. Press the lid centrally on top. Weight the lid while the glue dries.

**7** Apply white relief paint liberally to the lid. Sprinkle tiny pink star-shaped sprinkles on the lid. Set aside to dry.

**8** Pierce a hole through the centre of the lid using a bradawl. Knot the end of a 10cm/4in length of fine green thonging and thread it up through the hole. Glue the knot in place and dab glue on the thonging just above the hole. Thread on a 12mm/½in diameter red bead. Cut the thonging 2.5cm/1in above the bead.

# Japanese paper fans

*Origami paper is easy to fold sharply, so it is ideal for making tiny fans. It is available in traditional Japanese patterns in rich colours.*

### materials and equipment

- 3 sheets of patterned origami paper
- craft knife
- metal ruler
- cutting mat
- masking tape
- double-sided tape
- gold paper
- scissors
- 18cm/7in square of dark blue card (stock)
- green textured paper
- 8 x 16cm/3 x 6in rectangle of red mulberry paper
- bone folder
- glue stick
- glue dots
- small gold tassel

**1** Cut three 15 x 2.5cm/6 x 1in strips from the different origami papers, using a craft knife and metal ruler and working on a cutting mat. Make narrow accordion folds in each strip of paper to make fan shapes.

**2** Hold the end of one pleated paper tightly together and bind it with a thin strip of masking tape. Stick double-sided tape to the back of a small strip of gold paper and wrap this around the masking tape. Trim the ends neatly. Complete the other two fans in the same way.

**3** Fold the blue card in half and go over the crease with a bone folder to sharpen it. Tear the edges of the green paper against a ruler so that it is 5mm/¼in smaller all round than the red paper.

**4** Glue the red and green papers to the folded card using glue stick, then stick the fans in place with glue dots. Attach a small gold tassel just below the lowest fan.

# Embroidered flowers

*This simple design is a lovely way to make use of a collection of fine patterned and handmade papers. Even small scraps in your collection can be mixed and matched to create a bouquet of pretty flowers with jewelled centres.*

### materials and equipment

- A4 sheet of card (stock)
- bone folder
- selection of patterned and plain handmade papers
- scissors
- glue stick and ruler
- tracing paper and pencil
- embroidery needle
- metallic embroidery thread (floss)
- 3 large round jewellery stones
- adhesive foam pads

**1** Fold the A4 sheet of card in half. Cut a rectangle of patterned paper to fit the front and apply it using a glue stick. Tearing against a ruler to give a deckle edge, tear a rectangle of dark handmade paper 2cm/¾in smaller all round than the card, and glue it centrally on the front.

**2** Trace the flower template from the back of the book and cut it out. Use it to cut out three plain and three patterned flowers in different papers.

**3** Thread a large-eyed needle with two strands of metallic thread. Work a round of large stitches in the centre of the three patterned flowers, to represent veins.

**4** Arrange the flowers on the handmade paper and stick them down using a glue stick. Stick jewellery stones to the patterned flower centres using adhesive foam pads.

# Greetings for a gardener

*This clever card is quick to decorate using a flower-shaped paper punch, and embossed foil makes a perfect old-fashioned watering can.*

## materials and equipment

- tracing paper
- pencil
- 10 x 12cm/4 x 5in rectangle of craft foil
- embossing tool or blunt pencil
- ruler
- old scissors
- A4 sheet of sky-patterned card (stock)
- bone folder
- glue stick
- flower-shaped punch
- scraps of plain and patterned paper in red, purple and orange
- glue dots
- silver pen

**3** Use a flower-shaped punch to cut out at least 20 flowers from various coloured and patterned papers.

**4** Stick the flowers in place across the bottom of the card using glue dots. Using a silver pen, draw a sprinkling of water droplets spraying from the watering can.

**1** Trace the watering can template at the back of the book. Place it centrally on the wrong side of the craft foil and score around the curved parts of the outline with an embossing tool. Use a ruler as a guide to score the straight lines.

**2** Cut out the watering can using old scissors. Fold the sky-patterned card in half and rub over the crease with a bone folder. Stick the can at an angle in the top right corner of the card, using a glue stick.

# A card with a view

*This sweet picture with a nautical flavour is created from layers of torn tissue. The boat is a button, but it could also be cut out of paper or painted on card.*

**materials and equipment**

- 18 x 12cm/7 x 5in rectangle of white mount board
- craft knife and metal ruler
- cutting mat
- pencil
- hole punch
- 5 eyelets and eyelet pliers
- 18 x 12cm/7 x 5in rectangle of turquoise parchment
- scraps of blue and turquoise tissue paper
- glue stick
- double-sided tape
- blue corrugated card (stock)
- button with yacht motif
- glue dots
- coloured pencil

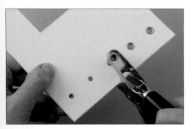

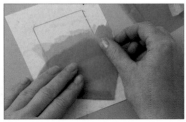

**1** Draw a 6cm/2½in square 3cm/1¼in down from the top of the mount board and centred between the side edges. Cut it out using a craft knife and metal ruler, working on a cutting mat. Mark five points evenly spaced along the lower edge of the card. Punch a hole at each point and insert an eyelet using eyelet pliers.

**2** Lightly mark the position of the square aperture on the turquoise parchment. Tear a few strips of tissue and arrange these across the lower part of the square, with the lightest colours at the back, to resemble a rough sea. Stick the tissue in place using a glue stick.

**3** Attach the parchment to the back of the board with double-sided tape, making sure the tissue paper is lined up with the square. Cut a frame from four strips of corrugated card, mitring the corners, and glue in place around the opening.

**4** Stick the button in place on the "sea" using glue dots and draw a few birds in the sky with a coloured pencil.

# Damask gift envelope

*Stencil this classic damask motif on a slim envelope designed to hold a gift token. Once you have made the stencil it is quick and easy to apply the design.*

**materials and equipment**

- jade green paper
- craft knife
- metal ruler
- cutting mat
- bone folder
- tracing paper
- pencil
- stencil board
- masking tape
- pale blue acrylic paint
- stencil brush
- kitchen paper
- 5mm/¼in-wide double-sided tape

**1** Referring to the techniques section, cut and fold a basic envelope 17cm/6¾in long and 8.5cm/3⅜in wide, using jade green paper. Open the envelope out flat.

**2** Use the template at the back of the book to draw the damask design on stencil board. Cut out the stencil using a craft knife, working on a cutting mat.

**3** Tape the stencil centrally to the front of the envelope. Pick up a small amount of pale blue paint with a stencil brush. Dab off the excess paint on kitchen paper. Dab the paint through the stencil, holding the brush upright and moving it in a circular motion. Leave to dry.

**4** Carefully remove the stencil to reveal the design. Apply 5mm/¼in-wide double-sided tape to the side edges of the back of the envelope, on the wrong side, between the fold and curves. Stick the back over the tabs. Apply a piece of double-sided tape to the flap to seal the envelope later.

# Embossed silver birthday card

*The texture of embossed wallpaper is a great surface to enhance with metallic wax. This card has an embossed motif highlighted with silver, on a subtle pink and grey background. Adjust the size of the card to suit your wallpaper motif.*

## materials and equipment

- grey and pale pink printed paper
- grey and pale pink card (stock)
- spray adhesive
- craft knife
- metal ruler
- cutting mat
- bone folder
- embossed wallpaper
- scrap paper
- silver metallic wax
- kitchen paper

**1** Stick the printed paper to grey card using spray adhesive. Cut a 28 x 14cm/ 11 x 5½in rectangle of the covered card using a craft knife and metal ruler. Score and fold the card across the centre, parallel with the short edges, using a bone folder.

**2** Resting on a cutting mat, cut a motif approximately 7.5cm/3in across from embossed wallpaper using a craft knife.

**3** Resting on a piece of scrap paper, rub silver metallic wax sparingly on the wallpaper motif, using kitchen paper, to highlight the raised areas.

**4** Cut a 9cm/3½in square of pale pink card. Use spray adhesive to stick the pale pink square diagonally to the front of the card then stick the wallpaper motif on top.

# Eightieth birthday card

*Hand embroidery on paper is very effective if the design is simple. A matching tag proudly announces the important birthday that the card celebrates.*

## materials and equipment

- lilac paper with a silver glitter pattern
- lilac, white and silver card (stock)
- spray adhesive
- cutting mat
- craft knife
- metal ruler
- bone folder
- tracing paper
- pencil
- masking tape
- bradawl
- 4mm/$^5$/$_{32}$in round diamanté sticker
- crewel embroidery needle
- pink and green stranded embroidery thread (floss)
- 4mm/$^5$/$_{32}$in crystal heart sticker
- 4mm/$^5$/$_{32}$in purple brad
- 5mm/$^1$/$_4$in-wide double-sided tape

**1** Apply patterned lilac paper to lilac card using spray adhesive. Cut an 18cm/7in square of the covered card using a craft knife and metal ruler on a cutting mat. Score and fold the card across the centre.

**2** Cut a 6 x 5cm/2½ x 2in rectangle of white card. Cut a tag from silver card. Trace the templates at the back of the book. Tape the tracings to the cards and pierce holes at the dots using a bradawl.

**3** Stick a round diamanté sticker to the centre of the flower. Thread a needle with pink embroidery thread and work lazy daisy stitch around the stone. Stitch the stem with running stitch and the leaves with single stitches, using green thread.

**4** On the tag, stitch the number 80 with back stitch using pink embroidery thread. Stick a heart sticker to the tag and attach the tag to the embroidered rectangle with a purple brad through the remaining holes. Stick the rectangle to the card front, 2cm/¾in below the upper edge, using double-sided tape.

# Pleated gift wrap

*This is an elegant way to wrap a boxed gift for an important birthday. Pearlized gift wrap is neatly pleated around the present, then decorated with a row of jewellery stones in co-ordinating shades.*

### materials and equipment

- turquoise pearlized gift wrap
- scissors
- pencil
- ruler
- clear adhesive tape
- double-sided tape
- 3 oval jewellery stones in shades of turquoise
- glue dots

**1** Cut the gift wrap large enough to cover the present, adding 8cm/2¼in to the depth to allow for the pleats. On the wrong side of the paper, draw lines across the gift wrap with a pencil and ruler 2cm/¾in then 1cm/⅜in apart three times. Draw a final line 2cm/¾in away from the previous one.

**2** Fold the gift wrap along the first line with right sides facing. Match the fold to the second line.

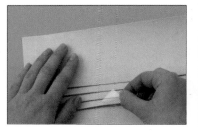

**3** Continue folding along the lines and matching the folds to the following lines. Stick two pieces of clear adhesive tape to the folds to hold the pleats in place.

**4** Wrap the boxed present, placing the pleats on the top of the box and sticking the gift wrap with double-sided tape. Stick three oval jewellery stones in a row on one of the pleats using glue dots.

# Ninetieth birthday card

*The shiny number 90 is made from fine embossed metal, with the neat finishing touch of a red star-shaped jewel.*

## materials and equipment

- gold card (stock)
- craft knife
- metal ruler
- cutting mat
- bone folder
- turquoise translucent paper
- spray adhesive
- tracing paper
- pencil
- paper scissors
- masking tape
- fine brass embossing metal
- old pair of scissors
- bradawl
- kitchen paper
- embossing tool or spent ballpoint pen
- all-purpose household glue
- red star jewellery stone sticker

**3** Place the numerals right side down on two sheets of kitchen paper. Use an embossing tool or a spent ballpoint pen to emboss a simple swirling design.

**1** Cut a 24 × 16cm/9½ × 6⅓in rectangle of gold card. Score and fold the card across the centre. Cut a 15 × 11cm/6 × 4¼in rectangle of translucent paper. Stick the rectangle centrally to the front of the card.

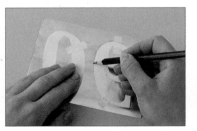

**2** Use the template at the back of the book to cut the number 90 from tracing paper. Tape the template face down on a piece of fine brass embossing metal. Draw around the numerals with a pencil, pressing firmly to make an indentation. Cut out the numerals using an old pair of scissors. To cut out the centres, make a hole with a bradawl first then cut outwards from the hole.

**4** Glue the numerals on the front of the card using all-purpose household glue. Stick a star sticker on the nought.

# Hundredth birthday card

*Frame a photocopy or a reprint of a family heirloom photograph to commemorate a landmark hundredth birthday.*

## materials and equipment

- apricot and silver card (stock)
- craft knife and metal ruler
- cutting mat
- bone folder
- spray adhesive
- tracing paper and pencil
- photocopy or reprint of family photograph
- bradawl
- 4 x 12mm/$^1$/$_2$in antique-style brads
- white paper
- double hole punch
- 40cm/16in of 15mm/$^5$/$_8$in-wide grey organza ribbon
- scissors

**1** Cut two 19 x 18cm/7¾ x 7in rectangles of apricot card using a craft knife and metal ruler and working on a cutting mat. Score and fold one rectangle, which will be the front of the card, 2.5cm/1in in from the long left-hand edge, using a bone folder, to make a hinge. The other rectangle will be the card back.

**2** Use the template at the back of the book to cut out the photocopy or reprint, following the broken lines. Cut the frame from silver card following the solid lines. Stick the photograph to the card front then stick the frame on top using spray adhesive.

**3** Resting on a cutting mat, pierce holes through the dots on the frame using a bradawl. Insert a brad through each hole. Splay open the prongs inside the card.

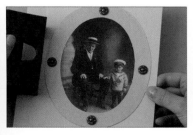

**4** Cut two 18 x 17cm/7 x 6½in rectangles of white paper for the inserts. Lay the inserts on the back then place the front on top, matching the left-hand edges. Punch a pair of holes centrally in the hinge using a double hole punch. Thread the ribbon through the holes and knot in a double knot. Cut the ribbon ends diagonally.

# Special occasions

Every landmark occasion deserves to be marked with a greetings card. This chapter presents cards for all of life's red-letter days, from welcoming a new baby to embarking on retirement, and everything in between.

There are witty ideas for the young at heart and elegant sophisticated designs too. There are also some pretty gifts to make and novel ideas for wrapping and trimming presents for christenings, wedding anniversaries and many other occasions.

# Birthstone card for a new baby

*Birthstones are paired with the months, so choose the relevant stone to welcome a new baby. An amethyst, the birthstone for February, is used here.*

materials and equipment
- beige paper with metallic fragments
- beige card (stock)
- spray adhesive
- craft knife
- metal ruler
- cutting mat
- bone folder
- silver textured paper
- cream handmade paper
- polished stone
- bradawl
- 20cm/8in of 0.8mm silver wire
- wire snippers
- double-sided tape

**1** Apply beige paper with metallic fragments to beige card using spray adhesive. Cut a 23 × 18cm/9 × 7in rectangle of the covered card. Score and fold the card across the centre, parallel with the short edges, using a bone folder.

**2** Against a ruler, tear a 7 × 6cm/3 × 2½in rectangle of silver textured paper and a 6 × 5cm/2½ × 2in rectangle of cream handmade paper. Stick the cream paper in the centre of the silver paper using spray adhesive.

**3** Place the paper rectangle on a cutting mat and hold the stone in the centre. With a bradawl, pierce about six holes around the stone to thread the wire through.

**4** Insert the wire through one hole and bend 2cm/¾in of the end back on the underside of the silver paper. Wrap the wire over the stone and insert it in another hole. Repeat to secure the stone in place, pulling the wire tight each time. Bend back the end of the wire on the underside of the paper. Snip off the excess wire. Stick the paper to the card front using double-sided tape.

# Lace pram baby congratulations card

*This delicate card uses scraps from the sewing basket to make a pretty pram motif. Use blue paper, as here, for a boy and pink for a baby girl.*

## materials and equipment

- beige and light blue handmade paper
- ruler
- bone folder
- tracing paper
- pencil
- fabric scissors
- scrap of cream lace
- spray adhesive
- cutting mat
- bradawl
- beige stranded embroidery thread (floss)
- crewel embroidery needle
- 4mm/$^5$/$_{32}$in cream pearl bead
- 2 x 12mm/$^1$/$_2$in mother-of-pearl buttons
- glue dots

**1** Tear a 20 x 13cm/8 x 5⅛in rectangle of beige handmade paper by tearing against a ruler. Score and fold the card across the centre, parallel with the short edges, using a bone folder.

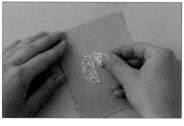

**2** Tear a 12 x 9cm/4⅝ x 3½in rectangle of light blue handmade paper by tearing against a ruler. Use the template at the back of the book to cut a pram and hood from a scrap of lace. Stick the lace pieces to the light blue rectangle using spray adhesive.

**3** Place the light blue rectangle on a cutting mat. Hold the tracing of the template on top and, using a bradawl, pierce the dots for sewing the handle. Sew along the handle through the holes with a back stitch, using stranded embroidery thread. Catch in a pearl bead with the end stitch and fasten the thread ends at the back of the paper.

**4** Glue the light blue rectangle to the card front with spray adhesive. Stick on two buttons for wheels using glue dots.

# Baby clothes card

*Although the arrival of a new baby means a never-ending round of washing, the sight of tiny clothes pinned to the clothes line never fails to enchant. The miniature versions on this card are equally endearing.*

## materials and equipment

- A4 sheet of white card (stock)
- bone folder
- jade green card (stock)
- scissors
- wooden coffee stirrer
- craft knife and cutting mat
- nail file
- glue dots
- bradawl
- fine string
- 2 sticky labels
- tracing paper and pencil
- 5 mini clothes pegs (pins)
- scraps of felt
- fabric scissors
- fine white cotton
- double-sided tape

**3** Cut out a vest and sock shapes from felt and hang from the washing line with pegs.

**I** Fold the card in half parallel with the short edges and rub over the crease with a bone folder to sharpen it. Open the card out flat. Cut a narrow strip of jade card to fit along the lower edge. Snip into one edge of the jade strip to make a grass fringe, then glue in place.

**2** To make the clothes prop, cut a V-shaped notch in the end of the coffee stirrer and trim the curve from the other end. Rub it down with a nail file to smooth any rough edges. Attach it to the card with glue dots. Pierce two holes in the sides of the card with a bradawl, just under a third of the way down. Thread the string through the holes and pull taut over the prop. Cover the ends with sticky labels on the inside.

**4** Cut a 6cm (2½in) square of fine cotton for the nappy (diaper) and peg to the line. Secure everything in place with double-sided tape and glue dots.

# Baby footprints card

*Celebrate a christening or naming day with this contemporary card of tiny stencilled footprints. The design is attached to the front of the card with star-shaped brads. Make a blue card for a boy and a pink card for a girl.*

## materials and equipment

- light blue mottled card (stock)
- craft knife
- metal ruler
- cutting mat
- bone folder
- tracing paper
- pencil
- stencil board
- white confetti paper
- masking tape
- mid-blue acrylic paint
- stencil brush
- kitchen paper
- orange polka dot paper
- spray adhesive
- bradawl
- 2 light blue 15mm/⁵⁄₈in star-shaped brads
- 5mm/¹⁄₄in-wide double-sided tape

**1** Cut a 35.5 × 17cm/14 × 6¾in rectangle of blue mottled card. On the wrong side, parallel with the short edges, score and fold the card 11.5cm/4¼in from the left edge and 12cm/4½in from the right edge.

**2** Use the template at the back of the book to cut the footprints from stencil board. Cut an 8.5 × 6cm/3⅜ × 2⅜in rectangle of white confetti paper. Tape the stencil to the paper. Pick up a little paint on the stencil brush and dab off the excess on kitchen paper. Apply the paint through the stencil, holding the brush upright and moving it in a circular motion. Leave to dry. Remove the stencil.

**3** Cut a 10 × 9cm/4 × 3½in rectangle of orange polka dot paper. Stick the stencilled panel centrally on top using spray adhesive. Open the card out. Position the panel on the card front (the middle section) and use a bradawl to pierce holes at the top and bottom of the stencilled paper.

**4** Insert the brads through the holes. Splay open the prongs inside the card. Fold the facing section inside the card front and secure the edges with double-sided tape.

# Naming day gift wallet

*Use this colourful wallet to present a christening or naming day gift. The sides of the wallet are joined with pastel-coloured safety pins and the top fastens with ribbon. Make it in pink for a girl or blue for a boy.*

### materials and equipment

- pink handmade paper
- ruler
- pencil
- cutting mat
- bradawl
- 8 pastel coloured safety pins
- double hole punch
- 50cm/20in of 8mm/$^5$/$_{16}$in-wide lilac ribbon
- fabric scissors

**1** Carefully tear a 30 × 18cm/12 × 7in rectangle of pink handmade paper by tearing against a ruler. If the paper is strong, dampen it first with a paintbrush, then tear the paper and allow to dry. Fold the paper in half, parallel with the short edges.

**2** With a pencil, mark a row of dots 1cm/⅜in in from one side edge, starting 2cm/¾in above the fold. Mark the dots 8mm/⁵⁄₁₆in then 2.5cm/1in apart three times. Mark the top dot 8mm/⁵⁄₁₆in above the previous one. Resting on a cutting mat and using a bradawl, pierce a hole at each dot. Repeat on the other side.

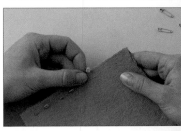

**3** Carefully fasten a safety pin through each pair of holes.

**4** Punch a pair of holes through both layers centrally at the top of the wallet. Slip the gift inside and fasten with ribbon through the punched holes. Tie the ribbon in a bow and trim the ends diagonally.

# Baby's naming day card

*By the time a baby's christening or naming celebration takes place, a few months after birth, you may have accumulated a collection of photographs, from which you can make a selection for this pictorial card, converting them to black and white for a timeless look. The dark blue card blank makes a smart change from baby pastels.*

## materials and equipment

- dark blue card blank
- photograph of baby
- photo corners
- glue stick
- contact or album sheet of small pictures
- scissors and pencil
- 3 swing labels
- bradawl
- 3 brass paper fasteners

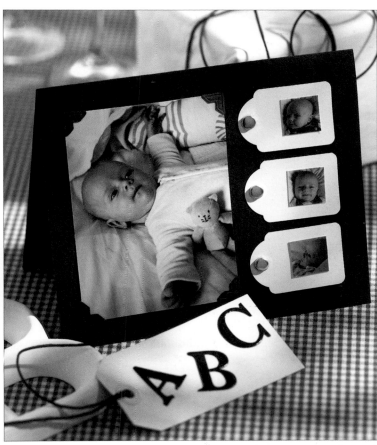

**1** Fix the main photograph to the left side of the card front using photo corners. You may need a little extra glue to hold the picture securely in place.

**2** Cut out three small images from the contact or album sheet using scissors.

**3** Glue the images to the swing labels so that the holes are on the left side. Snip off the ties and arrange the labels on the right-hand side of the card. Mark the positions of the holes.

**4** Use the bradawl to pierce the card at each of the three marks. Use brass paper fasteners to fix the tags in place, then glue them down to stop them sliding around.

# Confirmation gift box

*This beautiful wired flower is used to embellish a ready-made gift box in which to present a small confirmation gift. The beads are threaded on to wire so that they can be bent into petal shapes, and a cluster of twinkling crystal beads forms the centre of the flower. Punch a hole in the box first, if the cardboard shape is stiff.*

**1** Bend over one end of the wire for 5cm/2in to stop the beads slipping off. Thread on 35 rocaille beads and slip them along to the bend in the wire.

**2** Twist the wire around itself a few times at the bend in the wire under the beads, forming the first petal.

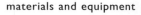

## materials and equipment

- 55cm/22in of 0.4mm silver wire
- 210 coral coloured pearlized rocaille beads
- 14 transparent 3mm/$^1$/$_8$in crystal beads
- wire cutters
- gift box
- bradawl
- co-ordinating paper
- spray adhesive
- silver cross sticker

**3** Thread on another 35 rocaille beads for the next petal. Twist the wire on itself as before. Make a total of six petals.

**4** Bring the long end of the wire up through the centre of the petals and thread on the crystal beads. Coil the beaded wire at the centre of the flower. Pull the end to the underside of the flower and twist the wire on itself a few times to secure.

**5** Pierce a hole in the lid of the box where you wish to place the flower. Insert the wire ends through the hole.

**6** To neaten the underside of the lid, cut a piece of paper slightly smaller than the lid and stick it in position using spray adhesive. Stick a silver cross sticker inside the box.

# Starting school gift tag

*Here is a great gift tag to tie on a good-luck present for someone who is about to start school. The colourful pencil can be used as a bookmark.*

## materials and equipment

- pen
- metal ruler
- beige laid card (stock)
- red paper
- cutting mat
- craft knife
- spray adhesive
- single hole punch
- 25cm/10in of 1cm/³/₈in-wide blue ribbon

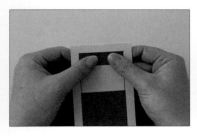

**1** Draw an 18 × 5cm/7 × 2in rectangle on beige card. From red paper, cut a 13.5 × 5cm/5¼ × 2in rectangle for the paint on the pencil and a 5 × 1.5cm/2 × ⅝in rectangle for the tip. Stick the papers on each end of the drawn rectangle using spray adhesive.

**2** Draw diagonal lines from the centre at the "tip" end of the rectangle to the corners of the "paint" to form the point of the pencil.

**3** Cut out the pencil shape using a craft knife and metal ruler and working on a cutting mat.

**4** Punch a hole with a single hole punch at one corner of the tag and tie a length of ribbon through the hole.

# Funky foam CD envelope

*The soft foam envelope of this design will protect its contents. It would be a great way to wrap a CD or a gift with hard but breakable edges. The envelope is designed to be reusable.*

### materials and equipment

- aquamarine Neoprene foam
- craft knife
- cutting mat
- masking tape
- black A4 sheet of Neoprene foam
- 2 metal eyelets
- eyelet tool
- tack hammer
- bradawl
- 60cm/24in of red plastic thonging
- scissors

**1** Cut a flower shape about 5.5cm/2¼in wide from aquamarine Neoprene foam using a craft knife and working on a cutting mat. Use masking tape to hold it in position at the centre of one short edge of a black A4 sheet of Neoprene foam.

**2** Insert a metal eyelet centrally through the flower and wallet and fit it using an eyelet tool and hammer. Remove the masking tape. Insert an eyelet in a matching position at the opposite edge of the sheet.

**3** Fold the wallet in half. Resting it on a cutting mat, pierce a row of holes 1cm/⅜in in from each side edge using a bradawl, starting 1cm/⅜in above the fold then piercing the holes 1.5cm/⅝in apart.

**4** Knot one end of the plastic thonging and lace it in and out of the holes. Tie a knot at the last hole and cut off the excess. Repeat on the other side. Insert the gift and tie the top with the remaining thonging.

# Handbag invitation

*This fun three-dimensional handbag is sure to be cherished. Unfold the bag to write an invitation on the underside, perhaps for a school friends' reunion.*

## materials and equipment

- pink snakeskin-effect paper
- deep pink card (stock)
- spray adhesive
- tracing paper
- pencil
- craft knife
- metal ruler
- cutting mat
- bone folder
- gold flower paper trim
- paper glue
- gold button
- glue dot

**1** Apply pink snakeskin effect paper to deep pink card using spray adhesive. Use the template at the back of the book to cut a handbag from the covered card, using a craft knife and metal ruler and working on a cutting mat.

**2** On the wrong side, score the handbag along the broken lines shown on the template, using a bone folder. Fold the handbag with the wrong sides facing, then open the handbag out flat again.

**3** On the right side of the bag, stick gold flower paper trim along the curved edge of the flap using paper glue.

**4** Stick a glittery gold button to the flap using a glue dot. Fold up the bag, tucking the flap through the handle.

**Tip**
Use stiff card for the base of this handbag so that it holds its shape once assembled. You could use it to add a small gift as well as an invitation.

# Portfolio congratulations card

*Send a message of congratulations on an exam pass with this portfolio greetings card. The vibrant crocodile skin-effect paper is strengthened with card and the corners and spine are bound with adhesive cloth tape.*

**1** Apply crocodile skin paper to green card using spray adhesive. From the card cut two rectangles each 21 x 13cm/8¼ x 5⅛in. On the right sides draw diagonal lines across the two outer corners, beginning 5cm/2in from each corner. Stick cloth tape diagonally across the corners, along the marked lines. Trim the tape level with the straight edges.

**2** Draw a line 1cm/⅜in in from the inner long edges on both sides of both pieces of card. To make the hinge, on the right side stick a length of cloth tape to one piece of card along the marked line, with 1cm/⅜in extending at the top and bottom. Stick the other long edge of the tape to the other card, along the marked line.

## materials and equipment

- green crocodile skin-effect paper
- green card (stock)
- spray adhesive
- craft knife
- metal ruler
- cutting mat
- black pen
- 5cm/2in-wide black cloth tape
- scissors
- 50cm/20in of 2.5cm/1in-wide black grosgrain ribbon
- 2.5cm/1in-wide double-sided tape

**3** On the inside, turn in the ends of the tape and stick down. Stick a 20cm/8in length of tape to the hinge, lining up the edges with the marked lines.

**4** Cut 2.5cm/1in slits 1cm/⅜in in from the long opening edges of the portfolio. Cut the ribbon in half and thread each length through a slit. Stick the ribbon ends inside the card with double-sided tape.

# Graduation accordion book

*An accordion book has plenty of room to write in and can be filled with messages at graduation time. Beautiful toile de jouy fabric is applied to the cover. The book is decorated with a golden rosette and fastens with ribbon.*

## materials and equipment

- white card (stock)
- craft knife
- metal ruler
- cutting mat
- toile de jouy fabric
- fabric scissors
- PVA (white) glue
- white paper
- bone folder
- 15cm/6in of 15mm/⁵/₈in-wide gold ribbon
- needle and thread
- 12mm/¹/₂in diameter gold jewellery stone
- glue dots
- 70cm/28in of 5mm/¹/₄in-wide gold ribbon
- hole punch and tack hammer

**1** For the back and front of the book, cut two 20 × 10.5cm/8 × 4¼in rectangles of white card using a craft knife and metal ruler and working on a cutting mat.

**2** Cut two 23 × 13.5cm/9¼ × 5½in rectangles of fabric. Place the fabric face down and place each cover on top. Turn in the corners of the fabric diagonally and stick them to the card using PVA glue, then fold in the edges and stick them in place.

**3** Cut a 60 × 19.5cm/24 × 7¾in rectangle of white paper for the pages. Score and fold the paper at 10cm/4in intervals, parallel with the short edges, using a bone folder.

**4** Spread PVA glue on one end page and stick one of the covers to it centrally. Stick the second cover on the other end page.

**5** Sew a running stitch along one edge of the 15mm/⁵/₈in-wide gold ribbon. Gather the ribbon tightly, overlapping the ends, and fasten off the thread securely.

**6** Stick a 12mm/¹/₂in diameter gold jewellery stone to the centre of the ribbon rosette with a glue dot.

**7** Fold a 12cm/4¾in length of narrow gold ribbon in half. Stick the fold with a glue dot behind the rosette and trim the ends diagonally. Stick the rosette to the front cover of the book with glue dots.

**8** Resting on a cutting mat, punch a 3mm/⅛in hole centrally in the right-hand edge of the front cover using a hole punch and tack hammer. Thread the remaining length of narrow gold ribbon through the hole and tie in a bow around the card.

# Driving test card

*Make a copy on a photocopier or computer of a photograph of a handsome old car for this card. It would be great to send to wish someone luck with their driving test or to congratulate them on passing.*

**1** Cut two 16 x 13cm/6½ x 5⅛in rectangles of grey card using a craft knife and metal ruler and working on a cutting mat. On the right side, score and fold one rectangle 2.5cm/1in from the short left edge, using a bone folder, to form the hinge. Open the rectangle out flat again. This will be the front of the card, and the other rectangle will be the back.

**2** Cut two 15.5 x 12cm/6 x 4⅝in rectangles of translucent white paper for the inserts. Assemble the card. Stack the inserts on the back, matching the short left edges. Place the front on top, with the folded edge on the left-hand side.

## materials and equipment

- dark grey card (stock)
- craft knife
- metal ruler
- cutting mat
- bone folder
- translucent white paper
- single hole punch
- 2 x 8mm/⁵/₁₆in black eyelets
- eyelet pliers
- photocopy or reprint of photograph of old car
- 4 black photo corners

**3** Punch holes in the hinge 2.5cm/1in in from the upper and lower edges, using a single hole punch. Insert a black eyelet in each hole using eyelet pliers.

**4** Slip a photo corner on to each corner of the photograph. Position the photograph on the card front. Moisten the photo corners and stick in place.

# New job wallet

*Coloured acetate is fun to use and gives very effective results. Use this smart wallet to give a present or card celebrating a new job. The wallet could then be used by the recipient to hold papers or receipts.*

**1** Fold an A4 sheet of turquoise acetate in half, parallel with the short edges, and crease the fold with a bone folder. Open the acetate out flat again.

**2** Cut two 8 × 3.5cm/3⅛ × 1⅜in diamond shapes of green acetate using a craft knife and metal ruler and working on a cutting mat. Resting on a sheet of white scrap paper so that you can see the shapes clearly, tape the diamonds centrally at each end of the turquoise acetate, 5mm/¼in from the edge, on the right side.

## materials and equipment

- A4 sheet of turquoise acetate
- bone folder
- green acetate
- craft knife
- metal ruler
- cutting mat
- white scrap paper
- masking tape
- 8 chrome diamond-shaped studs
- bradawl
- 35cm/14in of silver thonging

**3** Resting on scrap paper and a cutting mat, push a diamond-shaped stud into the centre of each acetate diamond. Remove the stud. Enlarge the holes made by the prongs with a bradawl. Replace the studs and push the prongs through both layers of acetate. Fold over the prongs to secure in place. Remove the masking tape.

**4** Fold the acetate in half. Resting on white scrap paper, position three studs, evenly spaced, down one side edge of the wallet. Push the prongs of the studs through the acetate and fold them over to secure. Repeat on the other side. Slip the contents inside. Fasten the wallet with thonging bound around the acetate diamonds.

# Painted pebbles leaving card

*This restful design of striped pebbles looks effective on lovely handmade paper but is simple to paint. Although the card is dark blue, an insert inside the card means that a message can be written on light coloured paper.*

## materials and equipment

- dark blue card (stock)
- craft knife
- metal ruler
- cutting mat
- bone folder
- mustard yellow handmade paper
- pencil
- medium and fine artist's paintbrushes
- acrylic paints in grey and off-white
- spray adhesive
- mottled yellow paper
- paper glue

**3** Draw three pebbles on the mustard paper panel with a pencil. Paint the pebbles with grey acrylic paint using a medium paintbrush. Leave to dry.

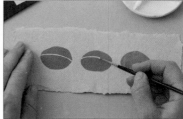

**4** Using a fine paintbrush, paint thin stripes across the pebbles with off-white paint. Stick the painting to the front of the card with spray adhesive. Cut a 20 × 17cm/7¾ × 6⅜in rectangle of mottled yellow paper and fold the paper in half parallel with the long edges. Run a line of paper glue along the fold and stick the insert inside the card, matching the folds.

**1** Cut a 21 × 18cm/8⅛ × 7in rectangle of dark blue card using a craft knife and metal ruler and working on a cutting mat. Score and fold the card across the centre, parallel with the long edges, using a bone folder.

**2** Lightly draw a 19.5 × 7.5cm/7½ × 3in rectangle on mustard yellow handmade paper. Moisten the outline with a medium artist's paintbrush and tear the paper along the line against a ruler.

# Chinese-stamped gift box

*The textured paper cover of this smart gift box gives it an Oriental feel, so it has been decorated with a stamped and embossed bamboo motif. A pair of chopsticks tucked into the tape binding completes the theme.*

## materials and equipment

- pale grey and black paper
- craft knife
- metal ruler
- cutting mat
- rubber stamp with bamboo design, measuring about 6.5 x 3cm/2¹/₂ x 1¹/₄in
- black ink pad
- scrap paper
- embossing powder
- embossing gun or other heat source, such as a toaster
- spray adhesive
- metallic copper and aluminium paper
- white gift box
- 2 chopsticks
- 5mm/¹/₄in double-sided tape
- black imitation suede tape

**1** Cut a 7.5 x 4cm/3 x 1¾in rectangle of pale grey paper. Press the rubber stamp on the ink pad. Stamp the motif centrally on the pale grey rectangle.

**2** Resting the motif on scrap paper, sprinkle embossing powder on the ink. Shake off the excess. Heat the image until the powder melts. Stick the panel on black paper using spray adhesive and trim to leave a 2mm/¹/₁₆in border around the grey paper.

**3** Cut a 3cm/1¼in-wide strip of metallic copper and aluminium paper. Position the strip 2cm/¾in in from one edge of the lid and stick the ends of the strip under the lid rim using double-sided tape. Stick the motif to the strip using spray adhesive.

**4** Stick two chopsticks to the lid with a few small pieces of 5mm/¼in-wide double-sided tape. Place the present in the gift box. Tie the box with two lengths of black imitation suede tape and stick the ends under the box using double-sided tape.

# Beaded engagement card

*The fabulous colours of the gift wrap chosen to cover this card determined the bright colours of the beads used. The shiny glass and metallic beads threaded on glossy gold thread are ideal for a celebratory engagement card.*

## materials and equipment

- green and turquoise gift wrap
- deep turquoise and white card (stock)
- spray adhesive
- craft knife
- metal ruler
- cutting mat
- bone folder
- pen
- crewel embroidery needle
- gold embroidery thread (floss)
- turquoise and lime green beads
- embroidery scissors
- 5mm/¼in-wide double-sided tape

**3** Apply a total of four threads threaded with beads across the square of card, arranging them at slight angles. Knot the thread securely on the underside.

**1** Apply gift wrap to deep turquoise card using spray adhesive. Cut a 34 x 18cm/13½ x 7in rectangle of the covered card. On the wrong side, score and fold the card 11cm/4¼in from the left short edge and 11.5cm/4½in from the right short edge. Open the card out flat. Draw a 5.5cm/2⅛in square centrally on the middle section, 3cm/1¼in down from the top. Cut out the square.

**2** Cut a 7.5cm/3in square of white card. Thread a crewel embroidery needle with gold embroidery thread and knot the end. Starting 5mm/¼in in from one side edge and about 2cm/¾in from the top, bring the thread to the right side of the card square. Thread on 9–10 assorted beads. Lay the thread diagonally across the card. Push the needle back through the card, 5mm/¼in in from the opposite side edge.

**4** Apply double-sided tape around the window on the wrong side of the card. Peel off the backing strips and stick the beaded square behind the window. Fold in the facing and secure with double-sided tape.

# Floral engagement card

*Here is a sophisticated and romantic card to celebrate an engagement. A pressed rosebud is wrapped with delicate Japanese paper and set off with lovely paper containing metallic decorations.*

## materials and equipment

- rosebud
- blotting paper
- flower press or heavy book
- beige paper with metallic fragments
- cream card (stock)
- spray adhesive
- craft knife
- metal ruler
- cutting mat
- PVA (white) glue
- white lightweight Japanese grid paper
- brown paper printed with silver glitter
- bone folder

**1** Press a rosebud between sheets of blotting paper in a flower press or within the pages of a heavy book for about 10 days. Apply beige paper with metallic fragments to cream card using spray adhesive. Cut out a 5 × 10cm/2 × 4in rectangle of the covered card using a craft knife and metal ruler and working on a cutting mat. Stick the rosebud centrally to the card using PVA glue.

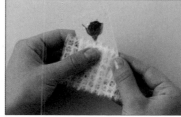

**2** Tear an 8 × 5cm/3¼ × 2in rectangle of Japanese grid paper between your fingers. Wrap the paper diagonally across the stem of the bud, folding the excess to the back of the card. Stick the ends to the back of the card using PVA glue.

**3** Apply brown paper printed with silver glitter to cream card using spray adhesive. Cut a 20cm/8in square of the covered card. On the wrong side, score and fold the card across the centre using a bone folder.

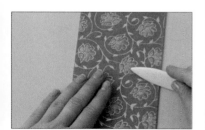

**4** Stick the wrapped rosebud panel to the card front, 2cm/¾in in from the folded edge and down from the upper edge, using spray adhesive.

# Slotted butterfly gift box

*Give a small engagement present in this pretty gift box. The box can be reused, as the butterfly on the top is in two halves that slot together. Accurate cutting and folding will ensure that the box is symmetrical once assembled. A few diamanté stickers decorate the wings of the butterfly.*

**1** Trace the template at the back of the book and transfer it to lavender card. Cut out the box using a craft knife and metal ruler, working on a cutting mat.

**2** Score the card along the broken lines using a bone folder. Rub away the pencil lines with a pencil eraser. Fold the box along the scored lines then open it out flat again.

## materials and equipment

- tracing paper
- pencil
- lavender card (stock)
- craft knife
- metal ruler
- cutting mat
- bone folder
- pencil eraser
- 1.5cm/⅝in-wide double-sided tape
- blue diamanté triangular stickers

**3** Apply double-sided tape to the end and base tabs on the right side. Stick the end tab inside the opposite end of the box.

**4** Fold in the base tabs. Fold down the base and press the edges firmly on to the tabs to secure it.

**5** Tuck the upper side tabs inside the box. Slot the two halves of the butterfly together to fasten the box.

**6** Stick blue diamanté triangular stickers on the tips of the wings. To place the stickers accurately, pick them up on the tip of a craft knife blade. Position them using the blade then remove it and press them firmly into place.

# Wedding cake card

*A special occasion deserves a special card. This exquisite yet elegantly understated card fits the bill when a wedding is being celebrated.*

## materials and equipment

- white ridged card (stock)
- craft knife
- metal ruler
- cutting mat
- bone folder
- pale yellow paper embedded with metal fragments
- spray adhesive
- gold glitter paint
- fine artist's paintbrush
- 6 tiny diamantés
- tweezers
- 10cm/4in of fine gold cord
- embroidery scissors
- glue dots
- tiny gold heart-shaped sticker
- masking tape
- 3mm/1/8in hole punch
- tack hammer
- 45cm/18in length of 3mm/1/8in-wide gold ribbon

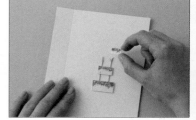

**3** Cut the fine cord in half. Arrange the cords 1.2cm/1/2in apart in the centre of the card front to form the cake columns. Stick the ends in place with glue dots. Stick the tiers on top with glue dots. Stick a gold heart-shaped sticker above the top tier.

**4** Tape the front of the card to the back with masking tape, matching the left-hand edges. Resting on a cutting mat, punch a hole at the centre of the hinge using a 3mm/1/8in hole punch and tack hammer, then punch two more holes 4.5cm/1¾in above and below the centre. Cut the gold ribbon into three. Thread each length through a hole and tie in a knot around the hinge. Remove the masking tape.

**1** Cut two 18 x 13.5cm/7 x 5¼in rectangles of ridged white card using a craft knife and metal ruler and working on a cutting mat. Score and fold one rectangle 2.5cm/1in in from the long left edge to make a hinge. This will be the front of the card. Apply pale yellow paper embedded with metal fragments to a small piece of white card using spray adhesive.

**2** Cut one 1.5 x 1cm/5/8 x 3/8in, one 2 x 1.2cm/3/4 x 1/2in and one 3 x 1.5cm/1¼ x 5/8in rectangle of the covered card for the cake tiers. Apply gold glitter paint along the upper edge of the smallest tier. Use a paintbrush to brush the glitter downwards. Place a tiny diamanté on the glitter using tweezers. Repeat to decorate the other tiers. Set aside to dry.

# Vintage charm card

*Search your needlework box for pretty scraps of fabric and ribbon to make this charming wedding card. A trio of jewellery charms hang from the card front.*

## materials and equipment

- light green card (stock)
- craft knife
- metal ruler
- cutting mat
- bone folder
- scrap of vintage fabric
- pinking shears
- spray adhesive
- 3 charms
- 1 x 8mm/$^5$/₁₆in jump ring
- 10cm/4in of 5mm/¼in-wide olive green ribbon
- fabric scissors
- glue dots

**1** Cut a 23 x 15cm/9 x 6in rectangle of light green card using a craft knife and metal ruler and working on a cutting mat. Score and fold the card across the centre, parallel with the short edges, using a bone folder.

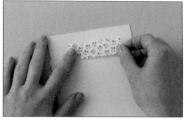

**2** Cut a 7.5 x 2.5cm/3 x 1in rectangle of fabric using pinking shears. Stick to the card front using spray adhesive, 2cm/¾in from the upper and left edges.

**3** Thread three charms on to a jump ring and close the ring.

**4** Tie a 10cm/4in length of 5mm/¼in-wide olive green ribbon through the ring. Cut the ends diagonally. Stick the knot of the ribbon to the fabric strip with a glue dot.

# Silver wedding anniversary card

*Handmade paper embedded with delicate petals creates a pretty background for pressed larkspur flowers, which are applied to silvered squares on this lovely silver wedding anniversary card.*

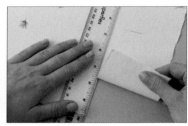

## materials and equipment

- 3 larkspur flowers
- blotting paper
- flower press or heavy book
- handmade paper with embedded petals
- ruler
- bone folder
- pencil
- flat paintbrush
- 15-minute gold size
- scissors
- sheet of aluminium Dutch metal transfer leaf
- soft brush
- PVA (white) glue
- tweezers

**1** Press three flowers between sheets of blotting paper in a flower press or within the pages of a heavy book. Set aside for about 10 days.

**2** Tear a 20cm/8in square of handmade paper by tearing against a ruler. Score and fold the paper across the centre, parallel with the short edges, using a bone folder.

**3** Lightly draw a line of three 3cm/1¼in squares down the card front with a pencil, starting 3cm/1¼in down from the upper edge and spacing them 2cm/¾in apart. With a flat paintbrush, apply gold size within the outlines. Set aside for 15 minutes until the size has become tacky.

**4** Cut a piece of aluminium transfer leaf slightly larger than the group of squares. Lay the aluminium leaf face down on the squares and gently press in place.

### Tip

Pressed flowers, in perfect condition, can be purchased from craft supply stores if time is short.

Flowers can also be pressed using a microwave, which speeds up the drying process. Use tweezers to handle small, delicate flowers in order to avoid damaging the petals.

**5** Peel off the backing paper. Sweep away the excess aluminium leaf using a soft brush. If the aluminium leaf has not adhered to the size in places, press a piece of the left-over leaf in place.

**6** Stick a pressed flower over the lower left corner of each square with PVA glue, positioning the flowers with tweezers.

# Silver wedding gift tag

*This exquisite gift tag is sure to become a treasured memento of a special day. The number 25 is outlined with tiny jewels on acetate.*

## materials and equipment

- tracing paper
- pencil
- clear acetate
- craft knife
- metal ruler
- cutting mat
- turquoise pearlized card (stock)
- 2mm/¹⁄₁₆in hole punch
- tack hammer
- masking tape
- silver jewellery stone star stickers
- 25cm/10in length of silver embroidery thread (floss)

**Tip**
Instead of buying a sheet of acetate, you could use a piece of stiff clear plastic packaging to make the gift tag.

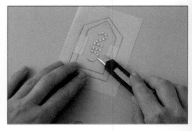

**3** Tape the acetate tag on the template. Stick jewellery stone star stickers along the outlines of the numerals, cutting between the stars on the backing paper with a craft knife. Use the craft knife to lift and position the stickers before pressing them down firmly with your finger.

**1** Trace the tag at the back of the book and use it to cut a small gift tag from clear acetate and a large gift tag from turquoise pearlized card, using a craft knife and metal ruler and working on a cutting mat.

**2** Resting both tags together on a cutting mat, punch a hole through both layers at the dot using a 2mm/¹⁄₁₆in hole punch and a tack hammer.

**4** Place the acetate gift tag on the card gift tag, matching the holes. Tie silver embroidery thread through the holes.

# Pearl wedding anniversary gift trim

*This three-dimensional flower with its pearl centre and hanging loops of pearly beads is the ideal trimming for a present given for a pearl wedding anniversary, celebrated after thirty years of marriage.*

**materials and equipment**

- tracing paper
- pencil
- white pearlized paper
- craft knife
- cutting mat
- glue dots
- 8mm/$^5/_{16}$in pearl bead
- 60cm/24in string of small pearl beads
- clear adhesive tape

**I** Trace the flower template at the back of the book and transfer the outlines of the large and small flowers to white pearlized paper. Cut out the two flowers using a craft knife and working on a cutting mat. Overlap the end petals of each flower and stick in place with glue dots.

**2** Stick the small flower on top of the large flower, arranging the small petals between the large ones, using a glue dot at the centre. Stick a pearl bead at the centre of the flower using another glue dot.

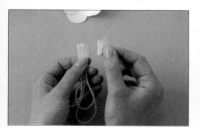

**3** Bend a 60cm/24in string of pearl beads into three loops of different sizes. Hold the loops together at one end and bind with clear adhesive tape.

**4** Stick the bound end of the loops to a wrapped present with glue dots. Stick the flower on top with glue dots.

**Tip**
This flower trim has a timeless quality. Experiment with different paper textures, patterns and colours.

# Pearl wedding anniversary card

*Three mother-of-pearl buttons subtly mark a pearl wedding celebration on this pretty card. This is a great project for a beginner.*

**materials and equipment**

- cream teardrop punched paper
- gold card (stock)
- spray adhesive
- craft knife
- metal ruler
- cutting mat
- bone folder
- pale blue patterned gift wrap
- 3 mother-of-pearl heart-shaped buttons
- glue dots

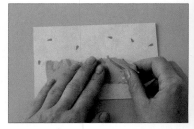

**3** Stick the torn paper to the card front using spray adhesive.

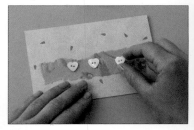

**4** Stick three mother-of-pearl heart-shaped buttons in a row to the torn paper panel using glue dots.

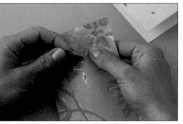

**1** Apply cream teardrop-punched paper to gold card with spray adhesive. (You could create your own punched paper using a hole punch.) Cut a 20 x 15cm/8 x 6in rectangle of the covered card using a craft knife and metal ruler and working on a cutting mat. Score and fold the card across the centre, parallel with the short edges, using a bone folder.

**2** Roughly tear an 11 x 3cm/4¼ x 1¼in rectangle of pale blue patterned gift wrap between your fingers.

# Ruby wedding anniversary card

*This lovely posy contains tiny flowers cut from coloured felts in shades of red, making it a great card to mark a ruby wedding anniversary.*

**materials and equipment**

- pale pink card (stock)
- craft knife
- metal ruler
- cutting mat
- bone folder
- tracing paper
- pencil
- scraps of red, maroon, dark purple and green felt
- fabric scissors
- tweezers
- round and flower-shaped sequins
- glue dots
- red relief paint
- 25cm/10in of 15mm/⅝in maroon organza ribbon

**1** Cut a 17 x 10.5cm/6¾ x 4¼in rectangle of pale pink card using a craft knife and metal ruler and working on a cutting mat. Score and fold the card across the centre, parallel with the short edges, using a bone folder.

**2** Use the templates at the back of the book to cut out a total of eight flowers and circles from red, maroon and dark purple felt. Cut four leaves from green felt. Arrange the flowers and leaves in a circular group on the card front, interspersed with round and flower-shaped sequins. Use tweezers to nudge the pieces into place.

**3** Stick the flowers, leaves and sequins to the card front with glue dots. Stick small round sequins on a few of the flower centres with glue dots, using tweezers.

**4** Dot red relief paint on a few flower centres and at random around the posy. Tie the ribbon in a bow and trim the ends diagonally with scissors. Stick the bow under the posy with a glue dot.

# Golden wedding anniversary card

*Luxurious creamy handmade paper is gilded with a pair of flamboyant hearts and tied with a dramatic ribbon on this super golden wedding card.*

## materials and equipment

- cream handmade paper
- ruler
- bone folder
- tracing paper and pencil
- flat paintbrush
- 15-minute gold size
- scissors
- sheet of gold Dutch metal transfer leaf
- soft brush
- double hole punch
- 80cm/32in of 4cm/1½in-wide gold organza ribbon
- fabric scissors

**1** Tear two 16 x 14cm/6¼ x 5½in rectangles of handmade paper by tearing the paper against a ruler.

**2** Score and fold one rectangle, which will be the front of the card, 2.5cm/1in in from the long left edge, using a bone folder, to make a hinge. The other rectangle will be the card back.

**3** Using the template at the back of the book, lightly draw two hearts at angles on the card front with a pencil. With a flat paintbrush, apply gold size to the hearts. Set aside for 15 minutes until the size has become tacky.

**4** Cut a piece of transfer gold leaf slightly larger than the pair of hearts. Lay the gold leaf face down on the hearts and gently press in place.

**5** Peel off the backing paper. Sweep away the excess gold leaf with a soft brush. If the gold leaf has not adhered in places, press a piece of the left-over leaf in the gaps.

**6** Lay the card front on the back. Punch a pair of holes centrally in the hinge using a double hole punch.

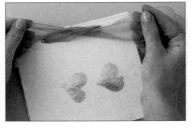

**7** Thread the ribbon through the holes and tie in a bow at the front of the hinge. Cut the ribbon ends diagonally.

# Golden wedding card

*Against a background of cream and gold paper, a frayed silk square displays a golden metal heart-shaped plaque. Tiny jewels are a delicate finishing touch.*

## materials and equipment

- turquoise pearlized card (stock)
- craft knife
- metal ruler
- cutting mat
- bone folder
- cream and gold printed paper
- medium artist's paintbrush
- spray adhesive
- scrap of turquoise silk dupion
- fabric scissors
- 2.5cm/1in-wide double-sided tape
- gold heart plaque
- glue dots
- 3 tiny light blue jewellery stone heart stickers

**1** Cut a 23 x 16cm/9 x 6¼in rectangle of turquoise pearlized card using a craft knife and metal ruler and working on a cutting mat. Score and fold the card across the centre, parallel with the short edges, using a bone folder.

**2** Moisten the outline of a 13.5 x 9cm/5¼ x 3½in rectangle on a piece of cream and gold printed paper using a medium artist's paintbrush. Tear the paper along the moistened lines. Stick the paper centrally to the card front using spray adhesive.

**3** Cut a 5.5cm/2¼in square of turquoise silk dupion, cutting the edges along the grain of the fabric. Fray the edges for 1cm/⅜in. Stick a 3cm/1¼in length of 2.5cm/1in-wide double-sided tape to the back of the silk. Stick the silk to the front of the card 2.5cm/1in below the upper edge.

**4** Stick a gold heart plaque to the silk square with glue dots. Stick three tiny light blue jewellery stone stickers in a row below the silk square, using the tip of a craft knife blade to lift and position the stickers.

# Housewarming in style card

*A trio of 50s-style cocktail glasses suggest fun times ahead on this housewarming card. The glasses are cut from translucent papers and accompanied by colourful metallic plastic discs.*

### materials and equipment

- lime green card (stock)
- craft knife
- metal ruler
- cutting mat
- bone folder
- 5 assorted blue, silver and pink 12mm/¹/₂in diameter metallic plastic circles
- glue dots
- tracing paper
- pencil
- turquoise, pink and mauve translucent paper
- white scrap paper
- spray adhesive

**1** Cut a 20 x 18cm/8 x 7in rectangle of lime green card. Score and fold the card across the centre, parallel with the short edges, using a bone folder.

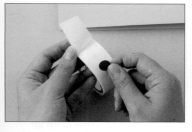

**2** Stick five assorted blue, silver and pink metallic plastic circles along the left edge of the card front using glue dots.

**3** Trace the cocktail glass templates at the back of the book and transfer to turquoise, pink and mauve translucent paper Resting on white scrap paper (so that you can see the outlines clearly) on a cutting mat, cut out the glasses using a craft knife.

**4** Arrange the glasses on the card front. Stick them in place using spray adhesive.

# Key charm new home card

*This rustic key charm is a super motif for a new home card. The key is tied to a ready-made luggage label and hangs in front of a band of striped gift wrap.*

**materials and equipment**

- copper-coloured card (stock)
- craft knife
- metal ruler
- cutting mat
- bone folder
- striped gift wrap
- spray adhesive
- luggage label
- purple hemp string
- key charm
- 5mm/¹/₄in hole punch
- tack hammer
- scissors
- cream paper
- paper glue

**1** Cut a 22 × 15cm/8½ × 6in rectangle of copper card using a craft knife and metal ruler and working on a cutting mat. Score and fold the card across the centre, parallel with the short edges, using a bone folder.

**2** Cut an 11 × 6.5cm/4¼ × 2½in rectangle of striped gift wrap. Stick the gift wrap across the card front, 5cm/2in below the upper edge, using spray adhesive.

**3** Discard the string on the luggage label. Slip a length of purple hemp string through the key and the label. Open the card out flat and punch a 5mm/¼in hole centrally 1cm/⅜in below the upper edge of the front.

**4** Insert the string through the hole and knot the ends so the label and key hang in the centre of the front. Cut off the excess string. Cut a 21 × 14cm/8 × 5½in rectangle of cream paper and fold it in half. Run a line of paper glue along the fold and stick the insert inside the card, matching the folds.

# Coffee break retirement card

*This card evokes a relaxing chat between friends over mugs of coffee and would be a charming theme for a card marking a well-deserved retirement.*

## materials and equipment

- tracing paper
- pencil
- light blue translucent paper
- broad grey felt-tipped pen
- white and blue star-printed paper
- black relief paint
- craft knife
- cutting mat
- pale orange card (stock)
- metal ruler
- bone folder
- blue and white gingham gift wrap
- spray adhesive

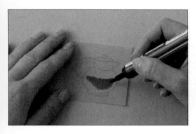

**1** Use the template at the back of the book to draw the solid lines of the percolator on light blue translucent paper with a pencil. Turn the paper over and colour the "coffee" with a grey felt-tipped pen. Leave to dry then turn the percolator to the right side.

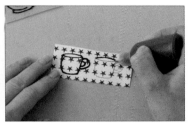

**2** Use the template to draw two mugs on white and blue star-printed paper with a pencil. Redraw the outlines of the percolator and mugs with black relief paint. Set aside to dry, then cut out the pieces, outside the black lines, using a craft knife.

**3** Cut out a 21 × 16cm/8½ × 6¼in rectangle of pale orange card (stock) using a craft knife and metal ruler and working on a cutting mat. Score and fold the card across the centre, parallel with the short edges, using a bone folder.

**4** Cut a 16 × 3cm/6¼ × 1¼in strip of gingham gift wrap. Stick the strip to the lower edge of the card front using spray adhesive. Stick the percolator and mugs to the front using spray adhesive.

# Embossed fish retirement card

*You could send this graphic card to a keen angler to celebrate their retirement. The bold fish is fun to make from fine embossing metal.*

## materials and equipment

- white corrugated card (stock)
- craft knife and metal ruler
- cutting mat
- bone folder
- tracing paper and pencil
- masking tape
- aluminium embossing metal
- embossing tool or spent ballpoint pen
- kitchen paper
- old pair of scissors
- blue spotted paper
- all-purpose household glue
- spray adhesive

**1** Cut a 17 × 15cm/6⅝ × 6in rectangle of white corrugated card, with the short edges parallel with the corrugations, using a craft knife and metal ruler and working on a cutting mat. Score and fold the card across the centre, parallel with the short edges, using a bone folder.

**2** Trace the fish template at the back of the book and lightly tape the tracing face down on a piece of fine aluminium embossing metal. Draw the details and around the outline with a sharp pencil, using the tracing lines, pressing firmly to make an indentation. Remove the template.

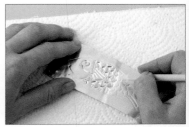

**3** Cut a 5.5cm/2¼in square of metal using old scissors. Place the square and the fish, right side down, on two sheets of kitchen paper. Use an embossing tool or ballpoint pen to emboss the details on the fish and dot the square at random. Cut out the fish.

**4** Cut a 12 × 5.5cm/4¾ × 2¼in rectangle of blue spotted paper. Arrange the metal square on the card front, overlapped by the blue paper, 5mm/¼in in from the edges of the card front. Stick the metal square with all-purpose household glue and the spotted paper with spray adhesive. Stick the fish on the spotted paper with all-purpose glue.

# Watercolour stamped retirement card

*Use a rubber stamp with a peaceful design to make this retirement card. The motif is printed with watercolour stamp paints, which can be subtly blended together on the stamp before it is applied to the paper.*

## materials and equipment

- watercolour paper
- ruler
- medium artist's paintbrush
- bone folder
- 7.5cm/3in square rubber stamp of a peaceful scene
- purple and green watercolour stamp paints
- scrap paper

**1** Tear a 22 × 14cm/8⅞ × 5½in rectangle of watercolour paper, first drawing a moistened paintbrush along the intended tear lines to weaken them, then tearing against a ruler. Score and fold the card 10.5cm/4¼in from one short edge, parallel with the short edges, using a bone folder.

**2** Paint the stamp with purple and green watercolour stamp paints, using a medium artist's paintbrush and blending the colours together on the stamp.

**3** Stamp the image on the front of the card, which is the narrower section. Make a firm impression. Leave to dry.

**4** Open the card. Resting on scrap paper, moisten the right edge of the lower section. Pick up some green watercolour paint on a moistened paintbrush and run it along the wet edge. Set aside to dry.

# Heartfelt sentiments

Sometimes it's good just to send a card to say "hello" and catch up with friends and relatives or convey snippets of news. Telephones and emails have largely superseded the sending of handwritten notes, but it is worth taking the trouble to remedy that, as receiving them is always a joy.

This chapter has cards to make for special friends, to say good luck or best wishes, to wish a loved one good health and send condolences for life's sad occasions too.

# 1950s-style spotted and striped postcards

*It is so simple to make these retro-style postcards that you will be able to produce a whole set very quickly. Use them to send quick heartfelt notes to friends and family, who will instantly recognize another message from you in their mail.*

**1** To make the black postcards, cut 15 × 10cm/6 × 4in rectangles of black card using a craft knife and metal ruler and working on a cutting mat.

**2** Cut a 14 × 9cm/5½ × 3½in rectangle of white paper for each black postcard. Stick the white paper rectangles centrally to the back of the black cards to provide a surface light enough to write a message on.

## materials and equipment

- black card (stock)
- craft knife
- metal ruler
- cutting mat
- white paper
- spray adhesive
- white and black relief paint
- plain white postcards
- scrap paper
- fine artist's paintbrush

**3** Decorate the black postcards with white relief paint and the white postcards with black relief paint. Applying spots of various sizes at random over the surface is one of the simplest methods of decoration.

**4** Resting on scrap paper, draw stripes across the postcards, angling them slightly and extending them a little beyond the edge of the card so that they do not stop short of the edge.

**5** To make the shorter stripes, draw irregular short lines on the postcards, staggering their spacing.

**6** Draw out the ends of the painted lines using a fine paintbrush. Leave all the postcards to dry.

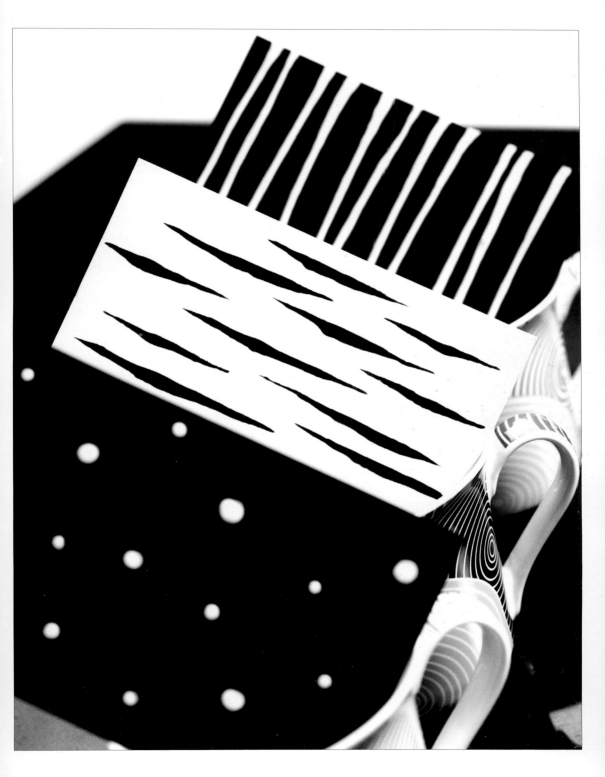

# Swedish felt motif card

*Send a "thinking of you" message with this tactile felt motif card. The angular shape of the design is inspired by traditional Swedish cross-stitch pictures.*

**materials and equipment**

- red card (stock)
- craft knife and metal ruler
- cutting mat
- bone folder
- tracing paper
- black pen
- 11cm/4¹/₄in square of iron-on interfacing
- masking tape
- pencil
- white paper
- scissors
- red and fawn felt
- iron
- spray adhesive
- pinking shears
- fawn textured paper
- paper glue

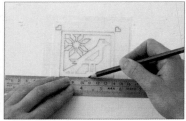

**1** Cut a 25 x 12.5cm/10 x 5in rectangle of red card using a craft knife and metal ruler and working on a cutting mat. Score and fold the card across the centre, parallel with the short edges, using a bone folder.

**2** Trace the template at the back of the book with a black pen. Tape a piece of iron-on interfacing, shiny side down, to the wrong side of the tracing using masking tape. Trace the motif on to the interfacing with a pencil, working on a sheet of white paper so that the image shows clearly.

**3** Cut out the pieces roughly, leaving a margin all round. Iron the motif on to red felt and cut out the pieces. Cut a 9.5cm/3¾in square of fawn felt with pinking shears. Stick this square to the card front then stick the motif on top using spray adhesive. Cut a 24 x 11.5cm/9½ x 4½in rectangle of fawn textured paper with pinking shears and fold it in half. Run a line of paper glue along the fold and stick the insert inside the card.

# Bleached letterheads

*Household bleach lightens coloured papers and card and can be used to create very effective decoration for a friend when applied with a brush. This ethnic stationery with its distinctive African designs demonstrates the technique well.*

### materials and equipment

- household bleach
- non-metallic container
- fine artist's paintbrush
- brown and beige handmade writing paper and envelopes
- ruler
- spray adhesive

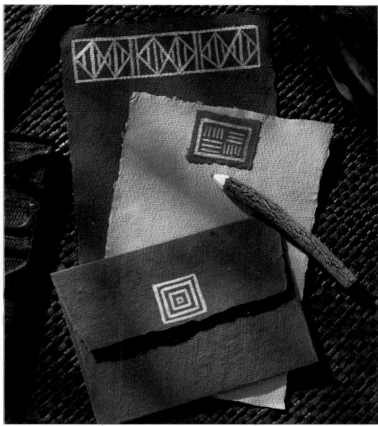

**1** Pour some household bleach into a non-metallic container. Dip a fine artist's paintbrush into the bleach and use it to paint the outline of a rectangle across the top of a sheet of brown handmade writing paper. Divide the rectangle into thirds with pairs of lines. The more thickly the bleach is applied, the lighter the colour will be.

**2** Using bleach, paint the outlines of two diamond shapes within each of the three sections. Paint vertical stripes in the diamonds to complete the letterhead.

**Tip**
When using household bleach, work in a ventilated area, keep away from the reach of children and wash your hands after use.

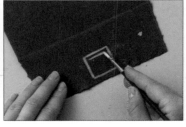

**3** Using a fine paintbrush dipped in bleach, paint the outline of a rectangle on the flap of a matching envelope. Paint a simple design within the rectangle.

**4** To decorate the beige writing paper, tear a 4.5 x 4cm/1¾ x 1½in rectangle of brown writing paper by first moistening the intended tear lines with a paintbrush then tearing along them against a ruler. Paint a design in bleach on the rectangle then stick it to the writing paper using spray adhesive.

# Lion friendship card

*There are lots of interesting textures on this card, which is suitable for many occasions, or simply for keeping in touch with a friend.*

## materials and equipment

- black and blue handmade paper
- medium artist's paintbrush
- ruler and bone folder
- fabric scissors
- scrap of natural linen
- spray adhesive
- cutting mat
- brass lion charm
- bradawl
- fine hemp string
- double-sided tape
- beige paper
- craft knife and metal ruler
- paper glue

**1** Tear a 23 × 16cm/9 × 6¼in rectangle of black handmade paper, moistening the outline with a paintbrush first, then tearing the paper against a ruler. Score and fold the card across the centre, parallel with the short edges, using a bone folder.

**2** Cut a 14 × 9cm/5½ × 3½in rectangle of natural linen, cutting the edges along the grain of the fabric. Fray the edges for 1cm/⅜in. Tear an 11 × 6cm/4¼ × 2¼in rectangle of blue handmade paper against a ruler, moistening the outlines first.

**3** Stick the blue rectangle centrally to the frayed linen rectangle using spray adhesive. Resting on a cutting mat, hold the lion charm centrally on the blue rectangle. Pierce a hole through the card under the hole on the charm and another hole 8mm/⁵⁄₁₆in above the first, using a bradawl.

**4** Thread fine hemp string through the two holes and tie on the charm. Trim the ends of the string. Stick the linen to the front of the card using double-sided tape. Cut a 22 × 15cm/8½ × 5¾in rectangle of beige paper and fold it in half. Run a line of paper glue along the fold and stick it inside the card.

# Flower garland gift trim

*This beautiful gift wrapping idea is very simple to achieve and ideal for a grandmother's birthday. The smaller flowers form a spray of silk delphiniums, threaded on to fine ribbon to form a garland across the top of a wrapped gift.*

### materials and equipment

- spray of silk delphinium flowers
- 3mm/¹/₈in-wide blue ribbon
- 2 x 6mm/¹/₄in lilac beads
- large-eyed needle
- fabric scissors

**1** Dismantle the silk delphiniums and select the flowers that suit the size of the wrapped present. Set aside the larger flowers for other craft projects.

**2** Thread about four flowers on to a length of narrow blue ribbon long enough to tie around the gift.

**3** Bind the ribbon around the wrapped gift and tie the ribbon ends together in a bow. Adjust the threaded flowers so that they lie in a line on the front of the gift.

**4** Thread one small flower on to each end of the ribbon. Thread one ribbon end on to a large-eyed needle and thread on a 5mm/¹/₄in bead. Knot the ribbon under the bead and trim the end below the knot. Repeat on the other ribbon end.

# Pressed flowers friendship card

*Assemble pressed flowers, leaves and scraps of sequin strings and ribbon to make a charming card for a special friend. Pressed flowers are available from craft suppliers if you do not have time to press your own: dyed pressed flowers will add extra splashes of vibrant colour to this eclectic design.*

## materials and equipment

- assorted flowers and small leaves
- blotting paper
- flower press or heavy book
- light blue A5 handmade paper
- bone folder
- sequin strings in assorted colours
- 15mm/⅝in-wide pink organza ribbon
- fabric scissors
- PVA (white) glue
- cocktail stick (toothpick)
- ruler
- double-sided tape

**1** Press a selection of flowers and leaves between sheets of blotting paper in a flower press or within the pages of a heavy book. Set aside for about 10 days. Once pressed, choose the best colours for your card, and discard any that have discoloured or are in poor condition.

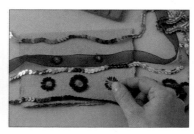

**2** Fold an A5 sheet of light blue handmade paper in half, parallel with the short edges, and rub over the fold with a bone folder. Arrange strings of sequins, a length of 15mm/⅝in-wide pink organza ribbon and the pressed flowers and leaves in bands across the front of the card.

**3** To stop the sequin strings unravelling, cut the strings approximately 4cm/1½in longer than the width of the card front. Pull a few sequins off each end. Stick the string under the last few sequins using PVA glue, applied with a cocktail stick.

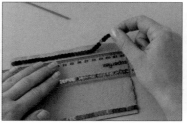

**4** Lay a ruler across the card front as a guide to help you. stick each sequin string in a straight line. Stick the sequin strings to the card front using PVA glue.

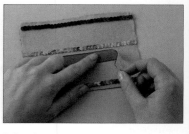

**5** Cut the organza ribbon 2cm/¾in longer than the width of the card front. Stick double-sided tape to the ribbon. Peel off the backing strip and stick the ribbon across the card front.

**6** Cut the ribbon ends level with the card edges using scissors.

**7** Stick the flowers and leaves to the card using PVA glue applied with a cocktail stick.

# Button friendship card

*Here is a charming card to send to a friend. The colourful buttons will
particularly appeal if the friend is a keen needleworker.*

materials and equipment

• cream laid card (stock)
• craft knife
• metal ruler
• cutting mat
• bone folder
• light green handmade paper
• spray adhesive
• 4 blue, red and yellow
  buttons, including
  flower shapes
• glue dots
• bradawl
• green stranded embroidery
  thread (floss)
• crewel embroidery needle
• embroidery scissors
• 5mm/¹⁄₄in-wide
  double-sided tape

I Cut a 29.5 x 14cm/11¾ x 5½in rectangle
of cream laid card using a craft knife and
metal ruler and working on a cutting mat.
On the wrong side, score and fold the card
parallel with the short edges, 9.5cm/3¾in
from the left edge and 10cm/4in from the
right edge.

2 Tear an 8 x 3cm/3¼ x 1¼in rectangle of
green handmade paper between your
fingers. Stick the torn paper to the middle
section (which will be the front of the card)
using spray adhesive.

3 Arrange the buttons on the card front
then stick them in place with glue dots.
Open the card out flat on a cutting mat.
Use a bradawl to pierce holes in the card
front at the ends of the intended stems.

4 Stitch the stems with single stitches
through the pierced holes using green
stranded embroidery thread and a crewel
embroidery needle. Stick the facing inside
the front using double-sided tape.

# Lace best wishes card

*Here is a great way to use up small scraps of pretty white edging lace in assorted designs. The lace is beautifully set off by the lovely choice of handmade and marbled papers used for the background.*

### materials and equipment

- silver marbled paper
- grey card (stock)
- spray adhesive
- craft knife
- metal ruler
- cutting mat
- bone folder
- grey handmade paper
- scraps of edging lace
- fabric scissors

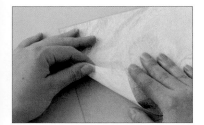

**1** Apply silver marbled paper to grey card using spray adhesive. Allow to dry. Cut a 28 × 14cm/11 × 5½in rectangle of the covered card using a craft knife and metal ruler and working on a cutting mat. Score and fold the card across the centre, parallel with the short edges, using a bone folder.

**2** Tear a 22 × 7.5cm/8⅝ × 3in rectangle of grey handmade paper by tearing the paper against a ruler. Stick the paper diagonally across the card front using spray adhesive.

**3** Turn the card over. Resting on a cutting mat, cut the excess grey paper level with the card edges using a craft knife.

**4** Stick lengths of edging lace to the grey paper using spray adhesive. Trim off the excess lace at the edges of the card using fabric scissors.

# 3D dragonfly card

*This richly coloured sparkling dragonfly looks quite intricate, but the technique is simple: the wings are cut around then lifted a little to add an extra dimension and show the contrasting coloured card underneath. The shimmering effects are created with glitter paint and sequin dust.*

## materials and equipment

- purple and jade green card (stock)
- craft knife
- metal ruler
- cutting mat
- bone folder
- tracing paper
- pencil
- purple glitter paint
- medium and fine artist's paintbrushes
- green, purple and blue sequin dust
- four white photo corners

**1** Cut a 32 × 13.5cm/12½ × 5½in rectangle of purple card using a craft knife and metal ruler and working on a cutting mat. Score and fold the card across the centre, parallel with the short edges, using a bone folder.

**2** Cut a 13 × 10.5cm/5 × 4in rectangle of jade green card. Use the template at the back of the book to transfer the dragonfly to the rectangle. Apply purple glitter paint to the wings, spreading the glitter paint sparingly with a medium artist's paintbrush. Set aside to dry.

**3** Paint the body with purple glitter paint. Use a fine artist's paintbrush to draw out the antennae.

**4** Sprinkle green, purple and blue sequin dust on the body before the paint dries. Set the dragonfly aside to dry then shake off the excess sequin dust.

**5** Resting on a cutting mat, cut around the edges of the wings using a craft knife, leaving the wings attached at the body. Gently lift the wing tips upwards.

**6** Paint the photo corners with purple glitter paint. Sprinkle green, purple and blue sequin dust on the photo corners before the paint dries. Set aside to dry.

**7** Slip each photo corner on a corner of the jade green rectangle. Moisten the back of the photo corners and press the rectangle centrally to the card front.

# Starry good luck card

*The shooting stars on this glittering good luck card are attached to coloured wires bursting out of a window in the card front. A star paper punch creates the cut-outs on the lower edge. As an extra surprise, punch more stars from coloured paper to make some confetti to slip inside the card.*

## materials and equipment

- deep pink glitter card (stock)
- craft knife and metal ruler
- cutting mat
- bone folder
- 1cm/³/₈in star paper punch
- light green, yellow and turquoise pearlized card (stock)
- paper glue
- tracing paper and pencil
- 0.6mm turquoise wire
- wire snippers
- clear adhesive tape
- 5mm/¼in-wide double-sided tape
- light pink paper

**1** Cut a 29.5 × 18cm/11¾in × 7in rectangle of deep pink glitter card using a craft knife and metal ruler and working on a cutting mat. On the wrong side, score and fold the card, parallel with the short edges, 9.5cm/3¾in from the left edge and 10cm/4in from the right edge.

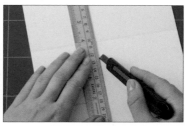

**2** Open the card out flat again. Draw a 5.5cm/2¼in square on the central section, which will be the front of the card, 2.5cm/1in down from the upper edge. Cut out the square.

**3** Punch a row of five stars along the lower edge of the front using a paper punch. Make a clean cut each time, and space the stars evenly.

**4** Cut a 9.5 × 2cm/3¾ × ¾in rectangle of light green pearlized card and stick it to the wrong side of the facing (the left section) along the lower edge, using paper glue. The pearlized card should be visible through the cut-out stars.

**5** Use the template at the back of the book to cut three stars from light green, yellow and turquoise pearlized card. Snip three 9cm/3½in lengths of turquoise wire. Stick the end of each wire to the back of a star using clear adhesive tape.

**6** Stick the other ends of the three wires behind the window using clear adhesive tape. Apply double-sided tape around the window on the wrong side and peel off the backing strips.

**7** Cut a 7.5cm/3in square of light pink paper and stick the paper square behind the window.

**8** Apply double-sided tape to the outer edges of the facing. Peel off the backing strips and fold it behind the front. Punch stars in light pink paper using a paper punch to make confetti.

# Starburst congratulations card

*Embossing paper is known today as parchment craft. This fabulous starburst is embossed through a stencil and the raised surface is coloured with silver metallic wax. The vibrant colours are a great choice for a congratulations card.*

**2** Turn the paper over. Rub through the stencil cut-outs with a small ball embossing tool or the handle end of a fine artist's paintbrush. The design will be embossed on the right side.

**3** Turn the paper over leaving the stencil attached. To highlight the embossing, rub silver metallic wax sparingly on the starburst using kitchen paper. Draw around the stencil. Remove the stencil and cut out the circle. Cut a 7.5cm/3in diameter circle of silver card.

## materials and equipment

- tracing paper and pencil
- stencil board
- cutting mat
- craft knife
- masking tape
- pink paper
- small ball embossing tool or fine artist's paintbrush
- silver metallic wax
- kitchen paper
- silver and orange card (stock)
- metal ruler
- bone folder
- spray adhesive

**1** Trace the template at the back of the book and transfer the design to stencil board. Resting on a cutting mat, cut out the starburst and circle using a craft knife. Tape the stencil to the right side of a piece of pink paper using masking tape.

**Tip**
Clashing pink and orange perfectly complement the spiral motif of the stencil. Use colours with a similar tonal value.

**4** Cut a 21 × 13.5cm/8¼ × 5¼in rectangle of orange card using a craft knife and metal ruler and working on a cutting mat. Score and fold the card across the centre, parallel with the short edges, using a bone folder. Using spray adhesive, stick the embossed circle to the circle of silver card, then stick the panel to the card front.

# Four-leaf clover for luck

*The meaning is clear with this simple good luck motif. The wire leaf is formed using round-nosed pliers and then sewn to the card front with fine wire.*

## materials and equipment

- white laid card (stock)
- craft knife
- metal ruler
- cutting mat
- bone folder
- round-nosed pliers
- 35cm/14in of 0.8mm green wire
- wire snippers
- bradawl
- 20cm/8in of 0.4mm green wire
- 5mm/¼in-wide double-sided tape

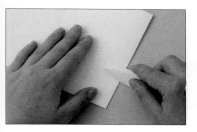

**1** Cut a 28 × 13.5cm/11 × 5¼in rectangle of white laid card using a craft knife and metal ruler and working on a cutting mat. On the wrong side, score and fold the card, parallel with the short edges, 9cm/3½in from the left edge and 9.5cm/3¾in from the right edge. Open the card out flat again.

**2** With a pair of round-nosed pliers, bend the 0.8mm green wire into the four-leaf clover shape, referring to the template at the back of the book. Snip off the excess wire with wire snippers.

**3** Lay the card right side up on a cutting mat and hold the clover on the centre of the middle section (which will be the front). Pierce a hole with a bradawl on each side of the wire between the two side leaves and at each side of the end of the stem.

**4** Use 0.4mm green wire to sew the four-leaf clover to the card, bending the ends of the wire on the back to start and finish, to hold it in place. Snip off the excess wire with wire snippers. Fold in the facing section and stick it behind the front with double-sided tape along the edges.

# Silvered thank you notelets

*Masses of images are readily available in copyright-free books for craftwork. These découpage notelets combine copyright-free vintage motifs with silvered circles. They are quick to make, so a whole series would be easy to produce.*

## materials and equipment

- lilac card (stock)
- craft knife
- metal ruler
- cutting mat
- bone folder
- pair of compasses
- pencil
- flat paintbrush
- 15-minute gold size
- scissors
- aluminium Dutch metal transfer leaf
- soft brush
- image from copyright-free book
- spray adhesive

**1** Cut a 20 × 15cm/8 × 6in rectangle of lilac card using a craft knife and metal ruler and working on a cutting mat. Score and fold the card across the centre, parallel with the short edges, using a bone folder.

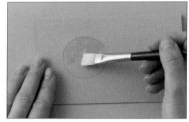

**2** With the fold horizontal, lightly draw a 4.5cm/1³/₄in diameter circle on the card front using a pair of compasses and a pencil, 2.5cm/1in in from the fold and left edge. Using a flat paintbrush, apply gold size to the circle. Set the card aside for 15 minutes until the size has become tacky.

**3** Cut a piece of aluminium transfer leaf slightly larger than the circle. Lay the aluminium leaf face down on the circle and gently press in place, then peel off the backing paper.

**4** Sweep away the excess aluminium leaf using a soft brush. If the aluminium leaf has not adhered in places, press pieces of the left-over leaf into the gaps.

**5** Select an image from a copyright-free book and cut it out with a craft knife, resting on a cutting mat.

**6** Stick the image to the card front using spray adhesive, overlapping the circle.

# Busy bee thank you card

*This charming card is also a wonderful thank you gift. The polymer clay bumble bee is held on the card with a magnet and can be removed to attach to another magnetic surface such as the refrigerator door. Adhesive magnetic sheets are available from craft suppliers and can be cut to any size.*

**materials and equipment**

- yellow, black and white polymer clay
- baking parchment
- kitchen knife
- light blue card (stock)
- craft knife
- metal ruler
- cutting mat
- bone folder
- adhesive magnetic sheet
- black felt-tipped pen

**1** Roll a 1.5cm/⅝in diameter ball of yellow polymer clay. Roll the ball into an oval to make the bee's body.

**2** On baking parchment, flatten the oval to 2cm/¾in long. Roll a 4mm/³⁄₁₆ diameter log of black polymer clay. Flatten the log to 1mm/¹⁄₂₄in thick. Lay the flattened log in two bands across the bee and cut off the excess clay using a kitchen knife.

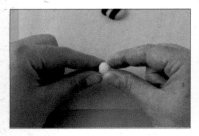

**3** Roll a 1cm/⅜in diameter ball of white polymer clay. Cut the ball in half. Squeeze one side of the clay to a point to make a wing. Make a second wing to match, then press the wings to the top of the bee. Bake the bee following the clay manufacturer's instructions. Leave to cool.

**4** Cut a 21 × 16cm/8¼ × 6¼in rectangle of light blue card using a craft knife and metal ruler and working on a cutting mat. Score and fold the card across the centre, parallel with the short edges, using a bone folder.

**5** Cut two 1.5 × 1cm/⅝ × ⅜in pieces of adhesive magnetic sheet. Stick one piece to the underside of the bee. Stick the other piece to the card front.

**6** Place the bee on the card front. Draw a looping broken line from the bee with a black felt-tipped pen. To protect the clay bee, send the card in a padded envelope.

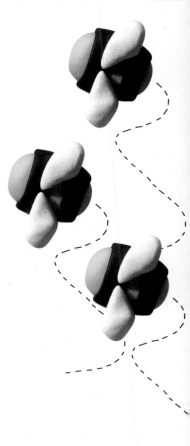

# Pin-pricked letterhead

*Writing paper with an unusual decorative heading is often expensive to buy, but you can create your own stationery for special letters using this easy pin-pricking technique. Experiment with the design: the pricked motif can be positioned at a corner or a single element of the design can be used as a repeating pattern if you prefer.*

**1** Trace the template at the back of the book with a pencil. Tape the tracing right side down to the top of a sheet of writing paper using masking tape. Draw over the outline to transfer it.

**2** Remove the tracing. Resting the writing paper on a cutting mat, cut the upper edge with a craft knife.

## materials and equipment

- tracing paper
- pencil
- A5 sheets of beige writing paper
- masking tape
- cutting mat
- craft knife
- 2mm/$^1$/$_{16}$in hole punch
- tack hammer
- bradawl

**3** Tape the tracing right side up on the writing paper using masking tape. Resting on a cutting mat, punch a hole at each large dot using a 2mm/$^1$/$_{16}$in hole punch and a tack hammer.

**4** Pierce holes at the small dots using a bradawl. Remove the tracing. If you wish, carefully enlarge some of the holes with the bradawl. You could cut the flap of an envelope to match the letterhead.

# Musical instrument stickers card

*Outline stickers are finely detailed adhesive motifs that are available in lots of themes, and they are a very useful way to personalize your greetings cards quickly and easily. The electric musical instrument stickers used here would be ideal decorations for a "miss you" card to send to a music-mad friend.*

## materials and equipment

- bright green card (stock)
- craft knife
- metal ruler
- cutting mat
- bone folder
- lime green paper
- spray adhesive
- musical instrument outline stickers

**1** Cut a 24 x 17cm/9½ x 6½in rectangle of bright green card using a craft knife and metal ruler and working on a cutting mat. Score and fold the card across the centre parallel with the short edges using a bone folder.

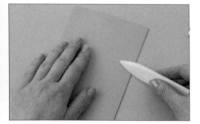

**2** Cut out triangles from lime green paper. Arrange the triangles on the front of the card and stick in place using spray adhesive.

**3** Peel the instrument stickers from the backing paper and apply to the card front.

**4** As a finishing touch, stick a few music note stickers inside the card.

# Retro photo and cross-stitch card

*Remind a friend of happy times by using a favourite old photograph to make this charming card. A '50s-style printed paper was chosen for the background as it suits the period of the photo. Photocopy an original photograph or scan and reprint it using a computer, and adjust the size and shape of the card to suit your print.*

**1** Apply printed paper to pale yellow card using spray adhesive. Allow to dry. Cut a 28.5 × 21cm/11¼ × 8¼in rectangle of the covered card using a craft knife and metal ruler and working on a cutting mat. Score and fold the card 13.5cm/5¼in from, and parallel with, one short edge, using a bone folder.

**2** Cut out the copy of the photograph and a 17 × 10.5cm/6¾ × 4in rectangle of pale yellow card using a craft knife and metal ruler and working on a cutting mat. Stick the image in the centre of the card rectangle using spray adhesive.

## materials and equipment

- 1950s-style printed paper
- pale yellow card (stock)
- spray adhesive
- craft knife
- metal ruler
- cutting mat
- bone folder
- photocopy or reprint of photograph
- bradawl
- crewel embroidery needle
- green stranded embroidery thread (floss)

**3** Resting on a cutting mat, use a bradawl to pierce two rows of holes to make three cross stitches 1cm/⅜in in from the top and bottom edges of the photograph.

**4** Thread a crewel embroidery needle with green stranded embroidery thread. Sew cross stitches at the pierced holes, knotting the thread on the underside of the card to start and finish.

**5** Stick the pale yellow rectangle centrally to the card front using spray adhesive.

**6** Tear a strip of the printed paper approximately 8mm/⅜in wide. Stick the strip to the inside back of the card using spray adhesive, aligning the straight edge with the right edge of the card. Trim the ends level with the card.

# Flowery get well card

*This pretty design, with its fresh, springlike colours and simple flowers, makes a great card to send to a friend to cheer them up and wish them well. It is very simple to make, as the flowers are punched from glittery papers in assorted colours with a flower-shaped punch and then dotted with glitter paint.*

**1** Cut a 20 × 15cm/8 × 6in rectangle of pearlized yellow card using a craft knife and metal ruler and working on a cutting mat. Score and fold the card across the centre, parallel with the short edges, using a bone folder.

**2** Tear a 10 × 5cm/4 × 2in rectangle of Japanese grid paper by tearing the paper against a ruler. Stick the paper centrally to the card front using spray adhesive.

## materials and equipment

- pearlized yellow card (stock)
- craft knife
- metal ruler
- cutting mat
- bone folder
- white lightweight Japanese grid paper
- spray adhesive
- turquoise, lilac and pink glitter paper
- 15mm/$^5$/$_8$in flower-shaped paper punch
- 5mm/$^1$/$_4$in adhesive foam pads
- silver glitter paint

**3** Punch a total of eight flowers from turquoise, lilac and pink glitter papers, using a flower-shaped punch.

**4** Apply a 5mm/$^1$/$_4$in foam pad to the back of each flower.

**5** Peel the backing papers off the foam pads and stick the flowers along the long edges of the Japanese paper.

**6** Dot the flower centres with silver glitter paint. Set aside to dry.

# Stencilled coral gift wrap

*Coral is believed to have healing qualities so is a good choice as a motif when giving a get well gift.*
*These jaunty branches of coral are stencilled on sea blue paper to use as gift wrap.*

### materials and equipment

- tracing paper
- pencil
- stencil board
- craft knife
- cutting mat
- light blue paper
- masking tape
- orange acrylic paint
- stencil brush
- kitchen paper

**3** Remove the stencil. Move it to a new position on the paper and tape in place.

**4** Stencil the coral again. Repeat to cover the paper. Leave to dry.

**1** Trace the coral motif template at the back of the book and transfer it to stencil board. Cut out the stencil using a craft knife, working on a cutting mat.

**2** Tape the stencil to light blue paper with masking tape. Pick up a little paint on the stencil brush and dab off the excess on kitchen paper. Holding the brush upright, apply the paint through the stencil, moving the brush in a circular motion.

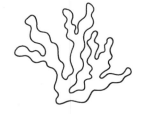

# Convalescence card

*Create a restful scene of a beach hut to wish a friend a successful convalescence. The beach hut is stamped on balsa wood.*

## materials and equipment

- striped canvas effect gift wrap
- cream card (stock)
- spray adhesive
- craft knife
- metal ruler
- cutting mat
- bone folder
- 2mm/¹/₉in-thick balsa wood
- beach hut rubber stamp, about 5cm/2in square
- dark blue ink pad
- red paper
- all-purpose household glue

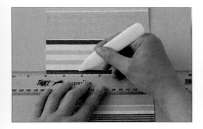

**1** Apply striped gift wrap to cream card using spray adhesive. Cut a 30 × 15cm/12 × 6in rectangle of the covered card using a craft knife and metal ruler and working on a cutting mat. Score and fold the card across the centre, parallel with the short edges, using a bone folder.

**2** Cut a 7.5 × 7cm/3 × 2¾in rectangle of balsa wood using a craft knife and metal ruler and working on a cutting mat. Press a beach hut rubber stamp on to a dark blue ink pad. Stamp the image centrally on the balsa wood rectangle. Leave to dry.

**3** Cut an 8.5 × 8cm/3½ × 3¼in rectangle of red paper and stick it centrally to the card front using spray adhesive.

**4** Stick the balsa wood panel on top using all-purpose household glue.

# Foam elephant get well card

*Amuse a sick child with this colourful card decorated with a bright blue elephant wearing a real cotton bandage around his trunk.*

## materials and equipment

- pale green card (stock)
- craft knife
- metal ruler
- cutting mat
- bone folder
- tracing paper
- pencil
- pen
- blue Neoprene foam
- 15cm/6in of 15mm/⅝in-wide white cotton tape
- fabric scissors
- all-purpose household glue
- yellow relief paint

**1** Cut a 24 × 18.5cm/9½ × 7¼in rectangle of pale green card using a craft knife and metal ruler and working on a cutting mat. Score and fold the card across the centre, parallel with the short edges, using a bone folder.

**2** Trace the template at the back of the book and use it to draw the elephant and its ear on blue Neoprene foam with a pen. Cut out the pieces using a craft knife and working on a cutting mat.

**3** Tie cotton tape in a knot around the elephant's trunk for a bandage. Trim the ends of the tape with fabric scissors.

**4** Stick the elephant to the card front using all-purpose household glue.

**5** Apply all-purpose household glue to the top of the ear on the wrong side. Stick the ear to the elephant.

**6** Dot the eye with yellow relief paint. Set aside to dry.

# Olive bon voyage card

*Quilling is the traditional craft of creating pictures with coiled paper strips. This simple motif of a sprig of olives is a great introduction to the craft and makes a charming card to send to someone who is leaving on a trip.*

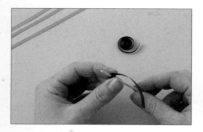

**1** Using a craft knife and metal ruler and working on a cutting mat, cut two strips of black paper and three of green paper, each 4mm/³⁄₁₆in wide and 20cm/8in long. Coil the black paper strips and two of the green paper strips tightly around a cocktail stick. Release the coils so that they spring open.

**2** Use a cocktail stick to apply PVA glue to the inner surface of one black strip at the outer end of the coil. Stick the end against one side of the coil to form a circle. Repeat with the other coils.

## materials and equipment

- craft knife
- metal ruler
- cutting mat
- black and green paper
- cocktail stick (toothpick)
- PVA (white) glue
- A5 beige handmade paper
- bone folder

**3** Gently squeeze the black circles to form ovals for the olives.

**4** Squeeze and pinch the green circles to a point at each side to form the leaves.

**5** Cut the remaining green strip in half. Fold each part in half and hold the fold between a thumb and finger. Starting at the fold, pull the strips between your other thumb and a finger to curl them for the stems.

**6** Glue the end of the outer curve 3mm/⅛in from the end of the inner curve.

**7** Fold an A5 sheet of beige handmade paper in half, parallel with the short edges, and rub over the fold with a bone folder. Arrange the olives, leaves and stems on the card front. Spread glue on the underside of each coil with a cocktail stick and stick the pieces to the card front.

# Anchor bon voyage card

*Wish bon voyage to a traveller leaving for a seaside destination with this card depicting an anchor on a shell-strewn beach.*

## materials and equipment

- cream card (stock)
- craft knife
- metal ruler
- cutting mat
- bone folder
- light blue translucent paper
- spray adhesive
- 20cm/8in of 1mm blue wire
- round-nosed pliers
- wire snippers
- masking tape
- bradawl
- 20cm/8in of 0.4mm blue wire
- 5mm/¹⁄₄in-wide double-sided tape
- 4 small shells
- glue dots

**1** Cut a 35.5 x 13cm/14 x 5in rectangle of cream card using a craft knife and metal ruler and working on a cutting mat. On the wrong side, score and fold the card parallel with the short edges, 12cm/4¾in from the left edge and 11.5cm/4¼in from the right.

**2** Cut a 13 x 6cm/5 x 2¼in-wide strip of light blue translucent paper. Tear one long edge of the strip between your fingers to create an irregular edge.

**3** Use spray adhesive to stick the strip to the middle section, which will be the card front, matching the long cut edge to the fold next to the narrower section, which will form the facing.

**4** Bend one end of the 1mm blue wire around the widest part of one prong of a pair of round-nosed pliers, forming a ring. Bend the extending end of the wire at right angles to the ring and snip the wire 4cm/1½in below the ring to make the upright part of the anchor.

**5** Snip a 5cm/2in length of 1mm wire and bend it into a gentle curve between your fingers. Snip a 2cm/¾in length of 1mm wire for the crosspiece.

**6** Open the card out flat on a cutting mat. Arrange the wire pieces on the front to form the anchor. Stick them temporarily in place with masking tape. Using a bradawl, pierce a hole on each side of each intersection, then on each side of the curved wire, 5mm/¼in from the ends.

**7** Use 0.4mm blue wire to sew the anchor to the card front, bending over the ends of the wire on the inside of the card to start and finish to hold it in place. Snip off the excess wire with wire snippers. Remove the masking tape.

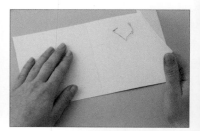

**8** Fold in the facing section and stick it behind the card front using double-sided tape along the edges. Stick four small shells to the front of the card with glue dots.

# Welcome home card

*Welcome a world-weary traveller home with this evocative card. Make a photocopy or a computer print-out of an old map for the background paper, and use postage stamps saved from correspondence from your friend's travels.*

**materials and equipment**

- copy of an old map
- lilac card (stock)
- spray adhesive
- craft knife
- metal ruler
- cutting mat
- bone folder
- translucent purple paper
- pale grey fibrous writing paper
- 3 postage stamps
- adhesive foam pads

**1** Apply a copy of a map to card using spray adhesive. Cut a 23 × 18cm/9 × 7in rectangle of the covered card using a craft knife and metal ruler and working on a cutting mat. Score and fold the card across the centre, parallel with the short edges, using a bone folder.

**2** Cut a 13 × 5.5cm/5¼ × 2¼in rectangle of translucent purple paper and a 12 × 4.5cm/ 4¾ × 1¾in rectangle of pale grey fibrous writing paper. Stick the fibrous paper rectangle centrally to the purple rectangle using spray adhesive.

**3** Stick the purple rectangle to the right-hand side of the card front using spray adhesive.

**4** Stick three postage stamps in a row on the fibrous paper rectangle using adhesive foam pads.

# Letter of sympathy

*However much you want to convey your feelings to the recipient, a letter of sympathy is always difficult to compose and demands time and thought. The understated design of this paper uses a seedhead motif, with its associations with ripeness and the natural cycle – a comforting thought in the face of a sad loss.*

### materials and equipment

- seedhead rubber stamp
- yellow and orange watercolour stamp paints
- medium artist's paintbrush
- A4 handmade writing paper and envelope
- scrap paper

**1** Paint the stem on the stamp with yellow watercolour stamp paint using a medium artist's paintbrush.

**2** Blend orange and yellow paint together on the seedhead.

**3** Stamp the image on the writing paper. Leave to dry.

**4** Resting on scrap paper, moisten the upper edge of the writing paper. Run a line of yellow, then a thinner orange line along the moistened edge. Decorate an envelope to match. Set aside to dry.

# Accordion leaf card

*An accordion or concertina card, sometimes known as a "leporello", allows you to write a long letter within the card. The subdued colours of this elegant version are suitable for a letter of apology or sympathy. The card fastens with ribbon, which can be loosened to allow it to stand upright for display.*

## materials and equipment

- thick grey paper
- craft knife
- metal ruler
- cutting mat
- bone folder
- 3mm/¹/₈in hole punch
- tack hammer
- tracing paper
- pencil
- dark blue, bright olive green and jade green paper
- masking tape
- spray adhesive
- 60cm/24in of 3mm/¹/₈in-wide jade green ribbon

**1** Cut a 36 × 18cm/14 × 7in rectangle of thick grey paper using a craft knife and metal ruler and working on a cutting mat. Score the card at 9cm/3½in intervals, parallel with the short edges, using a bone folder.

**2** Fold the card in accordion folds along the scored lines using a bone folder.

**3** Resting on a cutting mat, punch a hole on each side through all the layers, 8cm/3⅛in from the lower edge and 1cm/⅜in inside the folds, using a 3mm/⅛in hole punch and a tack hammer.

**4** Trace the template at the back of the book and transfer the outline of the outer leaf to dark blue, the leaf to bright olive green and the leaf details to jade green paper. Cut them out using a craft knife on a cutting mat.

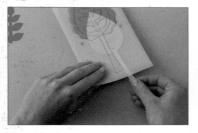

**5** To judge the position of the motif on the card, tape the traced template to the top of the card front. Slip the pieces underneath, matching their positions, and stick in place with spray adhesive.

**6** Thread the punched holes with ribbon and fasten in a bow on the card front.

# SCRAPBOOK PAGES

# DECORATIVE ALBUM PAGES

In the early days of photography, having a picture taken was a notable event. It generally involved a visit to a professional photographer's studio, and the resulting prints – though they might be small and hard to see in tones of sepia or grey – were treasured and displayed in silver frames or ornate albums. Now we live in an age where photography is all around us. It is easier than ever before to take beautiful, detailed, interesting photographs whenever we want, and yet many good prints languish in boxes or drawers. The burgeoning craft of scrapbooking is all about displaying them as they deserve to be seen. But scrapbooks are more than just photograph albums: on their pages you can present your favourite pictures in beautiful, creative settings, accompanied by all the details you need to keep your memories of special times alive and fresh, to enjoy now and to pass down to future generations.

This comprehensive guide includes everything you need to get you started, whatever your artistic ability, with practical tips and inspiring suggestions for pages of originality and style. The opening

▼ *Christmas is a good subject for scrapbooks and there is always plenty of decorative material to hand.*

▲ *Old black-and-white photographs show how times change when compared to today's colour prints.*

section details the different kinds of materials and equipment you can choose from to make your pages and sets out easy techniques for mounting and editing photographs, creating backgrounds and making decorations. It also explores a range of styles and shows how to achieve each look. Following on are 120 step-by-step projects which put the basic techniques into practice, with inspirational results. They are grouped around popular themes such as Children, Weddings, Travel and Family History, to help you decide how to organize your own collections.

Before you begin work on your first page, you need to decide on the size of the album you will use, as this will dictate the size of the layout. Most of the projects in this chapter are based on 30cm/12in square pages, on which there is plenty of space to mount a good selection of pictures and embellish them creatively. Scrapbooking suppliers offer a huge range of paper, card and other materials in this popular size. Alternatively, you could go for the slightly smaller 21 x 28cm/8½ x 11in. This has the advantage that you can print material on A4 paper to fit it, but it can be more difficult to arrange all the items you want on a single page or double-page spread. Smaller size albums are also available, such as 20cm/8in square, and can be useful if you want to create mini-albums as gifts. Of course, you can also make your own albums and covers in any size you wish, and there are some great ideas in this section for displaying your designs in one-off albums.

Albums use a number of different binding systems: with three-ring bindings it is easy to move pages around, but they hold a limited number of pages, and the rings make it difficult to display double-page layouts effectively. This is not a problem with post-bound or strap-bound albums, which can expand to take more pages as your collection grows. Whatever you choose, always look for albums and papers that are of "archival" quality, made with acid-free and lignin-free materials, so that your precious prints don't deteriorate once they are mounted.

Like many other aspects of life, the digital revolution plays a vital part in many areas of scrapbooking. Digital cameras and image-editing software have opened up all kinds of photographic possibilities. With no need to buy film, you can take

▲ *Photographs of a family trip to the seaside take on a nostalgic appearance when embellished with 1950s memorabilia.*

as many experimental pictures as you like and play around with novel formats, colour and special effects. An internet connection gives you access to online craft suppliers, sources of templates and fonts, and special interest groups with whom you can discuss your projects and display your favourites in virtual galleries. There is now a growing trend towards virtual scrapbooking, in which stickers, borders and charms are replaced by digital versions entirely assembled and displayed on screen.

However, it's certainly not necessary to have a computer in order to enjoy scrapbooking to the full. This craft's great attraction derives from the fact that it is a wonderfully back-to-basics pastime. Good layouts combine artistic flair with genuine hands-on skills with paper, card, fabrics and natural materials. Like the quilting and knitting bees of previous generations, communal scrapbooking events (known as "crops") are strengthening social networks everywhere. As you assemble the elements of your pages, you can rediscover all the enthusiasm and satisfaction you felt when compiling a scrapbook as a child, in the knowledge that you are safeguarding and enhancing your treasured family memorabilia for your own children and for future generations.

▼ *Children are a perennially popular subject for scrapbooks, and when they are older will love looking at their own photographs.*

# Getting started

Creating album pages is about encapsulating life's precious moments in a way that feels right for you. As you gain experience you'll have plenty of ideas for presentation and develop your own personal style. There are lots of ways to make exciting scrapbooks, and there are tips to guide you through your ideas to help you make the best of irreplaceable prints and memorabilia.

   Craft stores are bursting with seductive pieces of kit and decorative materials, and it's very easy to get carried away buying stickers, die stamps and fancy cutters that appeal to your sense of colour and style before you have any clear idea of what you'll do with them. This section offers a guide to the materials and equipment available, to help you match the possibilities to the items you want to display. Step-by-step instructions will take you through all the different photographic and craft techniques you need to make beautiful, meaningful pages.

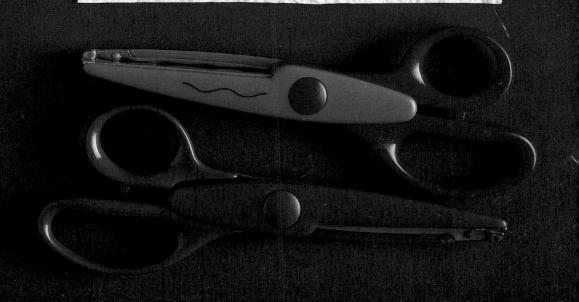

# EQUIPMENT AND MATERIALS

It's easy to get carried away by the vast range of fancy punches, stamps and stickers available for scrapbooking. Start with the basics – album pages, scissors and adhesive – and add to your collection gradually as you develop your themes.

## Cutting tools

*Whatever the style of your albums, impeccably accurate cutting is essential for good-looking results. Bad trimming can ruin your precious pictures, so invest in good scissors and knives.*

### Metal ruler and craft knife
These give total control over where and how you cut. The knife blade should always be retracted or covered when not in use. If safety is a concern, a guillotine or trimmer may be a better option.

### Straight trimmer or guillotine
Use this to trim paper or photographs with straight edges. All trimmers have a grid printed or embossed on to the cutting surface, to help you measure accurately. Some have interchangeable blades that cut patterned lines as well as straight ones.

### Speciality cutters
There are all kinds of cutters available that make it easy to cut photographs and mats into decorative shapes. Placing a template over a photograph allows you to see what size to cut. Templates and cutters are only suitable for use together.

*Guillotine*

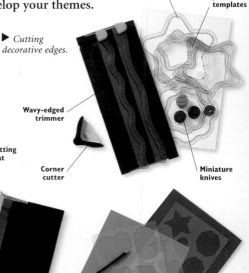

▶ *Cutting decorative edges.*

Template sheets
Shaped plastic templates

Wavy-edged trimmer

Corner cutter

Miniature knives

▼ *Cutting straight lines.*

Decorative-edged scissors

Scissors

Cutting mat

Small scissors

Metal ruler

Craft knife

Straight trimmer

Plastic templates

▶ *Cutting small decorative shapes.*

Punches

### Templates
A wide range of lightweight templates provide different cropping options, and are easy to store. Use a pencil with the template to trace a shape on to a photograph or paper, then cut along the drawn line with scissors.

### Punches
Simple small shapes look striking when punched in coloured card. Larger shapes can also be used to cut out the important part of a photograph. Shaped punches are available in hundreds of designs, and can be combined for added impact: for example, several hearts can be assembled together to create the petals of a flower.

### Scissors
It is useful to have two pairs of scissors: a large pair for cutting straight lines and a small pair for trimming around decorative shapes and templates. Blades with pointed tips make it easier to cut out intricate shapes.

### Decorative-edged scissors
Used sparingly, these add a fancy touch to mats and trims, although it is advisable not to use them on photographs. They work best when cutting a straight edge or a gentle curve.

# Adhesives

*Many different kinds of adhesive will work well on paper and card (card stock). Make sure any you use are labelled acid-free so that your photographs will not deteriorate when in contact with them.*

### Glue sticks

These are a cheap and easy way to stick light items such as punched shapes, but some glue sticks are not strong enough to hold photographs in position permanently. Although the glue takes some time to dry, it does not need to be left flat while drying.

### Spray adhesive

Both permanent and repositionable adhesives are available in spray form – the latter allows for something that is stuck down to be peeled off and then reapplied. Spray outside or in a well-ventilated room, so that the fumes can disperse. To prevent the spray going everywhere, it is a good idea to place items in a large box, and direct the spray into that. No drying time is required.

### Foam pads

These can be used to raise an element on a layout, making it appear three-dimensional. For greater height, you can stick two or more pads together before mounting your item. Use scissors to trim the pads if they are too large, but clean the scissor blades afterwards.

### Glue dots and glue lines

These are available in different sizes and thicknesses, and with permanent or repositionable adhesive. The glue is tacky and will hold most items securely. No drying time is required.

### Double-sided tape

Whether as a single sheet, pre-cut into squares, or on a continuous roll, this is a clean, easy way to glue most items. Long strips can be used to created borders, by applying a piece of tape, removing the backing, then pouring beads or glitter over the exposed tape. Use the same technique with small shapes punched from a sheet. No drying time is required.

### Tape applicators

These dispensers allow for the convenient application of a square or line of adhesive, making it easy to glue the edge of unusual or angled shapes.

Refills are available for most designs, making them economical too. No drying time is required.

### PVA (white) glue

This will hold most items in place, including awkward or three-dimensional items such as shells or charms. The work must be left flat while the glue dries. To cover an album or box, brush glue diluted with water over a sheet of paper and wrap it around the sides.

### Photo corners

If you prefer to avoid gluing your photographs permanently, mount them with photo corners. Because the adhesive is on the corner and not the photograph, the picture can be removed later if necessary. Clear photo corners are the most useful, but coloured ones are also available. Gold, silver or black look good on heritage or wedding layouts. No drying time is required.

### Masking tape

This is useful for temporarily attaching stencils to a layout, or for lifting stickers from their backing sheet.

Sticker sheets

Sticker borders

▲ *Stickers.*

### Glue for vellum

Specially made "invisible" glue dots are needed when working with vellum, to avoid the adhesive showing through the sheet. Alternatively, it can be attached using spray adhesive.

### Stickers

As well as being a decorative element, stickers can be positioned to attach vellum, photographs or journaling blocks to a layout. Choose large scale stickers if you want to stick a heavy item down.

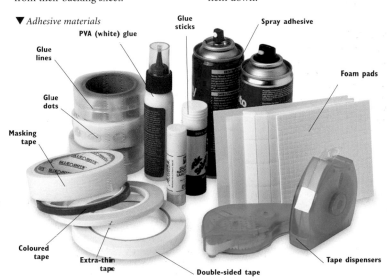

▼ *Adhesive materials*

Glue lines

PVA (white) glue

Glue sticks

Spray adhesive

Glue dots

Masking tape

Foam pads

Coloured tape

Extra-thin tape

Double-sided tape

Tape dispensers

# Paper and card

*Good paper makes a world of difference to your designs, so always buy the best quality you can afford, and make sure it is acid-free to keep your photographs in perfect condition.*

### Page kits

Sometimes helpful for beginners, page kits combine paper with matching stickers or other embellishments and offer an easy way to create co-ordinated layouts quickly. They are designed to suit a range of themes and cover many different subjects.

### Self-coloured card (stock)

This is the basis for many scrapbook pages, and its firmness provides an ideal surface to support photographs and embellishments. Card may be smooth or textured to resemble natural surfaces such as linen. It is available from art and craft suppliers, as single sheets or in multi-packs. Save scraps for paper piecing and matting photos.

### Patterned paper

There are thousands of patterned papers available to match almost any theme, event or mood. Papers may be purchased individually, in books or multi-packs; the latter offer better value, but not all the sheets may be to your taste. A folder of patterned paper scraps is useful since many layouts can be attractively embellished using small scraps of paper.

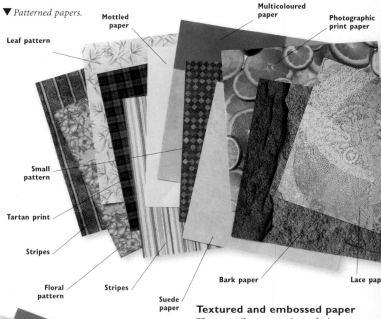

▶ *Mini-album materials.*

Blank notebook

Pack of pre-cut coloured cards

▼ *Patterned papers.*

Mottled paper

Multicoloured paper

Photographic print paper

Leaf pattern

Small pattern

Tartan print

Stripes

Floral pattern

Stripes

Suede paper

Bark paper

Lace paper

### Textured and embossed paper

These tactile papers give a design texture and depth without adding bulk. Some papers resemble leather or fabric, while others have stitching or metallic embossing to add richness.

### Mulberry paper

The fibres used to create this paper are light but very strong. Do not use scissors to cut the paper; instead, "draw" a damp paintbrush across the paper, then tear apart, leaving soft, feathery edges.

### Photographic print paper

Some patterned papers offer photographic or naturalistic representations of everyday objects. These can overwhelm a layout if they compete with your own photographs, so restrict them to accents.

▼ *Self-coloured card.*

Glitter card

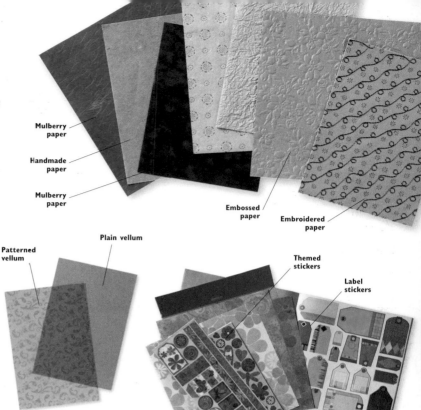

▶ *Textured and embossed papers.*

Mulberry paper
Handmade paper
Mulberry paper
Embossed paper
Embroidered paper

## Suede paper
This mimics the texture and appearance of real suede, and so is perfect for representing that material.

## Glitter and pearlescent paper
The soft sheen of pearlescent paper is ideal for baby or wedding layouts, while brighter glitter sheets can be used as colourful accents for party pages.

## Cut and mini-album packs
Pre-cut small paper packs are available for matting or mini-albums.

## Lace papers
These delicate papers mimic the soft colours and patterns of lace without adding weight to the pages, and are perfect for wedding or heritage layouts.

## Vellum
Being translucent, vellum gives a soft look to paper or photographs placed underneath it. Patterned vellum can be layered over plain or patterned paper to create a romantic look, and mini-envelopes made from vellum half-conceal the souvenirs they hold. If a photograph you want to use is a little out of focus, you can disguise this by slipping it behind vellum.

Plain vellum
Patterned vellum
Themed stickers
Label stickers

▲ *Vellum sheets.*

▶ *Sheets of decorative stickers.*

## ALBUM BINDINGS

Your album can be of any size, but you will probably find that a 30cm/12in square format offers the best scope for creating satisfying layouts. Loose-leaf albums give the most flexibility, and there are basically three methods of binding pages into them.

**Ring binder albums**
These are the cheapest way to display layouts, which can be slipped into clear plastic page protectors. Extra page protectors can be added to expand the album. As the ring binding lies between the two pages and distracts the eye, ring binders are best used to present single-page layouts.

**Post-bound albums**
These albums conceal the posts binding the page protectors together, so a double layout can be viewed without distracting elements. They are available in a wide range of sizes and designs. Extra page protectors may be inserted by unscrewing the posts and adding extenders.

**Strap-hinge albums**
Plastic hinges slide through loops on the spines of these album pages to create an infinitely extendable album. Each page is an integral part of this kind of album, so background paper needs to be glued on top (known as "wallpapering") to change the layout base.

**Notebooks**
Any kind of notebook may be used as a scrapbook, especially if a smaller gift album is being created. Decorate plain notebooks by painting or covering with paper, and add embellishments for a unique look. Don't forget to leave room for a title page before the first layout.

# Embellishments

*This is where the fun really starts, but it's important to keep the focus of attention on your own photographs and memorabilia: make sure the decorative elements enhance the theme of your page rather than dominate it.*

▶ *Stickers and adhesive borders.*

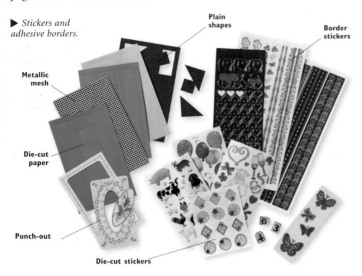

Metallic mesh

Die-cut paper

Punch-out

Die-cut stickers

Plain shapes

Border stickers

Multi-shape template

Adhesive mesh strip

Slide mounts

▶ *Photo mounts and templates.*

Memorabilia pockets

Frames

Snap fasteners

Zippers

Rings

Charms

Keys

▲ *Fabric pockets and attachments add interest to a layout.*

## Stickers

A staple of scrapbooking, stickers are available in every conceivable colour, size and design, and make it easy to embellish a page quickly. Popular characters are represented on stickers, as well as traditional themes such as Christmas and weddings. If you want to make a sticker more substantial, apply it to white card and cut round it, then mount the shape on a foam pad.

## Fabric stickers

These are printed on fabric to add textural interest to a layout. For a homespun look, fray some of the threads at the edges of the sticker.

## 3D stickers

These are built up from two or more layers of card, ready to be added to a page. Popular themes include babies and travel, and many are also suitable for making greetings cards.

## Punch-outs

Shapes die-cut from sheets of card are known as punch-outs, as they need to be pressed out of the backing sheet. They are usually simple shapes, and may be coloured.

Printed shapes, or those carrying titles, embellish a layout quickly, and can create a consistent style throughout an album.

## Stamping

Use stamps to create a theme on background paper. Stamped images can be coloured, cut out and used like stickers to lend an accent colour or design to a layout. Choose inks in colours that complement the layout, or scribble a felt-tip pen over a stamp, spray lightly with water, then press down. Alphabet stamps are useful for titles.

▼ *Collect postcards, currency and timetables as travel mementoes.*

## Paint

Acrylic paint can be used to create any design on backing paper, and the huge range of colours available means you can match any shade in a photograph. Ready-mixed paint in tubes is easy to apply and very fine lines can be drawn using the nib.

## Templates

All kinds of templates are available to help you customize layouts. They are an economical option since it's easy to create many different looks with just one template.

## Fibres

Lengths of fibre add softness and texture to layouts, and provide contrast with the flatness and hard edges of card and paper. Luxurious knitting wool or ribbons can also be used. Mixed packs can be bought already colour co-ordinated. Try wrapping fibres round the bottom of a photograph, or threading a handful through a tag.

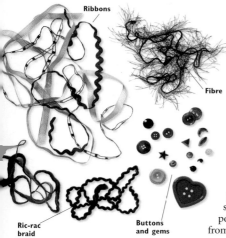

Ribbons

Fibre

Ric-rac braid

Buttons and gems

▲ *Fibres, braids and buttons can be used as borders for pictures or to hold items in place.*

## Buttons and gems

Stitch or stick these to a layout as embellishments, or to anchor journaling blocks. You could use a gem to dot the "i" in a title, or scatter several in the corner of a photograph. Delicate pearl buttons are especially suited to baby themes or heritage layouts.

## Memorabilia

Real or replica memorabilia adds significance to a layout. When you go travelling, for example, save ephemera such as tickets, timetables and restaurant bills to combine with your photographs. Failing the real thing, you can buy a replica pack. Foreign stamps, used or unused, and paper currency are other authentic additions.

### Memorabilia pockets

Tuck small items of memorabilia in pockets to keep them safe but accessible. Pockets that have clear fronts allow you to see what's inside without taking it out.

### Attachments

There are lots of specialist attachments available now, which can be kept as they are or further embellished by sanding, painting or stitching. Tuck a special souvenir in a pre-made pocket, or hang a key or zipper pull from a length of ribbon.

### Metal

Embellishments sold for scrapbooks have been specially coated to prevent damage to layouts. Use brads or eyelets to fix vellum or tags in place. Thread ribbon or fibres through charms, or place a tiny key next to a heart. Photo turns are attached with brads and can hold hidden journaling closed but accessible. For quick attachment of ribbons, use coloured staples.

### Adhesive mesh

This is available in strips or sheets and quickly adds texture to a layout. Dab ink or chalk over the surface then peel off, to give a shadowed texture pattern on paper.

### Slide mounts

Cover these in paper or paint, then use as tiny picture frames or to highlight part of a photograph.

### Paper charms

Embossed printed and foiled charms can be cut out and added to layouts.

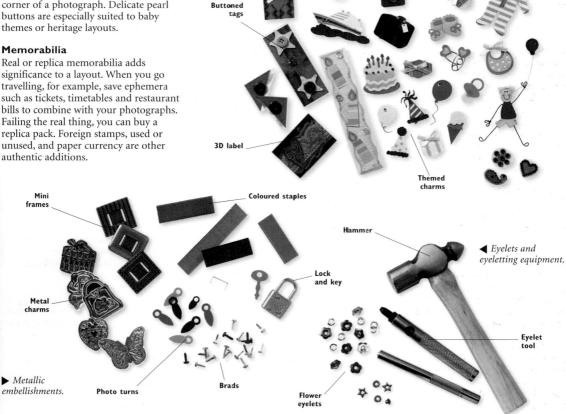

▼ *Paper charms.*

Buttoned tags

3D label

Themed charms

Mini frames

Coloured staples

Hammer

◀ *Eyelets and eyeletting equipment.*

Metal charms

Lock and key

Eyelet tool

▶ *Metallic embellishments.*

Photo turns

Brads

Flower eyelets

# Lettering

*The words you add to your layouts add an all-important dimension. Use the title to establish the theme of the page, bringing out the character of the layout in your treatment of the main word or perhaps an illuminated initial.*

### Letter templates

Use these in reverse to trace individual letters on to the back of your chosen paper, then flip over, to avoid having to erase pencil lines. Or use right side up to trace a title directly on to a layout, then colour with pencils or pens.

### Letter stickers

The quickest and easiest way to add titles to your pages is with adhesive stickers. Align the bases of the letters along a ruler or use a special plastic guide for curved lines of lettering. Mix colours and styles for a fun approach. Letter squares can be used in both positive and negative forms, making them versatile and economical. Tweezers or a crocodile clip are useful in helping to place letter stickers accurately.

### Cut-out letters

These are available in sheets or as part of themed paper collections, and make good decorative initials. Cut them out individually and glue down, or mount on foam pads for added dimension. A large number of styles are available to suit any scrapbook theme.

### Buttons

Some manufacturers offer sets of letters in a range of different formats, such as small buttons. You could glue or stitch them on to a layout, or thread a name on thin ribbon and drape it over a photograph. Use a single button for the initial letter of a word to highlight it.

▼ *Lettering stickers and tools.*

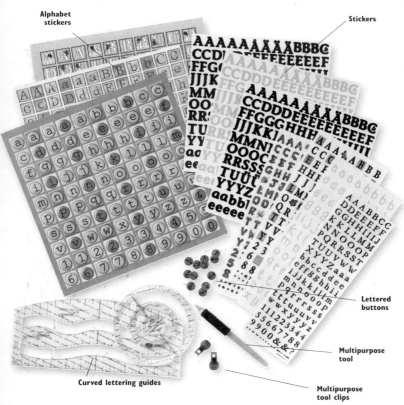

Alphabet stickers

Stickers

Lettered buttons

Multipurpose tool

Curved lettering guides

Multipurpose tool clips

▲ *Use lettering templates to trace individual letters for titles, then fill in with ink or pens or cut out and glue in place on the page.*

# Tools for journaling

*While titles and captions can identify the people in the pictures, journaling goes further, explaining the background to an event and capturing its mood. Writing by hand adds a personal touch.*

▶ *Fibre-tipped pens are easy to use and available in a wide range of colours and widths.*

**Plain lettering**

**Wedding template**

**Decorative lettering**

▲ *Plastic templates and stencils are available in a wide range of different styles of lettering and themes.*

◀ *Printed journaling blocks can be filled in by hand and then glued on to the album page.*

## Templates

Scrapbooking templates in decorative shapes can be used to help you fit and align journaling. Trace one of the shapes on to the page and draw in guidelines with a soft pencil. Rub out the lines when the text is complete. Alternatively, draw round the shape and cut it out of contrasting paper. Add the journaling, erase the guidelines, then glue the paper shape on the layout.

## Writing guide

Rest this on the paper and rest your pen lightly on the top of the wire loops as you write. The flexible loops will bend out of the way for the tails of letters descending below the level of the line.

## Pens

Fibre-tip pens give good, even coverage. Use the tip for fine writing, and the side to create striking titles.

## Fine-tipped pens

Use these when a lot of information has to be written in a small space, as their fine point allows for very neat writing. Fine tips can also be used to decorate titles drawn with thicker pens.

## Gel pens

Manufactured in a wide range of colours, gel pens are a scrapbooker's staple. Metallic shades look good on dark paper.

## Paint pens

These draw a wide, opaque line of colour, perfect for large titles or for outlining photographs instead of matting.

## Computer fonts

A computer will give you access to an almost limitless range of fonts and sizes available for titles and journaling. Titles can be printed out and mounted on a layout, but for a more striking effect, print a title in reverse and cut it out, then flip it over and add to the page. Printing in reverse means any lines will not be seen on the finished layout.

## Printed journaling boxes

Sets of journaling boxes offer pre-made titles and sayings to add to a layout, along with some blanks for you to record personal information. These are often produced to coordinate with paper sets, making it easy to complete a layout.

▶ *Fibre-tipped and gel pens are suitable for titles and journaling.*

**Flexible nylon loops**

▲ *A writing guide keeps your handwriting horizontal when journaling without obstructing the movement of the pen.*

**Fine-tipped pens**

**Round-tipped pens**

# CREATIVE IMAGE-MAKING

Whether you're sorting through boxes of old family pictures or taking new ones with your album in mind, these ideas will help you develop your visual sense and explore imaginative ways of using photographs to create some really arresting images.

## Taking good photographs

The craft of scrapbooking sprang from a desire to present photographs of family and friends in a creative and meaningful way, and good photographs are the heart of every album page. So here are some tips to help you take more effective pictures for really stunning layouts. Modern cameras, equipped with high-quality lenses, built-in automatic exposure meters and sophisticated auto-focusing systems, can do nearly all the work for you. Unless you choose to manage your camera's settings manually for creative effects, you really can just point and shoot terrific pictures. However, technical quality is meaningless if your pictures are badly composed, coarsely lit or just lifeless.

Whether you're using a state-of-the-art SLR or a disposable camera, you need to train your eye to make the most of light, colour and form, and learn how to see your subject as the camera sees it to achieve the effective results you want.

Even if you are a good photographer, you are bound to have some pictures that don't come out right, with too much background or foreground, subjects disappearing off the edge of the photo or, if you've used flash, people with red eyes. All is not lost: there are ways of improving many pictures that will enable you to display them.

## Photographing people

Whether they're formally posed or candid shots, photographs of people should aim to convey their true character. Most people feel ill-at-ease or put on some kind of show when you first point a lens at them, so it's best to take lots of pictures. Children, especially, will soon forget about the camera's presence if they're busy playing, leaving you to get your best photographs.

For candid shots, a telephoto or zoom lens means your subjects need not be aware of the camera at all. It will also throw the foreground and background out of focus, adding emphasis to the subject, which is just what you want.

## Lighting

The traditional instruction to "shoot with the sun behind you" when taking pictures outdoors tends to produce the flattest effect. If your subject is a person looking at the camera, this position will leave them squinting uncomfortably. It can be much more effective to move them into the shade of a tree or a building, where the indirect light will be much more flattering and the contrasts less extreme, making it possible to capture every detail.

If you are taking pictures in direct light, it's best to move yourself or your subject so that the light is coming from one side. This is easiest to achieve when the sun is low in the sky – early in the morning or in the late afternoon (which photographers call the "magic hour"). Indoors, a similar atmospheric sidelight can be provided by daylight coming through a window, which is wonderful for portraits.

## Composing pictures

As you look through the viewfinder, or at the LCD screen of a digital camera, it's easy to concentrate too hard on the main subject of your picture, but it's important to see how the whole picture works within the frame. Before you focus and shoot, move the camera around to find the best angle. If necessary, change your position entirely to get a better angle, or to bring in some foreground interest.

Think about the background too: try to find an angle that gives a background that's attractive but not distracting, and look out for ugly details like power lines. If anyone appears to have a tree growing out of their head, move slightly to one side to avoid the problem.

▼ *Here the photographer has successfully used the rule of thirds to make a visually interesting image, but has tilted the camera so that the horizon is not level.*

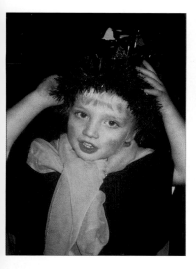

If you're photographing people, move in as close as you can to fill the frame. Alternatively, use a zoom lens – this also has the advantage of flattening perspective, which has a flattering effect. With children, crouch or kneel to get yourself down to their level.

Try turning the camera on its side. A vertical, or "portrait", format is often better for pictures of people, but that's not always the case. If you're taking the photograph in an interesting setting,

*▼If you forget to check what's going on in the background of a picture while focusing on smiling faces, you can end up with an object appearing to grow out of someone's head.*

*◀▲ Red eyes appear when a subject is looking directly at the camera when the flash goes off. The problem is easy to rectify with a red-eye pen. Use it like a felt-tipped pen to mask out the unwanted red tones.*

including more of the the surroundings in a "landscape" format may convey more information about your subject. For example, you might portray a keen gardener in the context of the garden that they have created.

The most interesting pictures rarely have the main subject right in the centre. Photographers tend to follow the "rule of thirds", which involves visualizing a grid dividing the picture vertically and horizontally into three. Placing your subject on one of the four points where the imaginary lines intersect gives a harmonious composition.

## Cropping prints

If you have a photograph where the main focus is too far off to one side, or the subject is set against a busy, distracting background, it is easy to crop the picture to eliminate the unnecessary parts and balance up the composition.

Rather than cutting off the unwanted part of the picture by eye and ending up with a lopsided picture, cut out two L-shaped pieces of black card (card stock). You can use these to form a rectangular frame of any size so that you can judge the part of the picture you want to use. Adjust the L-shapes backwards and forwards until you find the crop that looks best, then mark the print with a pencil. Cut along the marked lines using a craft knife and metal ruler and working on a cutting mat. Cropping pictures will give you a variety of different-sized prints, which can often add interest to album pages. You can

even remedy pictures that are crooked by cropping a little: draw a new frame parallel with the horizon in the photograph and trim all the edges to produce a straight image.

### Red eyes

If people are looking straight at the camera when you take pictures using flash, the light reflects on their retinas, causing their eyes to shine red. Professional photographers use lights set at a distance from the camera to avoid this problem, and some compact cameras that rely on inbuilt flash have a "red-eye reduction" setting, which can help. Another solution is to take pictures when your subjects are not looking directly into the lens.

If you do want to use photographs in which people looking directly at the camera have red eyes, you can improve your prints using a red-eye pen, available from photograhic suppliers. This is a dark green marker pen that successfully counteracts the red, leaving the eyes looking dark. Simply colour in all the red eyes visible on the photograph, taking care not to mark the rest of the faces. The ink is permanent so the colour will not smudge, and your pictures will look much better.

*▲ Everyone has the odd print like this in their collection: most of the sky can simply be cropped away to focus on the main subject.*

*▶ Many badly framed pictures can be redeemed by judicious cropping, but try out your ideas with an adjustable frame, easily made from two pieces of black card, before you start cutting up a print.*

# Tinting photographs

*Black-and-white photographs, particularly those that have not faded with age, can sometimes look stark in a photograph album. One way to enliven them and give them more interest is to tint them with coloured inks.*

**1** Select the photographs to be hand-tinted. Pour some water mixed with the ink thinner solution into a shallow tray. Using a pair of tweezers, add one photograph at a time to the solution.

**2** Place the wet photo on a board and wipe the excess water from it using a cloth. The photo should be damp rather than wet, or the ink will run where the water is rather than where you want it to go.

**3** Pour a little thinner solution into a palette and add a drop of ink. Apply the colour gently using a fine paintbrush and wait for it to be dispersed by the damp print before adding more. Test the colours to see how different they appear once dry.

**4** Add touches of colour to the hair, eyes and lips. Darken the colour as necessary to suit the person in the photograph. Finally, add a few touches of colour to the clothing. Leave the photograph to dry thoroughly before mounting it.

## COLOURING MEDIA

Oil-based inks specially formulated for colouring photographs are available in a range of colours and are sold with a thinner solution that can be used to prepare the surface of the print and to dilute the colour. Special marker pens are also available, and can be easier to use for small areas of colour, though the use of a brush can give a more authentic period look. You could also experiment with other media, such as coloured pencils.

The degree to which the colour "takes" will depend on the type of paper used to make the print: if possible select matt prints for colouring as the surface has more grip and will hold the ink more successfully than gloss.

Traditionally, when all photography was in black and white, the most common use for hand-colouring was to add flesh tones to portraits, and doing this will give your prints a period feel. When painting faces, however, take care not to overdo the inking, or your pictures will end up looking like caricatures. If you add too much colour to start with it cannot easily be removed. Use very dilute inks and test all the colours first on a copy of the photograph to ensure that you are happy with the effect and so that you do not risk ruining the original print.

## VIRTUAL HAND-TINTING

If you have image-editing software, such as Adobe Photoshop, on your computer, you can apply all kinds of colour effects before making prints. In the example shown here the colourful background was felt to be too dominant and has been selectively converted to black and white so that the album pages stand out more strongly. If you wish to "age" existing black-and-white prints digitally you can scan the images into the computer and add effects such as sepia toning, vignetting or hand-tinting, then print new copies.

# Making a photographic mosaic

*Try this simple technique to give added interest to an image with bold shapes and colours, or to create an overall pattern from a more detailed picture. Simply cut the print up into a series of small squares and then reassemble it on a coloured background, leaving narrow spaces between the shapes. Mosaic works best on more abstract subjects, or shots of the natural world like these two flower pictures. If you are working with pictures of people, don't make any cuts through the faces as this will alter their proportions.*

**1** Working on a cutting mat, use a clear ruler and a sharp knife to cut the picture into strips of equal width, 2.5–3cm/1–1¼in wide. Cut each strip into squares, keeping them in the correct order as you work to avoid ending up with a jigsaw. A 10 x 15cm/4 x 6in print can be divided into 24 squares each measuring 2.5cm/1in; larger prints can be cut into more squares, or larger squares, as desired.

**2** Decide how much space you want around the completed mosaic and how wide to make the distance between the squares. Lightly rule a border on to your chosen backing paper. Starting at the bottom left corner, stick down the first row of squares, making sure that the gaps between them are regular. Continue working upwards until you reach the end of the last row.

**3** For a less structured approach, try using a punch to cut out the squares. This method leaves larger, irregular spaces between the picture elements and the finished look resembles a traditional mosaic made from tesserae. Adhesive foam pads add an extra dimension to the finished image. Make sure you are going to punch out a complete square by opening the little flap underneath the cutter and inserting the photograph face down in the punch.

## NOW TRY THIS

These two mosaics show complementary variations on the technique. A photograph of russet, gold and green branches takes on an abstract feel when divided into squares, while a picture of rich autumnal foliage provides the perfect frame for a study of a noble tree.

# Making a photographic patchwork

*Traditional patchwork blocks have a strong geometry, which provides a ready-made framework for floral photographs. Designs such as the hexagonal "Grandmother's Flower Garden" are ideal for showing off your favourite garden pictures, and flowers such as primulas, pansies and apple blossom are reminiscent of the pretty prints on old-fashioned dressmaking fabrics. Look for formal carpet bedding, fields of colourful crops or wild flowers, and take both wide-angle and close-up photographs of them to use in creating your own interpretations of these patterns.*

**1** Use a patchwork template to cut out a series of hexagons from your prints – you will need to make several copies of each photograph. The centre of each motif is cut from a single close-up and the six hexagons that surround it are made from pictures of massed flowers in a bed.

**2** Take time to arrange the shapes before sticking them down, making sure that you have enough of each type. Starting at the bottom left corner, glue six patterned hexagons around a plain coloured one. Leaving a 6mm/¼in space all around, make more interlocking motifs to fill the page. Trim the edges flush with the background.

# Weaving photographic images

*This technique requires planning, but the results are well worth it and often produce unexpected effects. Experiment by combining a black-and-white and a coloured copy of the same photograph to create extra depth, as shown with the picture of a Japanese news stand, or by weaving an abstract photograph of texture with a landscape. Weaving works best on landscape or abstract images: as with photographic mosaics, avoid using close-up portraits.*

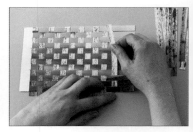

**1** For a square weave, cut the black-and-white version of the picture into horizontal strips 2cm/¾in wide, stopping just short of one end so that they remain joined together. Use a sharp knife and a transparent ruler, and work carefully on a cutting mat. Cut the coloured picture into separate vertical strips of the same width.

**2** Weave the first strip from the left of the coloured picture under and over the black-and-white strips. Take the second strip and weave it under the alternate strips: repeat this to the end, making sure that they are all at right angles and that the space between them is minimal. Secure the ends of the strips with double-sided tape and display the finished piece in a window mount.

**3** To create a basket weave, in which the horizontal strips form rectangles and the vertical ones squares, leave a 3mm/⅛in gap between the short strips. Two very different pictures – one of a stunning coastal sunset and the other of a rusting iron shed – are combined in this weave. They work well together because they have very similar colour schemes.

# Making panoramas and compositions

*Panoramic cameras are fun to use but you don't actually need one to make your own panorama. If you take two or more photographs from the same viewpoint, turning the camera slightly each time, you can then trim and stick the photographs together to make a long, narrow view. You can also use variations on this technique to create extended panoramas from just a single image or use your imagination to combine different images, with surprising results.*

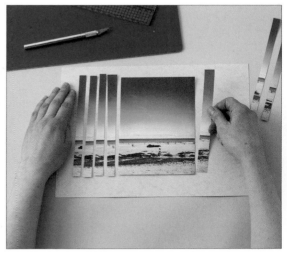

▲ If you are making a joined panorama remember that photographs tend be slightly darker towards the edges (a natural consequence of producing a rectangular image with a round lens) so it's best not to butt untrimmed vertical edges together. Instead, overlap the pictures to see how much of the image they share, then trim half this width from one picture. Put them together with the trimmed photo on top, align a ruler with the trimmed edge, slide away the top picture and trim the bottom one.

▲ Turn a single portrait-format view into an extended landscape, or composite panorama, by combining two identical prints. Cut strips of varying width from each side of one photograph and mount them either side of your main image. If you leave narrow spaces between them, it is less obvious that they simply repeat the image rather than extending it.

▲ An interesting variation on the composite panorama is to use two very different but related pictures to encapsulate memories of an event or place. Here a photograph of a Greek flag is interspersed with a geometric abstract view of buildings clinging to the steep hillside of the Cycladic island of Syros. Staggering the strips adds to the geometric nature of the images.

▲ A quick way to join two similar pictures is to find an obvious vertical line or strong outline along the edge of one of them and cut along it. You can then overlay this edge across the other picture. Although the two pictures used here were not taken from the same spot, they share the same colours and tonal range, so give the effect of two people appearing in the same photograph.

▲ *A great way to produce a multifaceted image of an event or scene is as a photo-composite, in the style of artist David Hockney. To do this, take lots of pictures from different angles and combine them in a collage. This view of the lake and Palm House at the Royal Botanic Gardens in Kew, London, includes several photographs of the same pair of swans, creating the illusion of a larger flock.*

# Transferring photographs on to fabric

*Several types of special paper are available for transferring photographs on to fabric. Your pictures will not be damaged by the process but it must be undertaken at a photocopy bureau. Copy several photographs together on to one sheet. Make sure you have enough transfers to allow for experimentation and mistakes. Some photographs do not work well on transfer paper, such as those with dark backgrounds or lots of contrast, so be prepared for some trial and error.*

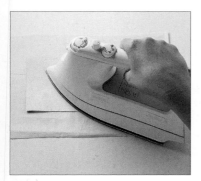

## NOW TRY THIS

This endearing photograph of a much-loved pet required special treatment. The image was transferred on to a piece of natural linen and the vintage-style fabric that forms the frame was carefully selected to echo the paisley quilt the kitten is sitting on. A narrow lace edging and pearl buttons complete the frame.

**1** Stick the photographs lightly on to a piece of plain paper. Take this to a colour copy bureau together with the transfer paper, which needs to be fed one sheet at a time through the paper tray. (Have the photographs copied using a normal colour process to check the colour before they are copied on to the transfer paper.) Trim around a transfer and place it face down on a plain natural fabric with a close weave, such as calico, which will withstand heat and pressure. Referring to the manufacturer's instructions, press with a hot iron. If a lot of pressure is required, it may be advisable to work on a sturdy table protected with several layers of blanket.

**2** Carefully peel off the transfer backing in an even movement to reveal the transferred image. Allow the fabric to cool before using it. Refer to the transfer paper manufacturer's instructions for washing and aftercare. A more expensive, but generally foolproof method of photo transfer is to have the process done professionally at a copy bureau that prints T-shirts with your own images.

## NOW TRY THIS

This sophisticated cloth book would make a wonderful keepsake for a young child. Take close-up photographs of familiar scenes around the child's house and garden and transfer them on to a coarsely woven fabric such as linen or calico to give them a canvas-like texture. Trim each one to 12.5cm/5in square and tack (baste) it to a 16.5 x 18cm/6½ x 7in felt rectangle, allowing a 2cm/¾in border around three sides and a wider border at the spine. Attach with a decorative machine stitch, then assemble the pages and stitch along the spine. You could also embellish the pages with embroidered messages, printed text or other appliquéd decoration.

# Making a kaleidoscope

*The multi-faceted image inside a kaleidoscope is created by reflecting an image between two angled mirrors to produce a repeating, symmetrical pattern. With patience it is possible to make your own photographic version: the effect is stunning, complex, and can be slightly surreal, as with this reinterpretation of a Venetian canal scene. You will need eight prints of the same picture, four of them reversed.*

**1** Draw a square on acetate or tracing paper and divide it diagonally to make a triangular template. Cut it out and use to make two sets of four triangles from the photographs. Clear acetate will enable you to position the template accurately so that the images are identical, with one set a mirror image of the other.

**2** Mark a square sheet of paper into eight equal sections: these will be your guidelines for assembling the pattern. Matching the sides of the images exactly, glue the segments in place, making sure that each one lies next to its mirror image.

**3** You can then trim the finished pattern as you wish: into a square, a four-point star or, as here, a circle. Mark the circumference with a pair of compasses and cut around the pencil line.

**4** If you choose an image that is already symmetrical you can make a kaleidoscope from four, six or eight prints without having to reverse them. Here, the iconic image of the Eiffel Tower is surrounded by pictures of a period shop front to create a unique souvenir of Paris.

## NOW TRY THIS

Here, eight diamonds form the design known in patchwork as the LeMoyne Star, giving the original flower image an abstract quality.

# Framing and mounting photographs

*There are many possible ways to frame your favourite photographs and cards. All the ideas shown here are quick and easy to do and look very effective, both in album pages and as fresh ways of displaying photographs in frames. Try them on your own layouts, or use them as inspiration for your original ideas.*

## CUTTING PAPER FRAMES

Single or multiple borders in paper or thin card (stock), known as mats, are a simple way to present a picture, but must be accurately cut for successful results. Choose colours that match or contrast effectively with the dominant colours in the photographs, and make sure that each successive border balances the photograph and is evenly positioned around the picture.

▲ *On this album page attention is focused on a single image by mounting it in a double mat in two colours. The opening in the top layer is cut a little larger to expose a narrow contrasting inner border.*

▲ *In this charming treatment the paper border is arranged some way away from the edge of the photograph, so that the background acts as an inner frame. A spray of die-cut daisies completes the effect.*

▲ *Multiple paper frames in a simple colour scheme are a great way to give unity to a diverse collection of photographs and other memorabilia. Extra layers can be added to disguise differences of size.*

▼ *For this stacked technique the subject is cut out first and used as the template for the border shapes, each drawn 6mm/¹/₄in larger than the layer above. The careful choice of graduated tones, complementing the bird's plumage, gives a subtle three-dimensional effect.*

▲ *Here the background colour matches the vehicle, and contrast is provided by the square black frames, each of which has a window a little larger than the cut-out photograph, leaving a striking band of colour around each picture.*

# USING TEMPLATES

Plastic templates are available in a host of different shapes and sizes, from simple geometric forms to outlines of cats and Christmas trees. You can also draw and cut your own from many sources. Basic shapes such as ovals are useful guides for trimming photographs accurately, and are easy to use.

**1** Position a template over the part of the photograph you want to use and draw around the outline with a pencil.

**2** Use a small, sharp pair of scissors to cut carefully around the pencil line.

▲ *Use a set of templates in graduated sizes to cut a series of mats or frames to fit around your picture.*

**1** Cut out a narrow frame from a photograph with a lot of background to draw attention to the focal point.

**2** Turn the cut-out section by 45 degrees and replace it between the central area and the border to complete the frame.

▲ *Alternatively, cut away the outer sections of the picture in regular shapes, then offset them slightly and glue to a backing sheet.*

▲ *For a rainbow effect, use a template to cut a succession of circles, then offset them.*

▲ *Make a frame to suit your subject, like this porthole for an underwater theme.*

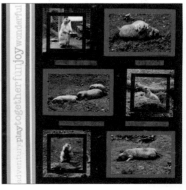

▲ *Different framing methods are unified here by consistent use of colour and shape.*

# TEARING PAPER FRAMES

Torn paper shapes can add softness and a change of texture to your layouts, but it's a good idea to use the effect sparingly, as it can easily become too dominant. Combine it with neat, straight edges for contrast, or make a mosaic of lots of small-scale torn edges using different colours for a subtle collage.

**1** Tearing paper or card (stock) that is coloured the same shade all through gives a soft textured edge. The feathery lines are good for recreating textures such as teddy bear fur, or for layering to create backgrounds resembling water, clouds or grass. Tearing with the grain of the paper gives a straighter edge than tearing against the grain, so practise to see the effects you can achieve. To make it easier to tear a shape, try drawing with a dampened paintbrush along the line you want to tear.

**2** Patterned paper is usually printed and has a white core. Tearing the paper will reveal this. Tearing towards yourself with the pattern uppermost produces a white edge, which highlights the tear. If you don't want to make a feature of this, tear the paper from the other side so that the rough white edge is concealed under the printed top layer. This is a good choice when you want to create a softer line, perhaps when overlapping torn edges to create a change of colour.

▲ *A sheet of torn mulberry paper in a toning colour makes a lovely textural border for a picture. Tearing this paper pulls out the fibres to make a softly fringed edge. The paper should be dampened where you want it to part. For a straight tear, fold it and wet the folded edge then gently pull it apart. For the more random tearing used here, dampen the paper by drawing curves and shapes with a wet paintbrush or cotton bud (swab).*

# DECORATING PAPER FRAMES

You can use pre-printed stickers, but it is easy to make your own frames to suit a particular theme. Trace motifs from books or magazines on to plain paper and adjust the scale on a photocopier if necessary to make a template. Draw around or trace the design on to coloured paper and cut out as many shapes as you need, then glue them on to your album page.

▲ *Specially shaped edging scissors are available in many different designs, and you can use these to create smart decorative effects on coloured paper frames.*

▲ *You can decorate the corners of frames with a punched motif, or punch rows of decorative holes all round the edge. Keep the shapes to decorate the rest of the album page.*

▲ *Use a template to cut decorative shapes from appropriately coloured paper to highlight the theme of an album page, and let them overlap the picture frames.*

▲ *Create an informal look by making a frame from printed stickers. Mount the photograph on a plain background then mass the stickers in groups around it, overlapping the edges and each other.*

▲ *A pricked design makes a pretty, lacy edging for a simple paper frame. Draw the design lightly in pencil then prick evenly along the lines with a bodkin, resting the frame on a soft surface such as a cork tile.*

▲ *Use a stamp of a frame and bright ink to make a frame on plain coloured paper. Cut out a wavy edge for a funky look.*

## NOW TRY THIS

Instead of framing pictures, try mounting them over blocks of bright colour to create a collage effect, then frame them with groups of flowers in co-ordinating shades. These could be stickers or your own photographs, carefully cut out.

1 Select individual flowerheads to match the colours in your pictures and cut them out, carefully eliminating any background.

2 Arrange the coloured paper shapes for the background and glue in place, then position the photographs.

3 Arrange the flower cut-outs to create a scattered effect over the background areas, co-ordinating the colours and allowing the petals to overlap the edges of the photographs.

# BACKGROUND TREATMENTS

Rather than have plain backgrounds to the pages in your album, decorate them with stamps, stencils, stickers and paint effects in colours and themes that are sympathetic to your photographs. Choose subdued, muted shades for subtle compositions, or be more adventurous and experiment with unusual combinations of colour and pattern.

## Choosing colours

*The background should flatter the photographs rather than overpower them and its style needs to be in keeping with the subject matter. But you need not restrict your choice to a single colour or design: try making up collages of interesting textures and patterns. Include greetings cards, wrapping paper, children's artwork, and even fabric swatches.*

▲ *Once you have decided on the images you want to mount, think about colours and motifs that underline their theme. These gold papers suit a wedding layout and the heart is a traditional symbol. Play around with combinations of papers until you find a good balance between images and background.*

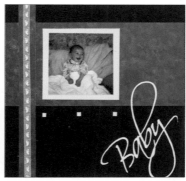

▲ *Blue is the traditional colour scheme for a baby boy, but the dark blue background overlaid with simple bands of lighter tones, with only tiny dashes of baby blue, give this simple treatment a modern look.*

▲ *Do not shy away from patterned backgrounds; these scraps of delicately patterned wallpaper work beautifully with each other and the warm tones of the cat.*

▲ *If you place the same images on a different background, with colours that clash with the photographs, you can instantly see that it is an unsuitable combination.*

### COMPLEMENTARY COLOURS

1 Allow the photographs to dictate your choice of background colours, rather than choosing a paper and hoping the pictures will match it. Hold your images against a wide variety of colours and patterns before making your choice. Here the photograph is overpowered by the colour of the background paper.

2 Orange and green are opposite each other on the colour wheel, so they complement each other well and the cooler colour tends to recede, making the picture of the pumpkins stand out as the focal point. Against this background you could use accents of orange and other warm, toning colours such as peach and gold to accompany the image.

# Using patterns

*Patterned backgrounds help to give layouts a distinctive style, but need to be carefully chosen to avoid dominating the images and other elements that you may choose to add to the page. Make sure the colours and contrasts in the photographs are strong enough to stand out from the background.*

## MONOCHROME SCHEMES

An easy way to begin experimenting with pattern is to restrict your use of colour.

**1** Gather together a selection of papers, patterned and plain, in a single colour. Experiment by overlapping them or placing them next to each other until you find an arrangement you like. Choose one as the background, and cut a few rectangles or strips from the other papers.

**2** For this layout, cut a rectangle of plain blue paper 18 x 25cm/7 x 10in and a strip 5 x 30cm/2 x 12in from another pattern. Stick the rectangle to the left-hand side of the page, 2.5cm/1in from the top, bottom and left side. Arrange the patterned strip horizontally across the page so it overlaps the lower part of the rectangle. Mat the photographs and add them to the layout.

▲ *Using the same design in a different colour scheme and with different subjects changes the look entirely. Here, the monochromatic green layout includes touches of pale yellow in the flower and buttons to pick up the yellow details in the photographs.*

## COMBINING PATTERNED PAPERS

Many ranges of patterned paper are specially designed to be used in combination, making it easy to create interesting backgrounds.

**1** This design mimics a wall with wallpaper and a dado rail, the perfect place to display a few photos. Choose a 30cm/12in square sheet of paper for the background and cut a strip of another paper 10cm/4in wide.

**2** Glue the strip to the bottom of the page and cover the join with a length of toning ribbon. Arrange two large photographs on the upper part of the page. With a button and an extra length of ribbon, suspend a smaller photo from the ribbon "rail".

▲ *These two papers harmonize perfectly because although the patterns contrast in shape and scale they are printed in the same range of colours. When mixing patterns, go for colours in the same tonal family and try teaming stripes with floral designs, or look for the same motifs in different sizes.*

# USING STRIPES AS BORDERS

If you are combining striped and patterned paper, the stripes can be cut up to form a border around the page and frames for the photographs.

**1** Choose a paper with wide stripes, and cut four identical strips 4 x 30cm/1¹/₂ x 12in. Mount one on each side of the page, matching the stripes. Glue another along the bottom and mitre the corners by cutting diagonally through both layers.

**2** Add the last strip at the top of the page, making sure the strips correspond as before, and mitre the two top corners. Mat your selection of photographs in toning shades and mount on the page.

▲ *Four black-and-white photographs of disparate subjects are neatly unified with this simple treatment, which does not distract attention from the pictures.*

# USING BOLD PATTERNS

Some patterned papers are bold and dramatic but won't overwhelm photographs if they are paired with strong images or colours. Close-ups of faces or objects work best.

**1** Choose a patterned paper that includes as many of the colours in your choice of photographs as possible. Here the bright pinks and oranges pick up the colours of the flowers and the vivid stripes convey the exuberance of spring blossom.

**2** Pick shades from the patterned paper to mat the photos: this will help them stand out from the background. Add embellishments that match the colour and theme of the layout.

▶ *The pretty ribbons on this page are chosen to match the striped paper, while the little flower buttons echo the springtime theme.*

# Collage techniques

*Building up a multilayered background using different papers allows you to introduce a satisfying variety of texture and colour.*

## USING MULBERRY PAPER

Mulberry paper is available plain or printed, and some sheets incorporate pieces of flowers or leaves, making perfect backgrounds for pictures with a pastoral or garden theme. Its soft feathered edges are very attractive.

**1** Choose a selection of papers that match the tones of the photograph. Strips of paper will be used to extend the bands of colour in the sky. To tear them, dip a paintbrush in water then trace a line on the paper. Pull the paper apart while it is wet.

**2** Build up the scene with torn strips of mulberry paper; a different shade is created when two colours of the paper overlap. Mat the photograph in black, so that its straight edges form a striking contrast with the soft outlines of the mulberry paper, and mount it on the background.

▲ *This lovely photograph of a sunset has an almost abstract quality, and the collage background made with torn strips of mulberry paper extends the scene very effectively. The dark foreground, reduced to a silhouette in the fading light, is matched by a sheet of black paper covering the lower part of the page.*

## MAKING A PAPER COLLAGE

Subtle colour effects can be achieved by building up small pieces of torn paper in a range of toning colours. Begin by tearing a good quantity of the colours you need before applying any glue.

**1** Tear the paper into small pieces of a fairly even size, aiming to make rounded shapes. Tear away the straight edges of the paper so that they are roughly torn on all sides.

**2** Glue the pieces to the background in a group, overlapping them and mixing the colours at random. If you want to create the effect of falling leaves, you could add a scattering of isolated pieces.

**3** Add details to the collage if you wish by stamping motifs or drawing them in with a fibre-tipped pen in a toning colour.

▶ *Here a photograph is enhanced by a colour-co-ordinated collage in subdued colours that has been aged with stamping.*

# USING COLLAGED PAPER

Some patterned papers have a collage-effect design, with elements scattered across the paper. If you cut around parts of these, you can slide photographs underneath to look as if they are part of the overall design.

**I** Mark with a pencil where a corner or edge of the photograph intersects with an element in the pattern. Use a craft knife to trim along the edge of the pattern.

**2** Make more slits across the page to accommodate the photographs you wish to include. Mat the photos and slide them under the flaps.

▲ *Single elements, such as the suitcase on this travel-themed layout, can be trimmed from another sheet of patterned paper and added as embellishments.*

# COLOUR BLOCKING

This is an easy technique to master, especially for beginners and when using a monochromatic colour scheme. Photographs and other elements can sit neatly within one block or overlap across several. This design for a 30cm/12in album page is based on a grid of 8 x 8 squares.

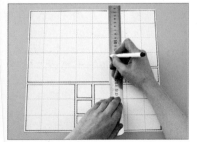

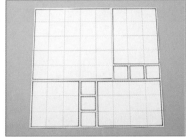

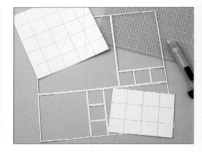

**I** Using a grid of 4cm/1½in squares, design the blocks for your layout.

**2** Rule 6mm/¼in margins between the blocks and all round the edge of the sheet.

**3** Use a craft knife and ruler to cut each template piece out of the grid.

**4** Draw round each template on the back of patterned paper and cut out. Use a different paper for each section.

**5** Glue the cut-out papers on to a background sheet of 30cm/12in card (stock), following the original layout.

**6** Add photographs, embellishments and journaling as desired.

## NOW TRY THIS

Traditional patchwork patterns include lots of designs that can be adapted to scrapbooking. This one is called "Shoo Fly" and is a simple combination of squares and triangles in a balanced design to which photographs can be added.

**1** Choose one 30cm/12in square paper for the background. From a different paper, cut three 10cm/4in squares. Cut two of these in half diagonally.

**2** Position the background square centrally on the page, and arrange one triangle diagonally across each corner. Glue in place.

**3** Add lines of "stitching" around the patches with a black pen to mimic running stitch and blanket stitch. Glue the remaining square in the centre.

**4** Arrange the photographs and embellishments between the patches.

◀ *The patchwork theme is enhanced with drawn-in stitching and lettering designed to resemble appliqué.*

# MAKING A SILHOUETTE

This makes an interesting treatment for a photograph of someone in profile. Cut the profile out of black or coloured card (card stock) to form an accompaniment to the photo. You can use the photograph as your guide for the silhouette, or you could draw your own version.

**1** Using a computer or photocopier, enlarge the photograph to the desired size for the silhouette and glue to a sheet of dark card.

**2** Cut carefully around the outline of the person in the print using a pair of sharp-pointed scissors.

**3** Reverse the silhouette and add it to the layout, positioning it to balance the original photograph.

# Adding paint, chalk and ink

*Instead of using printed paper, you can create your own unique patterns to form tailor-made backgrounds for your collections. If you don't feel confident about your painting and drawing skills, just choose from the host of ready-made stencils and stamps available, and work with colour-washed backgrounds.*

## PAINTING BACKGROUNDS

For interesting textural effects, make patterns in wet paint. You can try a variety of objects such as the blunt end of a paintbrush, a cocktail stick (toothpick) or a wooden skewer, drawing simple curls, spirals and stars. Or cut a comb from stiff cardboard and draw it through the paint.

**1** Mix some acrylic paint with wallpaper paste to make a thick paste. With a wide brush, paint the surface of a sheet of heavy cartridge (construction) paper using even strokes in one direction. Use a comb to make patterns in the wet paint.

**2** Draw the comb in two directions for a woven pattern, or use random strokes for bark-like effects. Allow the paper to dry completely. If it buckles, press the back with a cool iron, then leave it between heavy books to keep it flat.

## ANTIQUING

Paper with an aged look can be useful for heritage layouts, either as a background, as part of a collage, or for titles and journaling.

**1** To achieve an antique effect, brush a strong solution of tea over the surface of white paper. Allow to dry, then press with a cool iron if necessary to flatten. The paper can then be torn or cut up to use in a collage. You could also try singeing the edges to add to the effect.

## RUBBER STAMPING

There are literally hundreds of rubber stamps available on the market nowadays, so you will always be able to find something to complement your album page designs. You could use small motifs for surface decoration, or large scale designs that form an all-over background pattern.

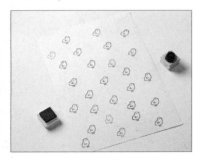 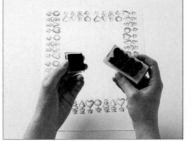 

**1** Use a single motif to stamp an all-over design on to plain paper to create a patterned background. Press the stamp in the ink pad, then press it on the paper, taking care not to smudge. Repeat as desired. Apply the images in a random pattern, or rule faint pencil guidelines.

**2** The elongated shape of this topiary stamp makes it ideal for a border design. If you want a symmetrical design, measure the stamp and work out how many repeats will fit the page. Ensure the stamp aligns with the edge, and that each new print lines up with the designs already stamped.

**3** Rubber-stamped designs can be enhanced very simply by colouring the motifs lightly with coloured pencils. You could also try using various kinds of paint to achieve different effects.

# USING CHALKS

Sets of acid-free chalks are available in various ranges of different shades and can be used to create very soft colour effects on very light or very dark papers. To extend the tones of a photograph across a full layout, use chalks to recreate the scene, or use them to tint embossed paper.

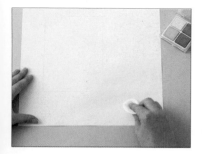

**1** Measure the photograph, subtract 1cm/⅜in from each side, and trace the dimensions on to a 30cm/12in square sheet of white card (stock). With a pad of cotton wool (ball), pick up some coloured chalk and rub it across the page.

**2** Continue to build up the chalk scene, matching the shades used in the photograph and using a clean pad for each new colour. For details such as the path and fence posts, use a cotton bud (swab) or the applicator supplied with the chalk to draw finer lines.

**3** Leave the page overnight, to allow the chalks to settle into the paper. Finally, add the photograph in the marked area.

# COMBINING CHALKS AND STAMPING

Used together, rubber stamps and chalks enable you to combine fine pictorial detail with soft colouring. You can either use the chalks to fill in the stamped motifs or rub them over the paper to create a mist of colour over the whole page before applying the stamped image.

**1** Choose rubber stamp motifs to match the theme of the page and stamp them at random over the background sheet using a range of coloured inks. Using a cotton wool pad (ball) rub chalks in toning colours across the page to create a soft wash of background colour. Leave the page for a few hours to allow the chalk to settle into the paper, then add the matted photographs and embellishments.

▶ *The smaller photograph of a leafy country track inspired the choice of leaf stamps in soft autumn shades for this background. The chalks harmonize well with the horse's colouring, and a length of real ribbon provides the finishing touch.*

# STENCILLING

Charming backgrounds can be created using stencils, which work well with paints, oil sticks or chalks. Stencils are easy to cut from manila card or clear acetate, and you can work from templates or draw your own. Hundreds of ready-cut designs are also available in craft stores.

**1** Trace the design and transfer it to stencil card. Working on a cutting mat and using a craft knife cut out each shape, taking care not to cut through any "bridges" holding elements of the design in place.

**2** Using an oil stick or appropriate paint, and a large stencil brush, dab paint on to the chosen area using the stencil. Lift the stencil carefully to avoid smudging the edges and leave to dry.

**3** Add details with a second stencil. Leave to dry.

▼ *Stencilled animals and a Noah's ark make a lovely setting for a young child's picture.*

# EMBELLISHING THE PAGES

Adding the final decorative touches is often the most enjoyable part of assembling your album pages. The elements you use should enhance the photographs and complement the background.

## Papercraft

*Keep a collection of offcuts of interesting papers for these delicate decorations, which use precise folding and cutting to create pretty three-dimensional ornaments, from decorative tags and envelopes to classic origami flowers.*

### PAPER ROLLING

Rolled paper edgings and frames work particularly well when you use paper that is printed differently on each side, as the rolling exposes the contrasting pattern or colour.

▲ *The photographs here have been enhanced with rolled paper frames.*

1 To create a rolled heart, draw the shape on the back of the paper and cut a series of slashes from the centre to the edge.

2 Roll a dampened cotton bud (swab) along the cut edges to soften the fibres. Turn the paper over and roll each section towards the edge of the shape.

3 Glue a photograph or embellishment in the centre of the heart motif.

### MAKING A LACÉ DESIGN

Pronounced "lassay", this technique works best when cut from two-sided card (stock). It can be cut using a metal template (you can buy lots of different designs) or you can devise your own using a pair of compasses or a protractor. Small patterned cuts are made in the card and the cut piece is bent over to form a bicoloured design.

1 Transfer the template to the wrong side of the card using a pencil (the lines will be erased later).

2 Using a sharp craft knife, cut neatly along the lines from end to middle. Erase the pencil marks and turn the card over.

3 Lift one petal and fold it backwards. Once all the petals are folded, tuck each one under the edge of the previous point.

# PAPER APPLIQUÉ

Appliqué literally means "applied". Usually appliqué is a technique used with fabric in the art of patchwork. Here it is used with paper. Cut-out shapes in paper or card (stock) of different colours or patterns can be stacked together to create three-dimensional motifs. Here the appliqué effect is emphasized by lines of decorative "stitches" drawn around the card patches. Attaching the motif by means of sticky foam pads raises it a little above the surface, so that the butterfly seems to hover over the flowers.

**1** Trace the outlines of the butterfly and the applied panels for the wings and copy them on to a sheet of card to make templates. Cut out all the pieces.

**2** Select sheets of card in four different colours. Draw round the templates for the basic shape and the body in one colour, and divide the smaller coloured details between the remaining sheets, keeping the design symmetrical.

**3** Cut out all the pieces of the butterfly.

**4** Using a fine-tipped black pen, draw lines of small "stitches" around the edge of each coloured shape. Glue the shapes to the butterfly's wings. Create a pair of antennae from a length of fine silver wire, curling the ends tightly, and glue to the head. Attach the body to the wings using foam pads to give a three-dimensional effect, and use more foam pads to anchor the butterfly to the background.

▶ *This cut-out butterfly, floating a little above the surface of the album page, softens what would otherwise be a very rigid layout of squares, and is perfectly in keeping with the floral theme. The colours of the panels on its wings are repeated in the picture mats.*

# QUILLING

Thin strips of finely rolled paper are arranged into pictorial images suitable for scrapbooking. This traditional craft requires a special tool and narrow strips of plain coloured paper, which you can buy specially cut. It is possible to cut them yourself but they must be precisely the same width all along their length. Once you've mastered your first roll (it's very easy) you can make this pretty flower.

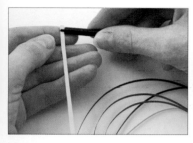

**1** Make the leaves first. Slide one end of a green strip into the notch on the quilling tool.

**2** Roll the paper tightly and evenly on to the tool.

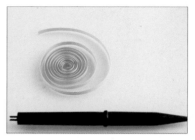

**3** Gently ease the rolled paper off the tool and allow it to uncoil to the desired size. Glue the end and hold until dry.

**4** Pinch the edges of the circle on opposite sides, using your thumbs and forefingers.

**5** Make four red coils for the petals. Make two pinches close to each other and press the rest of the circle down towards them.

**6** Roll a tight black coil for the centre. Cut a stem from green paper and assemble the pieces to complete the poppy.

# DECORATING TAGS

Tags are quick-to-make scrapbook embellishments and use only small quantities of materials. You can use a die-cutting machine or templates, or make the shape by just snipping the corners off a rectangle.

**1** Snip two corners off a rectangle of card. Punch a hole for the string and shape the other two corners with a corner cutter.

**2** Embellish the tag as desired. In this case ribbons and ribbon roses were used and the tag was tied with coloured fibres.

▲ *Use simple tags to hold pictures or text, or just as decoration. They can be glued to a page or hung by ribbon ties.*

# MAKING POCKETS

As vellum is translucent, you can use this simple pocket for photos, or just slip some journaling or souvenirs such as tickets inside.

**I** Cut out a pocket template and draw around it on vellum.

**2** Fold in the side and bottom flaps. Glue the flaps and attach to the layout.

▼ *Vellum allows you to see what's inside the pocket without taking it out.*

# MAKING MINI-ENVELOPES

A tiny envelope adds excitement to a page, and could be used to hold small treasures such as a handful of confetti in a wedding album, a scrap of lace or even a lock of hair. Or you could inscribe a secret message on a little card and tuck it inside.

**I** Draw around an envelope template and cut out.

**2** Fold in three of the corners and glue the overlapping edges. Fold down the top.

▶ *For a page celebrating the arrival of a baby girl, you could decorate some little envelopes with pretty labels and tiny pink bows.*

## PLASTIC POCKETS

Cut a pocket from the lower edge of a stationery folder. Staple the sides together and insert a memento. Staple the top closed or leave it open so that the contents can be taken out.

Cut two squares from a plastic folder and pierce holes around the edges. Attach a memento or decorations to one piece using double-sided tape. Lace the sides together with cord and knot the ends.

# MAKING POP-UP PAGES

Proper pop-ups like these party balloons work only on pages that aren't in page protectors, since it's the action of the pages opening out that makes the pop-up rise. You can, however, arrange lifting flaps on single pages inside page protectors, either by cutting a slit for them or by sticking them to the outside with another, cut-down, page protector to cover them. These pages are good for children's themes.

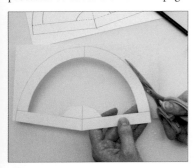

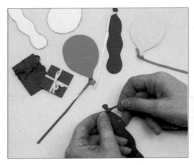

**1** Transfer the pop-up template at the back of the book to white card (stock) and cut it out. Score along the dotted lines. Fold the bottom struts up and the arch back.

▼*A pop-up is a dramatic ornament for a strap or post-bound album.*

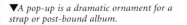

**2** Apply adhesive to the bottom of the two struts, then glue the whole pop-up in place across two pages of the album. Following the templates, cut out the four balloons and two presents from plain card in a range of bright colours.

**3** Wrap a ribbon round each present and tie ribbons round the ends of the balloons. Stick the parcels on the base of the pop-up, and balloons on the arch, making sure they will not jam the pop-up when it closes. Stick the tails of the balloons behind the parcels. Add photographs to the layout.

# MAKING AN ORIGAMI SHIRT

This traditional craft of paper folding can be successfully exploited for scrapbooking designs. This clever little design really does look just like a tiny shirt, and makes a lovely embellishment for pictures of children playing at dressing up, or perhaps dressed for a special occasion. All the creases need to be sharp and accurate.

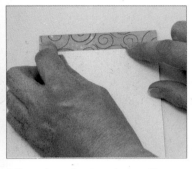

**1** Cut a piece of patterned paper 10 × 20cm/4 × 8in. Fold in half lengthwise, then unfold. Fold down 1.5cm/½in from the narrow top edge. Fold over again.

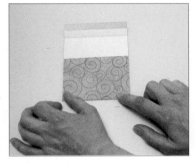

**2** Unfold the two folds at the top, and fold up 7cm/2¾in from the bottom edge.

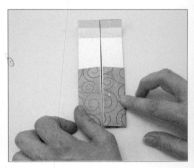

**3** Fold the two long edges in to meet in the centre.

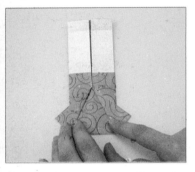

**4** Fold out the bottom corners (these will form the sleeves).

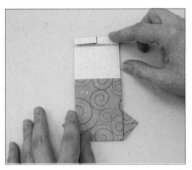

**5** Turn over and fold the top edge down once, along the pre-existing crease.

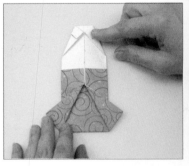

**6** Turn over again and fold the top corners into the centre to form the collar.

**7** Fold in half horizontally, so that the original lower edge just touches the outer corners of the collar.

**8** Tuck the points of the collar over the folded edge to complete the shirt. Add a bead necklace or a ribbon tie.

▲ *For this page the shirt is neatly trimmed with a necklace threaded with a child's initial, and is accompanied by a little skirt made by concertina pleating a strip of paper in a toning colour. Photo mats using the two papers tie the whole scheme together.*

# TEA BAG FOLDING

This technique gets its unusual name because its inventor made her first fold using a colourful tea bag envelope. It's also known as miniature kaleidoscopic origami, and you can buy or download sheets printed with small patterned squares. The easiest design is a rosette, which can be used as a decorative element or as the "O" in a word like "snow" or "love".

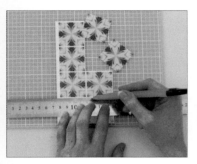

**1** Cut out eight patterned tea bag squares from a printed sheet.

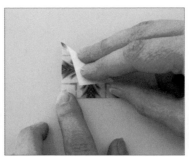

**2** Fold the first square diagonally, with the patterned side inside.

**3** Unfold and turn the paper over so the back of the square is facing you.

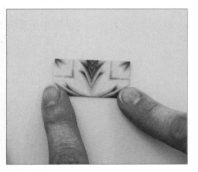

**4** Fold the square in half horizontally, taking the bottom edge up to the top edge.

**5** Unfold it, then fold it in half vertically, taking the right edge to the left edge with the patterned side inside. Unfold.

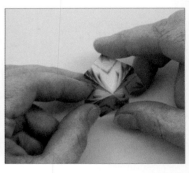

**6** With the patterned side facing you, push the valley folds in and bring the two uncreased quarters of the square together.

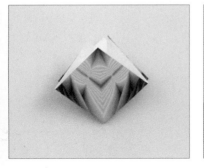

**7** Fold all the remaining squares in the same way, then take one in your fingers, with the peak down and the open folds to the top.

**8** Open the fold on one side, and spread some glue on it. Slide the next square, peak down, in between these two sticky sides, and press to make the glue stick.

**9** Go round the circle, adding each square in the same way until the rosette is complete, then glue the last section over the first.

**10** Glue a cluster of beads or sequins in the centre to complete the decoration.

▲ *Adding green paper stems and simple leaf shapes to these tea bag rosettes turns them into stylized flowers to decorate a layout with a garden theme.*

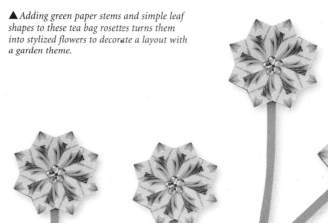

# IRIS FOLDING

This technique creates intricate spiralling designs using folded strips of paper arranged like the panels of a camera iris. It is an ingenious method of creating curved forms using only straight components, and looks very effective when mounted inside an aperture. Experiment with combinations of plain and patterned paper or contrasting colours.

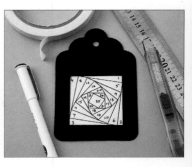

**I** Choose four different shades of paper and cut into strips 2cm/¾in wide.

**2** Fold each strip in half lengthwise and glue the two sides together, right sides out.

**3** Cut a 5cm/2in aperture in black card (stock) and use low-tack masking tape to fix the template temporarily within the aperture. The pattern will be built up backwards, so place the black card face down on the table, with the template below.

**4** Cut a piece 6cm/2¼in long from a length of brown paper. Line it up to cover the triangle labelled 1, with the folded edge towards the centre. Glue the edges of the strip to stick it down (be careful not to get any adhesive on the template below).

**5** Take a 6cm/2¼in length of pink paper, and glue it in position to cover the section marked 2 on the template.

**6** Take a 6cm/2¼in length of blue paper, and glue it in position to cover the section marked 3 on the template.

**7** Take a 6cm/2¼in length of green paper, and glue it in position to cover the section marked 4 on the template.

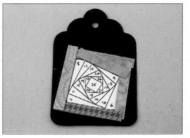

**8** Continue round the spiral, adding paper strips as follows: brown (5), pink (6), blue (7), green (8), brown (9), pink (10), blue (11), green (12), brown (13), pink (14), blue (15), green (16), brown (17), pink (18), blue (19), green (20), brown (21), pink (22) blue (23), green (24).

**9** The strips spiral into the centre, leaving a square hole (section 25 on the template).

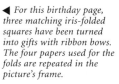

▲ *This six-petalled flower design accentuates the spiralling shapes created in iris folding. This time just three different papers have been used, and a paper stem and leaves have been added to complete the picture.*

◀ *For this birthday page, three matching iris-folded squares have been turned into gifts with ribbon bows. The four papers used for the folds are repeated in the picture's frame.*

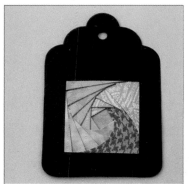

**10** Cover the central hole by gluing on a square of brown paper.

**11** Turn the card over and remove the template to reveal the completed design.

**12** Turn the square into a house with a brown triangle for the roof and a folded paper chimney.

# Adding metal and wire

*Eyelets, wire decorations and metal tags add lustre and a change of texture to your layouts. Make sure hard materials of this kind are well protected and positioned so that they will not damage your precious photographs.*

## EMBOSSING METAL

Foil of around 38 gauge is suitable for embossing, working on the back to create a raised pattern, or on the front to indent a pattern.

**1** To make a tag, draw round a card tag on a sheet of foil using an embossing tool or dry ballpoint pen and a ruler.

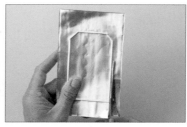

**2** Cut out the tag with old scissors, trimming 2mm/¹/₁₆in outside the embossed line. Punch a hole in the top of the tag.

▲ *A simple outline of evenly spaced dots makes a pretty decoration for small metal picture frames.*

**3** Place the tag face down on thick cardboard and emboss a row of dots inside the marked line. Add other motifs as desired and glue on a photograph or message.

◀ *For extra charm add some small motifs such as stylized flower shapes or these simple stars.*

## USING WIRE

Fine wire in silver, gold and other colours can be twisted into delicate coils and curls and used in conjunction with paper decorations, fabric or ribbon flowers, sequins or clay ornaments.

**1** To make a coil, wrap some coloured wire around a pencil, then slide it off and trim.

**2** Flatten the coils with your fingers and glue the wire in place on the layout.

▲ *A wire coil makes an offbeat stem for a punched flower decoration in shiny plastic.*

# INSERTING BRADS

Brads or paper fasteners are a decorative way to attach pictures.

**1** To attach a picture to a tag, cut a small slit in each corner of the picture, and corresponding slits in the tag.

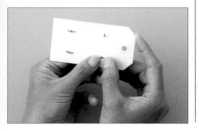

**2** Push in the brads and open out the pins on the back, pressing them flat. Cover with small pieces of sticky tape if desired.

▲ *Brads can be used to hold layers of papers and embellishments together or they can be used for purely decorative purposes.*

▼ *This picture is held in place on its mount with eyelets in each corner, through which a length of fibre fringe has been threaded.*

# INSERTING EYELETS

Eyelets can be used to hold several layers of paper or card together; in addition they provide holes through which ribbon or string can be laced.

**1** Glue the picture to the card, then place it on a block of wood. To make holes for the eyelets, place an eyelet punch in one corner of the picture and tap it sharply with a tack hammer. Repeat at each corner. Insert an eyelet into the first hole, through both picture and card.

**2** Turn the card over Place the pointed end of the eyelet setter into the collar of the eyelet, and tap it sharply with a tack hammer. This will split and flatten the collar. Repeat for the remaining eyelets.

▶ *Outsize coloured metal eyelets threaded with string make an eye-catching trimming for a plain frame.*

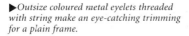

# Adding texture and ornament

*Relief effects add subtle interest to a page. Embossed motifs can underline a theme and draw attention to the tactile quality of lovely paper, while glitter and sequins add a change of texture as well as sparkle. Use tiny beads or model your own motifs for three-dimensional embellishments.*

## BLIND (DRY) EMBOSSING

If you are using good paper with an interesting texture, embossed motifs make the most of its quality and lend an extra dimension to a layout.

**1** Draw your chosen motif on a piece of card (stock). Using a craft knife and working on a cutting mat, cut out the motif to make a stencil for embossing.

**2** Place the stencil on a lightbox, if you have one, and lay a sheet of watercolour paper on top. Use an embossing tool to press into the paper, through the stencil. This is now the back of your paper. Reposition the paper to repeat the embossed motif as many times as required.

▲ *It's possible to use real objects as templates for embossed designs. On very smooth paper you could try a finely detailed object such as a coin, while on heavily textured paper greater relief is needed. Here, a flat scallop shell has been used to embossed rough handmade paper with a bold design.*

◄ *Embossed on thick, soft watercolour paper this simple heart motif gains complexity when repeated and overlapped in a soft curve, creating an engaging interplay of light and shade.*

---

### SHRINKING PLASTIC

**1** Using felt-tipped pens, draw a design on the rough side of a piece of shrink plastic. If the plastic does not have a rough side, sand it lightly first with fine glass paper. The image should be no larger than 12.5 x 10cm/5 x 4in. Bear in mind that it will become seven times smaller and the colours will intensify.

**2** Cut out the image, leaving a narrow border all round. Bake the plastic in an oven for a few minutes following the manufacturer's instructions. It will twist and turn then become flat. Remove the image, which will be pliable, and place a weight such as a book on top for a few moments to keep it flat while it cools and sets.

# GLITTER AND SEQUINS

If you want to add a little sparkle to a photograph, glitter paint is easy to control, allowing you to highlight fine details of the image. This product is particularly effective on black-and-white photographs.

I Apply glitter paint to selected areas of a picture via the nozzle of the container or using a fine paintbrush.

2 Attach some small cabouchon jewellery stones to the glitter paint, using a pair of tweezers to position them accurately.

3 Gently drop sequins and sequin dust on the glitter paint. Shake off the excess.

# RAISED (WET) EMBOSSING

In wet embossing, a design is stamped on the paper then coated with embossing powder, which is fused with the stamped design using heat to produce a raised motif. Embossing powders and inks are available in many colours as well as metallic and pearlized finishes.

# LOOSE GLITTER

Glitter needs to be attached to the paper using glue, usually painted on with a brush, so broad effects are easier to achieve than fine detail.

I Press the stamp into the ink pad and stamp an image on to the paper where required. While the ink is still wet, sprinkle embossing powder over the image. Make sure it is completely covered, then pour the excess powder back into the pot.

2 Use a dry paintbrush to gently brush away any excess embossing powder from the paper.

3 Switch on a heat gun. Holding it about 10cm/4in from the surface of the paper, gently blow heat over the embossing powder until it melts and flows together to make a raised image.

I Using an old paintbrush, draw the design in PVA (white) glue. Sprinkle on the glitter.

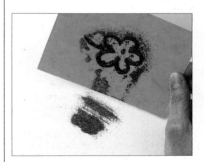

2 Shake off the excess glitter on to a sheet of scrap paper then pour it back into the container.

# BEADS

Small glass beads can be strung on thread using a beading needle or threaded on to fine wire: 0.4mm is a suitable thickness to use.

◀ Mount a photograph on card using spray adhesive. Resting on a cutting mat, use an awl to pierce holes at each end where you wish to add wires. Thread coloured wire up through one hole, bending back the end on the underside to keep the wire in place. Thread on a few beads. Insert the wire through the next hole. Bend back the wire to hold it in place on the underside, and snip off the excess with wirecutters. Repeat to attach wires between all the holes.

▲ *In this celebratory layout, coils of fine wire frame the pictures in the central panel.*

# BEADED FLOWER

Glass rocaille beads are available in a range of exciting colours and add sparkle and colour to layouts. When threaded on wire they can be manipulated easily to make motifs.

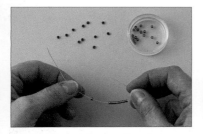

**1** Bend back 3cm/1¼in of one end of a 12.5cm/5in length of fine wire to stop the beads slipping off. Thread on rocaille beads to a point 3cm/1¼in from the other end.

**2** Twist the wire ends together under the beads to make a loop. Repeat to make four petals. Pierce the centre of a piece of card and poke the wire ends through the hole.

**3** Stick the wire ends to the underside of the card with sticky tape. Splay the petals open on the front of the card and sew on a button to form the centre of the flower.

# TASSELS

Little tassels made of silky thread are a charming trimming for elements such as small books containing journaling. They are quick and easy to make using embroidery thread (floss).

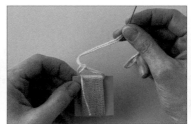

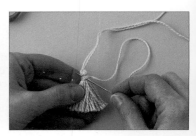

**1** To make a tassel 4cm/1½in long, cut out a rectangle of card (card stock) measuring 8 x 4cm/3¼ x 1½in and fold it in half, parallel with the short edges. (Cut a larger rectangle of card to make a bigger tassel.) Bind thread around the card many times.

**2** Fold a 40cm/16in length of thread in half and thread the ends through the eye of a large needle. Slip the needle behind the strands close to the fold then insert the needle through the loop of thread and pull tightly.

**3** Slip the point of a scissor blade between the card layers and cut through the strands. Thread the needle with single thread and bind it tightly around the top of the tassel. Insert the needle into the tassel to lose the end of the thread. Trim the ends level.

# Using modelling clay

*Polymer and air-drying clays are ideal for moulding small three-dimensional motifs. Their fine texture enables you to create very detailed objects. Polymer clay needs to be baked in a domestic oven; air-drying clay hardens over about 24 hours. Glue motifs in place using strong epoxy glue.*

## CUTTING CLAY

For flat motifs, roll the clay out on a smooth cutting mat using a rolling pin. Rolling guides, such as two pieces of plywood placed on each side of the clay, guarantee an even thickness.

I Cut the clay with a craft knife. Cut straight edges against a metal ruler.

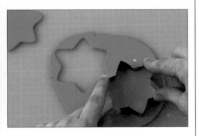

2 Use cookie cutters to stamp motifs then pull away the excess clay.

## MAKING POLYMER CLAY MOTIFS

Complex motifs are easier to make if you first break the shapes down into a series of geometric forms, such as cylinders, cones, spheres and rectangles. These basic shapes can be pressed together and refined using modelling tools.

I To make a flower, roll a ball of polymer clay for the centre and six matching balls for the petals. Flatten all the balls and press the petals around the centre.

2 Shape the petals by impressing them close to the flower centre using the pointed handle of an artist's brush.

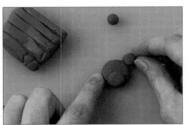

3 Roll a ball for a bear's head. and three smaller balls for the muzzle and ears. Flatten all the balls and press together. Impress the ears with the handle of an artist's brush.

4 Press on a tiny ball of black clay for the nose. Stamp the eyes with the glass head of a dressmaker's pin and use the point to indent a line down the muzzle.

## STAMPING CLAY

For repeated motifs, flat shapes of polymer or air-drying clay can be stamped with any object with an interesting profile. Novelty buttons, for example, make good stamps. If the button has a shank, you can hold this to stamp the button into the clay. Bonsai wire (from specialist nurseries) is ideal for making wire stamping tools for curls and spirals as it is thick but very pliable.

◀I To make a wire stamping tool, shape the wire using jewellery pliers. Bend the free end up at 90 degrees to form a handle.

▶ 2 Hold the handle and stamp the motif on to polymer or air-drying clay.

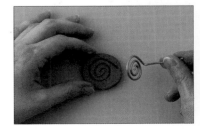

# SEWING AND FABRICS

You can use fabrics and fibres of all kinds to add texture and variety to your album pages, and all can be enhanced with decorative stitching and embroidery, by hand or machine. Bold stitches also look good on paper and card (stock). If you are machine sewing on paper use a new needle.

## STRAIGHT STITCH

Use plain machine stitching to join fabrics to paper or card (stock).

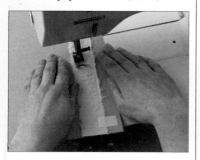

▲ For decorative effect or to apply a contrast coloured border, tear or cut a strip of paper or fabric. Tape it to the background with masking tape at the top and bottom. Stitch the strip with a straight stitch either in a straight line or meander in a wavy line. Remove the masking tape. Pull the thread ends to the wrong side and knot them. Cut off the excess thread.

## ZIG-ZAG

In a contrasting colour, zig-zag stitch makes a decorative border.

▲ Stick a photograph in place with paper glue. Stitch along the edges of the photo with a zig-zag stitch, pivoting the stitching at the corners. Pull the thread ends to the wrong side and knot them. Cut off the excess thread.

## SATIN STITCH

Decorative lines of satin stitch can be worked on paper, card or fabric.

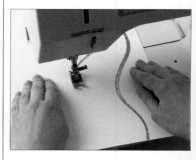

▲ To work a line of satin stitch on card (card stock) or fabric, gradually increase and decrease the width of the zig-zag stitch as you stitch. These lines are sewn with a shaded thread in random wavy lines. If you prefer, draw guidelines lightly with a pencil first. Pull the thread ends to the wrong side and knot them. Cut off the excess thread.

## SATIN STITCH MOTIF

For a simple fabric motif, work the outline in satin stitch, using either matching or contrasting thread, then cut it out and attach with glue.

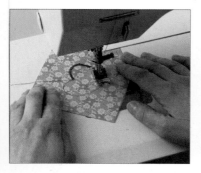

I Draw the outline of the motif on fabric. Stitch along the line with a close zig-zag stitch, pivoting the stitching at any corners, until you return to the starting point. Pull the ends of the threads to the wrong side and knot them. Cut off the excess thread.

2 Use a pair of sharp embroidery scissors to cut away the fabric close to the stitching.

# RUNNING STITCH

To keep your stitches perfectly even and avoid tearing paper or card (card stock), it's best to make the holes first using an awl.

**1** Stick the photograph in place with paper glue. Resting on a cutting mat, pierce a row of holes along two opposite edges of the picture, using an awl or paper piercer.

**2** Knot the end of a length of fine cord. Thread the cord in and out of the holes. Knot the cord on the last hole and cut off the excess. Repeat on the opposite edge.

# GUIDE HOLES FOR HAND SEWING

Instead of piercing holes individually, try using your sewing machine, set to a long stitch length: the holes will be perfectly even and straight.

**1** To create a frame or line of evenly spaced holes to sew through, first draw your design lightly with a pencil. Stitch with a straight stitch but no thread. Rub away the pencil marks with an eraser.

**2** Sew in and out of the holes with thread. Knot the thread ends on the underside to start and finish. A photo or charm can be stuck within the frame.

# CROSS STITCH

Use thick embroidery thread (floss) to make large-scale cross stitches.

**1** Stick the photograph in position with spray adhesive and "sew" along the top and bottom edges with a row of large cross stitches using embroidery thread. To make it easier to sew, pierce a hole at each end of the cross with an awl, resting on a cutting mat. Knot the thread ends on the underside to start and finish.

▲ *A felt cover with a border of bold blanket stitching is a pretty treatment for a mini-album containing baby pictures.*

# Working with fabric

*A box of fabric scraps can be a real treasure trove when you are designing layouts. Materials such as net won't fray and looks lovely when gathered. Sheer organza is especially useful for subtle effects.*

## APPLIQUÉ

Bonding web is a fusible webbing used to apply fabric to fabric. It is simply ironed on, prevents fraying and is ideal for appliqué work.

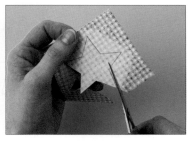

**I** Draw your motif, in reverse if not symmetrical, on the paper backing of the bonding web. Roughly cut out the shape and iron it on to the wrong side of the fabric.

**2** Cut out the design. Peel off the backing paper and position the motif right side up on the background. Press with a hot iron to fuse it in place. Oversew the edges by hand or with a machine satin stitch if you wish.

▲ *To make a pretty net spiral decoration, cut a 50 x 1.5cm/20 x ⁵⁄₈in strip of net. Run a gathering thread along one long edge. Pull up the gathers until the strip is 15cm/6in long. Curl the strip and glue it in a spiral shape to your background using all-purpose household glue.*

## ORGANZA LAYERS

This sheer fabric is available in many colours, some shot with silver or gold for exciting effects.

**I** Cut a motif such as this tree from fabric or paper and stick it to the background card (card stock) with spray adhesive.

**2** Tear strips of organza fabric. Use spray adhesive to stick the strips across the card overlapping or singly in bands. Trim the organza level with the edges of the card. Glue on sequins to complete the picture.

▶ *Sheer fabrics such as organza can be layered to create depth and interesting tonal effects. Here the raw edges also suggest grass.*

## TIE-DYEING

**1** Wash and dry a piece of 100 per cent cotton fabric. Roughly gather the fabric in tight accordion folds and bind tightly with elastic bands where you want paler stripes in the design.

**2** Dampen the fabric. Wearing protective gloves, plunge the fabric bundle into a bowl of cold water dye made up according to the manufacturer's instructions.

**3** After the required soaking time, wash the fabric, rinse until the water runs clear, remove the bands and smooth it out to reveal the effect. Leave to dry then press with a hot iron.

# NET SKIRT

A scrap of gathered net can be turned into a beautiful ballgown in no time.

▼ Cut a 14 x 6cm/5½ x 2½in rectangle of net. Gather one short edge tightly. Press a piece of iron-on interfacing to the wrong side of some matching fabric and cut out a bodice shape about 2.5cm/1in across. Glue the bodice and skirt to the background and attach a stick-on jewel at the waist.

# RIBBON WEAVING

It's worth experimenting with ribbons of different widths to see what effects you can create. Once you're happy with the design, iron-on interfacing keeps it in place.

**1** Cut a piece of iron-on interfacing to the finished size of your panel adding a 1cm/⅜in margin at each edge. Matching the depth of the interfacing, cut enough lengths for the "warp" ribbons to fit along one edge. Lay them on the adhesive side of the interfacing and pin them in place along the top edge.

▶ **3** Press the ribbons with a hot iron to fuse them to the interfacing, removing the pins as you work. Press the raw edges under.

**2** Cut enough lengths of contrasting "weft" ribbons to fit along one side edge. Weave the first ribbon in and out of the warp ribbons, passing it over one and under the next until you reach the opposite edge. Repeat to form a chequered pattern and pin all the ends in place.

◀ *A tiny evening dress, easily made from scraps of fabric, would make a romantic detail for a party or prom layout.*

# LETTERING SKILLS

While pictures are the focal points of scrapbook layouts, titles, captions and written details are crucial to creating lasting souvenirs that keep your memories intact. Word-processing software and the thousands of available fonts enable you to establish a host of different moods and characters for your pages, but writing by hand stamps them with a unique personality – yours. Perfect calligraphy isn't essential, but practising a few of the techniques that go towards mastering this traditional skill can be helpful in improving the grace and legibility of your own handwriting.

## BASIC PENMANSHIP

A broad nib, pen or brush is the essential tool for calligraphy. When you hold the pen in your hand the flat tip forms an angle to the horizontal writing line (called the pen angle). It takes some adjustment to use this sort of tool after using pointed pens and pencils, so practising basic strokes is helpful.

### Writing position
To produce beautiful work you need a relaxed posture, so spend some time adjusting your position so that you are comfortable. You may like to work on a drawing board resting on a table top, or secured to the edge of a table so that the paper is on gentle slope. If you prefer, you can rest the board on your lap, or flat on a table, resting your weight on your non-writing arm so that you have free movement with your pen.

Remember to place some extra sheets beneath the paper you are working on to act as padding: this will help the flexibility of the nib and stop it scratching the paper and spattering ink. Attach the writing sheets securely to the board with masking tape.

Light should fall evenly on your working area; although good daylight is best, you can also use an adjustable lamp to light the page.

### Terminology
Calligraphy uses special terms to describe the consituent parts of letters and words and the way they are written. The style or "hand" in which the writing is created is composed of "letterforms". These are divided into capital, or "upper-case" letters and smaller "lower-case" letters. Most text is written in the latter because they are easier to read than solid blocks of capitals.

The "x-height" is the height of the full letter in capitals or the main body of small letters, excluding "ascenders" and "descenders", which extend above or below the line of the text.

Calligraphers use pencil guidelines to ensure that their strokes are correctly placed on the page, and the two most important are those drawn to mark the top and bottom of the x-height.

◀ *Calligraphy pens are available with different size nibs. This type of pen can be used with different colours and consistencies of ink.*

### Forming strokes
When you write with a normal pen, it can easily be moved round the page. When you are using a calligraphy pen this is not possible because the nib resists against the paper and may cause an ink blot or mark. For this reason, letters are made from several separate strokes, lifting the pen between them. For example, the letter "o" is made using two strokes, with one pen lift, while a small "d" is made in three strokes and other letters may require four. Practise slowly to start with.

---

**WRITING WITH THE LEFT HAND**

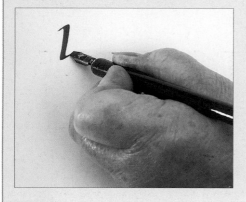

If you are left-handed you should sit to the right of the paper and tuck the left elbow into the waist, twisting the wrist so as to hold the pen at the required angle. Special left-oblique nibs are available to minimize the amount that the wrist needs to be bent, but if you can manage with straight-edged nibs the left-hander will have a greater choice of nibs available to them.

Three strokes                    Four strokes

## PRACTICE STROKES

To begin with it is helpful to practise just keeping the whole nib edge against the paper.

Practise simple curves and angles before you form any letters. Zig-zag patterns will show you the thinnest and thickest marks the nib is capable of.

## PEN ANGLES

Holding the pen at the same angle to the writing line for every letter is an essential discipline to create letters that work well together. Practise first on spare paper. A line of differently angled letters will look odd.

Resist the temptation to move the wrist as you would in standard writing. As you complete each letter, check that you are keeping the same pen angle: it is easy to change without noticing. Zig-zag patterns, made at the correct angle for the alphabet you are using, can be a useful warming up exercise before writing.

## LAYING OUT TEXT

Having decided what you are going to write, you need to plan where each word will fall and work out how much space it will take up, so that the page looks balanced and harmonious. Think about the relative importance of titles – and hence which will be larger or smaller.

**1** Determine the x-height of an alphabet using a "ladder" of nib widths. Holding the nib at 90 degrees to the baseline, make a clear mark, then move the pen up and repeat for the required number of widths.

**2** Measure the height of the ladder and use this measurement to mark the x-height down both sides of the paper, then join the marks up with a ruler and pencil. If you have a T-square you can mark one side only.

**3** When ruling guidelines for lower-case letters, leave the equivalent of two x-heights between each line of text to allow for ascenders and descenders. For capitals, you can leave one x-height or even less.

**4** When you are going to write mostly in lower case with the occasional capital, rule as for lower case and gauge the height of the capital letters by eye.

**5** Once you start writing, it is important to be aware of letter spacing and awkward combinations, such as the "r" and "a" above: move them closer to create a natural space.

**6** Adjusting letter spacing helps to make the text more legible by evening out the frequency of downstrokes: leave more space between adjacent uprights, as above.

# Foundational hand

*To grasp the principles of calligraphy it is best to start by learning an alphabet. The Foundational, or Round, hand was devised by the British calligrapher Edward Johnston (1872–1944), who is credited with reviving the art of penmanship and lettering in the modern age.*

▶ *The numerals and letters of the alphabet are written in a specific order. Follow the numbers on the digits and letters opposite to achieve the best effect.*

The Foundational hand is simply crafted, based on the circle made by two overlapping strokes of the pen, and is written with a constant pen angle of 30 degrees and few pen lifts. It is the constant angle that produces the characteristic thick and thin strokes of the letterforms. Johnston based his design for the lower-case letters on the Ramsey Psalter, a late tenth-century English manuscript now in the British Library. The capitals, however, are based on carved letterforms used in ancient Rome, and their elegant proportions relate to the geometry of a circle within a square.

### The basic rules

Foundational hand is a formal, upright script, in which each letter is made up of two or more strokes. The letters should be evenly spaced for easy reading. An important characteristic of this hand is that the top curves of "c" and "r" are slightly flattened to help the eye travel along the line of writing.

The x-height is four nib-widths. Turn the pen sideways to make four adjacent squares with the nib, then rule your guidelines that distance apart. The ascenders and descenders should be less than three-quarters of the x-height (two or three nib-widths). The capital letters should be just two nib-widths above the x-height and do not look right if they are any higher. Hold the nib at a constant angle of 30 degrees for all letters except for diagonals, where the first stroke is made with a pen angle of 45 degrees.

### Practice exercises

Almost all the letterforms of this hand relate to the circle and arches, so practise by drawing controlled crescent moon shapes, beginning and ending on a thin point. These semicircles can then be attached to upright stems to create rounded letterforms, or they can be extended into a downstroke to form arches. Begin high up and inside the stem to create a strong, rounded arch. Rounded serifs are used on entry and exit strokes to embellish the letters.

## GROUPS

### Round or circular

**cbpdqoe**

Note where the thin parts of the letters are. The first stroke of these letters should be a clean semicircular sweep, producing a shape like a crescent moon. Start at the top and move the pen downwards. The left and right edges of the pen form the circles.

### Arched

**lmnrhau**

The arch joins the stem high up. Beginning with the pen in the stem, draw outwards in a wide curve, following the "o" form. Start the letters with a strong, curved serif and end with a smaller curved serif. Keep the pen angle at 30 degrees throughout.

### Diagonal

**wxyzkv**

For the first stroke, hold the pen at the steeper angle of 45 degrees. This will prevent the stroke from being too thick. Take care not to make any curve on this stroke. Revert to a pen angle of 30 degrees for the second stroke.

### Ungrouped

**fgsijt**

Keep the pen angle at 30 degrees for these letters. Follow the smooth shape of the "o" when drawing curves. Crossbars should sit just below the top line, and should protrude to nearly the width of the curve.

## STROKES

(1st = red, 2nd= blue, 3rd = green)

The letter "o" is made by two overlapping semicircular strokes, which produce the characteristic oval shape inside the letter. The back of the "e" does not quite follow the "o", but is flattened so it appears balanced. The top joins just above halfway.

For "a" draw an arch continuing into a straight stroke. The bowl begins halfway down the stem. The "u" follows the same line as an "n" but upside down, producing a strong arch with no thin hairlines. Add the stem last.

Start the ascender for "k" three nib-widths above the x-height. The second stroke is a continuous movement forming a right-angle. The pen angle is steepened for the first stroke of "v" and the second begins with a small serif. The two should sit upright.

The base of the first stroke of the "j" curves inwards to cup the preceeding letter "i". The second begins with a small serif and joins the base. The dot above the j is formed last. Start the "t" above the top line. The crossbar forms the second stroke, just below the top line.

1 2 3 4 5 6 7 8 9 0

A B C D E F G
H I J K L M N
O P Q R S T U
V W X Y Z & Æ

a b c d e f g
h i j k l m n
o p q r s t u
v w x y z &
? æ ĕ ŭ é ß . ,

# DIGITAL SCRAPBOOKING

There is a whole range of software available for digital scrapping. Some of the programs that came free with your computer, printer or digital camera, such as simple layout software, or image-viewing and editing programs, are essential scrapbooking tools. Specific digital scrapbooking software is also available and is easy to use to import photographs and design elements to your pages. For those wishing to work at an advanced level, professional image-editing software enables you to create a vast range of effects on photographs and layouts.

## SCRAPBOOKING SOFTWARE

If you enjoy scrapbooking and also like working on a computer, you will enjoy all the possibilities of creativity offered by designing your scrapbook pages on screen. Being able to undo, redo, or make several different versions of your ideas and see them side by side without wasting any paper, is a joy. Your computer and printer, with various software packages, give you all the basics you need to design and print great pages. If you also have a scanner, digital camera and access to the internet you will have even more creative options. There are many scrapbooking websites, which offer a variety of e-papers, borders and embellishments at high resolution, allowing you to make good-quality prints. They sell templates and even ready-made pages – so all you need to do is position your photos.

Each site has its own style: some elements look very high-tech and computer generated, whereas others have a more traditional feel. If you need inspiration you can browse through the galleries on the sites, which are full of exciting ideas. There are many software tutorials to help you out, too.

▼ *Scrapbooking websites such as scrapgirls.com offer themed collections of background designs, overlays, embellishments, and everything you need to compile your digital pages.*

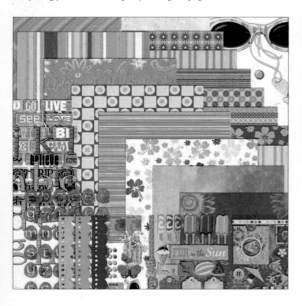

## CREATING DIGITAL PAGES

Even the most basic software can be used to create backgrounds and make different shapes and frames to contain photographs and journaling. You can either use these in traditional scrapbook layouts by printing all the elements individually to arrange together on paper, or print the finished page. You can buy a whole range of papers to print on, and experiment with coloured and textured papers, and even fabric.

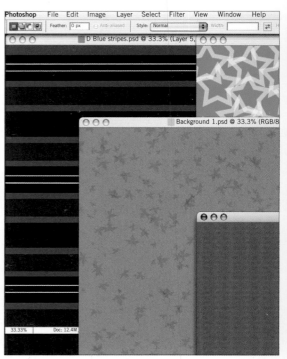

I To begin your page using image-editing software such as Photoshop, set the design area to 30 x 30cm/12 x 12in (it can later be reduced to 20 x 20cm/8 x 8in if you want to print on to A4 paper). For good printing quality use 300dpi (dots per inch) when creating and importing images, and experiment with different filters and effects. The stripes on the left were achieved by colouring rectangles then repeating down the page.

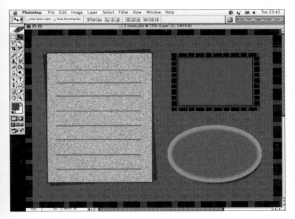

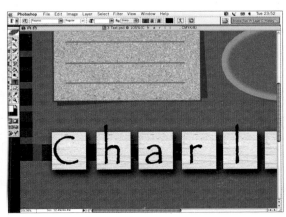

**2** Squares, circles, stars and more can be created to make boxes, borders and embellishments, then coloured and treated with different filters and effects. Here the striped background has been used to create a stripy border. In the journaling panel on the left, a textured surface and rules imitate notepaper. The shape was duplicated then twisted a little and re-coloured to give a shadow effect. Another shadow under the oval shape gives it a three-dimensional feel. You can resize and reshape the elements as much as you like, until you are happy with the basic layout.

**3** The beauty of creating journal boxes on screen is that you can type your story straight into the box, and then edit it and resize the type or the box until everything fits beautifully and you have exactly the look you want to achieve. Your computer will come with a basic range of fonts installed, and many more are available if you want to create a particular look. They can be enlarged, emboldened, italicized and capitalized and all will look different. Special effects for titles and other text include drop shadows, 3-D effects and outline lettering, and you can of course type in any colour to fit the mood of the layout. Alternatively, you can print the empty boxes and write the text by hand for a traditional look, or print your text on clear film and superimpose it on a printed background.

## DRAWING A SOLID OBJECT

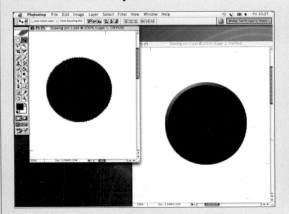

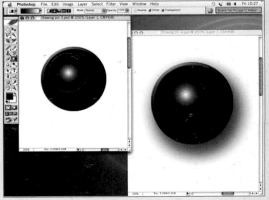

**I** Try using imaging software to create the illusion of solid objects such as this drawing pin (thumb tack). Create a circle and colour it, using the eyedropper tool to pick a colour from one of your photos. Create a bevel edge using the Bevel and Emboss layer style. Here a smooth inner bevel has been added with a shading angle of 120 degrees. Play with the settings until you are happy with the effect.

**2** To add a little shine to the surface of the pin, create a smaller circle on the surface. Choose Radial Gradient in the gradient tool menu and scale to make the area of shine as big or small as you want it. Here it has been set at 56 degrees. Finally add a shadow to relate the pin to the background, at the same angles of 120 degrees. You can now scale the image down to a realistic size and use it to "pin" your photograph to the page.

# Scanning and using digital images

*A scanner is definitely useful if you have an archive of traditional photographs you want to scrapbook digitally. All your old family photos can be scanned too, so all your relatives can have their own copies. As well as photographic prints, both colour and black and white, most scanners can also be used to copy transparencies and negatives. And of course your traditional paper scrapbook pages can be scanned, to be stored or refined digitally, or emailed to your friends.*

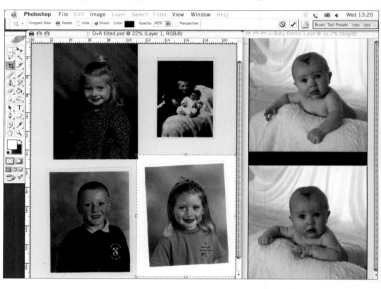

### Making a scan

**1** Fit as many photos on to the scanner bed as possible, as they can be cropped individually once they are scanned. Work at 300dpi or, for small photos that you may want to use at, say, three times the original size, at 900dpi. Save and name the scan.

**2** Crop out the picture you want to use, and save and rename it as a separate file. If the picture is a bit wonky, which often happens when scanning prints, or even upside down, it can be turned around easily in increments of 90 degrees or less, until it is straight. Check the alignments using the guides on the screen.

## DIGITAL PHOTO FILES

If you have a digital camera, all your photographs can be downloaded straight to your computer using the software supplied with the camera. The pictures are then ready to use on digital scrapbook pages, or can be printed to use traditionally. Store each set of digital photos in a folder and label as you would ordinary prints.

You can store your photographs, and other scrapbooking material, on your computer, but they will take up a lot of memory. You should certainly delete any bad pictures so they do not take up valuable space, and it is best to copy all your pictures on to CDs or DVDs, so that you have back-up copies.

Use your camera for backgrounds such as beach, grass and sky, as well as other elements such as signs, tickets, labels and buttons. With these and elements from other sources you can build up a library of digital papers, embellishments and typography to use whenever you want.

## NOW TRY THIS

1 Scan your photograph. Add a white border to imitate a print, by increasing the canvas size, before you bring it on to the album page. Duplicate the image box, twist by a few degrees, re-colour and put behind the photograph to give the semi-shadow effect.

2 Create stripes for the background, matching colours from the photo using the eyedropper tool.

3 Take a patch of colour from the photo background to use for the decorative boxes to the right of the photograph. Reshape one of these boxes to add the cross bands at the bottom and right of the page.

4 Create individual text boxes with shadows and add type to create the title.

5 You can make the drawing pins (thumb tacks) digitally as here, or print the page and then add buttons and other three-dimensional embellishments to the printed version. For best results use a good quality printing paper, and allow plenty of time for the inks to dry.

▲ The denim dungarees Jack is wearing in the colour photograph provided the inspiration for this layout. The background is a picture of the garment itself, digitally augmented with stripes and lettering, and the photograph has been vignetted in a shape that fits neatly on to the pocket.

▲ A single scanned photograph of this pampered pet on his favourite cushion has been used three times at different scales, and the tartan rug in the picture also forms the background design. Don't forget that you can use a scanner to create digital images of fabrics and printed papers as well as photographs. The frames, name tag and stitching are all digital embellishments.

# USING A SCANNER FOR SPECIAL EFFECTS

As well as creating digital images from your photographic prints and negatives, you can use a scanner like a camera to create pictures of a whole host of other items that you might want to use on your scrapbook page. Different patterns and textures for backgrounds, traditional embellishments such as buttons, bows, lace, ribbon or photo corners can all be scanned to be used on your pages. All those tickets and other ephemera from your travels can be scanned in to go with the photos. In fact, if you can pick it up, then you can usually scan it! The flatter the item, the better the scan.

▲ Woven fabric, denim from a pair of jeans, a piece of knitwear, flower petals and a child's painting have been scanned here. Fabric needs to be pulled taut across the scanner bed to avoid creases, unless of course you are after a creased effect. As with photographs, you can crop around the area that you want to use after making the scan. The scans can be used as they are, or layers, colours and other effects can be added to tone them down, creating more abstract patterns.

**1** Create a border around the knitwear background by duplicating the background, cutting out a row of stitching, copying this to the other side, then copying and rotating to make the other two sides of the square. Use the same method to make the edging around the photograph.

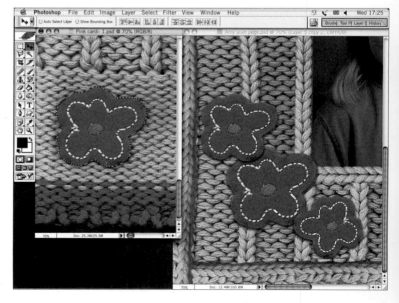

**2** A felt flower with contrasting stitching is used here to embellish the frame. Having scanned the motif, use the lasso tool to cut it out and drag it on to your page. It can be resized as necessary and dropped into position. It can also be copied and used again and again in different sizes. Add a little shadow behind the motifs to enhance the realistic effect.

▲ *The final touch to this pretty layout is a row of simple felt shapes embroidered with the letters of the child's name. The pink knitted frame is a good match for this photograph, but you could of course change the colour if you wanted to use this texture in a different context.*

# IMPROVING YOUR PHOTOS

Once you have your photos in digital format, there are a number of easy ways to enhance the quality of both black and white and colour photographs. Even the most basic picture-editing software packages will allow you to improve the colour or composition, or restore damaged prints. Always make a copy of the original scan to work on, so that you can refer back to it or start again if you don't like the new effect.

### Cropping out distracting objects

If you find you have an awkward or distracting object in the background, or foreground, like this overhanging roof, it can often easily be cropped out using the crop or selection tool. Experiment with cropping even further to focus more on the subjects.

### Improving colour

Here the picture on the left is too light and the contrast and colour have been improved using the automatic settings. To refine the result further you could alter the contrast and brightness controls manually, and add the colours individually in the colour balance panel.

### Improving the sky

A featureless or dull sky is easily improved. First select the sky area using the wand or lasso tool. Select a suitable sky colour to go with the foreground, then select linear gradient in the gradient tool. Draw a vertical line with the mouse to add the gradient colour – the longer the line the more colour there will be in the background. Experiment with the gradient until you are happy with it.

### Retouching

If you don't want to crop into the background of a picture, you may be able to remove a distracting object by retouching. Use the clone tool initially, to delete the object and match the area with the rest of the background. Then use the healing brush to soften any harsh edges. This method can be used to eliminate red eye, too.

## Making a focal point

You can blur the background if it is too distracting and you want to focus attention on the subject. Use the lasso tool to draw around the subject and make a clipping path. Invert the path to make the background the working area. Now choose Radial Blur in the filter menu. Decide how much blur to apply and position the blur centre: in this case it has been moved down below the centre of the image so that the effect circulates around the subjects.

### CHOOSING AND VIEWING PHOTOGRAPHS

Photo-viewing software is often supplied with your camera, printer or computer. It allows photographs to be imported from a digital camera and then viewed as large or small as needed. Viewing a group of photographs together as thumbnails makes it easier to make the best selection for a scrapbook page. You can arrange your picture library in folders or albums and add titles. Some software allows you to do a little picture editing too. You can rotate photos to view them the right way round, crop to improve framing and even create a slideshow. You can also import your finished digital pages to be viewed as a slideshow.

# IMPROVING BLACK-AND-WHITE PHOTOGRAPHS

As with colour photographs, black-and-white pictures can easily be improved with the addition of special effects.

## Brightening dark pictures

If a photograph is too dark, as on the left, make it brighter using the brightness control and lessen the contrast to lighten it. Use the curves and levels controls to refine the image. The sharpness can be improved too, which can be helpful with some older photos.

## Repairing creases and tears

When old photos have been stored for a long time, they may be creased or damaged. They may also be stained and spotted with damp or mould. The clone tool and the healing brush are both easy to use to retouch any damaged areas, and tears, spots and even small holes can be repaired very effectively.

## Creating tints and duotones

Copy the image (converting to greyscale if it is colour) then choose Duotone from the image menu. This allows you to create the photo in two, three or even four colours of your choice. Be careful – some colours, such as green, can make a photo look strange. Warm sepia works well with old photos. The duotones above show the effects created using orange (100y, 100m), yellow (100y) and finally magenta (100m).

## Eliminating creased corners

Old photos often have creased or bent corners. If the damage is too bad to retouch in the digital version, you could try this effect. Draw an oval shape around the subject, then invert the selection so the background is selected and delete it. The edge of the photo is softened, or vignetted, by feathering, in this case by 30 pixels, before hitting delete. This gives a soft, period feel to the picture.

## NOW TRY THIS

**1** Scan a sheet of brown paper for the background. Add brush marks around the edges to create the effect of antique paper.

**2** Add a white border to the photo, by increasing the canvas size before you bring it on to the page. Position it on the page, resizing to fit. Add a rectangular text box below and add the title.

**3** Make a tag, or download a tag from a scrapbooking website. Position it at an angle in the corner of the page. Select a rectangular section of the tag. Copy this and enlarge it down the left side of the page. Tone down the colour by adding a semi-opaque layer over it.

**4** Scan in photo corners, paper reinforcements and ribbon. Position the paper reinforcements, then add the ribbon as if threaded through them. Resize and crop to fit. Duplicate the ribbon and position it over the tag. Twist it around until it looks right and crop the length a bit. Add the photo corners. Finally, add a little shadow to all the elements to give a three-dimensional effect.

Dan & Joan

▲ The photograph of New York used as the background was given a painted effect using Fresco in the filter menu. In the main photo, Ink Outlines was used for the distant view, and Glass Distort noise effect has been added around the edge to soften it. A variety of city scenes have been added around the edges of the page to enhance the mood.

# CREATING A PHOTOGRAPHIC BACKGROUND

Photographic backgrounds can be very effective provided they don't distract too much attention from the main subject. There are many ways to avoid this, such as keeping the background to a solid colour, reducing the opacity of the background image, throwing it out of focus or applying a filter.

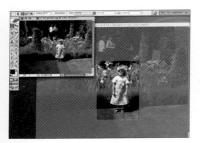

**1** Duplicate the background layer twice. On the top layer create a box around the area to be full strength, invert and crop out the background. You can check the crop by just viewing that layer. If you want to soften the edges, feather the crop.

**2** Click on the layer below. Reduce the opacity, or strength, of the background in the layers menu until you get the effect you want: in this case the background has an opacity of 60 per cent.

**3** To enhance the subject further, enlarge the full-strength area. Here this was subtly done by keeping the edge of the grass in line with the background. A soft shadow was added to lift it off the page.

# CREATING A PANORAMA AND MONTAGE

Various programs are available to stitch panoramas together, but you can do this yourself. It works best if the pictures are taken from the same standpoint.

**1** If you have an assortment of photos, choose the ones that match up best. Bring them on to the same page, resize as necessary and nudge along to find the best match. Enlarge the canvas to accommodate the photos.

**2** To add people to the scene, cut them out using the lasso tool, and move across to the panorama. They can be flipped, rotated and resized to fit. Use this method to add as many images as you need.

**3** After adding all the images and adjusting them to fit into the scene, look at the edge of the final photo. If it is uneven it can be cropped, and the page area altered so that it fits a page or across a spread.

# CREATING A TORN PAPER EFFECT

Torn paper is a good effect to master for use in your digital scrapbook pages. A real piece of paper can be torn and scanned, but it may not be quite the right shape. You can learn to alter the shape and size of a real paper scan or you can create a mock effect. Once you know how to create the effect with your software, this method can be used on any shape you need.

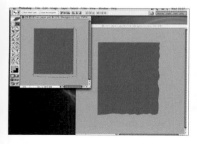

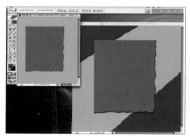

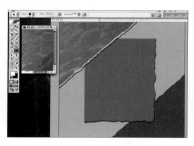

**1** Create and colour a rectangle. Make a jagged line around two sides with the lasso tool. Join up the shape and hit delete.

**2** Add noise in the filters menu and adjust the levels, making the torn area lighter or darker to suit your needs. This gives a jagged torn edge effect on two sides of the rectangular sheet.

**3** This effect can be added to the edge of a photograph. Apply the torn paper method as described in steps 1 and 2, then use the dodge tool along the jagged edge so that it appears white like a tear in a real print.

# CREATING A CALENDAR

Once you are into digital scrapbooking it is very easy to create your own calendar, adding seasonal effects. Scrapbooking websites offer many different calendar templates. Some can be created on the website and then downloaded to print (you will need broadband for this). Others are just like digital scrapbook templates and can be downloaded and designed as usual.

**1** For this October page, create an autumn background from leaf-patterned paper with an opaque layer over it to soften the colour. Add numbered boxes, duplicating the required amount. Add the days of the week above each column.

**2** Import the photos, resizing and moving them around until you are happy with the composition. Using the eyedropper to pick out a dark colour from one of the photos, add a border and shadows to both pictures.

**3** Add a contrasting band at the top by creating a rectangular box and using the eyedropper to colour it. Add noise to create texture and place it behind the top of the upper photo. Duplicate the band and position one at the bottom of the page. Duplicate again and position the middle band across the foot of the lower photo.

**4** Position the word "October" along the middle band, and add a shadow so that it stands out. Finally, using the leafy brush, spatter a few leaves in the bottom corner.

# UPLOADING PAGES

Having made your digital page, you can save it to disc for posterity, and print as many copies as you like. The brilliant thing about digital pages is that you can also email them to friends, and even upload them on to one of the many websites that allow you to show them. If your pages are saved at 300dpi you should first reduce the resolution to 72dpi. This generally makes your page small enough to be emailed and uploaded on to the web. Follow the instructions given on the website for uploading your material for display.

# Styles to suit

For inspiration for the style of your scrapbook pages you need generally look no further than the photographs you want to display and your knowledge of their subjects. So while a collection of old family photographs, for instance, might seem to warrant a "traditional" treatment, your partying forebears enjoying their cocktails might look happier in chic Art Deco black and silver frames to echo their sharp suits and stylish dresses.

The fun is in relating your backgrounds and decorations to the contents of the pictures, and it's important that the photographs always have a starring role: the thousands of patterns and ornaments available from scrapbooking stores should never be allowed to overwhelm the personal elements of your displays.

# Keeping it traditional

The photograph albums and scrapbooks of earlier generations have a wonderfully evocative look. It can be fun to adopt their look, either with squared up presentations of photographs, or with a twist, by adding in memorabilia that has been digitally scanned or enhanced. Keep the presentation quite formal, with the pictures squarely mounted in narrow borders or in old-fashioned photo corners, and add handwritten captions.

▼ This page crowded with lots of tickets and other bits and pieces evokes the eventful days of a memorable trip to San Francisco. It has been digitally created, and makes use of the standard elements of a traditional scrapbook.

▶ Athough created digitally, this layout looks back to an earlier era with its metal corners and hand-tinted black and white pictures.

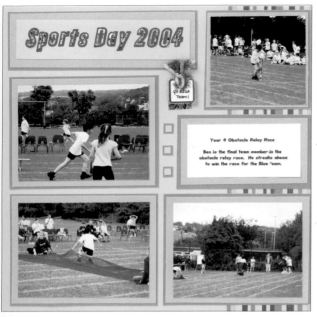

▲ The camouflage theme is taken from the uniforms in the picture and the titling and black border give a period feel.

▲ Here the pictures telling the story of the children's race almost fill the page, apart from a small panel describing what happened, and are squarely arranged with little embellishment.

▶ The dog's formal pose in this photograph has inspired an equally formal presentation in a double frame with bound corners.

▼ This record of a day at the zoo uses matching frames for all the pictures. The string detail is based on old album bindings.

▲ An old map has been used as the background to this Caribbean beach scene and neatly imitates the look of the sand where the boat sits in readiness to head out to sea.

# Bold graphics

*Crisp geometric shapes and repeating patterns can make really effective settings for strong images, or if you are using digital images, you could make a feature of the graphics within the photograph by repeating and blurring edges.*

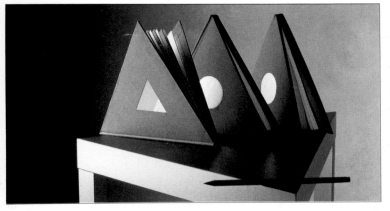

▲ *To create a smart, unified look for a multivolume set of family albums, go for matching or co-ordinated bindings in formal designs. Choose colours that suit your home décor so you'll want to have them on show.*

▲ *Albums need not be square: these striking triangular volumes have an Oriental feel and demand a modern, minimalist treatment on the pages inside.*

▶ *Papers printed in strong graphic designs like these make wonderful album covers. If you want to mix them up, look for designs of equal strength and scale, or use the same motifs in different sizes or colours.*

▼ *Die-cut patterns create a strong graphic effect when they are set against a background in a contrasting colour, as in this pretty ribbon-tied folder.*

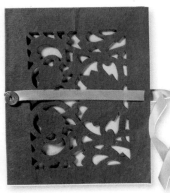

▲ Although the carousel is a very traditional subject, the modern technique of digital splicing has resulted in an image that forces you to take a second look.

◄ Image-editing software has been used to add some eye-catching stripes to this digitally created scrapbook page.

▼ Royalty-free images from old black and white engravings can be photocopied and added to paper collages to make lovely album covers, cards and gift tags.

# Fabric and stitch

*If you are skilled with a needle, there are lots of creative ways to introduce textiles and stitching into your scrapbooking, from embroidered album covers to painted or printed silk panels or braided embellishments.*

▼ *A small embroidery can become a front cover feature of a special album cover. This motif would be appropriate for a gardener.*

▶ *This small-scale book cover has been made by appliquéing small squares to a background fabric and satin stitching the raw edges.*

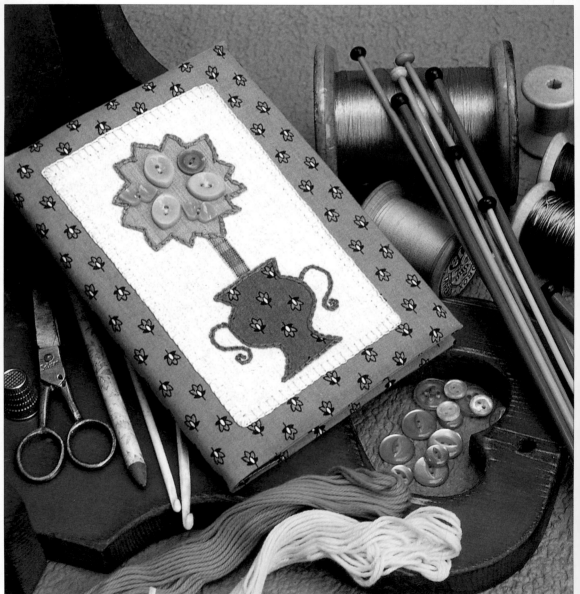

▲ Thick woven cotton or linen makes a lovely album cover, trimmed with embroidered titling and decorative blanket stitch and closed with two buttoned bands.

◀ For a contemporary decoration for the front of an album cover stitch small strips of evenly-spaced brightly coloured silk fabrics in a column to one side.

▶ Use transfer paper to copy a favourite photo on to fine fabric such as silk to form the centrepiece of an appliquéd panel.

# Heritage

*Most families have collections of photographs and ephemera handed down from previous generations, and it can be very rewarding to identify and mount them in albums to preserve them for the future. Good heritage layouts can be powerful evocations of the period when the pictures were taken.*

▼ *Copies of letters to home and other contemporary memorabilia make moving additions to wartime pages.*

▲ *Try to get older relatives to help you identify the subjects of photographs in your old family albums.*

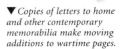

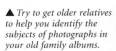

◄ *Treasured souvenirs of long-ago trips deserve to be properly displayed and preserved for the future.*

▼ *A decorative collage in period style can make the most of simple but precious family snaps.*

▲ When you're assembling a family group like this, the photographs themselves may all be simple portraits, but with personal knowledge of the subjects of the pictures you can choose appropriate backgrounds that help to show what the people were really like.

▼ For old photographs that are to be out on display, use old materials in muted colours to frame them. Here an antique cream piece of card (stock) immediately frames the photograph, and the outer frame is made from coloured corrugated cardboard, which picks up the darkest tones in the photograph.

▲ If you've inherited old family albums they're likely to be crammed with small black and white or sepia prints. It can be effective to reflect some of that style in your new album, but it's often possible to improve the images greatly by scanning and enhancing faded prints and reprinting them on a larger scale.

# Natural inspiration

*Don't forget your scrapbook when you're out and about: as well as bringing home photographs, gather natural objects such as shells, leaves and flowers that will help you build up a complete picture of the places you visited.*

▲ *This display box is a lovely way to bring together a photograph of a happy day on the beach with the collection of seashells you made while you were there.*

◀ *Instead of portraying a particular place, water has been chosen as the theme for this layout, bringing together diverse natural scenes. However, all the photographs used were taken in similar weather conditions, so the colours give the page a very unified feel.*

▼ *Handmade paper makes the perfect cover for an album on a natural theme. This sheet incorporates delicate scattered flower petals, and pressed flowers have been used to decorate the title panel. A simple undyed raffia tie holds it all together.*

▲ *This cover, decorated with a collage of leaves and flowers and bound with string, would be perfect for an album recording a garden tour.*

Cardigan Castle 2004

▲ *The complex frame-within-a-frame used in this layout, combined with the unusual view in the photograph, creates the effect of a window opening in the page, through which you can see the view of the tree beyond. The embellishment of leafy twigs is clearly related to the picture.*

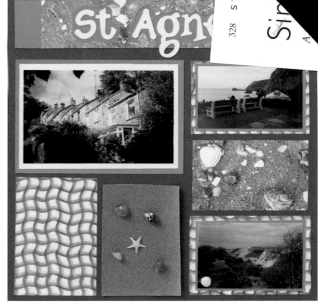

▲ *As well as taking photographs of views and landscapes when you're on holiday, you can use your camera to record interesting abstract images and close-ups for fantastic borders and backgrounds in future scrapbooks.*

◀ *Pretty pressed flowers form the focal point on this handmade album cover. The cover is made from textured paper, which has a handmade quality to it. The flowers can be collected fresh in spring and summer and pressed at home.*

▼ *Trinket boxes are a delightful way to store small treasures that are unsuitable for your album pages because of their shape. Beautify plain boxes with patterned papers and embellishments such as pressed flowers and leaves.*

# mple colour schemes

*monochrome treatment is an obvious choice for a collection of black-and-white photographs, but it can also be extremely effective with pictures in which the colour range is fairly limited. Don't limit your ideas to black and white but explore other single colours that match or contrast well with your images.*

▼ *A delicately decorated photograph box makes an elegant minimal presentation for a silver wedding souvenir.*

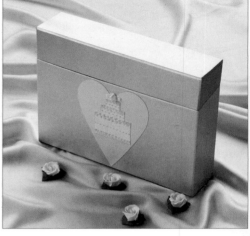

◀ *Although these striking seascapes are in colour the effect is almost monochromatic, and the simple black and white layout suits them perfectly.*

▼ *A crowded layout including photographs of all the members of a family is full of interest, and keeping it all in black and white gives a simple, graphic look.*

▲ *This all-white frame is intricately designed and texturally interesting, but doesn't distract attention from the photograph inside.*

▼ *Paper printed with a toile de Jouy design goes well with a strong collection of black-and-white photographs, though the plain black background is needed to keep all the images clear and well defined. The effect is softened with a purple border and ribbons.*

◄ *A fragile collection of old sepia prints can be overpowered by stark black-and-white or any strong colours, and looks best with gentle, faded tones.*

▲ *A photographic background, such as this drift of rose petals created for a wedding album, can have its opacity level reduced and be printed in just one or two colours, so that it does not compete visually with the photographs on the pages.*

◄ *In many older photograph albums the pages are of matt black paper, and this can still make a very effective and dramatic setting for both black and white and colour prints.*

▲ *A white wedding album luxuriously bound in white leather or vellum demands perfectly matted prints and a restrained approach to page layouts.*

# Bold colours

When you are mounting photographs of happy children playing with brightly coloured toys or running about on a sunny beach, your backgrounds can be as bold and bright as possible to create an explosion of colour. You can either pick up one of the strong colours in the pictures and use a matching or contrasting tone for the whole setting, or go for a multicoloured effect, using all the colours of the rainbow for a really eye-catching layout.

▲ The yellow background forming a frame around each of the cut-outs of this car has the effect of making them glow.

◀ Children's drawings and paintings, especially their self-portraits, make great additions to your layouts. Cut round both artwork and photographs to create amusing collages, and get them to help you with planning the pages.

▼ Here the layout is bold and bright but uses a limited colour palette and achieves a patterned quality by repeating two pictures all round the border. It also promises an irresistible surprise under the central flap.

▲ The two pictures on this layout are very different in character but the colour and black and white have been successfully linked by the shifting tones and consistent shapes of the frames and embellishments.

▶ Simple lacing through punched holes creates an eye-catching border for this name tag.

▼ This pretty garden of flower babies against a background the colour of a summer sky makes a sweet cover for a family album.

▲ This lovely page exhibits the finished results of the bold creative session that is in full swing in the photograph.

◀ The simplest shapes cut out of handmade or bark paper and cleverly combined make beautiful original tags and cards.

▼ Using a different bright colour for each page of a basic ring-bound album turns into it a really striking display that needs no further ornamentation.

▲ This digital scrapbook page takes the colour and movement of the sea as its theme, using a section of the photograph itself as part of the background.

# Pale and pastel

*Delicately coloured photographs can easily be overwhelmed by a layout that includes strong or dark colours. Softer, paler tones mix and match well with each other and can be used to create a very feminine look, or to give a period setting for a collection of old and perhaps faded prints.*

▼ *This pretty floral pattern looks right for the date of the photograph and its colours set off the sepia print perfectly. Toning stripes provide a crisp finishing touch.*

▶ *For a lovely, light-hearted wedding album cover, paste a scattering of tissue paper confetti shapes in mixed pastel colours over a sheet of soft handmade paper.*

*Florence*
Age 17.

*1940*

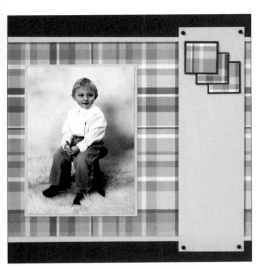

◀ *Pale blue for a boy is enriched by the framing bands of deep blue and the toning pale shades of olive and brown in the background, which carefully echo the soft colours in the photograph.*

◀ *The ice blues of this layout emphasize the coldness of the snow in the photograph. Although the picture was taken in sunny weather there is no colour to warm it up.*

Hayley

▲ *An enchanting little dog gets her own flowery setting in delicate colours that are just right for her light fur and small size. The daisy chain is threaded with a light touch across the bottom of the page. The simple colour scheme works well.*

▲ *Wearing a pale pink dress, this baby girl is given a traditionally coloured setting on a digitally created page. Touches of warmer pinks add interest to the treatment.*

▶ *The large spots on the girl's clothing were the starting point for this simple design, in which the colours are kept muted and pale so that the picture is the strongest element.*

# Shabby chic

*Mix-and-match patterns and textures with a confident hand for an eclectic, layered look with a timeless feel. This kind of treatment goes wonderfully with old family photographs and ornate memorabilia, evoking the richness of family history and the way in which possessions are gradually acquired and collected together in a home to make a harmonious whole.*

▲ *Handmade papers in soft colours, which can often be found with flower petals or leaves incorporated in their surface, mix beautifully with pressed flowers, ribbons and other scraps to make albums and folders.*

◀ *Scrapbooking websites offer a host of different patterned papers, which can be used for onscreen layouts or downloaded and printed. Ornate historical patterns set off the elaborate dresses of past generations.*

▼ *There are plenty of gift wrap papers or poster-size prints available that can be cut to size and reused as attractive and decorative covers for an album. Choose a print that is appropriate for the contents.*

▲ *Colour-printed die-cut scraps were collected in the 19th century to fill scrapbooks and make decorative collages on items such as trays and screens. Reproductions are now available to add instant Victorian charm to cards and tags.*

▼ *Richly patterned and gilded paper is ideal for embellishments such as envelopes and pouches to hold small treasures. Fasten their flaps with paper or silk flowers to complete the ornate effect.*

▲ *In the 19th century, the sending of greetings cards became extremely popular and many elaborate designs were produced, featuring flowers and hearts, intricate paper lace and ribbons. Their complexity and delicate charm provides inspiration for newly crafted displays in period style.*

▲ *A collage made up of old-fashioned items of ephemera immediately sets the tone for shabby chic. You could use this kind of background as a means of displaying old black-and-white photographs.*

▲ *The exuberant colours of mass-produced Victorian prints and scraps reflect the enthusiasm with which chromolithography, the first system of mass-market colour printing, was greeted when it appeared in the 1830s.*

◀ *Evoke the period of early photography with an abundance of intricate detail in scraps of lace and frills, printed patterns and rich textures. Delicate pressed flowers enhance the faded beauty of old textiles and photographs.*

# Journaling

*The text you add to your pages adds crucial meaning to the images, filling in all the details you know about when and where the pictures were taken and what was happening at the time, as well as identifying the people featured in them. There are many creative ways to add journaling so that it is not only informative but also becomes an intrinsic and attractive part of the design.*

▲ *If you have original letters to accompany your photographs, they can be copied and used as part of your display, or tucked safely into envelopes attached to the pages.*

▲ *In heritage layouts it's often important to explain the historical background to the photographs as well as establishing identities and locations.*

◀ *On this layout for a new baby the words encapsulating the feelings of the proud parents are addressed to the little boy, who will read them in the future.*

▲ *Old-fashioned wax seals and stamps can be purchased at craft stores. They can add the finishing touch to an album page.*

▶ *Instead of providing a commentary on these pictures, the journaling here is a collection of single words conveying the character of the child and all the aspects of a day on the farm.*

▲ *Beautifully formed lettering made with a calligraphy pen can become a focal point of a scrapbook design, or as here, the front of an album cover.*

▲ *Random words forming the background to this sequence of pictures convey ideas associated with the pleasures of travel, while a panel records the details.*

## My Great-Grandfathers
### Fathers of the Bride and Groom

**MY GRANDFATHERS**

Two old men in sepia
Stand with flowers in hand
At my parents wedding
My god how proud they stand

My Victorian grand-pa-pa's
With shining boots and heads of grey
Caught in a moment from the past
Prepared for the wedding day

If only they could tell us
Of the places they had been
Of mining tales and sailing ships
And places we've never seen

Perhaps a tale of comrades gone
When a great war swept like a flood
To leave young Uncle Tom
In the Gallipoli mud

Of my loved Victorian gents
The memory still remains
What noble lineage are we now
With such blood in our veins

By Bob Dufty

◀ *Writing in pen and ink takes time and practice to get right, but gives your work a beautiful hand-crafted, personal quality that cannot be replicated on a computer.*

▲ *If you have an aptitude for creative writing, an original poem can make a telling contribution. Or you could quote the work of others if the sentiments are appropriate.*

# Display and presentation

As well as making album pages for your scrapbook, you can also use your presentation skills to mount photographs and other family memorabilia for decorating album covers, memory boxes, memory quilts and even three-dimensional displays.

Archive albums in various formats and bindings are available from scrapbooking stores and other craft suppliers, but you can also buy all the fittings and materials you need to make your own. These unusual formats make particularly attractive gifts commemorating special occasions such as a wedding or the arrival of a baby.

# ALBUM COVERS

Designing a special cover for each album gives you a wonderful opportunity to establish its theme and character, so that everyone who sees it will want to look inside and will know instantly what the subject of the chosen album is.

## Baby girl album cover

*This charming project provides an ideal way to display your favourite baby pictures, and the album will become a family heirloom to be treasured. Make one for each new child in the family, or give them as presents to parents or doting grandparents.*

### materials and equipment

- metal ruler
- craft knife
- cutting mat
- self-adhesive mount board
- pencil
- polyester wadding (batting), 35 x 33cm/14 x 13in
- scissors
- two pieces of fabric, 35 x 33cm/14 x 13in
- glue stick
- masking tape
- photograph, 15 x 10cm/ 6 x 4in
- watercolour paper, 3 x 30cm/ 1¼ x 12in
- stickers
- hole punch
- 20 sheets of watercolour paper, 29 x 27cm/11¾ x 10¾in
- ribbon

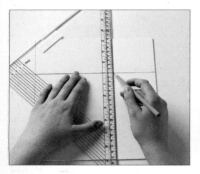

**1** Using a metal ruler and craft knife and working on a cutting mat, cut three rectangles each 30 x 28cm/12 x 11¼in and one 30 x 25cm/12 x 10in from self-adhesive mount board. On the smaller rectangle, use a pencil and ruler or set square to draw lines 8cm/3¼in in from each edge to form the aperture for the picture.

**2** To make the frame, use a craft knife to cut out the central rectangle and discard. Peel off the protective paper from the adhesive on the mount board and stick the piece of wadding, cut to size, over the frame. Using scissors, trim the wadding to the same size as the mount board.

**3** Place one rectangle of fabric right side down and lay the frame over it with the wadding underneath. Fold the surplus fabric to the wrong side of the mount board, mitring the corners carefully. Use a glue stick to secure the raw edges to the frame.

**4** Cut two diagonal slits in the centre of the fabric, fold the surplus fabric to the back and glue down. Tape the photograph face down over the aperture so that the picture is visible from the padded fabric side. Cover one of the larger rectangles of mount board with the other piece of fabric.

**5** Stick the narrow strip of watercolour paper down one long edge of a second large piece of mount board, then stick the frame in place over the rest of the board. Score along the line where the paper and frame join, so that the cover will open flat. Stick the remaining board to the wrong side of the fabric-covered board to form the back cover.

**6** Position a coloured sticker at each corner of the photograph at the front of the album to disguise any raw edges of fabric. For extra security for the stickers, dab a tiny spot of glue from a glue stick on to the fabric as well.

**7** Punch two holes centrally at the left edge of the front and back covers and the sheets of watercolour paper; the paper will form the album pages. Position the front and back covers on each side of the pages and lace them together with ribbon.

**8** Tie the ribbon ends in a bow. Add a few more stickers above and below the bow along the strip of watercolour paper to complete the cover.

# Christmas album cover

*A pair of square cake boards in a seasonal design, joined together by simple metal screw posts, form the cover of this festive album. A pair of Scottie dogs, cut from sticky-backed felt, complement the plaid design used here and make a charming motif for the front cover. Use this book when planning your Christmas celebrations: there is plenty of room for guest lists, seating plans, special recipes and gift ideas, and after the festivities you can add Christmas memorabilia such as greetings cards and photos.*

## materials and equipment

- 2 foil cake boards, 25cm/10in square
- double-sided carpet tape
- scissors
- metallic red corrugated cardboard
- self-adhesive felt in green, black and white
- leather hole punch
- 2 screw posts
- black card (stock)
- pencil
- black cotton tape
- tracing paper
- narrow ribbon
- PVA (white) glue
- self-adhesive black cloth tape
- bradawl (awl)
- 4 split pins

**1** Place the cake boards side by side, turning them to find the best position to join them (aiming to match the pattern). Stick a 2cm/¾in strip of double-sided carpet tape down each of the edges to be joined.

**2** Cut a strip of corrugated cardboard measuring 10 × 25cm/4 × 10in. Stick this over the tape, joining the boards but leaving a 1cm/⅜in gap between them to accommodate the pages.

**3** Turn the boards over and cut a rectangle of green self-adhesive felt large enough to cover the inside of the cover. Remove the backing paper and stick in place. Using a leather hole punch, make holes in the top and bottom of the back board, close to the edge of the corrugated cardboard strip. Push a screw post into each hole.

## VARIATION: Album cover with a window

Although this album cover has a different subject matter, it is constructed in the same way as the Christmas album cover. The difference is that this album has a window cut in the front, and it has been covered with green felt.

**4** From the black card cut 30 sheets 24cm/9½in square and 30 strips 4 × 24cm/ 1½ × 9½in. Make a hole gauge from a spare strip of card and punch out the holes in the card pages and strips. Slip them alternately on to the screw posts.

**5** Poke two small holes in the front of the corrugated spine. Thread black tape through the holes and tie in a bow for decoration.

**6** Draw a Scottie dog template and use it to cut out a black and a white felt dog. Cross a short length of narrow plaid ribbon at the neck of each dog and glue in position.

**7** Remove the backing from each dog. Stick the dogs on to the lower right corner of the front cover, so that the white one slightly overlaps the black one.

**8** Cut a rectangle of self-adhesive black felt to make a title plaque. At each corner, push a hole through the cloth, board and green felt using a bradawl. Insert a split pin in each hole and open it up on the inside.

# Wedding album cover

*The covers of this flamboyant album are made from sturdy silver cake boards, and the front cover is smothered in silk blooms that have been attached to a clear polypropylene sheet. Inside, the album is bound with screw posts, allowing you to add or remove pages as you wish.*

1 Using a craft knife and metal ruler on a cutting mat, cut a rectangle of polypropylene measuring 30 x 65cm/12 x 25⅝in. Score two parallel lines, 5cm/2in apart, across the mid-line, for the spine.

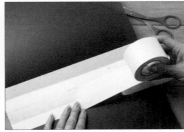

2 Reinforce the spine area on the inside with two lengths of self-adhesive cloth tape, positioning each one centrally over a scored line. Trim the ends flush with the cover.

## materials and equipment

- craft knife
- metal ruler
- cutting mat
- polypropylene sheet
- scissors
- self-adhesive cloth tape
- punch
- tack hammer
- assorted silk flowers, large and small
- split pins
- epoxy glue
- 2m/2¼yd wide satin ribbon
- double-sided carpet tape
- 3 silver cake boards, each 30cm/12in square
- weights
- 2 screw posts
- photographic refill pages

3 Using a punch and hammer, make two holes for the screw posts near the top and bottom of the back cover, in the area reinforced by the cloth tape.

4 Arrange the silk flowers on the front cover and mark the position of the centre of each large flower. Cut the bulbous end from the base of each flower using sturdy scissors. Press a split pin through the hole in the centre of each large flower.

5 Using a craft knife, make a small slit at one of the marks on the cover. (Start in the centre and work outwards.) Put your finger firmly on top of the split pin in a large flower and push the ends through the slit.

6 Open the ends of the split pin at the back. Repeat for the other large flowers. Once they are all in place, fill in any gaps by attaching single petals here and there using epoxy glue.

7 Use epoxy glue to attach smaller silk flowers and petals all around the edge of the cover, so that the plastic is completely hidden by them.

**8** Cut a length of ribbon long enough to wrap around the book and tie in a bow. Cut another piece to wrap over the spine. With the cover open, lay the longer piece horizontally across the centre of the spine, then wrap the other piece around the spine. Stick both pieces of ribbon in place using double-sided carpet tape.

**9** Punch holes in two of the cake boards to correspond with the holes made in the back cover for the screw posts. Sandwich the polypropylene cover, with the horizontal ribbon attached, between the boards, silver side out, and glue all the layers together. Leave the back boards under a weight until the glue is dry. Glue the front cover to the last cake board, with the ribbon sandwiched between and the silver facing out, so that the board forms the inside of the front cover.

**10** Position the board so that a narrow silver border is left all around the edge. Leave the glue to harden with the back cover hanging over a table edge and weight the front cover with small weights. Insert the screw posts through the back cover, slip on the photographic refill pages and screw to secure. Tie the ribbon in a decorative bow to close the album.

# Patchwork album cover

*You do not need to be a skilled stitcher to accomplish a patchwork cover, as the patches are held securely in place with bonding web before sewing. Follow the patchwork pattern known as "Log Cabin" to arrange fabric strips around a central image or position patchwork squares in a random arrangement.*

**materials and equipment**

- small album
- tape measure
- dressmaker's scissors
- extra-heavy non-woven interfacing
- fusible bonding web
- iron
- photograph printed on fabric using image transfer paper
- cotton print fabric in several colours
- pressing cloth
- sewing machine
- sewing thread
- dressmaker's pins

**1** Measure the opened book and add 2cm/¾in to the height and 10cm/4in to the width measurements to allow for hems and side flaps. Following these measurements, cut out a piece of extra-heavy non-woven interfacing and a piece of fusible bonding web. Following the manufacturer's instructions, iron the bonding web to the interfacing. Peel off the backing paper.

**2** Position your chosen image transfer so that it will appear centrally on the front cover. For the random arrangement, cut small squares of fabric and arrange them around the photo, overlapping them slightly.

**3** When you have covered the front and back completely, place a pressing cloth over the patchwork and iron to fuse the scraps to the interfacing.

**4** On a sewing machine, topstitch along all the joins between the patches with a satin stitch to cover the raw edges. Overcast around the the outer edges of the cover. With right sides together, turn in 5cm/2in down each short side and pin in place. Stitch along each end of these turnings with a 1cm/⅜in seam to make the side flaps, then turn right side out. Insert the album.

## VARIATIONS: Cloth covers and books

For a fabric album cover, measure the opened book and add 2cm/¾in to the height and width measurements for seam allowances. Cut two flaps from contrasting fabric. Turn in and stitch narrow hems on each flap. Decorate the front cover with appliqué and beads, then pin on the flaps, right sides together, stitch with 1cm/⅜in seams and turn.

A cloth book makes a lovely personalized gift album for a baby, and can be filled with familiar images transferred on to fabric. Cut out double pages from sturdy wool fabric or felt and stitch a picture on each page, using images of special people or animals. Add a favourite motif to the front cover and stitch all the layers together at the spine.

# ACCORDION ALBUMS

This ingenious and flexible format allows you to protect precious photographs and documents inside an album that closes between hard covers like a book, but can also be fully opened out to make a free-standing display on a table or mantelpiece.

## Concertina book

*Make this pretty accordion album to hold some of your favourite themed photographs. Choose a selection of luxurious decorative papers in similar shades of mauve for a really striking effect.*

### materials and equipment

- large rubber stamp in a leaf motif
- metallic ink stamp pad
- translucent paper
- craft knife
- metal ruler
- cutting mat
- thick cardboard
- decorative metallic paper
- glue stick
- bone folder
- handmade paper

**1** Stamp the motif on to a selection of papers to choose the effects you like best. To do this, press the stamp into the ink pad to coat the surface with ink, then press the stamp on the paper. Lift it up carefully to avoid smudging. In this case, the motif was stamped on translucent paper using metallic ink. Take care when stamping on to tracing paper, as some stamping inks do not dry well on the resistant surface. If you have difficulty, stamp on a lightweight handmade paper instead. Cut out the motif using a craft knife and metal ruler and working on a cutting mat.

**2** To make the front and back covers of the album, cut two pieces of thick cardboard to the required size using a craft knife and metal ruler, and working on a cutting mat. Then cut two pieces of decorative metallic paper 2.5cm/1in larger all round than the cardboard. Lay the paper right side down and glue one piece of cardboard to the centre of each piece. Cut across the corners of the paper, then glue the edges and carefully fold them over to stick them down securely on the cardboard. Turn the front cover over and glue the stamped leaf motif in the centre.

**3** Cut a long strip of translucent paper slightly narrower than the height of the cover boards. This will form the folded pages of the album. Measure the width of the album cover and make folds along the strip of paper to match. To do this, carefully and accurately measure the distance from one fold to another; use a metal ruler and bone folder to score and crease the paper to produce a succession of accordion folds. Trim off any excess paper at the end. When you have finished, ensure that the paper folds into a neat pile, and that it fits neatly inside the album.

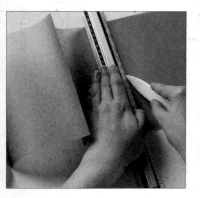

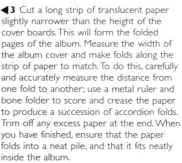

**4** Glue one end of the folded translucent paper on to the front cover of the album, then cover the whole with a sheet of handmade paper to coordinate with the rest of the album. Stick the other end of the translucent paper to the back cover and cover this with a second sheet of handmade paper. Fold up the book and place it under a heavy weight to prevent the papers from buckling as the glue dries.

# Accordion wrap

*This attractive book uses a folding technique developed in Japan to store long scrolls of paper. The paper used here for the covers contains fragments of coloured silk and threads, added to the paper pulp before forming the sheets.*

## materials and equipment

- 2 pieces of mounting board, 15 x 20cm/6 x 8in
- glue stick
- 2 sheets of handmade paper, 19 x 24cm/7½ x 9½in
- scissors
- craft knife
- metal ruler
- cutting mat
- narrow satin ribbon
- tapestry needle
- white cartridge (construction) paper 112 x 19cm/44 x 7½in
- bone folder

**1** To make the covers, apply glue to one side of each piece of mounting board. Place the board centrally on the wrong side of each piece of handmade paper.

**2** Cut diagonally across the corners of the two sheets of paper. Fold the excess paper over the boards and glue in place.

---

### VARIATION: Fan book

Fold a circle of paper into twelfths and cut down one fold to the centre. Trim the edge. Make two covers to fit the shape and glue to the end folds.

**3** Using a craft knife, metal ruler and cutting mat, cut a 1cm/⅜in slit in the centre of each long side on both covers.

**4** Cut four 25cm/10in lengths of ribbon. Using a tapestry needle, thread one through each slit and glue the end to the board.

**5** Using the bone folder, fold the cartridge paper into accordion pleats to form eight equal sections using accordion pleats.

**6** Glue the end sections of the paper to the inside of the covers, positioning them centrally. Make sure the two covers line up.

**7** Tie one pair of ribbons to create a book with turning pages.

# DISPLAY BOARDS

Rather than keeping all your creative ideas tucked away in albums, it can be fun to make scrapbook-style displays to go on the wall. Old prints fade easily, so it is a good idea to have copies made to use in this way and to keep the originals safely away from the light.

## Seaside memory board

*This collection of holiday memories serves both as a decorative feature for your wall and as a noticeboard to which other mementoes can be added from time to time. It could even be used as a memo board for day-to-day reminders. While you are on your trip, persuade the whole family to look for pretty souvenirs to remind them of your happy time on the beach together.*

### materials and equipment

- collection of seaside photographs
- pictures from printed sources of marine subjects such as sea, sand, sky, pebbles and shells
- old maps showing large areas of sea
- natural objects such as feathers and small shells
- scissors
- metal ruler
- craft knife
- cutting mat
- lightweight white board
- textured paper
- spray adhesive
- transparent photo corners

**1** Spread out your family photographs, together with printed pictures from other sources, maps and seaside ephemera, to decide which to use. Cut out some of the background material with scissors, tear some pictures to give them ragged edges, and trim others with a metal ruler and craft knife so that you have a range of different textures and edges to the collection.

**2** Assemble the larger, more abstract pictures of sky and sea on the board, overlapping them with areas of textured paper to make a background for the photographs. When you are happy with the arrangement, glue the background pictures down securely with spray adhesive. Arrange feathers and other pieces of seaside ephemera on the board.

◄ **3** Complete the memory board by adding your photographs to the arrangement, and secure them using transparent photo corners. If you are using duplicate prints you could stick them in position with glue once you have finalized the composition, but using photo corners enables you to place other mementoes behind the photos as your collection grows. Glue additional pieces of ephemera, such as small shells, around the photographs.

### VARIATION: Seashore album

For a seaside-themed album, cover the boards with an enlarged detail of a photograph of sand and sea, and glue a real seashell to the front – look for flat shells when you're on the beach.

# Pressed flower noticeboard

*Natural linen and linen tape tone beautifully with the pressed flowers and leaves
and the colour-washed wooden frame in this attractive design.*

## materials and equipment

- large, flat, rectangular wooden picture frame
- off-white emulsion (latex) paint
- medium-sized decorator's paintbrush
- pressed flowers and leaves
- measuring tape
- PVA (white) glue
- fine artist's paintbrush
- spray matt acrylic varnish
- natural linen or linen-look fabric
- scissors
- sheet of MDF (medium density fibreboard) cut to fit frame
- staple gun
- soft pencil
- linen dressmaking tape
- hammer
- decorative upholstery nails
- picture wire or cord for hanging

**1** Paint the picture frame with a coat of off-white emulsion (latex) paint. Apply the paint in a thin wash, so that the texture of the wood shows through. Leave to dry.

**2** Arrange the flowers and leaves with the help of a measuring tape. Starting in the centre of one short side of the frame and working outwards, apply a little PVA glue to the back of each flower and stick in place.

**3** When the design is complete, leave until the glue is dry then spray the frame with matt acrylic varnish. Repeat if necessary but take care not to flatten the flowers.

**4** Cut a piece of linen 5cm/2in larger all round than the MDF. Stretch the fabric over the board and secure it at the back with a staple gun, starting in the centre of each side and folding the corners neatly.

**5** On the right side, mark out a large central diamond using a soft pencil. Cut four lengths of linen tape to fit and lay in place, stapling them together at the corners.

**6** Arrange more lines of tape in a pleasing design, weaving them over and under each other. Trim the ends and secure at the back of the board with the staple gun.

**7** On the right side, secure the linen tape with upholstery nails spaced at regular intervals. Fit the decorated board into the frame and attach picture wire or cord.

# HERITAGE QUILTS

**Traditional quilts have often been used to record special events or memories by applying embroidery or incorporating symbolic patchwork shapes. With the latest range of transfer papers you can now create a photographic quilt made up of family pictures for posterity too.**

## Memory quilt

*This beautiful album quilt was made to commemorate the 70th birthday of the maker's mother. Some of the ivory silk fabric used was taken from a wedding dress, giving it particular sentimental value.*

**materials and equipment**

- black and white photographs
- scraps of ivory silk in a variety of textures and shades
- image transfer paper
- iron
- paper
- pencil
- dressmaker's scissors
- calico
- measuring tape
- dressmaker's pins
- sewing machine
- ivory sewing thread
- ivory silk for the quilt backing
- quilt interlining
- tacking thread and needle
- coffee silk for binding the edges
- metallic sewing thread

**1** Transfer the photographs on to silk, using a transfer paper suitable for the fabric. Decide on the finished block size and estimate how many blocks you will need to make by working out a plan on paper. Cut the block squares from calico, adding a seam allowance all around of 2cm/¾in. Trim each transferred photograph and pin to the block through the border to avoid damaging the prints.

**2** Cut random strips of different silks. Pin one strip right side down to one side of the photograph. Stitch the strip down, making sure the seam does not obscure the image, then flip the strip over to conceal the stitching and press lightly. Add the next strip at an angle, covering the end of the previous strip. Repeat, working clockwise round the image, and cut away excess fabric from each strip before adding the next.

**3** Complete each calico block in the same way, mixing the colours and textures of silk randomly. When you have added all the strips, press each patch then trim away the excess fabric with scissors, leaving a 2cm/¾in seam allowance around the block.

**4** Pin and stitch the blocks together in rows, adding extra strips of silk between them. Join the rows, then add a border. To assemble the quilt, place the backing right side down and the interlining on top. Finally place the quilt top right side up on top. Tack (baste) all three layers together.

**5** Decorate the quilt with machine or hand quilting before binding the edges with coffee silk. Finish the design with machine embroidery using metallic thread in a zig-zag or other embroidery stitch.

# Paper quilt wallhanging

*In this exciting and original hanging, the images are not just framed but actually become part of the vibrantly coloured handmade paper squares. Paper pulp and pigments for dyeing it can be bought from craft suppliers.*

## materials and equipment

- collection of photographs or other souvenirs such as tickets, labels or press cuttings
- aluminium mesh
- strong scissors
- 2.5cm/1in-wide masking tape
- absorbent non-woven kitchen cloths
- recycled paper pulp
- paper dyes in 2–3 colours
- 2–3 large plastic bowls
- paper string or embroidery thread (floss)
- 60cm/24in dowelling, 6mm/¼in diameter

**1** With your collection of materials in front of you, decide on a standard size for each patch and the number of patches that are required to make the hanging. In this case each patch will be 15cm/6in square.

**2** To make the moulds for the paper, cut a 17.5cm/7in square of aluminium mesh, and a strip 15 × 4cm/6 × 1½in. Fold strips of masking tape over each edge of the mesh shapes to cover the sharp edges.

**3** Cover a large board with several layers of non-woven kitchen cloth. Dye two or three batches of pulp following the manufacturer's instructions. Immerse the square mesh in the background colour pulp and lift the first square out of the bowl.

**4** Turn the mesh carefully to deposit the square in the top corner of the couching cloth. Repeat to make a total of nine squares, laying them in three rows of three. Use the masking tape binding as a guide for the spacing between the squares.

**5** Cut 36 lengths of paper string or embroidery thread 10cm/4in long, and lay them over the spaces to join the squares. Cut nine lengths 9cm/3½in long to make the hanging loops. Double these and arrange them along one side.

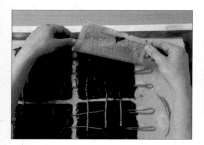

**6** Couch nine more squares of the same coloured pulp on top of the first set, to hold the strings or threads in place.

**7** Arrange your collection of images centrally on the squares of wet pulp.

**8** Using different coloured pulp and the smaller mould, couch strips of pulp over the edges of the images to hold them in place. Leave for several days to dry naturally, then thread the dowelling rod through the loops.

# KEEPSAKE BOXES

For small collections, or treasured three-dimensional objects that cannot be fitted into an album, a keepsake box is the answer. Look out for good quality packaging that can be recycled, or buy plain cardboard boxes from craft stores and decorate them to match the subject of your collection.

## Découpage memory box

*The art of decorating with paper scraps, which are overlaid and varnished to give the appearance of a hand-painted finish is known as découpage. This box is prettily decorated with pictures of coloured feathers, cats, flowers and fans, and finished with a pink ribbon border – every girl's ideal treasure box.*

### materials and equipment

- plain hexagonal cardboard box with lid
- acrylic or household emulsion (latex) paint in eau de Nil
- paintbrush
- scraps of old manuscript paper, or new paper aged by dyeing in tea
- glue stick
- selection of cut-out paper scraps printed with images of cats, fans, feathers and flowers
- acrylic matt varnish
- measuring tape
- scissors
- fabric ribbon
- fabric glue
- assorted buttons
- needle and thread

**1** Paint the box inside and out with two coats of eau de Nil paint and leave to dry. Tear the manuscript paper into scraps and glue these to the sides and lid of the box. Cover with the printed scraps, overlapping them as desired. Apply two to three coats of acrylic varnish, leaving each coat to dry.

**2** Measure the rim of the lid and cut a length of ribbon to this measurement. Using fabric glue, stick the ribbon around the rim. Using the same glue, stick a selection of buttons in assorted designs around the rim, on top of the ribbon.

**3** Make a simple rosette shape with another length of ribbon and secure by stitching through the central folds. Stitch a button in to the centre, then glue the rosette to the centre of the box lid.

### VARIATION: Travel memory box

To house a collection of holiday souvenirs, cover a travel-themed memory box with découpage using scraps of maps featuring appropriate destinations.

# Fabric-covered box

*Covering a box with a luxurious fabric such as linen, velvet or silk makes a very special setting for small treasures such as a collection of love letters and romantic trinkets. This box is cleverly constructed with ribbon ties so that it lies flat before assembly and could make a lovely surprise gift. If you are making the box as a memento of a family wedding you may even be able to obtain a little spare wedding dress fabric to make an extra-special reminder of the occasion for the bride.*

## materials and equipment

- craft knife
- metal ruler
- cutting mat
- strong cardboard
- squared pattern paper
- pencil
- scissors
- dressmaker's pins
- pale lilac linen
- dressmaker's scissors
- tacking (basting) thread
- needle
- narrow velvet ribbon
- grosgrain ribbon
- Ric-rac braid
- sewing machine
- sewing thread
- iron
- small embroidered motif
- fabric glue

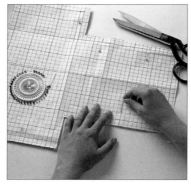

**1** Using a craft knife and metal ruler and working on a cutting mat, from strong cardboard cut out a base and a lid, each 19 × 15cm/7½ × 6in; two long sides each 19 × 7.5cm/7½ × 3in; and two short sides each 15 × 7.5cm/6 × 3in. These will be slipped inside the cover to make the box rigid.

**2** Make a paper pattern using the measurements on the template at the back of the book as a guide. Add a 1.5cm/⅝in seam allowance all around the pattern. Pin the pattern to a piece of lilac linen folded in half along the grain and cut out two matching pieces of fabric.

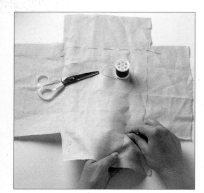

**3** Using a contrasting coloured thread, and working on the piece of fabric intended for the right side of the cover, tack (baste) the fabric to mark out the stitching lines for the different sections of the box, following the guides on the template. Cut eight 15cm/6in lengths of narrow velvet ribbon for the corner ties and two 30cm/12in lengths of grosgrain ribbon for the front ties.

## VARIATIONS: More fabric ideas

To memorialize a beloved pet, cover a box with fabric on to which you have transferred a favourite photograph.

Cover an old shoe box with decorative papers or fabrics appropriate for the occasion and add ribbons.

**4** On the right side of the fabric, pin and tack a length of Ric-rac braid along the seam line around three sides of the box lid. Pin the ties in place at the corners and pin one piece of grosgrain ribbon to the lid.

**5** Pin the last piece of grosgrain ribbon to the centre front section of the box base. Stitch the ribbon ties down with a straight machine stitch, turning the raw edges underneath to neaten.

**6** Pin the two pieces of fabric right sides together and stitch all around the edges of the box. Leave the long side at the front of the base open so that the cardboard sections can be slipped inside the cover. Clip the corners and trim the seam allowance, then turn the cover through to the right side and press.

**7** Push the first piece of cardboard for the lid through the opening along the long side. Neatly stitch along the lid edge to enclose it using a zipper foot on the machine. Insert the cardboard for the long side at the back and enclose with another line of stitches, followed by the pieces for the short sides and the large piece for the base. Enclose each piece of cardboard with a line of stitches. Finally, insert the last piece for the long side at the front of the box.

**8** When all the cardboard is in place, turn in the seam allowance of the opening and neatly slipstitch the seam. Glue an embroidered motif on to the box lid with fabric glue. Then tie the ribbon ties at each corner to assemble the box.

# THREE DIMENSIONS

The crafts of paper folding and paper sculpture open up many new avenues for creativity in scrapbooking. Here are two very simple ideas to start you thinking in three dimensions when devising themed settings for your photographs.

## Our house

*This fold-out display is an ideal showcase for photographs of a house renovation. Remember to preserve a piece of that ghastly old wallpaper that took you hours of work to remove.*

### materials and equipment

- three sheets of white cartridge (construction) paper, two measuring 38 x 60cm/15 x 24in and one 19 x 30cm/7½ x 12in
- bone folder
- pencil
- metal ruler
- craft knife
- cutting mat
- glue stick
- bulldog clips

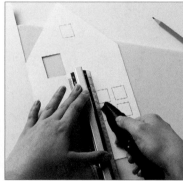

**1** To make the accordion-style house on the right of the design, fold the small sheet of paper in half lengthwise, then fold the long ends back to align with the centre fold. Crease the folds sharply using a bone folder. Open the paper out, then fold it in half widthwise. Open out the sheet and mark in the pointed roofs on the two centre sections, following the template at the back of the book. Using a craft knife and a metal ruler and working on a cutting mat, cut out the roof sections and cut out two small windows under each pointed roof. Fold the design widthwise and glue the two sides of each outer section together so that the house will stand up.

**2** To make the folded house at the left of the design, take a large sheet of paper and fold over a third of it at the right-hand side. On this third, lightly draw a pointed roof and windows. Cut out the roof and windows as before.

**3** For the background, fold in 2cm/¾in down one short side of the last sheet of white paper. Crease the fold sharply using the bone folder. Glue the plain section of the larger house to this flap so that the house can be lifted and turned like the page of a book.

**4** Glue one side of the smaller house to the right-hand side of the main album page. Secure the paper with bulldog clips while the glue dries. Arrange photographs and memorabilia on the background page and inside the left-hand house.

# Butterfly bonanza

*These two charming ideas for presenting a single photograph use matching butterfly motifs, which are folded and glued so that they appear to flutter around the picture. Punched holes give their wings a lacy appearance.*

## materials and equipment

- pencil
- paper
- scissors
- selection of pastel-coloured papers, including white
- cutting mat
- craft knife
- revolving leather punch
- fancy-edged scissors
- fine corrugated white cardboard
- glue stick
- heavy white paper
- coloured card (stock)
- photographs
- transparent photo corners

**1** Enlarge the butterfly template at the back of the book in three different sizes and cut them out. Place a template on a piece of folded coloured paper and trace around it. Cut out the small angled shapes in the wings using a craft knife and working on a cutting mat, and make decorative round holes in various sizes using a leather punch.

**2** Keeping the paper folded, cut round the outline of the butterfly with fancy-edged scissors. Make a selection of butterfly motifs in different sizes and colours. Do not flatten out the central folds. To make winged cards, cut out one wing only, then cut out a rectangle around the wing using fancy-edged scissors. Fold the wing outwards.

**3** To make a foundation on which to mount the butterflies, enlarge the frame template so that it is about 2.5cm/1 in larger all round than the photograph, then cut it out. Position it on a piece of white corrugated cardboard and draw round it lightly with a pencil. Cut out the shape, taking care not to crush the ridges of the cardboard. Glue the cut-out on to a slightly larger rectangle of heavy white paper and mount this on a larger piece of coloured card.

**VARIATION: Butterfly theme**

Butterflies are a perennially popular motif. They can be stencilled, stamped, cut out from paper and applied in different ways to album pages.

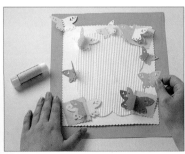

**4** Carefully make four tiny marks at the corners where you intend to mount the photograph, then arrange the butterfly motifs around the frame, slotting some individual butterflies inside the winged cards. Glue them in place using a glue stick. Finally, attach the photograph to the mount using transparent photo corners.

**5** To make the photo mailer, cut a long strip of heavy white paper slightly wider than the photograph and long enough to enclose it plus an overlap for the butterfly. Crease the vertical folds. Cut out one small and one large butterfly motif from coloured paper, then cut out a half large motif from the end flap. Using the photo as a guide, position and cut four diagonal slots to take the corners.

**6** Assemble the photo mailer by sticking the large butterfly to the front of the card in such a position that the wings slot through the folded half motif cut in the flap. The action of slotting the wings together will keep the card closed. Stick a small motif on the front of the card and mount the photograph inside.

# Children

Babies and children are of course among the most popular subjects for scrapbooking: all parents long to preserve their memories of their offspring as they grow up so quickly. For most people, it's also when they have their own children that they become most aware of the need to pass on the family history to future generations. There is nothing older children like more than revisiting their own earliest memories – seeing pictures of their former little selves and being reminded of special times they can just remember, or discovering what they were like as babies, before their memories begin. As well as photographs, of which you will have plenty to choose from, include some of the children's early works of art or attempts at writing.

# Album page for a baby boy

*Soft pastel shades dictate the look of this album page, which has a
contemporary style. Keep a tiny but important memento, such as the baby's
hospital identification tag, safely inside a small clear plastic envelope.*

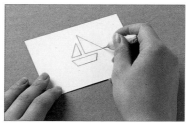

**1** Cut out rectangles of plain and printed paper, and arrange them on the heavy white paper. Use different-sized rectangles to make a pleasing layout. Glue in position. Arrange the collage items on the background. Small mementoes can be placed in clear plastic envelopes. Glue all the background items in place.

**2** Take a small piece of white card and draw a simple motif, such as a toy boat, on the wrong side of it. Working on a cork mat or corrugated cardboard to protect the work surface, use a bodkin or paper piercer to make pinpricks at regular intervals along the outline of the design using the pencil line as a guide.

### materials and equipment

- scissors
- plain paper in pastel colours
- striped printed paper, such as wallpaper
- heavy white paper
- glue stick
- baby mementoes
- small, clear plastic envelope
- white card (stock)
- pencil
- cork mat or corrugated cardboard
- bodkin or paper piercer
- fancy-edged scissors in wavy and postage stamp designs
- rotating leather hole punch
- lettering stencil
- craft knife
- cutting mat
- baby Ric-rac braid

**3** Cut out a rectangle of blue paper using wavy-edged scissors. Then cut out the pinpricked motif with fancy-edged scissors in a postage stamp design and glue it on the blue paper.

## VARIATION: A patchwork background

Simple photographs can be enhanced in many ways. Here a single photograph takes centre stage and the ephemera that is added is colour co-ordinated to hold the design idea together. The stripey pastel patchwork background is appropriately coloured for a baby boy and matches his clothing.

The zipper pocket at the bottom of the page is a good place to keep any small items of memorabilia, such as small cards expressing good wishes from friends and family. The cute faces are a fun addition to this light-hearted album page.

**4** Make a mount for the photograph by cutting out a piece of white card larger all round than the photograph, using wavy-edged scissors. Pierce small decorative holes all around the edges of the card using a rotating leather hole punch.

**5** Place a lettering stencil over a rectangular piece of blue paper and stencil the letter of your choice on the card. Cut the letter out carefully with a craft knife, working on a cutting mat. Trim the corners of the paper shape with scissors to round them gently.

**6** Mount the cut-out letter on a rectangle of pale yellow paper, then on a larger fancy-edged rectangle of white card. Pierce a small hole in the centre top of the label and thread it with a short length of baby Ric-rac braid. Tie this in a bow. Carefully glue everything to the background.

# Album page for a baby girl

*Pages dedicated to baby girls don't always have to be pale pink and frilly. This cheeky picture called for a bolder treatment, so the page uses bright colours and a stitched paisley motif with the sparkle of tiny gems.*

**materials and equipment**

- scraps of card (card stock)
- pencil
- felt squares in blue, lime green, light purple and dark purple
- scissors
- stranded embroidery thread (floss) in lime green, fuchsia and turquoise
- needle
- small self-adhesive gems
- tweezers
- 30cm/12in square sheet of bright pink card (card stock)
- glue stick
- small buckle
- self-adhesive foam pads
- photograph
- chipboard letters
- craft paint in purple
- artist's brush

**1** Draw three large and two small paisley shapes on card and cut them out. Use them as templates to cut out five felt shapes in assorted colours.

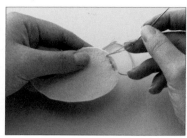

**2** Work a row of backstitch around the edge of each felt shape using six strands of contrasting embroidery thread. Work three lazy daisy stitches in the centre of each large shape and one on each small shape.

**3** Stick a small self-adhesive gem to the embroidery stitches in the centre of each paisley shape, grasping the gems with tweezers to make this easier.

**4** Cut a strip of purple felt 2cm/¾in wide and 30cm/12in long and glue it down the left side of the background card near the edge. Decorate a small buckle with more sticky gems and glue it to the felt belt.

**5** Glue the decorated felt shapes to the matching card shapes. Stick two foam pads on the back of each small paisley shape so that they will be slightly raised.

**6** Position the photograph centrally in the area to the right of the felt strip and glue it to the background. Arrange the three large paisley shapes down the left side of the picture, then position the small shapes between them. Glue all the shapes in place.

**7** Paint chipboard letters to spell the child's name in purple to match the felt shapes and leave to dry. Glue them in place at the bottom right of the layout.

# Schoolday memories

*This memento of your schooldays will bring back memories of past escapades, glories and disasters. Indulge yourself and relive all those carefree times by making a schooldays album page.*

## materials and equipment

- brick-effect dolls' house paper
- sharp scissors
- glue stick
- envelope
- selection of school photographs
- transparent photo corners
- small labels
- black pen
- striped grosgrain ribbon
- metal badge
- embroidered pocket and cap badges
- school reports
- star stickers

**1** Cut two sheets of brick-effect paper to match the size of your album pages and glue in position. Glue the envelope in one corner so that the flap faces upwards. Arrange the photographs on the page then secure with photo corners.

**2** Next to each photograph, stick a handwritten label giving the year each picture was taken (or use computer-printed labels if you prefer). The album pages here show three generations of schoolchildren.

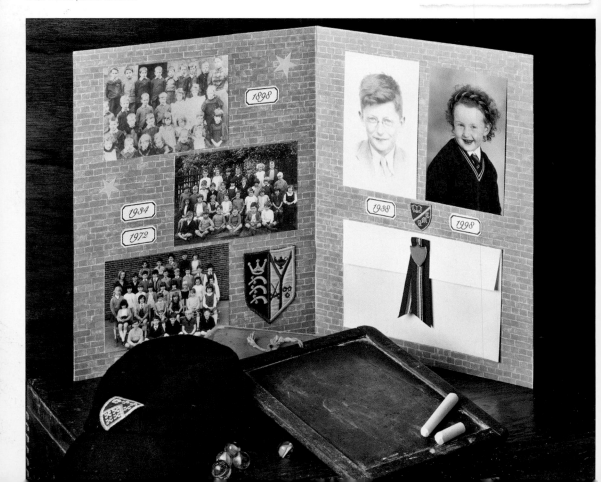

*Starting school is a major milestone for every child, but after just a few weeks they all seem to settle into their new life, making friends, learning new skills and starting on the path to independence. Mark the progress from the first uncertain day to being one of a trio of best friends with a special album page.*

## materials and equipment

- 30cm/12in square sheet of plain background paper
- brick-effect paper
- two or more photographs
- photo corners
- small labels
- alphabet fridge magnets
- photocopier
- scissors
- coloured pencils

**3** Fold the grosgrain ribbon in half and attach the metal badge to the top of the ribbon near the fold. Trim the ribbon ends to create a V shape. Glue the ribbon to the flap of the envelope. (Always keep a sheet of paper between the two album pages when they are closed to prevent the badge damaging the pictures.)

**1** Cut two 2.5cm/1in strips of brick-effect paper and stick them along the top and bottom of the background paper. Mount the photographs in the centre with photo corners. Add a printed or handwritten date label under each.

**2** Photocopy the fridge magnets and the pencils, reducing the size as necessary. Cut them out individually and arrange around the pictures. The letters can spell out a caption or be placed randomly. Glue everything in place.

**4** Glue the embroidered badges to the pages, positioning the cap badge just above the envelope. Fill the envelope with extra pictures and school reports. Finally, arrange a sprinkling of star stickers over the pages.

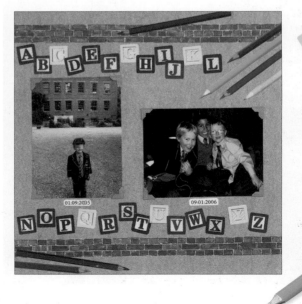

# Polka-dot mini-album

*This handy-sized accordion album, in its own brightly decorated matching box, could be filled with a selection of photographs from every stage of a child's life, to make an enchanting gift for a proud grandparent.*

## materials and equipment

- rectangular cardboard box
- handmade paper in orange, pink, turquoise and green
- small coins
- pencil
- scissors
- hole punch
- glue stick
- thick card (stock)
- metal ruler
- craft knife and cutting mat
- paper parcel tape
- thin green card
- pair of compasses
- thin satin ribbon

**1** Cover the box with orange handmade paper. Draw around small coins on to orange, pink, turquoise and green paper. Cut out all the circles. Punch small holes in the centre of some circles using a hole punch. Glue the circles to the top and sides of the box, overlapping some of them.

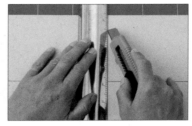

**2** Measure and mark out four identical rectangles of thick card to a size that will fit neatly inside the box. Cut them out using a craft knife and a metal ruler and working on a cutting mat.

**3** Place the rectangles side by side in a row, leaving gaps of about 3mm/⅛in between them. Cut six strips of paper tape, slightly longer than the card. Stick the tape to the cards, over the gaps, to join them together. Repeat on the other side. Leave to dry, then trim away the excess tape.

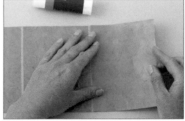

**4** Fold along the joins to make an accordion album. Cut eight pieces of turquoise handmade paper to the same dimensions as the cards. Glue one piece to the front and one to the back of each page of the album.

**5** Cut six strips of orange paper 2.5cm/1in wide to match the height of the pages. Glue a strip over the middle of each fold on the front and back.

**6** Decorate the front of the album with small multicoloured circles of paper to match the box.

**7** Draw a circle 6cm/2¼in in diameter on thin green card and cut it out. Trim a small photo into a slightly smaller circle and glue it to the green circle to make a tag.

**8** Punch a hole in the top of the tag and add a length of thin satin ribbon as a tie. Fill the album with photographs. Tie the tag around the album to keep it closed, then place the album in the box.

## VARIATION: Snow scene

Children playing in the snow are always full of fun and vitality, with bright smiles and rosy cheeks. Once the snow stops falling and the sun comes out, it's a great time to take photographs of them for your album, to store up memories of exciting days.

On this scrapbook page, blue and white spotted paper has been used to resemble a snowy sky, and the torn white edges and glittering stars, plus the pale colouring of all the elements, help to reinforce the cold, bright winter light in the photograph. You could create a similar snowy background for a winter page by sticking on individual self-adhesive dots in a random arrangement on plain paper.

# Growing up together

*Birthdays, Christmas and Easter holidays are family times that are especially important to grandparents, aunts, uncles and cousins. Keep a record of how the children are growing in the intervening months by collecting together pictures taken on these special occasions.*

**materials and equipment**

- six photographs
- coloured paper
- corner punch
- 30cm/12in square of background paper
- tear-off calendar
- glue stick

**1** Trim all the photographs to measure 7 × 9cm/2¾ × 3½in. Glue each on to a piece of coloured paper and trim the margins to 1cm/⅜in all around.

**2** Trim the corners with a decorative punch to give the frames a pretty, lacy look.

## VARIATION: Family secrets

Here's another idea for a family album page that shows all the children together yet allows each of them to make a personal contribution – if you can persuade them to take part.

Create matching mini-folders from thin card (stock), one for each child, and decorate the fronts with small photographs, each mounted on a torn square of handmade floral paper. Fasten each folder with a short loop of ribbon and a small button.

Inside the little folders you could insert a few folded pages of white paper and get each child to write something about themselves and what they have been doing, or make up a story or a poem, or draw some pictures. Alternatively, you could paste in more photographs or other memorabilia, or write your own account of your children's progress and achievements. Decorate the rest of the page with a few small embellishments and give it a title and a date.

You could make a page of this kind every year as an ongoing record of your growing offspring, with pictures shot specially for the album page. Both you and other family members, and the children themselves, will enjoy looking back over the years to see these snapshots of themselves as developing individuals within a family group.

**3** Arrange the pictures in two scattered rows of three, in chronological order, on the background paper.

**4** Add a few tear-off pages from the calendar, scattered over the page. Circle the dates when the pictures were taken on the calendar pages.

# Special occasions

Many of our most memorable and enjoyable experiences occur on the important annual festivals such as Christmas, Easter and Thanksgiving, which give a regular rhythm to family life and are traditionally times when everyone wants to get together with relatives and friends for informal and joyful celebrations.

As well as these parties, there are the very special occasions that mark life's milestones, such as graduation, engagement, marriage and the birth of a baby, to name but a few. All these high days and holidays demand to be commemorated by special pages in your albums, and all make great themes for which a wealth of decorative material is available, as well as a good collection of photographs of the event. The following pages include ideas for pages based on both seasonal festivities and more personal celebrations.

# Valentine's celebration

*The traditional imagery of Valentine's Day is perfect for an album page expressing the way you feel about your partner. Use the phrases on this layout as inspiration for your own special messages to the one you love.*

**1** Cut a 12 x 4in/30 x 10cm rectangle of pearl white paper and glue it to the left-hand side of the red card background, aligning the edges, to make a wide border.

**2** Print out all the words and phrases, except "Forever", on to white paper. Trim "I love you because…" and "…you're wonderful!" to thin white strips measuring 10 x 2cm/4 x ¾in. Glue to the top and bottom of the border.

**3** Glue two swing tags on to the back of a sheet of silver paper, and one on to red paper. Cut the papers to shape by cutting around the edges of the tags. Re-punch the holes with an eyelet punch.

**4** Cut out the three printed phrases and glue one to the front of each tag. Punch three small hearts from red vellum and glue these to the tags, over the text.

**5** Position the tags on the border. Mark the positions of the holes for the elastic at the sides of the tags and punch the holes with an eyelet punch. Thread the elastic to make crosses and tie at the back. Insert the tags with the red tag in the centre.

**6** To make the frame, draw a 12.5 x 15cm/ 5 x 6in rectangle on thick card. Draw a second rectangle inside it, 2cm/¾in smaller all round. Cut it out using a craft knife and metal ruler. Dry-brush a thin coat of parchment-coloured paint over the frame and leave it to dry.

**7** Cut out four small discs of white card. Inscribe the letters L, O, V and E on the discs using rub-on letters.

**8** Punch a small hole in the top of each disc using an eyelet punch. Insert an eyelet into each, then a length of ribbon. Glue the four discs to the top of the page.

**9** Cut out the printed words "you" and "me". Glue them to small heart-shaped tags. Attach the hearts to the page beside the border panel using white eyelets.

## materials and equipment

- scissors
- pearl white paper
- metal ruler
- pencil
- craft knife
- cutting mat
- 30cm/12in square sheet of thin red card (stock)
- spray adhesive
- computer and printer
- thin white paper
- 3 small swing tags
- silver and red paper
- small eyelet punch
- tack hammer
- red vellum paper
- heart punch
- thin round elastic in silver
- thick card (stock)
- acrylic paint in parchment
- paintbrush
- white card
- gold rub-on letters
- 6 eyelets
- thin red and silver ribbon
- 2 small heart tags
- white vellum
- thin steel wire
- strong clear glue
- photograph
- masking tape
- 4 photo corners

**10** Print the word "Forever" on to a sheet of white vellum. Trim closely, then glue with spray adhesive to a larger strip of white vellum. Attach the strip to the bottom of the page.

**11** Cut two pieces of steel wire 15cm/6in long. Bend into two hearts. Twist the ends of one heart together and loop the second heart through the first before twisting the ends. Glue the entwined hearts over the vellum pane using strong clear glue.

**12** Attach the photo to the back of the painted frame with strips of masking tape. Position the framed picture in the centre of the red area of the page and attach it using photo corners.

# An engagement

*This simple and beautiful layout expresses a single idea very clearly: the love and happiness of the newly engaged couple. The use of translucent vellum for the heart shapes creates a pretty, layered look. It's essential to use spray adhesive for the vellum, as any other glue will show through.*

## materials and equipment

- polka-dot paper
- metal ruler
- pencil
- craft knife
- cutting mat
- 30cm/12in square sheet of thin cream card (card stock)
- spray adhesive
- gold paper
- scallop-edged scissors
- red vellum
- light pink vellum
- dark pink paper
- 1 large photograph and 3 small ones

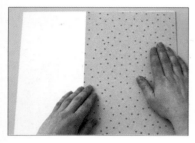

**1** Cut a 30 × 18cm/12 × 7in rectangle of polka-dot paper using a craft knife and metal ruler and working on a cutting mat. Glue the paper to the right-hand side of the cream card, aligning the outer edges.

**2** Cut three rectangles of gold paper 7 × 5cm/2¾ × 2in, and one 17 × 14.5cm/6¾ × 5¾in. Trim all the sides with scallop-edged scissors. Cut out the centres to make frames with narrow borders.

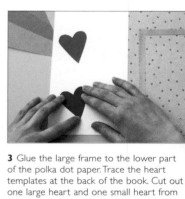

**3** Glue the large frame to the lower part of the polka dot paper. Trace the heart templates at the back of the book. Cut out one large heart and one small heart from light pink vellum, and one medium heart and one small heart each from red vellum and dark pink paper. Glue the small hearts down the left-hand side and the medium hearts to the right above the large frame.

**4** Glue the large pink heart to the middle of the page. Glue the small frames over the small hearts and glue the photographs in position in the frames.

**VARIATION: Other special occasions**

*Right:* This mosaic treatment is a good way to include plenty of individual shots of people who attend a farewell party. The scrapbook album page is a perfect record of those who attended as well as a good reminder of the occasion.

*Far right:* To mark the occasion of being voted lord mayor, this scrapbook album page is decorated with appropriately sombre colours.

*Below:* A handmade album cover for a special wedding anniversary is decorated with a ribbon of satin roses. The matt cream textured boards are appropriate for the subject.

# Christmas celebrations

*It's a treat to use the traditional festive colours of green and red for a Christmas layout, and deep red velvet-effect paper creates a fabulous rich background. Add plenty of gold and glitter for a thoroughly opulent look.*

## materials and equipment

- red velvet-effect paper
- ruler
- pencil
- scissors
- spray adhesive
- 30cm/12in square sheet of green card (stock)
- tartan border sticker
- sheet of gold glitter card (stock)
- Christmas photograph
- fancy-edged scissors
- glue dots
- star punch
- oval cutter
- gold paper ribbon

**1** Cut a rectangle measuring 28 × 22.5cm/ 11 × 9in from the red velvet-effect paper and glue it to the green card, leaving a narrow border of green at the top, bottom and right-hand side.

**2** Use a tartan border sticker to decorate the left-hand edge of the red velvet paper, sticking it centrally along the join.

---

### VARIATION: Digital Christmas

Online scrapbooking stores offer a host of backgrounds and other ingredients for seasonally themed digital pages, so it's very easy to put together a page including pictures of your Christmas festivities. You could even add pictures of the children opening their presents and email it to friends and family on the big day itself.

**3** Cut a piece of gold glitter card slightly larger all around than the photograph. Trim the edge using fancy-edged scissors. Glue the photograph to the gold card then glue in place on the background.

**4** Using the tree template at the back of the book cut a Christmas tree out of green card. Punch some stars from gold card and glue in place. Glue the tree to the background. Cut three gold oval baubles and punch a hole near one end of each for threading a short length of paper ribbon through. Glue all the decorations in place.

# Thanksgiving

*A collection of vintage scraps and a row of patches cut from homespun fabrics embody the traditional values of American Thanksgiving celebrations, suggesting comfort and warmth. A brown paper background and manila photo corners add to the old-time feeling of this autumnal page.*

## materials and equipment

- spray adhesive
- 20 x 30cm/8 x 12in rectangle of blue craft paper
- 30cm/12in square sheet of brown card (stock)
- scissors
- narrow double-sided tape
- striped ribbon
- 4 shirt buttons
- red thread and needle
- 2 portrait format photographs
- 8 manila photo corners
- reproduction Thanksgiving scraps and photocopies
- glue stick
- skeleton leaves
- check cotton fabric scraps

**1** Glue the blue craft paper to the centre of the background card. Cut two strips of double-sided tape and stick them over the two joins. Peel the protective layer from the tape and stick down two 32cm/13in lengths of ribbon, overlapping 1cm/½in at each end.

**2** Turn the ends of ribbon to the wrong side and stick them down. Sew on a button at each end of the ribbons using red thread. Stitch through the card as well as the ribbon and fasten off securely on the back.

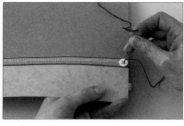

**3** Arrange the two photographs on the blue section of the background, then attach them to the page with photo corners.

**4** If you do not have enough original scraps, you can photocopy them, adjusting the sizes as necessary. Try reversing some copies to create a greater variety of images for the collage. Cut out the images accurately.

**5** Arrange the scraps on the page and glue lightly in place with a glue stick. Don't stick down the edges at this stage.

**6** Slip a few skeleton leaves in among the scraps. When you are happy with the arrangement, stick down both the leaves and the scraps securely.

**7** Cut out several small fabric squares, following the grain of the fabric carefully to create an accurate shape. Gently pull away a few threads from each side to create fringed edges.

**8** Arrange the fabric pieces evenly along the brown section at the lower edge of the page and stick down using a glue stick, leaving the fringed edges free.

# Hannukah

*The lighting of candles is an important part of the celebration of Hannukah, the Jewish festival of light. For impact, use one large photograph to fill one of the pages of this double-page spread. The title is arranged over both pages and uses a variety of letter styles. Metal embellishments with a Hannukah theme are available from scrapbooking suppliers.*

## materials and equipment

- 30cm/12in square sheet of pale blue card (stock)
- pencil
- scissors
- scrap paper
- patterned rubber stamp
- clear embossing stamp pad
- silver embossing powder
- heat tool
- 2 x 30cm/12in square sheets of navy blue card (stock)
- spray adhesive
- die-cut machine
- large label die
- 3 metal embellishments
- pale blue sheer ribbon
- assorted chipboard letters
- glue dots

**1** Draw a capital "H" on pale blue card and cut it out. Rest it on a sheet of scrap paper and stamp it randomly using a patterned stamp and clear embossing fluid.

**2** Place the pattern-stamped letter on a clean sheet of paper folded in the centre and sprinkle it liberally with silver embossing powder. (The paper will catch the excess powder and make it easier to pour back into the container.)

**3** Using the heat tool, heat the embossing powder until it turns from powdery to shiny. Keep the tool moving to avoid scorching the card.

**4** Glue the photograph in the centre of one of the navy blue sheets. Cut two 2.5cm/1in strips of pale blue card. Stick one down the left side of the page, centred in the margin. Trim the decorated initial and glue it at lower right, overlapping the photo.

**5** Use a die-cut machine to cut out three labels from pale blue card. Alternatively, make a template and cut out three labels by hand.

**6** Attach the metal embellishments to the tags using glue dots. Cut three lengths of ribbon to loop through the top of each tag.

**7** Arrange the remaining assorted letters along the bottom of the second page of the layout to finish the title. Make sure the heavy letters are firmly secured.

**8** Stick the remaining pale blue strip across the top of the second page. Place the three decorated tags in a row below it and use glue dots to attach them firmly to the card.

# Mum's birthday

*If the children have made a special effort to surprise their mum on her birthday, that's definitely worth recording in style. The tiny envelopes on this layout can conceal a few mementoes or additional pictures of the day.*

## materials and equipment

- 30cm/12in square sheet of pale blue card (stock)
- pencil and metal ruler
- craft knife and cutting mat
- pink, white, lilac, light yellow and light green paper
- glue stick
- pair of compasses
- scissors
- flower punch
- tracing paper
- white, pink and lilac card (stock)
- small coin
- eyelet punch and eyelets
- photograph
- narrow organza ribbon

**1** Draw a rectangle 15 x 10cm/6 x 4in on the blue card, 9.5cm/3¾in from the top and bottom edges, and 6cm/2½in in from the right edge. Cut out the rectangle using a craft knife and a metal ruler.

**2** Cut a 20 x 15cm/8 x 6in rectangle of pale pink paper. Glue the paper to the back of the card, over the aperture.

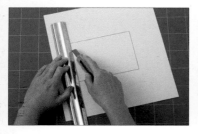

**3** Cut two 5cm/2in strips of white paper to fit across the page. Glue them in place, 2.5cm/1in in from the top and bottom edges, and trim any excess.

**4** Draw and cut out eight 4cm/1¾in diameter circles of paper, two each in lilac, pink, light yellow and pale green. Glue the circles to the white strips. Punch eight flower shapes in the same colours and glue them in the centres of the circles.

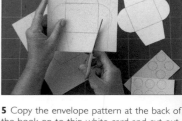

**5** Copy the envelope pattern at the back of the book on to thin white card and cut out to make a template. Draw around it once on pink and once on lilac card. Draw around a small coin twice on to pink card and twice on to lilac card. Cut them all out.

**6** On the inside of the envelopes, score the fold lines and fold in the sides and flaps. Use an eyelet punch to make holes in the envelope flaps and the pink and lilac circles. Attach the circles to the flaps using eyelets.

**7** Glue the photo in place inside the aperture, leaving equal amounts of pink border all round as a frame.

**8** Glue the envelopes to the left side of the page, with the flaps to the front. Fill the envelopes, then fold in the sides and flaps and wrap a length of ribbon around the circles to keep the envelopes closed.

# Father's Day

*You could make this layout to honour your own or your children's father on Father's Day. The little pull-out book attached to the page means that the journaling can be kept for his eyes only: get the children to write in the book.*

**materials and equipment**

- 3 x 30cm/12in square sheets of blue card (stock)
- 29cm/11½in square sheet of burgundy card (stock)
- tape runner
- 30 x 15cm/12 x 6in sheet of Argyll patterned paper
- photograph
- scissors
- silver embossing metal
- eyelet punch
- hammer
- screw brad
- metal ruler
- medium embossing tool
- pencil
- glue dots
- 30cm/12in burgundy ribbon
- 3 pale blue buttons

**1** Glue the burgundy card on to a sheet of blue card, leaving an even margin all round. Attach the Argyll patterned paper across the top half of the page. Cut out a piece of blue card a little larger than the photograph and mat the picture with it. Mount the photo towards the top left corner of the album page so that there is room below it for further decoration.

**2** Cut out an L-shaped piece of silver embossing metal to make a photo corner. Use an eyelet punch to make a small hole in the centre. Push the screw brad through and bend open the fasteners. Place in the top right corner of the layout.

**3** Cut a 9.5cm/3½in square of embossing metal. Lay it on top of a spare piece of patterned paper and emboss it by laying a ruler along the lines of the design and scoring with the embossing tool.

**4** To make the book, lightly mark the remaining sheet of blue card at 10cm/4in intervals along each edge. Fold up the first third using the marked edge as a guide. Crease the fold.

**5** Fold the remaining third back the other way to make an accordion fold.

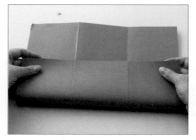

**6** Unfold and turn the card through 90 degrees. Repeat the two folds in the other direction. Unfold again.

**7** You should now have nine equal squares. Using scissors, cut out the top right square and the bottom left square.

**8** Fold the top left corner square to cover the centre square and crease sharply.

**9** Flip the card over and repeat with the opposite corner.

**10** The sheet can now be folded naturally into a square book shape, opening from left to right.

**11** Attach the embossed metal cover to the front of the book using glue dots.

**12** Stick a length of ribbon across the back of the book. This will be used to tie the book shut. Attach the book to your page using glue dots.

**13** To complete the layout, attach the three buttons using glue dots.

# Weddings

The history of wedding photography is almost as long as that of photography itself, as couples began to visit the photographer's studio for a picture to commemorate their marriage as early as the 1840s. However, the limits of technology meant that the camera did not leave the studio to cover the whole affair until the boom in weddings almost a century later.

It was not until the 1970s that the formal posed photographic style gave way to a more relaxed approach. Since then, weddings have been portrayed in a much more journalistic style, and the traditional album of posed shots is also giving way to much freer treatments, for which the skills of scrapbooking are extremely well suited. Many small reminders of the big day, such as menus, confetti and flowers from the bouquet, can now take their place in an album that captures the whole atmosphere of the wedding in a unique way.

# A traditional wedding

*This lovely reminder of a special day, featuring the wedding photograph and invitation, and decorated with cut-out doves and hearts, is simple yet effective in black, white and gold. This page can be the first in a wedding album, to be followed by other pictures of the happy day.*

## materials and equipment

- spiral-bound album
- craft knife
- metal ruler
- cutting mat
- heavy white paper
- fancy-edged scissors
- translucent glassine paper
- glue stick
- wedding photograph
- transparent photo corners
- scissors
- pencil
- gold paper
- gold card (stock)
- translucent envelope
- wedding mementoes: invitation, pressed flowers, ribbon, confetti

**I** Before starting work on the layout itself, make a protective page for the treasured photograph by cutting the preceding page out of the album to within about 2.5cm/1in of the spiral binding. Use a craft knife and a metal ruler, and work on a cutting mat.

**2** Cut another strip of paper slightly wider than the first strip from a sheet of heavy white paper. Trim one long edge with fancy-edged scissors. Cut a sheet of glassine paper or other translucent paper the same size as the album pages to replace the page you have removed.

**3** Glue the glassine paper to the tab in the album, then cover this with the single strip of paper with the decorative edge visible. The translucent protective sheet should now be sandwiched between the two tabs. Allow to dry.

**4** Assemble the photograph display. Using fancy-edged scissors, cut around the edges of a piece of heavy white paper slightly larger than the photograph. Mount the photo on this using transparent photo corners.

## VARIATION: Family weddings

Many family photograph collections include formal pictures of relatives' weddings, copies of which were usually ordered from the professional photographer and sent out to guests or to those unable to attend the wedding. Often these pictures are to be found, years later, tucked into a drawer or in a box of miscellaneous prints. Yet they are an important part of your family history, as well as being fascinating glimpses of the past, and deserve to be properly presented in your albums.

If old photographs include wedding guests unknown to you, try to find out who they are from older family members and gather all the information you can about the day. The page you design can include journaling to preserve all these memories. In the case of more recent events that you attended yourself, you can include souvenirs such as the invitation and order of service.

It's nice to design the page in a way that is appropriate to the period and the style of the wedding: you can usually get plenty of ideas from the clothes worn by the guests and the settings of the photographs. Many of these will be in black and white so will look best against subtly coloured backgrounds.

**5** Copy the dove and heart templates at the back of the book and cut them out. Draw round them on the wrong side of gold paper and heavy white paper. Reverse the dove motif so that they face in different directions. Cut them out.

**6** To assemble the album page, stick down a piece of gold card slightly larger than the mounted photo. Add a translucent envelope containing a memento of the occasion such as an invitation, together with any other small saved pressed flowers, ribbon, confetti or similar. Place some of the motifs you have cut out inside the envelope too. Glue down the mounted photograph. Stick the dove and heart cut-outs on to the page in a pleasing arrangement.

# An Indian wedding

*Traditional Indian weddings are celebrated on a huge scale, with a great deal of ritual, and hundreds of guests are often invited and lavishly entertained. The ceremony is full of vibrant colour and sparkle, with splendid clothes, flowers and food, and provides plenty of visual inspiration for a gorgeous album page ornamented in red and gold.*

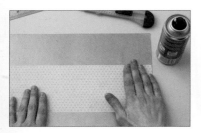

**1** Cut a rectangle of starry tissue paper measuring 30 × 10cm/12 × 4in and use spray adhesive to stick it to the sheet of gold card 7.5cm/3in from the top edge.

**2** Cut a 10cm/4in square of red embroidered paper. Glue it to the tissue paper panel on the left side of the page, matching the edges.

**3** Cut a length of gold braid and another of sequins to fit along the top and bottom of the panel and glue them in place. Glue the photograph in the centre of the panel.

## materials and equipment

- gold tissue with star pattern
- metal ruler and pencil
- craft knife and cutting mat
- 30cm/12in square sheet of thin gold card (stock)
- spray adhesive
- red embroidered paper
- fringed gold braid
- sequin strip
- PVA (white) glue
- 10cm/4in square photograph
- thin white card (stock)
- eyelet punch
- gold, red and green flower sequins
- star-shaped eyelets
- red and green shiny paper
- heart paper punch
- thin paper in gold and red
- small photos and mementoes
- gold marker pen
- thin gold ribbon

**4** To make the folders, cut three rectangles of thin white card each 16 × 8cm/6 × 3in. Lightly score a line down the rectangles, 4cm/1½in from each side. Fold the scored lines to make flaps.

**5** Punch a hole in the centre of each flap using an eyelet punch. Punch matching holes in two gold flower sequins. Attach the sequins to the flaps with star-shaped eyelets. Repeat for the other two folders.

**6** Punch eight hearts for each folder from red or green shiny paper. Stick the hearts to the flaps of the folders, four on each door.

**7** Cut two squares of red embroidered paper and one of thin gold paper to fit inside the folders and glue them in place. Draw a heart template to fit inside the squares and use it to cut out two gold and one red paper heart. Glue them into the folders and stick mementoes or photos of the bride and groom to the gold hearts.

**8** Inscribe the names of the bride and groom in gold on the red heart. Glue the folders in position on the page, beneath the border, with the red heart in the centre. Cut three lengths of gold ribbon and tie the ribbon through the holes in the sequins to keep the flaps closed.

# A contemporary wedding

*Using computer-printed kisses and light, bright colours, this layout reflects a modern take on a timeless ceremony, inspired by the unconventional wedding group photograph that forms its centrepiece. You could add some text to some of the panels instead of the printed kisses if you prefer.*

### materials and equipment

- 30cm/12in square sheet of white card (stock)
- computer and printer
- tracing paper
- metal ruler
- pencil
- craft knife
- cutting mat
- spray adhesive
- lilac, turquoise, blue, green and cream paper
- scissors
- glue stick
- heart punch

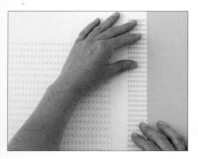

**1** Print kisses on to two sheets of tracing paper. Trim the paper to size. Glue to the white card with spray adhesive to make decorative areas.

**2** Cut three 30cm x 3mm/12 x ⅛in strips of lilac paper. Glue one strip down the middle of the card. Glue the remaining strips at each side of the card, 5cm/2in in from the edges.

**3** Cut a selection of rectangles and ovals on to turquoise, lilac, blue and green paper. Cut them all out.

**4** Assemble the layered shapes, gluing one colour on top of another.

**5** Print the bride and groom's names and large kisses on to tracing paper. Trim them to size and glue them to the rectangles and ovals.

**6** Punch hearts from cream, lilac and blue paper. Glue them to the rectangles.

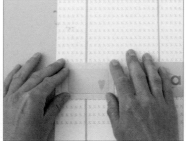

**7** Arrange the rectangles down the lilac "strings", then glue them in place.

**8** Trim the photo to size, rounding the corners. Glue it in place.

# Heritage wedding

*A heritage treatment for an old wedding photograph requires the use of colours and embellishments that are appropriate to the period of the picture. For this layout, fabrics and flowers in muted tones create a delicate background, and the look is subtle and stylish. Pieced calico was used here, but plain undyed fabric would be equally effective.*

## materials and equipment

- pieced natural calico fabric
- dressmaker's scissors
- 3 x 30cm/12in square sheets of kraft card (stock)
- spray adhesive
- large wedding photograph
- 30cm/12in square sheet of cream card (stock)
- craft knife and metal ruler
- cutting mat
- wide sheer cream ribbon
- jewelled stick pin
- pen and plain paper
- cork mat
- paper piercer or bodkin
- small pearl beads
- moulded paper flowers
- dimensional glaze
- stranded embroidery thread (floss) in cream
- needle
- sticky tabs

**1** Cut two 32cm/12¾in squares of calico to create the backgrounds for the pages. Cover one sheet of kraft card completely with the fabric, attaching it with spray adhesive and turning the raw edges to the back of the sheet. Cut the second fabric square approximately in half, cutting in a gentle serpentine shape, then glue it to a second sheet of kraft card, leaving the right-hand side of the card bare.

**2** Double-mat the wedding photograph on a sheet of kraft card and a larger sheet of cream card. Tie a loop of sheer cream ribbon to fit over the corner of the photograph and glue it at the back. Tie the ends into a bow at the front. Stick a jewelled stick pin through the knot of the ribbon bow. Attach the photograph to the centre of the left-hand page.

**3** To create the title, write the word "Wedding" or the names of the bride and groom in a flowing script on a piece of plain paper. Place the uncovered area of the right-hand page on a cork mat with the inscribed paper on top and prick evenly through the paper and the card using a paper piercer or bodkin, following the written line.

**4** Attach a pearl bead to the centre of each paper flower using dimensional glaze. Use a minimal amount of glaze, and leave it to dry thoroughly before attaching the flowers to the layout.

**5** Glue individual flowers down the pages following the lines of the pieced fabric, and in a line following the curved side of the fabric to cover the raw edge. Attach three more flowers to the card at the foot of the right-hand page. Stitch the title with three strands of embroidery thread, using back stitch and following the pre-pricked holes.

**6** On the back of the page, secure the ends of the thread with sticky tabs rather than tying knots, as these might create indentations visible from the front.

# Our wedding day

*A brightly coloured wedding dress and a fun photograph were the inspiration for this jolly layout, a radical departure from traditional wedding album pages. The red bodice of the dress was decorated with bold flowers and these motifs have been repeated in the page embellishments.*

## materials and equipment

- 2 x 30cm/12in square sheets white card (stock)
- craft knife and metal ruler
- cutting mat
- 2 x 30cm/12in square sheets red card (stock)
- spray adhesive
- large wedding photograph
- die-cut machine
- selection of flower dies
- large and extra large circle punches
- dark pink card (stock)
- medium pink card (stock)
- foam pads
- large and extra large daisy punches
- glue pen
- rub-on letters in pink
- embossing tool

**1** To make the background, trim one sheet of white card and glue it to a red sheet to leave a narrow border of red all round. Mat the photograph on red card and attach to the background towards the top right. Die-cut a selection of flower shapes and circles in red, pink and white card. Mix and match the flowers, centres and circles and glue them together.

**2** Attach foam pads to the backs of some of the completed embellishments to raise them on the page. Arrange all the flowers along the left side of the photograph so that they overlap. Stick in position.

**3** Punch out a selection of daisies in two sizes and in different colours.

**4** Using a glue pen, stick the small daisies to the centres of the large daisies, mixing the colours. Leave to dry.

**5** Place the daisies around and between the other flower embellishments and glue in position on the page.

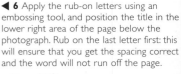

◀ **6** Apply the rub-on letters using an embossing tool, and position the title in the lower right area of the page below the photograph. Rub on the last letter first: this will ensure that you get the spacing correct and the word will not run off the page.

BESSIE LOVE.

# Family history

A heritage album is a delightful way to document your family's unique history and to preserve old photographs and mementoes for future generations. Most families have boxes of photographs just waiting to be unearthed and sorted out, and this in itself can be a fascinating journey back in time, particularly if you can ask your older relatives to help you identify the faces of long-lost family members and friends.

When you come to make selections of photographs for your pages, portraits and special occasions such as weddings and family parties will be central features, but try to include other shots that set them in context, such as pictures showing your forebears' houses or places of work, cars, gardens and home towns.

# Family tree

*This is a great way to record your family tree. Instead of drawing a diagram of names and dates, this family tree is decorated with pictures of each family member, glued on paper leaves with their details added alongside.*

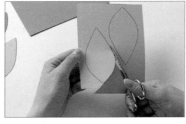

**1** Re-photograph the pictures on sepia-effect or black and white film, or scan them and convert to monotone or duotone, ensuring that all the faces are a similar size. Cut out each portrait carefully.

**2** Make a leaf template and draw around it on the wrong side of a piece of green paper. Cut around the outline. Repeat to make a leaf background for each picture, using paper in two shades of green.

## materials and equipment

- selection of family photographs or reprints
- scissors
- paper or card for template
- pencil
- paper in two shades of green
- glue stick
- sheet of marble-effect paper
- small labels
- pen
- green mount board (optional)

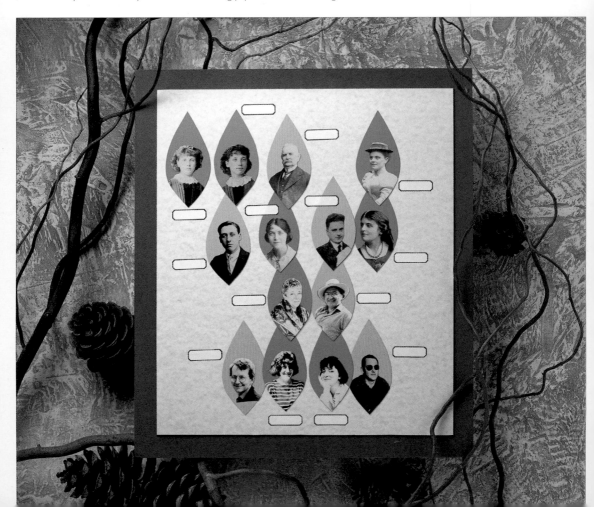

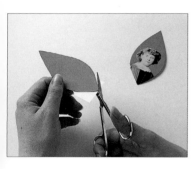

**3** Glue a photograph on to each leaf and allow to dry. Trim away the excess photograph to fit the leaf shape.

**4** Arrange the pictures on the marble paper background, with the youngest generation at the bottom. Glue in place. Next to each photograph stick a label on which to add names and dates. If desired, mount the family tree on green mount board to finish.

## FAMILY CARS

*Since the early days of the twentieth century, the car has been a prized family possession. Looking back through snapshots from holidays and outings over the years, you will find they crop up in pictures of your grandmother, father or aunt just as frequently as in those of younger relatives. Sort out all the photographs featuring cars, whether they are parked at picnics, driving along distant roads or being towed away on a breakdown truck, to make a record of your family motoring.*

### materials and equipment

- old road maps
- photocopier
- sheet of card (stock)
- glue stick
- driving handbooks
- scissors
- selection of photographs

**1** Photocopy the maps on the lightest setting. Stick them to the card to make the background, overlapping them so that all the card is concealed. Copy images of road signs from old driving handbooks or maps and cut them out.

**2** Arrange the pictures on the page, leaving space at the top and centre right. Glue lines of road sign cut-outs in these spaces, on bands of coloured paper if necessary so that they show up clearly. Stick down all the photographs using a glue stick.

# Victorian scrap album page

*Having a formal studio photograph taken was an important event for past generations, when cameras were prohibitively expensive and required the special skills of a professional photographer to operate them. The resulting portraits – like this charming oval picture – were framed and treasured. You can update an old family photograph in this way, or print out a contemporary picture in sepia to create a period-style picture.*

## materials and equipment

- original or reproduction sheet of coloured scraps
- photocopier
- scissors
- oval photograph
- 30cm/12in square sheet of coloured card (stock)
- paper glue
- paper doily
- coloured paper

**1** Photocopy the sheet of scraps, enlarging them if you wish. Make a second copy, this time with the image reversed (use the "iron-on" paper setting on your printer or ask your local copy shop to do this for you). Cut out each image carefully around the outline with small scissors, taking care to cut away all the white background.

**2** Cut out the photograph if necessary and glue it centrally to the background. Arrange the scraps around it, placing the mirror images on opposite sides. Overlap them to form a solid border, and glue them in place when you are pleased with the results. By adding a few that break out of the frame you will give movement to the design.

**3** Choose a motif from the paper doily for the corner decoration. It should be a part of the design that is repeated so that you can use it four times, and should be about 5cm/2in high. Cut out the four motifs roughly and glue a piece of coloured paper to the wrong side of each. Cut out the paper following the outline of the motif.

## VARIATION: Découpage boxes

If you have a collection of small trifles and keepsakes that have been handed down to you, give them safekeeping in a pretty box decorated with Victorian-style découpage. Plain cardboard boxes ideal for this purpose are available from craft suppliers in many shapes and sizes. Cut out small reproduction scraps of flowers, cherubs, butterflies and other pretty subjects, taking care to remove any white background, which would distract from the overall colourful effect, and glue them, overlapping, all over the base and lid. Apply several coats of glossy varnish to give a rich antique look.

**4** Stick one motif down near each corner of the background, pointing the designs towards the centre. Cut out eight more small matching shapes from the paper doily and glue a pair to each side of each corner shape to finish the decoration.

# Remember when...

*This heritage layout has a homespun look to it that suits the rustic scene in the old photograph. It has been achieved by using neutral colours, fabric, hand-stitching and twill tape printed with a nostalgic message. Photographs showing relatives at work are usually rarer than those depicting family and friends, and a good subject to record for posterity.*

**1** Mat the photograph on cream card. Place it on a cork mat and pierce holes, evenly spaced, all round the mat. Work a running stitch through the holes to make a border.

**2** Cut a heart shape from scrap card to make a template. Iron fusible bonding web to the wrong side of the fabric. Draw round the template on the backing sheet and cut out five fabric hearts.

## materials and equipment

- old photograph
- 30cm/12in square sheet of cream card (stock)
- craft knife
- metal ruler
- cutting mat
- spray adhesive
- cork mat
- paper piercer or bodkin
- stranded embroidery thread (floss) in cream
- needle
- scissors
- fusible bonding web
- patterned cotton fabric
- iron
- 30cm/12in square sheet of dark kraft card (stock)
- tape runner
- printed twill tape
- small brown buttons in two sizes
- glue dots

**3** Arrange the hearts in a row across the bottom of the layout and use a tape runner to stick them in place.

**4** Cut two lengths of printed twill tape and stick them to the layout, one 10cm/4in from the top and the other below the row of hearts. Attach the photograph to the layout, gluing it over the upper length of tape.

**5** Tie stranded embroidery thread through the holes in the buttons. Trim to leave short ends and fluff out the strands.

**6** Attach the buttons to the tape between the printed words, using glue dots, and add more buttons beside the photograph.

**7** Pierce two holes on each side of and through each heart and stitch with three strands of embroidery thread.

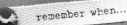
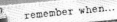

# Mother and child

*This evocative sepia print of a serene mother and her robust baby boy, taken in 1909, is faded and fragile, and has to be stored carefully away from the light. To preserve the memory, it was copied and enlarged at a slightly darker setting, then cropped to remove the damaged area. The "shabby chic" style used for this layout is perfect for very old family photographs.*

## materials and equipment

- 35cm/14in length of fine lace, 10cm/4in wide
- scissors
- iron
- spray adhesive
- 30cm/12in square sheet of kraft card (stock)
- piece of floral-patterned fabric
- photocopier
- white A4 paper
- photograph
- glue stick
- tracing paper and pencil
- heavy pink paper
- letters and other ephemera
- 2 Victorian scraps or other pictures
- tiny paper flowers

**1** Press the lace to remove any creases and trim the raw edge. Spray the wrong side with spray adhesive, and attach to the lower part of the background card with the scalloped edge facing downwards. Fold the ends of the lace to the back of the card and stick down.

**2** Photocopy the fabric on to A4 paper, setting the printer to a lighter than normal setting to give a faded appearance to the design. Glue to the upper part of the background so that the lower edge lies along the top of the lace.

**3** Enlarge the photograph so that it is about 17.5cm/7in high, trimming off any areas that were damaged in the original and darkening the print if necessary. Using spray adhesive, stick it down on the right-hand side of the floral paper.

**4** Trace the envelope template at the back of the book on to tracing paper and transfer it to heavy pink paper. Cut out, then fold all four flaps to the centre along the broken lines. Glue the bottom flap to the side flaps.

**5** Stick the front of the envelope to the layout at the lower left. Fill the envelope with letters, postcards and other ephemera, displaying them so that the stamps and addresses face outwards.

**6** Glue the two scraps in place, one on each side of the page.

**7** Finish off the layout by gluing a scattering of tiny paper flowers across the page.

## VARIATION: Family group

For this more recent photograph of a mother and her children, a more abstract setting has been chosen, using layers of torn paper in a subtle blend of buff and brick red inspired by the marbled paper used as the background. A black border around the picture adds definition to the rather soft grey tones of the photograph, and the assortment of letters in the title includes some black and white to match the central subject.

# Edwardian childhood

*The formal clothing of Edwardian childhood – bonnets, buttoned boots, frilly petticoats and fitted jackets – and the strict routine of the classroom were balanced by hours spent playing in the nursery with dolls, dolls' houses, toy cars and train sets. Record this lost era with a family photograph, pages from copy books and engravings from a contemporary shopping catalogue.*

## materials and equipment

- hand-marbled paper
- craft knife and metal ruler
- cutting mat
- 30cm/12in square sheet of white card (stock)
- spray adhesive
- photograph
- scanner and printer
- white paper
- scissors
- gummed black paper photo corners
- photocopier
- old copy book
- glue stick
- old engravings of toys

**1** Cut a square of marbled paper to fit the background sheet, and stick in place with spray adhesive.

**2** Enlarge the photograph so that it measures about 16cm/6½in high. Alter the brightness and colour balances if necessary to enhance the image if it is faded. Slip four old-fashioned paper photo corners on to the picture and place it in position on the left side of the layout.

**3** Photocopy and cut out four pages from an old handwriting copy book. Cut two narrow strips from one of the pages.

**4** Arrange the other three pages on the right side of the page so that they overlap each other and the edge of the layout.

**5** Place one of the copy book strips at the top and one at the bottom of the left side and glue in place.

**6** Cut out engraved images of dolls, train sets, rocking horses and other toys, cutting as close as possible to the outer edges.

**7** Arrange all the toys on the layout over the background and the copy book pages.

**8** Double check the position of all the various elements and when you are pleased with the design, glue everything securely in place.

# University revue

*Your pictures may not always be the perfect shape for square album pages. This production photograph from a student musical sums up all the glamour and excitement of amateur dramatics, but the upright, portrait format is not ideal. With a little photocopying and clever cutting, however, a single dancer can be turned into a chorus line that fills the stage.*

## materials and equipment

- theatrical photograph
- photocopier
- white paper
- scissors
- glue stick
- curtain from toy theatre kit
- heavy red paper
- wavy-edged scissors
- old sheet music
- 30cm/12in square sheet of gold card (stock)
- tracing paper
- pencil
- scraps of thin black and gold card (stock)

**1** Photocopy the image five times, enlarging it if necessary. Cut around the figure to be reproduced on four of the copies. Glue the pictures together so that the figures overlap realistically.

**2** Cut out the printed curtain from a toy theatre kit, or cut out a paper curtain shape, and glue it to the top of the picture. Mat the picture on a square of red paper trimmed with wavy-edged scissors.

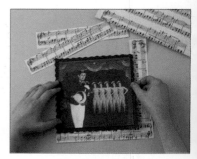

**3** Cut four strips from a page of old sheet music and mount them on the back of the red paper to form a square frame. Glue to the centre of a sheet of gold card.

**4** Trace the spotlight template at the back of the book and use it to cut out two spotlight silhouettes from black card and two oval discs from gold card. Glue the discs to the lights and fix in position at the top corners of the music.

## VARIATION: Period detail

A page photocopied from an illustrated trade catalogue of the appropriate period makes a fascinating and evocative background for a heritage layout.

# Family and friends

Happy times spent with your nearest and dearest are perfect subjects for your album pages, and you can include lots of informal snapshots of adults and children having fun and just being themselves – a world away from the formal posed photographs taken at special events such as weddings. For these pages you can go out armed with a camera with possible layouts already in mind, ready to look out for good subjects for backgrounds and embellishments as well as the focal points of the pages.

If you discuss your ideas with your friends and relatives you might also be able to get them to co-operate by posing together, larking about for action shots or even dressing up. If you have a digital camera you can easily take lots of pictures to give you plenty of choice at your next scrapbooking session. And if they know they've been involved, your friends will be eager to see themselves immortalized on the resulting pages.

# Picnic in the park

This fun collage combines snapshots of an al fresco *picnic* with cut-outs of cutlery, wine bottles, plates and a picnic basket to tell the story of a good outing. This is a really enjoyable and simple way to record a memorable day; you could make similar pages about a trip to the zoo or a child's birthday party by creating collages in the same style. It's worth building up a stock of cuttings by saving promising pages from magazines with good colour photography. Alternatively, when you're snapping away during a picnic, take some pictures of small details such as the basket, rug, bottles and food, as well as general shots of your surroundings for the background.

### materials and equipment

- magazine pages with pictures of picnic items
- scissors
- sheet of green paper
- glue stick
- snapshots of a family picnic
- transparent photo corners

**1** Assemble the motifs for the design. Carefully and accurately cut out pictures of a picnic basket, picnic rug, plates, cutlery, glasses and food, using sharp scissors. Ensure there is no background showing once you have completed the cutting out.

**2** Glue a picture of a travel rug down in one corner of the green background paper. Arrange photographs of the picnic on the paper, and when you are happy with the design, attach the pictures to the page with transparent photo corners.

**3** Arrange the other cut-outs decoratively around the photographs to fill in the spaces. Some cut-outs can be placed on the rug, and others displayed in groups scattered around the picnic photographs. Glue them all in place.

## VARIATIONS: Family outings

*Below*: Memories of childhood trips to the seaside invariably invoke pangs of nostalgia for traditional pleasures such as building sandcastles, eating ice creams and paddling in the sea, while the grown-ups looked on from their deck chairs. This digital album page captures the retro feel of those old memories by reproducing the photographs in a small square format with white borders like early colour prints. Behind them, an atmospheric photograph of a sandy beach is reproduced with a reduced opacity so that it fades into the background. A few marine embellishments complete the picture.

*Above and Below*: When you are portraying outings with children, include pictures of the animals or plants you saw as well as the children themselves, as reminders for them when they look at your album in future years.

# Trip to the farm

*In this small accordion album, photographs of a visit to a farm are mounted on tags slotted into pockets, and no child will be able to resist pulling them out to find his or her picture on each one. Close-up shots of crops and animals have been used to cover the pockets, conveying the flavour of the trip in near-abstract images that are all about texture and colour. A naive illustration created using rubber stamps provides the finishing touch.*

**materials and equipment**

- 2 sheets of A4 card (stock) in lime green
- tracing paper
- pencil
- metal ruler
- craft knife
- cutting mat
- self-cling unmounted stamps
- clear acrylic block
- coloured ink pads
- gift wrap or magazine pages
- glue stick
- daisy punch
- white paper
- eyelet punch and eyelets
- thin card (stock) in pale blue, turquoise and lilac
- photographs
- narrow ribbon
- gift wrap

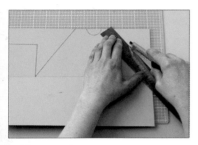

**1** Fold one green card in half lengthwise. Press the fold firmly to make a sharp crease. Trace the album template at the back of the book and transfer the tracing to the green card, matching the central line to the crease. Cut out the album.

**2** Fold the card where marked to create the album. Press all the folds firmly to make sharp creases.

**3** Press the self-cling stamps one by one on to the acrylic block and stamp the flower and butterfly design on the large pocket.

**4** Cut sections from gift wrap or pictures cut from magazines to fit the remaining pockets and glue in place.

**5** Punch a small daisy from white paper.

**6** Use an eyelet punch to make holes in the corners of the pockets, and in the daisy. Insert eyelets through the holes to fix the album together.

**7** Trace the tag templates at the back of the book. Transfer the shapes to thin, coloured card and cut them out.

**8** Punch four daisies from white paper. Glue one to the top of each tag.

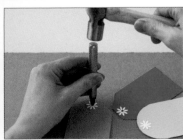

**9** Punch a hole through each daisy with an eyelet punch. Trim the photos to size and glue them to the tags.

**10** Cut lengths of ribbon and tie one through the hole in the top of each tag.

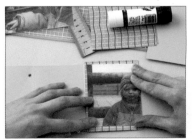

**11** Cut two covers slightly larger than the album from the remaining sheet of card and cover them with gift wrap. Glue the covers to the front and back of the album. Trim and glue photos to the front and back covers. Cut a length of ribbon and tie it around the album to keep it closed.

# A day in the garden

*Summer days are often spent in the garden, having lunch or a drink and chatting with family and friends. Keep a record of this part of life by making a collage using photos of your loved ones relaxing outside, decorated with stamped garden designs and pressed flowers and leaves.*

**1** Stamp several versions of garden-themed designs on a selection of coloured and textured paper, using black and dark green ink. Clean the stamps between different colours with paper towels. Allow to dry.

**2** Cut out some of the stamped motifs with fancy-edged scissors and others with ordinary scissors. Tear around some of the motifs to create rough edges.

## materials and equipment

- selection of rubber stamps with a garden theme: plant pots, flowers, garden tools
- selection of papers in shades of green, brown and off-white
- ink pads in black and dark green
- paper towels
- fancy-edged scissors
- scissors
- photographs
- sheet of brown paper
- glue stick
- gummed brown paper photo corners
- selection of pressed flowers and leaves

## VARIATION: Summer in the garden

For a digital scrapbook page, create the feel of a summer garden with a photographic montage in fresh greens and blues. You can find themed collections on scrapbooking websites offering suitable colourful borders and embellishments such as these jolly sunglasses, or make up your own borders and collage elements using the image-editing software on your computer. In the example on the right, all the images were cropped from one photograph, then enlarged and superimposed for a montage effect. The simpler treatment below could be achieved equally easily in digital or traditional form.

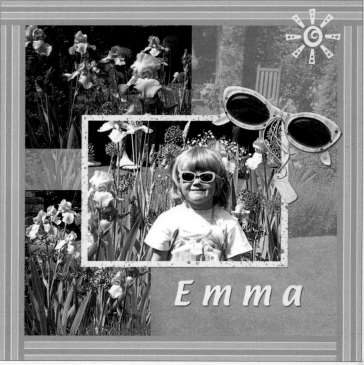

**3** Arrange the photos on the foundation page. When you are happy with the arrangement, stick the pictures down with the photo corners.

**4** Assemble the collage by adding the different stamped motifs, pressed flowers and leaves. Glue each item in position.

# Gone fishing

*Capture the magic of a long afternoon spent by the water's edge with this fun layout featuring a fond grandfather with his young grandson. Even if they didn't manage to hook anything with their makeshift rod, you can crop the photograph and add a catch consisting of a few embossed silver fish.*

**1** Cut a square of patterned paper to fit the background card and attach it with spray adhesive. Cut a 7.5cm/3in strip of dark blue paper to fit along the bottom of the page. Cut along the top edge with wavy-edged scissors and stick it in place.

**2** Use the wavy-edged scissors to cut out a few "waves" from the pale blue paper and glue them at intervals across the "water".

**3** Decide on the best position for the two photographs and stick them to the patterned background using a glue stick.

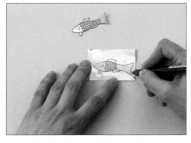

**4** Trace the fish template at the back of the book and cut out around the outline. Cut a small rectangle of embossing foil and, using a fine waterproof pen, draw around the template, then fill in the detail.

### materials and equipment

- patterned paper
- 30cm/12in square sheet of card (stock)
- spray adhesive
- craft knife
- metal ruler
- cutting mat
- thin paper in dark and pale blue
- wavy-edged scissors
- 2 photographs
- glue stick and sticky tape
- tracing paper
- fine waterproof pen
- silver embossing foil
- thick card or cork mat
- embossing tool or empty ballpoint pen
- old scissors
- large needle
- stranded embroidery thread (floss) in cream or fine string

**5** Lay the foil on a piece of thick card or a cork mat and trace over the lines with a stylus or old ballpoint pen, pressing firmly.

**6** Use an old pair of scissors to cut out the fish. Make another three fish in the same way, reversing some of them so that they appear to swim in opposite directions.

**7** Stick the fish to the dark blue paper with a glue stick, spacing them evenly between the waves.

**8** Thread a large needle with thread or fine string. Bring the needle out at the tip of the fishing rod and take it back in c ose to the fish, allowing the thread to loop gently. Tape the ends to the wrong side.

# Birthday party

*Children's birthday parties are big events to organize so it's nice to have a record of the day, as well as of your children's favourite friends, so that you can see how the the celebrations and children change as the years pass.*

materials and equipment

- selection of toning papers
- 6 photographs
- 30cm/12in square sheet of card (stock)
- cutting mat
- craft knife and metal ruler
- spray adhesive
- corner cutter
- purple metallic ink pad
- 5 tags
- glue dots
- stamp rubber stamp design
- flower and heart cutters
- brads
- sequins
- small floral stickers
- number template
- scissors

**1** Choose a selection of toning papers in colours that match your photographs and the background card. Working on a cutting mat and using a craft knife and metal ruler, cut one 12.5cm/5in square and mat it to the top left-hand corner of the background.

**2** Cut frames for your main photographs, 1cm/½in larger all around than the photographs. Use a corner cutter to trim the corners. Trim the photographs in the same way.

**3** Tint the edge of the main photograph frame using a purple metallic ink pad. Allow to dry. Mat the photographs to the frames, then mat the frames in position on the background.

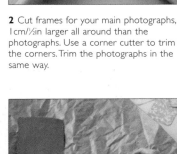

**4** Choose different papers to cover each of the five gift tags. Working in a ventilated area and with scrap paper on the work surface, use spray adhesive to coat the tags and mat each to coloured paper. Allow to dry, then carefully cut each out.

**5** Cut and trim three photographs and their corners to fit the tags. Cut slightly larger frames for each. Stick each of the three photographs to a frame, and a frame to a tag using glue dots or spray adhesive.

**6** For a tag without a photograph, decorate a plain frame with a stamped design. Add stickers to decorate the other tag without a photograph.

**7** Cut four flower motifs and one heart motif as additional decoration for the tags. Make a hole in the centre of each flower and in the top of four tags.

**8** For the tags without photographs, thread a sequin on a brad, then a flower, a frame and a tag. Open out the wings of the brad. Stick the tag to the background.

**9** For the centre tag, stick a heart to the top of the frame. Decorate the remaining tags as you like.

**10** Add small floral stickers to the background and the frames, as desired.

**11** Cut out the child's age from coloured paper using a template. Decorate the edges with the ink pad as before. Stick in place.

# Magic carpet

*With a little imagination you can transform an ordinary afternoon in the garden into a fairytale fantasy. All you need is a photograph of your family or best friends sitting out in the sunshine and a picture of the hearthrug. When taking the photographs, get everyone to sit close together in a solid group, and photograph the rug from a low angle. Cut them out, mount them together on an idyllic blue sky and you have a magic carpet to take you all on a wonderful adventure.*

**materials and equipment**

- group photograph
- computer and printer
- scissors
- photograph of rug
- hard and soft pencils
- tracing paper
- A4 sheet of thin silver card (stock)
- craft knife
- cutting mat
- scraps of coloured paper
- 60cm/24in metallic braid
- glue stick
- 30cm/12in square of sky-printed background paper
- tiny silver star stickers
- scrap of silver paper
- 4 small silver fabric motifs

**1** Enlarge the group photograph so that it measures approximately 15cm/6in from side to side and cut it out, following the outline of the figures as closely as you can.

**2** Enlarge the picture of the carpet to about 25cm/10in wide and cut out carefully, eliminating the original background.

**3** Trace the template from the back of the book, enlarging it to 30cm/12in wide. Transfer the outline to silver card. Cut along the skyline with scissors and cut out the windows with a craft knife on a cutting mat.

**4** Glue a small piece of coloured paper behind each window opening.

**5** Cut two lengths of metallic braid and glue them along the top and bottom edges of the sky-printed background sheet.

**6** Stick the silhouette to the background, just above the braid. Glue the family picture on to the carpet, then move it around the card until you are happy with its position. Stick it in place using a glue stick.

**7** Scatter the silver star stickers across the sky. Cut out a small crescent moon from silver paper and stick it low down in the sky near the buildings.

**8** Stick a silver motif on each corner, to cover the ends of the braid.

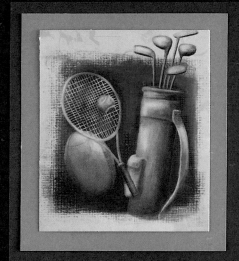

# New Year's Eve

*Beads, coiled wire and silver embellishments add a touch of sparkle to pictures of New Year's Eve celebrations. Lots of little ready-made ornaments are available to match this theme, so decorating the page is really easy. If the photographs are busy, keep the background simple so that there aren't too many things to distract the eye.*

**1** Cut a 30 × 15cm/12 × 6in rectangle of white card and mount all three photographs on it, cropping them a little if necessary to leave a narrow border of white between and around them.

**2** Stick the panel of photographs in the centre of the black card. Punch four squares of black and white patterned papers and four squares of pale grey card and arrange them, alternating, down each side.

### materials and equipment

- craft knife
- metal ruler
- thin card (stock) in white and pale grey
- cutting mat
- 3 photographs, each 15 × 10cm/6 × 4in
- tape runner or glue stick
- 30cm/12in square sheet of black card (stock)
- black and white patterned papers
- 5cm/2in square punch
- fine silver wire
- thin dowel rod
- wire cutters
- small glass beads in assorted colours
- paper piercer or bodkin
- sticky tabs
- label maker
- black label tape

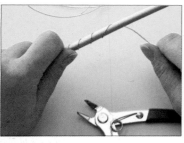

**3** Wrap a length of wire around the dowel to form a coil. Stretch it to the length of the page, leaving 5cm/2in of straight wire at each end. Make a second coil to match.

**4** Thread an assortment of small beads on to the wires. Use a generous amount as the wires are quite long.

**5** Pierce holes at the the top and bottom of the layout where you wish to anchor the wires. Push the straight ends of the wires through the card and anchor them at the back of the layout with sticky tabs. Add the sticker embellishments to the plain grey squares.

**6** Use a label maker to punch out a title for each photograph and the date on black tape. Stick the labels to the pictures and add the date in the corner of the layout.

# Sports

Whether your family members are active participants in sports, or fanatical supporters of a local team, sporting subjects make for rewarding layouts. This is a great theme for pages about children, where you can present them taking part in team games and school sports days, or showing off their daredevil skills on skateboards or bikes.

All kinds of games and sports make very satisfying subjects for scrapbooking pages, as they are all easily identified by the images and accessories associated with them, and there is plenty of strong colour in team strips, pitches and equipment. Add to these features the dramatic action shots you can capture in your photographs, and you can easily produce really eye-catching pages in this theme.

# Cycling

*This very simple double-page spread uses black ink trails to suggest the muddiness of a cycling trip in the countryside. Die-cut cog shapes and screw decorations reflect the mechanics of the bike.*

## materials and equipment

- black ink pad
- 2 x 30cm/12in square sheets of white card (stock)
- toy vehicle with rubber tyres
- sheet of metallic silver card (stock)
- craft knife and metal ruler
- cutting mat
- die-cut machine
- assorted cog dies
- matt silver paper
- 5cm/2in square punch
- photographs
- corner rounder
- glue stick
- paper piercer
- 5 screw brads

**1** Brush the black ink pad around the edges of the sheets of white card to give the pages a "muddy" appearance.

**2** Pat the ink pad on to the tread of a large wheel on a toy vehicle. Run the wheel across the card in different directions to create tyre tracks.

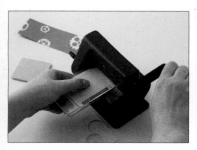

**3** Cut two strips of metallic silver card 5cm/2in wide: these will form a band across the two pages. Using a die-cut machine, cut out a selection of cogs from the matt silver paper. Stick all the shapes to the strips, allowing some to overlap the edges and trimming them flush.

**4** Punch details from photographs to create six square blocks. Round the two left-hand corners of the large photograph for the left-hand page, and the right-hand corners of a large photo for the right-hand page. Arrange all the pictures on the pages.

**5** Position the silver strips under the photographs. Trim them so that the ends align with the pictures and round the corners. Glue everything in place. Pierce holes in the positions where you will insert the screw brads.

**6** Push the brads into the holes and fold back the fasteners on the back of the pages to hold them in place.

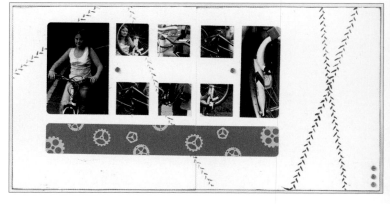

# Basketball

*The bright colours contrast with the black and white action photographs and the repeated circle motif clearly links with the ball game but also gives a sense of motion to the pages.*

## materials and equipment

- circle cutter
- thin card (stock) in lime green, turquoise and deep pink
- repositionable tape runner
- 2 x 30cm/12in square sheets of burnt orange card (stock)
- scissors
- eyelet tool kit
- letter stickers
- photographs
- 2 x 30cm/12in square sheets of chocolate brown card (stock)
- label maker
- black label tape

**1** Cut out circles from the lime green, turquoise and deep pink card in assorted sizes. If you don't have a circle cutter to do this you can draw and cut out a number of templates or draw round plates and cups of various sizes.

**2** Apply repositionable tape to the backs of the circles. This will allow you to move them around on the layout until you are happy with their positioning. Stick the circles to both sheets of burnt orange card in a random arrangement.

**3** Allow some of the circles to overlap the edges of the sheets and trim off the excess with scissors. On the inner edges of the pages, stick the circles to one side and trim, then stick the remaining parts to the opposite page, aligning them accurately.

**4** Use an eyelet tool to punch out small circles around parts of the large circles. If you have different sized punches try to use them all to add variety.

**5** Create the title using letter stickers. When placing these, always work from the outer edge of the page towards the middle, which will sometimes mean spelling the word backwards, to ensure that each word is accurately positioned.

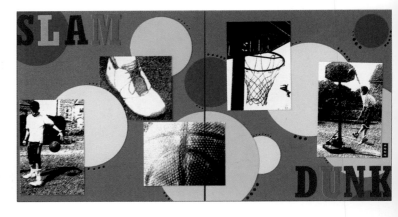

**6** Position the photographs so that they overlap the card circles, taking care to avoid any of the punched circles.

**7** Stick the finished pages to sheets of chocolate brown card, which will show through the punched holes.

**8** Use a label maker and black tape to punch the date and stick the label beside one of the photographs.

# Skateboarding

*Grunge and funky colours go hand in hand with skateboarding, and this double page spread has plenty of both. Inks, fabric, curly paperclips and roughly torn paper combine to create a great background for these pictures.*

**materials and equipment**

- 2 x 30cm/12in square sheets of turquoise card (stock)
- 2 x 30cm/12in square sheets of bright patterned paper
- thin lime card (stock)
- craft knife and metal ruler
- cutting mat
- ink pads in black and red
- hole punch
- roughly torn strips of woven cotton fabric
- "S" letter sticker
- die-cut "K"
- rub-on number "8"
- 4 round paperclips
- 4 photographs
- glue stick

**1** Cut both sheets of turquoise card in half. Tear away a strip approximately 4cm/1½in wide from each side, tearing at a slight angle. Always tear towards yourself to expose the inner core of the card on the right side.

**2** Moisten your finger and use it to roughen the torn edges of the card strips. Roll the edges back, without trying to do this too evenly. Stick the card strips on top of the squares of patterned paper.

**3** Cut four strips of lime card 6mm/¼in wide and 30cm/12in long. Roughly ink the edges of each strip using the black ink pad, then glue to the turquoise cards, aligning the strips across the two pages. Punch pairs of holes to tie the fabric strips through.

**4** To create the "S" for the title "skate", use the paper frame of a letter sticker as a template. Stick it gently to the layout (so that it can be peeled off later) and stipple through it using a red ink pad.

**5** When the ink is dry, pull away the template. Add the die-cut "K" and rub on an "8" to complete the title.

**6** Slide a paperclip on to the edge of each photograph. Arrange the photos at random angles across the centre of both pages and glue in position.

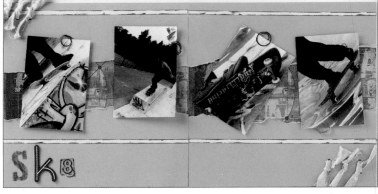

# Skiing

*Photographs of sunny days on the slopes demand pages with a touch of winter sparkle. This is a very simple layout, but the combination of snowflakes with silver patterned paper and an ice blue background gives a crisp, snowy look.*

## materials and equipment

- silver patterned paper
- guillotine (or craft knife, metal ruler and cutting mat)
- 2 x 30cm/12in square sheets of pale blue card (stock)
- eyelet punch
- tack hammer
- 24 silver eyelets
- foam brush
- acrylic paint in cobalt blue
- 6 sparkly snowflake buttons
- large white rub-on letters
- 4 photographs
- white card (stock), optional
- glue dots

**1** Cut 12 strips of silver patterned paper measuring 2.5 x 18cm/1 x 7in. If you don't have a guillotine, mark out the strips and cut them using a craft knife and metal ruler and working on a cutting mat.

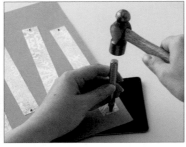

**2** Lay the strips across the two sheets of blue card at uneven heights and angles. Use the eyelet tools and silver eyelets to attach them to the card at each end.

**3** Using a foam brush, swipe a broad stripe of cobalt blue acrylic paint across the top left and bottom right corners of the layout. Leave to dry.

**4** Dab the edges of the snowflake buttons with the blue paint to make them stand out more on the page.

**5** When the paint is dry, rub on the white letters over it to create the titles.

**6** Print the photographs with a white border or mat them on to white card. Glue them at angles across the pages and stick on the snowflake buttons using glue dots.

# Tennis

*If you or others in your family enjoy getting to grips with the game, make this tennis court layout to celebrate your skills. You could personalize the page by using your own club colours for the background.*

## materials and equipment

- 30cm/12in square sheet of green card (stock)
- 2 x 30cm/12in square sheets of purple card (stock)
- craft knife and metal ruler
- cutting mat
- spray adhesive
- photographs
- white acrylic paint
- paintbrush
- alphabet foam stamps
- 2 purple and 4 green photo turns
- paper piercer or bodkin
- 6 dark green brads
- date stamp
- black ink pad

**1** Cut two wide and one narrow strip of green card and glue them vertically to the purple sheets to make the background. Glue the photographs in position on both pages. Brush white acrylic paint on to foam stamps to print the titles.

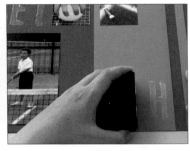

**2** On the right-hand page stamp the letters in reverse order from right to left so that you do not run out of space for the title. Take care not to overload the letters with paint or it will smudge. The words "game", "set" and "match" are used here.

**3** Lay a photo turn over the edge of each picture and pierce a hole in the card through the eye of the turn.

**4** Push a brad through the hole and fold the fasteners down at the back of the card to anchor the turn to the page.

**5** Add the date in the corner of the layout using a date stamp and a black ink pad.

# School sports day

*Make a first school sports day special for your child by creating a spread in your album to celebrate their determination, whether or not they managed to win any prizes. Your choice of photographs can emphasize what a good time everyone had taking part in the fun races.*

## materials and equipment

- large square punch
- photographs
- large dinner plate
- pencil
- 30cm/12in square sheet of patterned card (stock)
- scissors
- craft knife and metal ruler
- cutting mat
- 30cm/12in square sheets of cobalt and navy blue card (stock)
- glue stick
- computer and printer
- pale blue card (stock)
- 2 metal sports embellishments
- glue dots

**1** Use a large square punch to cut out three interesting sections from your photographs. Move the photos around in the window of the punch until you find the area you want. (If you don't have a punch, cut out the details using a craft knife and metal ruler, working on a cutting mat.)

**2** Draw round a large dinner plate on the patterned card and cut out the circle using scissors. Cut the circle in half and position each semicircle at the outside edge of the cobalt blue pages. Cut two wide strips of navy card and glue them next to the semicircles. Glue a strip of patterned paper at the inner edge of the right-hand page.

**3** Print the title "determination" in reverse on pale blue card and cut out the individual letters using a craft knife. The letters are less likely to tear if you cut out the centres before the outlines. Take your time and make sure the blade is sharp.

**4** Glue the letters up the right-hand side of the layout using a glue stick. Position the whole word first to help you space the letters evenly.

**5** Mat all the photographs on pale blue card and arrange them on the layout. Print a caption on pale blue card and add it to the first page.

**6** Tie the metal embellishments together with a thin strip of pale blue card and attach them to the layout using glue dots.

# Family pets

Dogs, cats and other animals are important and much-loved members of many families. If you have pets, they're sure to feature often in your photographs of outings, celebrations at home, and fun and games in the garden, but it can also be rewarding to devote some special pages of your scrapbook to your animals, making them the stars rather than the supporting cast.

Animals' lives are far shorter than ours, and this is a lovely way to remember them in later years. Children usually have a special connection with their pets and love to look back at photographs of their antics, or to find out about pets that were around before they were born or when they were very small. Album pages can paint vivid pictures of your pets' lives if you include shots of them in youth and age, at play, at rest, enjoying their favourite toys and doing their party tricks.

# My pet rabbit

*Sometimes it's difficult to find the perfect ready-made embellishments for your pages, especially if you're working on an unusual subject. Why not make your own? Polymer clay is the ideal material with which to create easy small-scale pieces to decorate your album.*

## materials and equipment

- polymer clay in orange and green
- baking tray
- 2 rabbit photographs
- craft knife
- metal ruler
- cutting mat
- 30cm/12in square sheets of card (stock) in mid- green, dark green and lime
- spray adhesive
- large square punch
- green vellum
- tape runner
- rub-on faux stitches
- embossing tool
- wire cutters
- 3 rabbit buttons
- glue dots

**1** Mould a carrot shape in orange polymer clay and add some green leaves. Place the carrot on a baking tray and harden in an oven according to the manufacturer's instructions. Leave to cool.

**2** Crop the photographs as necessary and mount on a large piece of mid-green card. Punch out three squares from dark green card and add them to the arrangement.

**3** Create the left-hand border by layering a strip of torn green vellum with a narrower strip of torn dark green card. Glue the border to the background 2cm/¾in from the edge of the page.

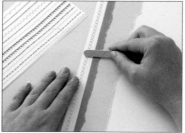

**4** In the 2cm/¾in gap use an embossing tool to rub on a line of faux stitches, taking care that they are straight.

**5** Use wire cutters to snip the shanks off the backs of the rabbit buttons. Stick one to each dark green square using a glue dot.

**6** Carefully tear green vellum into oval "lettuce leaves". Stick them overlapping at the bottom of the page.

**7** Attach the polymer clay carrot near the lettuce leaves. Use a generous quantity of glue dots as it is quite heavy.

# Folk art cat

*The colours in these photographs of a favourite cat suggested they would work well with the natural blues, rusts and ochres characteristic of American folk art. This in turn inspired the simple embellishments of cut-out hearts and paper animal shapes, and the drawn "stitches" around the woodgrain panel, which are a reminder of traditional patchwork.*

**1** On a background sheet of off-white paper, assemble a background collage using woodgrain design and complementary coloured papers. Cut out four triangles of patterned paper to go across the corners. Copy the templates of the cat, heart and dove motifs at the back of the book and transfer them to the back of the patterned papers. Cut them out using scissors.

**2** Glue the collage elements on to the background paper. Leave a narrow border around three sides and a wider strip down one side on which to place the cut-outs. Glue the cut-out motifs in position. Attach the photographs to the woodgrain panel using brown gummed photo corners. Finish the page by drawing "stitching" lines around the edges of the collage with a black marker pen.

## materials and equipment

- off-white heavy paper
- patterned papers in woodgrain and check designs
- craft knife
- cutting mat
- tracing paper
- pencil
- scissors
- glue stick
- photographs
- **brown paper photo corners**
- **black fine-tipped marker pen**

# Best friend

*Create a pet montage with cut-out photographs and conventional snapshots, and decorate the whole thing with fun paw prints and cute stickers. Using a combination of rectangular snapshots and cut-outs adds interest to the overall page, while the paw prints and stickers provide extra colour.*

## materials and equipment

- photographs of dog
- scissors
- 2 sheets of white card (stock)
- glue stick
- selection of children's stickers of dogs and puppies
- thin card in blue and green
- craft knife
- metal ruler
- cutting mat
- rubber stamp with paw print motif
- coloured ink pads
- paper towel

**1** Decide on the general layout of the album page, then work out which photographs you want to use. Either make extra colour copies or, if you have enough, cut around some of the dog images with scissors. Arrange the pictures on the plain paper then, when you are happy with the arrangement, glue all the pictures in position. Decorate with stickers of other breeds of dog.

**2** For the second page, mount the two main photographs of the dog on different coloured pieces of card, then add stickers all around the photographs to frame them. If you prefer not to place stickers directly on the original photographs, use copies.

**3** Decorate both pages with paw prints, either stamping a border design or making random prints at different angles. Wash the stamp between colours and pat dry with a paper towel.

# Bill and Ben the goldfish

*Pet fish are quiet and unassuming compared with larger animals, but are often valued family members, so give them their own moment of glory in your album with a special page dedicated to themselves. The background paper used for this layout had a squared design, making it very easy to create a scrapbook "aquarium" for this friendly pair.*

## materials and equipment

- craft knife
- 30cm/12in square sheet of scrapbook paper
- gold glitter paper
- bubble effect paper
- metal ruler
- cutting mat
- square patterned paper
- spray adhesive or paper glue
- pencil
- coin
- goldfish photographs
- scissors
- star tags
- printed names
- blue ribbon
- card tags
- self-adhesive shiny paper
- plain self-adhesive alphabet stickers
- patterned card alphabet stickers
- PVA (white) glue

**1** Cut a panel of gold glitter paper to fit at the top of the scrapbook paper and a panel of bubble paper to fit at the bottom. Glue both of them in place.

**2** Cut a thin band of square patterned paper to go on top of the bubble panel and glue in place.

**3** Draw around a coin on to the photos of your fishes, positioning it over their faces. Cut out the circles and glue one to each star tag. Print out the fishes' names, trim to size and glue one above each picture.

**4** Trim the large photograph to fit the central panel, then glue it to the left side of the page.

**5** Add short lengths of ribbon to the star tags and glue them in position on the right side of the page.

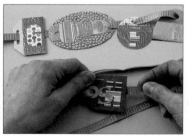

**6** Decorate five tags in assorted shapes with pieces of self-adhesive shiny paper. Spell out the word "goldfish" on the tags with alphabet stickers. Thread all the tags in sequence on to a length of blue ribbon.

**7** Position the ribbon across the top of the page then tuck the ends to the back of the page and glue them down with PVA glue.

# Purry puss

*This pampered fellow gets a very luxurious furry page to himself. If your cat is co-operative you should be able to get him to provide a paw print in paint with which to sign the page, but be sure to wipe the paint off his paw afterwards.*

## materials and equipment

- spray adhesive
- 30cm/12in square sheet of thin card (card stock)
- short pile fun fur or fleece
- scissors
- coin
- pencil
- thin card (stock) in red and green
- eyelet punch
- tack hammer
- gold rub-down letters
- 1cm/⅜in tartan ribbons
- PVA (white) glue
- 3 small swing tags
- gold paper
- glue stick
- photographs
- paw print
- narrow red ribbon
- collar bell
- 3 small gold safety pins
- thin red card
- metal ruler and pencil
- craft knife and cutting mat
- 4 photo corners

**1** Spray adhesive on to one side of a sheet of card. Press the card firmly on to the wrong side of a piece of fun fur. Using scissors, trim the excess fabric from around the edges, as close to the card as possible.

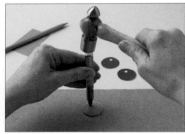

**2** Draw around a coin on to red and green card to make discs, one for each letter of your pet's name. Cut them all out. Punch a large hole at the top of each disc with an eyelet punch.

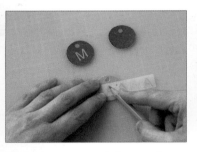

**3** Rub a letter on to each disc to spell your pet's name, alternating the colours of the discs as you go.

**4** Tie each disc to a length of tartan ribbon. Use PVA glue to attach the ribbons to the right side of the page, turning the raw ends to the back.

**5** Glue three tags to the wrong side of a piece of gold paper and trim away the excess paper. Re-punch the holes in the tags with an eyelet punch. Glue a small photo of your pet to one tag, and a paw print to a second. Tie a small collar bell to the third with thin red ribbon.

**6** Pin the three gold tags to the bottom left corner of the page, attaching them with small gold safety pins.

**7** Cut a rectangle of red card measuring 1cm/⅜in larger all round than the large photograph.

**8** Attach photo corners to the picture and and stick it to the mount, leaving an even border all round. Glue the mount to the page.

# Prize-winning pony

*If you have ponies that win rosettes for you or your children you'll want to honour their achievements by creating a special page. This is a very simple design using brightly coloured paper, with no other embellishments.*

## materials and equipment

- craft knife
- 30cm/12in square sheets of card (stock) in green and orange
- metal ruler
- cutting mat
- glue stick
- red, blue and yellow paper
- circle cutter or circular templates and pencil
- scissors
- photographs

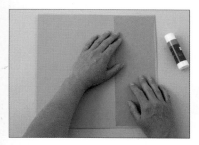

**1** Cut a rectangle of orange card measuring 29 × 10cm/11½in × 4in and glue it to the right-hand side of the green card, leaving very narrow borders of green around three sides.

**2** Cut three rectangles measuring 20 × 7cm/8 × 2¾in from red, blue and yellow paper. Glue them to the left side of the page, spacing them evenly, with the yellow at the top, then red, then blue.

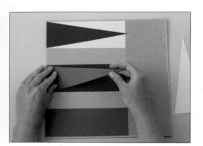

**3** Cut three triangles 20cm × 7cm/8in × 2¾in from red, blue and yellow paper. Glue them on top of the rectangles, placing red on yellow, blue on red and yellow on blue.

**4** To make the rosettes, cut three large and three small circles of red, yellow and blue card. Glue the smaller circles on top of the large circles. Cut two thin rectangles in the same colours of each paper. Snip the ends diagonally to make ribbons. Glue the ribbons to the backs of the rosettes.

**5** Draw a circle around each horse's head in a small photograph and cut it out.

**6** Glue a horse's head in the centre of each rosette.

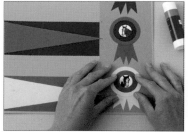

**7** Glue the rosettes to the orange panel on the right of the page, with the red one at the top, blue in the middle and yellow at the bottom.

**8** Glue two large horse photographs to the panel on the left side of the page, spacing the pictures evenly.

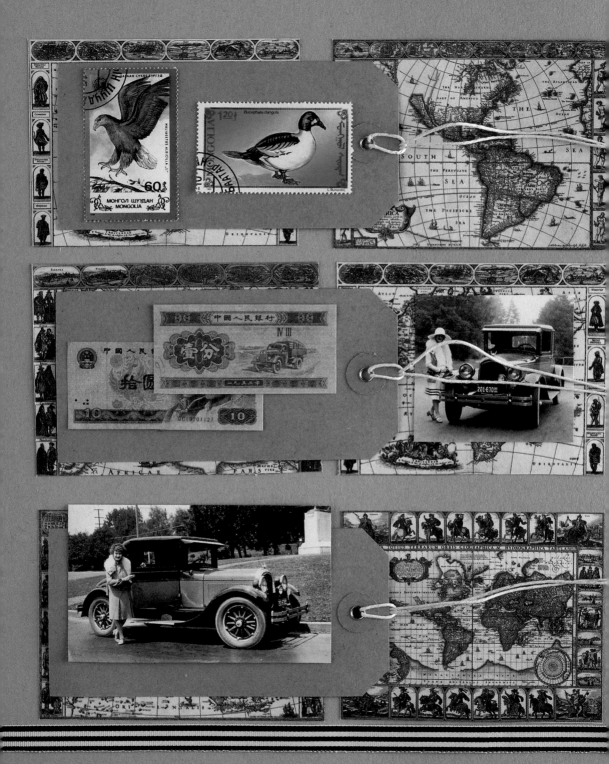

# Travel

Trips and vacations are prime themes for scrapbooks: everyone's feeling relaxed, you have time to take lots of good pictures and – with luck – the weather's wonderful. If you're touring there will be new sights to see every day and new experiences to inspire you. Keeping your scrapbook in mind while you're away you'll remember to hoard lots of good-looking holiday ephemera, such as tickets, menus, hotel bills, little natural objects such as shells and pressed flowers, and maybe some exotic food packaging and foreign newspapers or magazines that you can take cuttings from.

Jot down plenty of notes so that you don't forget the name of that perfect beach or what you ate at your favourite restaurant. The more detailed your journaling the more memories you'll preserve, and the more fascinating your travel albums will be for you and your family in the years to come.

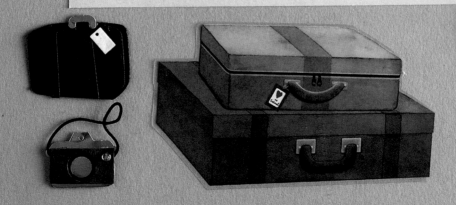

# Beside the sea

*A summer trip to the seaside is an intrinsic part of family life. The leisurely pastimes that make up a day's outing or a week's stay by the sea – paddling, swimming, beachcombing and building sandcastles – have remained unchanged over the years, and this album page brings together snaps of three generations of the same family having fun on the beach.*

## materials and equipment

- graph paper
- fine pen
- ruler
- A4 sheet of thin card (stock)
- craft knife
- cutting mat
- tracing paper
- selection of colour and black and white photographs and postcards
- watercolours
- fine paintbrush
- 30cm/12in square sheet of coloured card (stock)
- glue stick

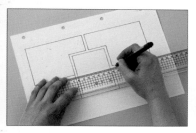

**1** Using the template at the back of the book as a guide, draw the postcard frame on graph paper, leaving margins of 5mm/¼in between all the shapes and 1cm/⅜in around the outside. Cut a rectangle of white card to the exact size of this rectangle.

**2** Trace each of the five segments on to a separate piece of tracing paper with a ruler and a fine pen. These templates will act as guides for selecting which images to use and where to crop them.

**3** Place each tracing over your chosen pictures until you find a composition that will fit well within the outline. You may need to enlarge or reduce the photographs.

**4** Black and white pictures can be hand-tinted with watercolour so that they blend in with the newer photographs. Use a fine brush to build up delicate layers of colour – without letting the paper become too wet.

**5** Cut out the centre rectangle and one of the corner segments from the graph paper template. Draw around these segments on your chosen photographs and cut out around the outlines.

**6** Glue the segments on to the white card rectangle, making light pencil guidelines to ensure that they are positioned correctly.

**7** Photocopy and cut out other pictures that have not been used on the "postcard" then arrange these, along with the postcard itself, on the coloured card. Glue everything in place using a glue stick.

78342

# Sightseeing in the States

*The Stars and Stripes make a really colourful background, but this simple idea could easily be adapted using the flag of whichever country you have visited. The folded airmail envelope opens to reveal a mini-album of extra pictures.*

## materials and equipment

- dark blue paper
- craft knife
- metal ruler
- cutting mat
- 30cm/12in square sheet of white card (stock)
- silver star stickers
- pencil
- glue stick
- red paper
- 5 luggage labels
- photocopy of denim fabric
- hole punch
- photographs
- natural twine
- two airmail envelopes
- adhesive tape

**1** To make the background flag, cut a 15cm/6in square of blue paper and glue it in the top left corner of the white card, matching the top and side edges exactly.

**2** Stick 50 silver stars in nine rows to the blue square. For the first row space six stars evenly, starting 1.5cm/½in from the left-hand side, with their lower tips 2.5cm/1in below the top edge. For the second row position five stars between the stars of the first row.

**3** Cut four strips of red paper 15 × 2cm/6 × ¾in, and three strips 30 × 2cm/12 × ¾in. Glue the strips to the white card to form the American flag, butting the short ones against the blue square, and leaving the same depth of white background between each horizontal strip.

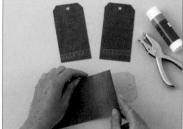

**4** To make the tags, remove the string from five luggage labels. Cover each label with denim paper and trim the paper to size. Make a new hole at the top of each label using a hole punch.

**5** Trim a photograph to fit across the centre of each luggage label and glue in place. Tie a short length of twine through each hole.

**6** To make the mini-album, fold two airmail envelopes into three. Tape the ends together to make a six-page album.

**7** Trim the remaining photographs to fit the pages of the mini-album and glue them in position.

**8** Glue all the tags in place on the flag page, then stick the mini-album in the centre of the lower row.

# Irish castles

*Ireland is known as the Emerald Isle, but as well as being green and lush, the rolling hills are crammed with impressive old buildings. The heraldic imagery and clear colours used to embellish this page reflect the country's historic sites and beautiful unspoilt landscape.*

## materials and equipment

- 30cm/12in square sheet of pale blue mottled paper
- craft knife
- metal ruler
- cutting mat
- 30cm/12in square sheet of dark green paper
- spray adhesive
- three photographs printed with white borders
- wavy-edged scissors
- tracing paper and pencil
- scissors
- thin paper, such as origami paper, in blues and greens
- glue stick

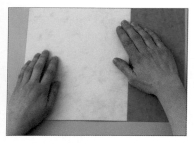

**1** Cut a strip of pale blue mottled paper to fit across two-thirds of the green background paper. Glue it in place with spray adhesive, aligning the edges.

**2** Trim the white borders of the photographs with wavy-edged scissors to give them a narrow decorative border.

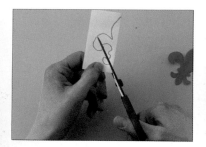

**3** Trace the fleur-de-lys template at the back of the book. Fold a small square of blue paper in half, with right sides facing, and transfer one half of the outline on to the wrong side. Cut out the motif. Cut a second fleur-de-lys from green paper.

**4** Glue two rectangles of different coloured paper together to make a small square, then stick the blue fleur-de-lys centrally along the join.

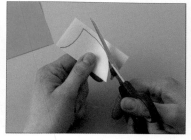

**5** Use the shield template at the back of the book as a guide to cut out a small shield shape from pale blue paper.

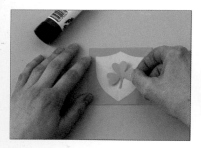

**6** Following the template, cut out a green shamrock and glue it to the centre of the shield. Glue the shield on to a square of darker blue paper.

**7** Glue the three photographs in position on the page, overlapping them slightly so that the join between the two background papers is concealed.

**8** Stick the two decorated squares and the second fleur-de-lys into the spaces between the pictures.

# Trip to Japan

*There is always something exciting about discovering a new country and its culture. Record your journey by collecting interesting ephemera as you travel; when you get back home, display it on a series of luggage labels.*

## materials and equipment

- patterned origami paper
- 30cm/12in square sheet of deep red card (stock)
- scissors
- spray adhesive
- photocopier
- old atlas
- emphemera including tickets, bills and wrappers
- luggage labels
- photographs
- fine permanent marker pen
- hole punch
- narrow black ribbon
- self-adhesive foam pads

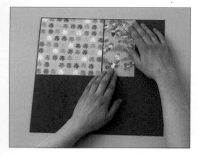

**1** Cut one sheet of origami paper in half, then glue one and a half sheets to the top left corner of the background card with spray adhesive, leaving narrow margins between them and around the outer edges.

**2** Photocopy a map of Japan from an atlas, reducing the size as necessary to fit into the bottom right-hand corner, and cut out, shaping the upper edge in a gentle curve. Glue in place using spray adhesive and add two tickets overlapping parts of the map.

**3** Remove the string from a luggage label. Place it over a photograph and draw round the edge with a fine waterproof pen.

**4** Mark the position of the hole, then cut out around the outline and punch a hole at the centre top.

**5** Cut a 20cm/8in length of narrow ribbon and loop it through the hole. Make one or more additional labels in the same way.

**6** Small items of memorabilia can be displayed by sticking them on to plain labels. Larger pieces, such as a calendar page, can be reduced in size on a photocopier.

**7** Tie all the labels together loosely in a bunch. Attach the knot to the top left corner of the card and then anchor the labels on the page with foam pads.

# A day in the countryside

*Machine stitching on card is a very quick way to add colour, pattern and texture to your page, and you can use a variety of stitches to real effect. This simple page uses fresh colours to echo the springlike tones of the photographs.*

**materials and equipment**

- sewing machine
- light purple thread
- scrap card (stock)
- 2 x 30cm/12in square sheets of lilac card (stock)
- pencil
- scissors
- flower-shaped punches in two sizes
- light and dark purple card (stock)
- photographs
- glue dots
- pink rub-on letters
- embossing tool

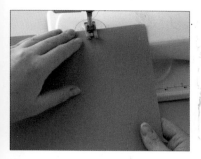

**1** Thread the machine with light purple thread and do a test on spare card to get the tension right. Stitch slowly across the lower part of the page to create two gently waving lines. Align the starting points on the second page with the ends of the first lines.

**2** Punch a selection of flowers from light and dark purple card using a large and a small punch.

**3** Crumple the flowers to add texture. Flatten out and stick the smaller ones on top of the larger ones. Use glue dots to stick them along the lines of stitching.

**4** Double-mat the photographs on light and dark purple card and glue to the pages. Rub on the title lettering in one corner.

# A weekend in Paris

*This is an excellent way to combine a large number of photographs and your journaling on one page. The paper bag book contains pockets for mini-pages displaying more photographs as well as tickets, maps and other souvenirs.*

**materials and equipment**

- guillotine
- photographs
- 30cm/12in square sheet of red card (stock)
- 3 flat-bottomed brown paper bags
- heavy-duty stapler
- selection of coloured card (stock)
- glue stick
- two-hole punch
- binder clip
- file tabs
- tickets, stamps and other travel memorabilia
- glue dots
- letter and number stickers

**1** Using a guillotine, crop a selection of photographs into 6cm/2½in squares.

**2** Arrange the photographs in a grid on the square card, using repositionable tape so that you can adjust them as necessary. Leave space for the title and the paper bag book on the right-hand side.

**3** To make the book, stack the three bags together with the flat bottoms facing upwards and at alternate sides.

**4** Fold the whole pile in half and make a crease at the fold. Staple along the fold to make the spine of the book.

**5** Cut a piece of card to fit the height of the book and fold it over the spine. Glue in place using a glue stick. Punch two holes through the spine and insert the binder clip.

**6** Cut out squares of card to fit the pockets created by the paper bags. Staple file tabs to the edges and fill the pages with pictures, ephemera and journaling.

**7** Decorate the front of the book and place all the cards inside the pages.

**8** Attach the book to the layout with a generous number of glue dots to support its weight. Use stickers to create the title and the date.

# Spanish memorabilia

*This collection of memorabilia from a vacation in Spain is attractively displayed in a practical way, with functional pockets in which to slip airline tickets, restaurant bills, postcards and other bits and pieces picked up during the trip. A photo-montage of attractive places can be made from a duplicate set of pictures to fill another page of the album.*

**materials and equipment**

- craft knife
- metal ruler
- cutting mat
- 4 x 30cm/12in square sheets of red card (card)
- masking tape
- pencil
- eyelet punch
- tack hammer
- small nickel eyelets
- scissors
- tickets, stamps and other travel memorabilia
- bone folder
- glue stick
- assorted paperclips
- photographs

**1** Using a craft knife and metal ruler and working on a cutting mat, cut out a 12.5cm/5in square from red card and tape it in the centre of one large square of card. Mark the positions for eyelets in each corner of the small square. Punch a hole at each marked point using an eyelet tool. Insert the eyelets through both layers of card. Tickets, pictures and travel memorabilia can be slipped under the small square.

**2** To make a pocket, cut a larger square of red card and attach a smaller piece to it with an eyelet. Score around two adjacent edges of the square. Trim away the corner between the scored lines and fold in the edges sharply with a bone folder to make two flaps. Glue these to a large card square. Memorabilia, such as tickets, stamps and notes can be inserted in the flap pocket or attached to the pocket with paperclips.

**3** For the photo-montage, use duplicate prints or make extra copies so that you can cut them up as necessary to make an effective composition. Arrange all the photographs and other pictures in a pleasing way on the last square of red card. Trim away any unnecessary parts of the photographs using a craft knife and a metal ruler, and working on a cutting mat. Once you are happy with your arrangement, glue all the pictures in place using a glue stick.

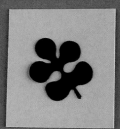

# Celebrating the seasons

Though the seasons return to delight us year by year, no two days are ever truly alike, and nature is always ready to astonish us with its beauty. For photographers, the desire to capture fleeting effects of light and colour in the natural world is a powerful impulse, and successful attempts are well worth framing beautifully on your scrapbook layouts.

Pages with seasonal themes can make an album in themselves, perhaps highlighting your favourite landscapes or country walks, or tracing the annual round in your own garden. Or you can use them to punctuate more general collections of photographs, to place your family activities and celebrations in a seasonal context.

# A seasonal mosaic

*Photographic mosaic is a lot easier than it looks as long as you take your time and measure accurately before cutting up your pictures. Special sheets marked with a grid take care of all the spacing and lining up for you. This is a wonderful way to create an impressionistic image of seasonal flowers.*

### materials and equipment

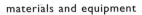

- photographs
- repositionable tape runner
- cutting mat with printed grid
- craft knife
- metal ruler
- 30cm/12in square sheet white mosaic grid paper
- computer and printer
- thin card (stock) in white and mid-green
- scissors
- glue dots
- 5 metal charms with a garden theme

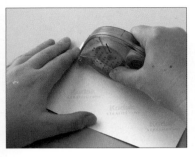

**1** Cover the back of each photograph with repositionable adhesive. Be generous with this as it will make the cutting easier.

**2** Stick each photograph to the cutting mat, aligning it carefully with the printed grid, and use a craft knife and metal ruler to cut it into 2.5cm/1in squares.

**3** Reassemble the photographs on the mosaic grid. If you want any pictures to occupy blocks of squares, remember to allow for the spaces between the squares when calculating the size to cut.

**4** Blend the edges of the photographs into each other a little, remembering to leave rectangular spaces for the titling as you arrange the pieces.

**5** Print the titles on to white card. Carefully measure the spaces you need to fill on the grid and cut out the titles. Cut slightly larger rectangles from green card for the mats.

**6** Mat the titles "bloom", "seasons" and "flower" and stick them in place in the spaces on the grid.

**7** Use glue dots to attach the metal charms to the layout.

# Spring in bloom

*The bold colour scheme and geometric lines in this eye-catching picture of a tulip bed required an equally dramatic treatment. Red, green and white tracing papers, which have a translucent, matt finish, echo the colours of the flowers, and the spiral-petalled flower punch gives the finished page a strong, contemporary look. The white flower label bears the botanic name of the tulip species, but you could also use it to record the date or place where the picture was taken.*

## materials and equipment

- A4 sheet of white tracing paper
- 30cm/12in square sheet of green card (stock)
- glue stick
- 2 A4 sheets of lime green tracing paper
- scissors
- flower picture
- glue dots
- flower-shaped punch
- thin white card (stock)
- A4 sheet of red tracing paper
- fine marker pen or computer and printer
- pencil

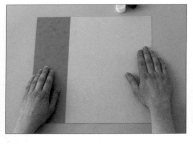

**1** Position the white tracing paper on the right-hand side of the green background card and glue it in place.

**2** Position a sheet of green tracing paper so that it covers the lower part of the card and glue in place. Trim the edges as necessary so that they are all level.

**3** Position the photograph centrally within the lime green square and stick in place with glue dots.

**4** Using the flower-shaped punch, make five flowers from white card and stick them down with a glue stick to form an evenly spaced row down the centre of the green rectangle on the left.

**5** Punch seven red and seven green flowers from the coloured tracing paper. Arrange them in two rows across the top rectangle, alternating the colours, and glue in place with the glue stick.

**6** Copy the plant marker template at the back of the book and cut out two green and two red shapes from the remaining tracing paper.

**7** For the named marker, either cut out a white label and write a name across the centre with a fine marker pen, or print the name on white paper. Place one of the tracing paper markers over it so that the name lies centrally in the top part, then draw round it and cut out the shape.

**8** Arrange the coloured markers down the left side of the page and the named marker at the bottom right corner of the photograph, and glue in place.

# Glorious summer

*This bougainvillea-clad house, replete with peeling paintwork and faded wooden shutters, epitomizes the languid days of high summer and is a reminder of a happy holiday spent on the shores of an Italian lake. A photograph taken in the garden of the adjoining villa shared the same colour scheme: this was cut up into squares to make a mosaic-style frame, and the background was chosen to harmonize with the flowers.*

## materials and equipment

- transparent ruler
- pink mulberry paper
- glue stick
- A4 sheet of pale green paper
- spray adhesive
- 30cm/12in square sheet of purple card (stock)
- marbled paper in toning colours
- craft knife
- cutting mat
- main photograph, measuring 17.5 x 12.5cm/7 x 5in
- two copies of a second photograph

**1** Using the edge of a ruler to give a deckle edge, tear two strips of mulberry paper each measuring about 2 x 30cm/¾ x 12in.

**2** Glue one strip behind each long edge of the pale green paper so that about 8mm/⅓in is visible. Using spray adhesive, glue the paper to the centre of the purple background card and trim the ends.

**3** Using a craft knife and transparent ruler, cut four narrow strips of marbled paper, each measuring 6mm x 31cm/¼ x 12½in.

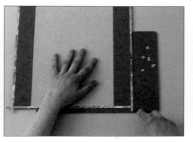

**4** Glue two of the strips to the top and bottom edges of the card, to conceal the edges of the other papers. Glue the remaining strips to the side edges and mitre the corners neatly.

**5** Glue the main photograph to the centre of the green paper, making sure that it lies completely flat.

**6** Cut the other two photographs into 2.5cm/1in squares, using a craft knife and ruler and working on a cutting mat.

**7** Glue these small squares around the main picture, alternating the light and dark tones to create a chequerboard effect.

# Autumn colour

*The fall in New England is world renowned for its glorious display of colour. Capture the hues of this "season of mists and mellow fruitfulness" with a special album page and make your own drift of dried leaves by using a special punch to cut shapes from duplicate pictures and toning card. As a finishing touch you could make a tiny luggage tag, using the leaf punch to make the hole and threading it with garden string, to record the date and location of your photographs.*

## materials and equipment

- spray adhesive
- 20 x 30cm/8 x 12in sheet of heavy cream tissue
- 30cm/12in square sheet of manila card (stock), plus extra for tag (optional)
- 3 autumnal photographs, plus an extra copy of each
- manila photo corners
- leaf-shaped punch
- glue stick
- coloured paper in matching autumnal shades
- self-adhesive foam pads
- garden string (optional)

**1** Spray the heavy tissue lightly with adhesive and smooth it down across the centre of the manila background card.

**2** Position the three photographs on the central panel and secure them using manila photo corners.

**3** Use the leaf-shaped punch to cut out a few leaf shapes from the duplicate copy of the topmost photograph.

**4** Scatter these around the edges of the main picture so that they appear to be tumbling down through the sky and glue them in place using a glue stick.

**5** Punch more leaves from the side and bottom edges of the other two photographs and stick them down randomly around the pictures, matching the colours.

**6** Cut a few leaves from the remaining tissue paper and fix these along the bottom of the card.

**7** Punch a selection of leaves from the coloured card and arrange them in a drift, with the darker colours towards the darker areas of the pictures.

**8** Overlap the leaves for a naturalistic effect and use foam pads for some, to give a three-dimensional effect. Add a manila tag tied with string if you wish.

# Winter wonderland

*Though it may be the most monochromatic of the seasons, winter is rich in texture: dazzling icicles, the beauty of snowflakes and the dense whiteness of fallen snow. These three snow scenes are mounted on a background flecked with gold and silver leaf, and brought to life with golden snowflakes, some handmade and others from a peel-off sheet.*

## materials and equipment

- three wintry photographs printed with white borders
- crinkle-edged scissors
- 30cm/12in square sheet of mottled grey paper
- spray adhesive
- tissue paper flecked with gold and silver
- scissors
- glue stick
- 12 small white paper fasteners
- A4 sheet of pale blue tracing paper
- gold pen
- sharp pencil
- peel-off gold snowflake stickers

**1** Trim the borders of each photograph using crinkle-edged scissors to create a decorative, frosted border.

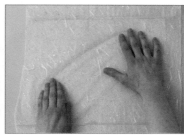

**2** Spray the background paper lightly with adhesive and cover it with metallic-flecked tissue. Trim the edges flush with the card.

**3** Position the pictures on the background, overlapping and angling them if you wish to create an interesting arrangement. Glue in position with a glue stick.

**4** Insert a small white paper fastener just inside each corner of the three pictures.

**5** Photocopy the snowflake templates from the back of the book. Place a sheet of blue tracing paper over the first snowflake and draw in the details with a gold pen. Trace the outline with a pencil, then cut out. Make another two or three snowflakes in the same way.

**6** Arrange the snowflakes in the largest space on the layout and stick them down using a glue stick.

**7** Finish off the design by sprinkling a few golden peel-off snowflakes across the page.

# The four seasons

*These four shots of family and friends enjoying country walks reflect the changing moods and colours of the seasons. Choose papers that echo these hues for mounting and add a border of punched motifs – the simple square format pulls together the different compositions and styles of the pictures.*

## materials and equipment

- light green, dark green, brown and ice blue paper
- ruler
- craft knife
- cutting mat
- pencil
- 4 seasonal motif punches
- thin coloured paper
- glue stick
- photograph for each season
- 4 sheets of tracing paper to match coloured paper
- 16 small coloured paper fasteners
- 30cm/12in square sheet of card (card stock)

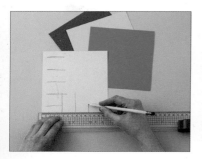

**1** Cut a 6in/15cm square from each of the coloured papers. Pencil in five equally spaced marks along two adjacent sides of each square.

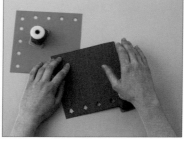

**2** Using these marks as guides, punch motifs around the two sides. Choose designs that reflect the season or location of each picture – such as a snowflake for winter and a sun for summer.

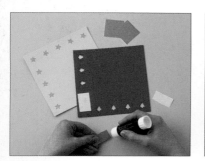

**3** Choose a complementary coloured paper for each main square and stick a small piece behind each cut-out motif.

**4** Glue each photograph to a piece of toning tracing paper, leaving a margin of at least 3cm/1⅛in all round.

**5** Tear the tracing paper against a ruler to create a narrow border with a deckle edge on all sides.

**6** Glue the photographs to their respective backgrounds so that the innermost edges line up exactly.

**7** As a decorative detail, attach a small coloured paper fastener to each corner of each picture.

**8** Glue the four squares to the background paper, aligning them carefully.

# TEMPLATES

*Enlarge the templates on a photocopier, or trace the design and draw a grid of evenly spaced squares over your tracing. Draw a larger grid on to another piece of paper and copy the outline square by square. Draw over the lines to make sure they are continuous.*

New Year celebration
page 65

Scandinavian Valentine
page 69

Winged heart Valentine
page 71

New Year calendar
page 64

Valentine shoe
page 70

Chinese New Year
page 68

Envelope Valentine
page 72

Easter card with
velvet chicks
page 75

St Patrick's Day wallet
page 74

Millefiori Easter cards
page 76 and Easter egg
card page 77

Mother's Day appliqué
page 83

Greetings for Diwali
page 86

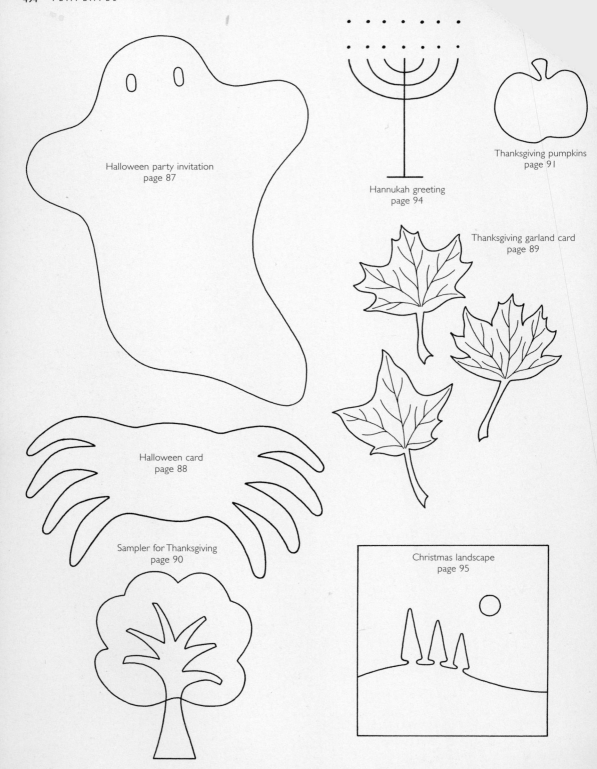

Halloween party invitation
page 87

Hannukah greeting
page 94

Thanksgiving pumpkins
page 91

Thanksgiving garland card
page 89

Halloween card
page 88

Sampler for Thanksgiving
page 90

Christmas landscape
page 95

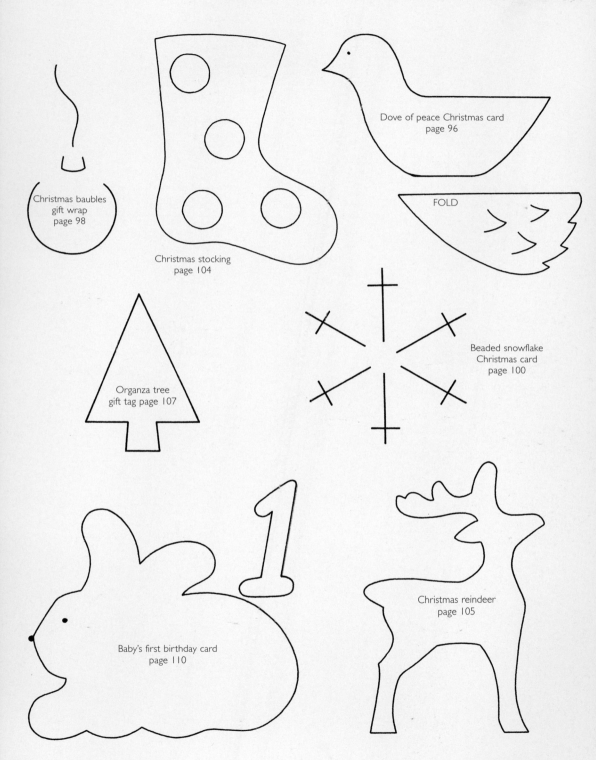

Christmas baubles
gift wrap
page 98

Christmas stocking
page 104

Dove of peace Christmas card
page 96

FOLD

Organza tree
gift tag page 107

Beaded snowflake
Christmas card
page 100

Baby's first birthday card
page 110

Christmas reindeer
page 105

FOLD

FOLD

Concertina caterpillar
page 112

Stencilled birthday car
page 114

FOLD

Cowboy card
page 120

Cutey birthday dog
page 116

Flying fairy birthday card
page 130

Butterfly birthday card
page 126

Funky foam monster birthday card
page 128

Russian dolls
page 124

Origami gift box
page 148

BASE

BASE BASE

BASE

BOX

LID

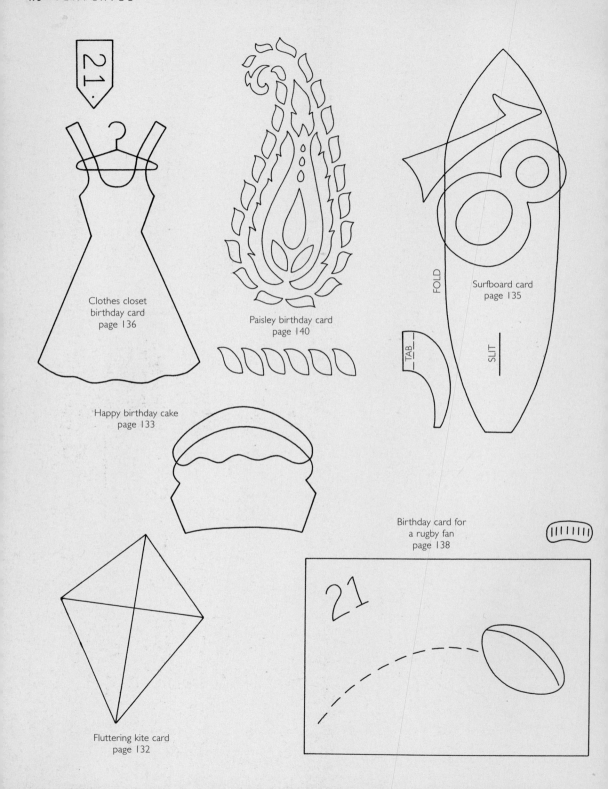

Clothes closet
birthday card
page 136

Paisley birthday card
page 140

FOLD

Surfboard card
page 135

TAB

SLIT

Happy birthday cake
page 133

Birthday card for
a rugby fan
page 138

Fluttering kite card
page 132

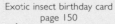

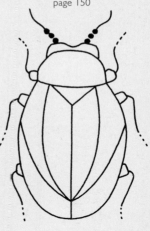

Greek urn card
page 145

Greetings for a gardener
page 156

Embroidered flowers
page 155

Damask gift envelope
page 158

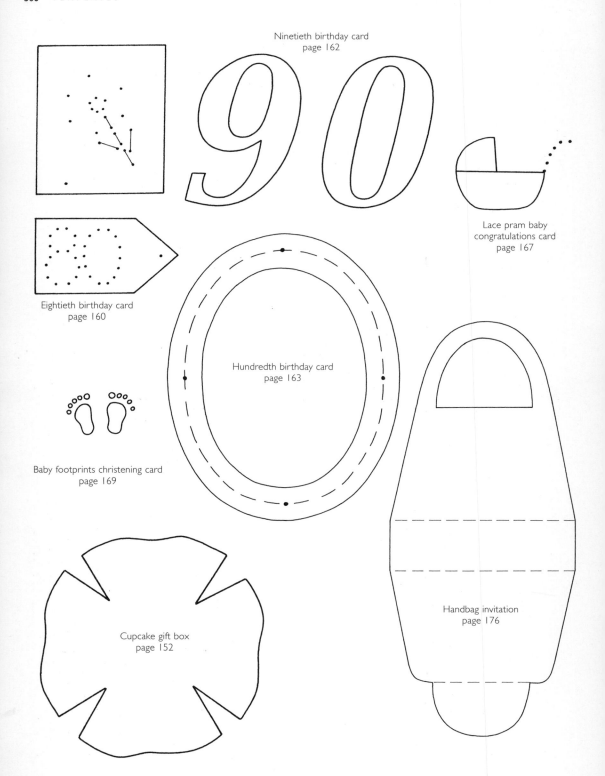

Ninetieth birthday card
page 162

Lace pram baby
congratulations card
page 167

Eightieth birthday card
page 160

Hundredth birthday card
page 163

Baby footprints christening card
page 169

Cupcake gift box
page 152

Handbag invitation
page 176

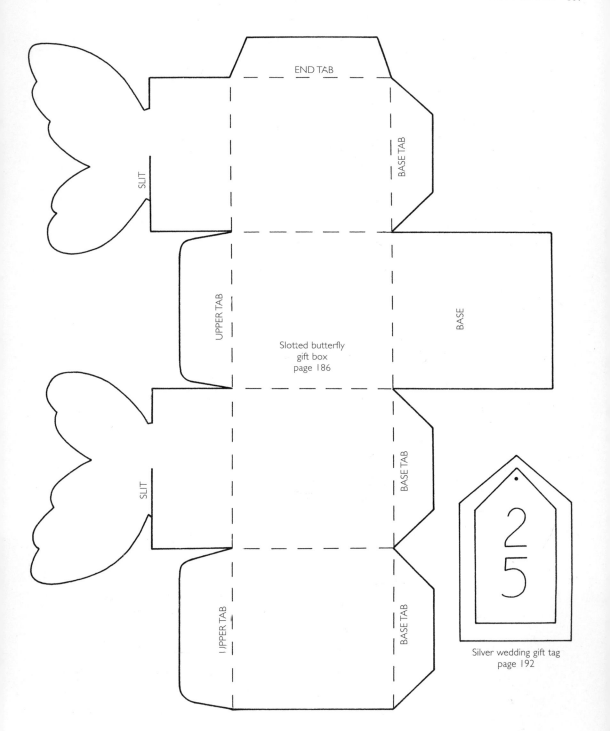

END TAB

BASE TAB

SLIT

UPPER TAB

BASE

Slotted butterfly
gift box
page 186

SLIT

BASE TAB

UPPER TAB

BASE TAB

BASE TAB

2
5

Silver wedding gift tag
page 192

Pearl wedding anniversary gift trim
page 193

Ruby wedding anniversary card
page 195

Starry good luck card
page 218

Golden wedding anniversary card
page 196

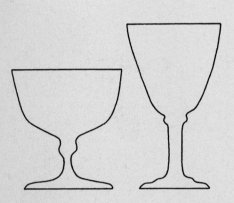

Housewarming in style card
page 199

Coffee break retirement card
page 201

Four-leaf clover for luck
page 221

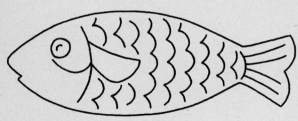

Embossed fish
retirement card
page 202

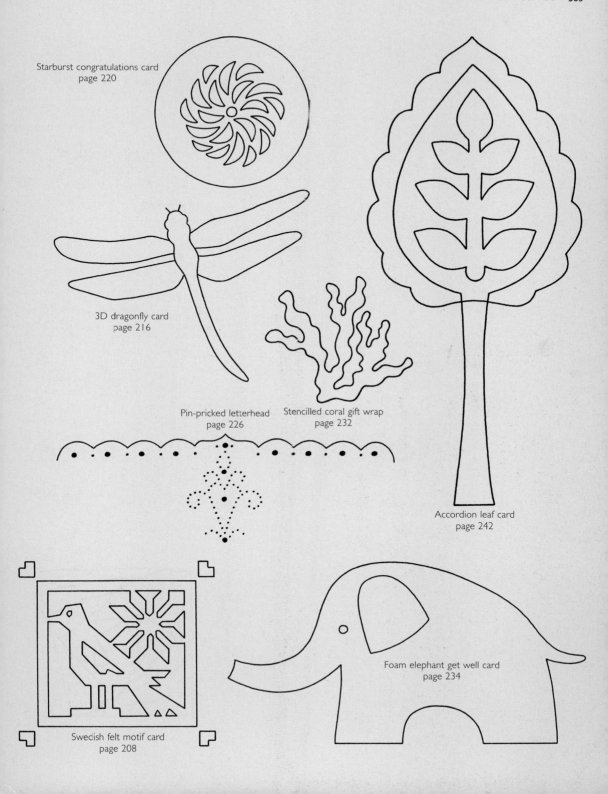

Starburst congratulations card
page 220

3D dragonfly card
page 216

Pin-pricked letterhead
page 226

Stencilled coral gift wrap
page 232

Accordion leaf card
page 242

Swedish felt motif card
page 208

Foam elephant get well card
page 234

Making a kaleidoscope
p265

Decorating paper frames p268

Stencilling p278

Stencilling p278

Paper appliqué p280

Iris-folding p288–9

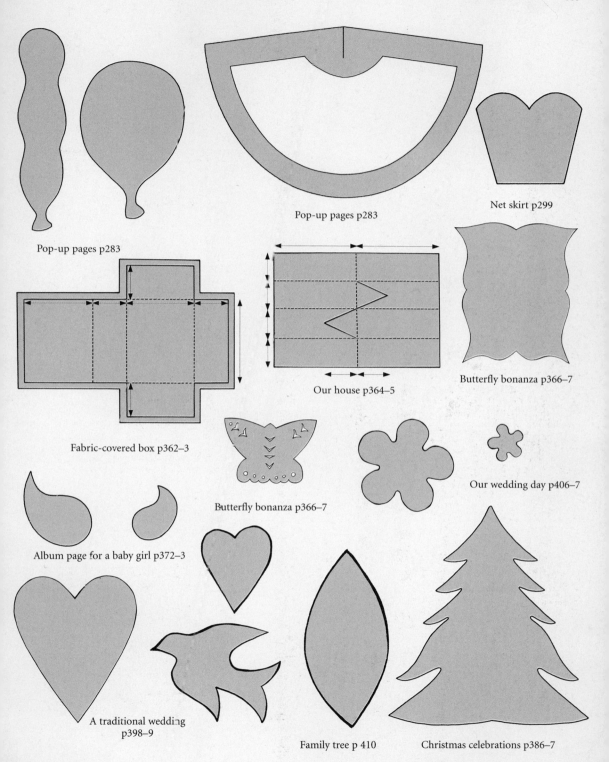

Pop-up pages p283

Pop-up pages p283

Net skirt p299

Fabric-covered box p362–3

Our house p364–5

Butterfly bonanza p366–7

Butterfly bonanza p366–7

Our wedding day p406–7

Album page for a baby girl p372–3

A traditional wedding
p398–9

Family tree p 410

Christmas celebrations p386–7

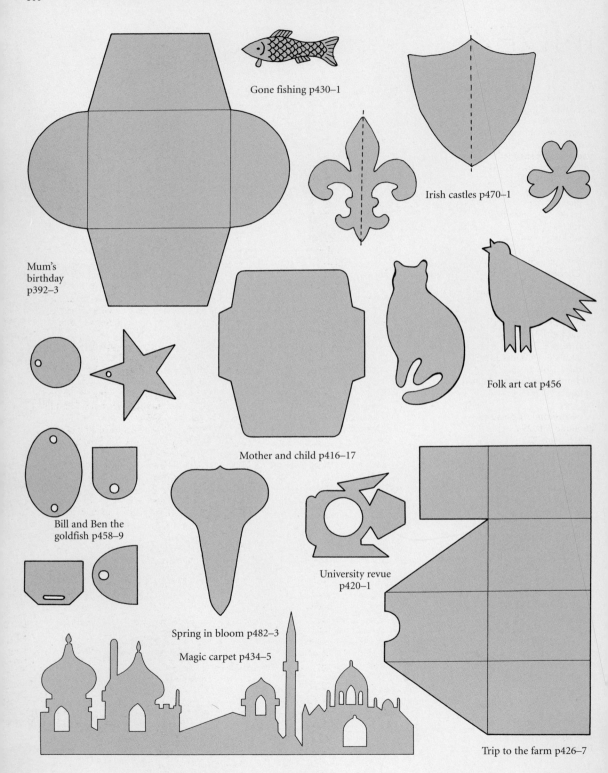

Gone fishing p430–1

Irish castles p470–1

Mum's
birthday
p392–3

Folk art cat p456

Mother and child p416–17

Bill and Ben the
goldfish p458–9

University revue
p420–1

Spring in bloom p482–3

Magic carpet p434–5

Trip to the farm p426–7

# INDEX

This edition is published by Southwater,
an imprint of Anness Publishing Ltd,
Blaby Road, Wigston, Leicestershire
LE18 4SE; info@anness.com

www.southwaterbooks.com; www.annesspublishing.com

If you like the images in this book and would like to investigate using them for publishing, promotions or advertising, please visit our website www.practicalpictures.com for more information.

Publisher: Joanna Lorenz
Editorial Director: Helen Sudell
Editor: Simona Hill
Designer: Ian Sandom
Photographers: Mark Wood
    and Paul Bricknell
Production Controller: Wendy Lawson

© Anness Publishing Ltd 2012

PUBLISHER'S NOTE

# Acknowledgements

Joy Aitman p260b, p294tr, p297br, p372–3, p390–1, p394–5, p404–7, p414–5, p432–3, p436–7, p440–1, p454–5, p475, p476–7, p480–1.

Penny Boylan, p260t, p264tl, p268b, p269, p270l and c, p276, p278, p282cr, p348–9, p352–5, p360–1, p362 tint box left, p364–7, p370–1, p385b, p398–9, p424–5, p428–9, p456–7, p474.

Pauline Craik p324 April in Paris, p326 Water, p328 Dartmouth 1997, p333 Danielle.

Sue Davies p336 Victory in Europe V.E. Day celebrations, p337 My great-grandfathers, p398 Aunty Janet and Uncle John Clarke 1960.

Marion Elliot p376–7, p382–4, p392–3, p400–3, p426–7, p430–1, 458–63, p468–9.

Sue Hallifax p346–7, p356–7.

Elaine Hewson p304–15 and all other digital scrapbook pages.

Lucinda Ganderton p68, p69, p76, p77, p79, p80, p93, p95, p136, p137, p146, p147, p150, p151, p158, p159, p160, p161, p172 p175, p340–1, p362 tint box right, p374–5, p378–9, p388–9, p410–3, p416–21, p434–5, p466–7, p470–1, p472–3, p482–3, p484–91.

Cher King p268 Tearing paper frames layout, p317 Mothers love, p378 Private lives.

Alison Lindsay p250, p251, p252, p253, p254, p255, p256, p257, p258, p259, p261, p262, p263, p264tr and b, p265, p269tr, p270 tint box, p271, p272, p273, p274, p275, p277, p279, p280, p281, p282, p283, p284, p285, p286, p287, p288, p289.

Mary Maguire p342–5, p350–61.

Gloria Nichol p362–3.

Cheryl Owen All greetings cards projects and techniques unless stated otherwise, p290, p291, p292, p293, p294, p295, p296, p297, p298, p299.

May Taylor p266 Penny for your thoughts, p267 I'd like to be under the sea and Adventure play together fun joy wonderful, p291 Chinese family portrait, p319 Sports day 2004, Stretcher race, Zoo, and Ticket to ride, p327 Cardigan Castle 2004, p333 Winter, and Daisy chain, p337 Travel mini accordion book, p370 Special delivery, p385 Au revoir, p426 Yardley Gobion 1997, and Zoo.

Thanks to the following suppliers:
Hot Off the Press, Inc., Paper Cellar Ltd, Glue Dots, Efco Hobby Products, Arty's, Fibermark, Grassroots, Magic Mesh, F. W. Bramell & Co Ltd, Creative Memories, Junkitz, Clearsnap Inc and Scrapgirls.com.